Programming Kotlin

Familiarize yourself with all of Kotlin's features with this in-depth guide

Stephen Samuel
Stefan Bocutiu

BIRMINGHAM - MUMBAI

Programming Kotlin

First published: January 2017

Production reference: 1130117

Published by Packt Publishing Ltd.
Livery Place
35 Livery Street
Birmingham
B3 2PB, UK.
ISBN 978-1-78712-636-7

www.packtpub.com

Credits

Authors

Stephen Samuel
Stefan Bocutiu

Reviewers

Antonios Chalkiopoulos
Alexander Hanschke

Commissioning Editor

Aaron Lazar

Acquisition Editor

Kirk D'costa
Sonali Vernekar

Content Development Editor

Nikhil Borkar

Technical Editor

Subhalaxmi Nadar

Copy Editor

Safis Editing

Project Coordinator

Vaidehi Sawant

Proofreader

Safis Editing

Indexer

Tejal Daruwale Soni

Graphics

Abhinash Sahu

Production Coordinator

Shraddha Falebhai

About the Authors

Stephen Samuel is an accomplished developer with over 17 years of experience. He has worked with Java throughout his career, and in the past 5 years has focused on Scala. He has a passion for concurrency and Big Data technologies. Having spent the last few years in investment banking, he is currently working with Kotlin on a major Big Data ingestment project. Stephen is also active in the open source community, being the author of several high profile Scala and Kotlin libraries.

I would like to thank my wife for being patient with all the days and nights spent on the computer, developing. I would also like to thank Stefan for kindly agreeing to co-author this book with me.

Stefan Bocutiu is a Big Data consultant with over 13 years of experience in software development. He enjoys coding in Scala, C#, and has a passion for stream processing technologies. With the team at DataMountaineer--a consultancy company offering delivery of solutions for streaming/ fast data platforms - he focuses on providing scalable, unified, real-time data pipelines allowing reactive decision making, analytics, and Hadoop integration.

Stefan is passionate about motorsports, and while his racing skills are not good enough to allow him to compete, he tries to attend as many MotoGP races as possible. When he is not coding, he can be found at the climbing wall or at the gym. Occasionally, hiking and scrambling trips are on his calendar, and during the winter season, skiing trips are a must for him.

About the Reviewers

Antonios Chalkiopoulos is a distributed systems specialist, engineering Big Data systems in the past 5 years on Media, Betting, Retail, Investment Banks, and FinTech companies in London. He is the author of Programming MapReduce with Scalding, one of the first books presenting how Scala can be used for Big Data solutions, and an open source contributor to a number of projects.

He is the founder of LANDOOP, a company that specializes in Fast Data and Big Data solutions and provides numerous tools and capabilities around Apache Kafka and real-time streaming systems.

Alexander Hanschke is a co-founder and CTO at techdev Solutions GmbH, a software company based in Berlin. He graduated from University of Mannheim and has worked in the financial sector, building Java enterprise applications for 8 years.

At his company, these days Alex is working on web applications written in Java and Kotlin. He frequently talks at user groups and conferences and is writing about Kotlin-related topics.

You can find him on Twitter at `@alexhanschke`.

www.PacktPub.com

For support files and downloads related to your book, please visit www.PacktPub.com.

Did you know that Packt offers eBook versions of every book published, with PDF and ePub files available? You can upgrade to the eBook version at www.PacktPub.com and as a print book customer, you are entitled to a discount on the eBook copy. Get in touch with us at service@packtpub.com for more details.

At www.PacktPub.com, you can also read a collection of free technical articles, sign up for a range of free newsletters and receive exclusive discounts and offers on Packt books and eBooks.

https://www.packtpub.com/mapt

Get the most in-demand software skills with Mapt. Mapt gives you full access to all Packt books and video courses, as well as industry-leading tools to help you plan your personal development and advance your career.

Why subscribe?

- Fully searchable across every book published by Packt
- Copy and paste, print, and bookmark content
- On demand and accessible via a web browser

Customer Feedback

Thank you for purchasing this Packt book. We take our commitment to improving our content and products to meet your needs seriously—that's why your feedback is so valuable. Whatever your feelings about your purchase, please consider leaving a review on this book's Amazon page. Not only will this help us, more importantly it will also help others in the community to make an informed decision about the resources that they invest in to learn. You can also review for us on a regular basis by joining our reviewers' club. **If you're interested in joining, or would like to learn more about the benefits we offer, please contact us**: `customerreviews@packtpub.com`.

Table of Contents

Preface

Kotlin is typically associated with Android development, and most discussion about it revolves gravitates around that. But the language has much more to offer and is ideal for modern server side developers. While any Android developer will find useful snippets in this book, the book is targeting Java and Scala developers primarily. The book will start with a introduction to Kotlin and explain how you set up your environment before moving on to the basic concepts. Once the basics are out of the way, the focus will shift towards more advanced concepts, and don't be surprised if you see a few bytecode listings. Once you have completed the book you should have all the knowledge required to start using Kotlin for your next project.

What this book covers

`Chapter 1`, *Getting Started with Kotlin*, covers how to install Kotlin, the Jetbrains Intellij IDEA, and the Gradle build system. Once the setup of the tool chain is complete, the chapter shows how to write your first Kotlin program.

`Chapter 2`, *Kotlin Basics*, dives head first into the basics of Kotlin, including the basic types, basic syntax, and program control flow structures such as if statements, `for` loops, and `while` loops. The chapter concludes with Kotlin-specific additions such as `when` expressions and type inference.

`Chapter 3`, *Object-Oriented Code in Kotlin*, focuses on the object-orientated aspects of the language. It introduces classes, interfaces, objects and the relationship between them, subtypes, and polymorphism.

`Chapter 4`, *Functions in Kotlin*, shows that functions, also known as procedures or methods, are the basic building blocks of any language. This chapter covers the syntax for functions, including the Kotlin enhancements such as named parameters, default parameters, and function literals.

`Chapter 5`, *Higher Order Functions and Functional Programming*, focuses on the functional programming side of Kotlin, including closures--also known as lambdas--and function references. It further covers functional programming techniques such as partial application, function composition, and error accumulation.

`Chapter 6`, *Properties*, explains that properties work hand in hand with object-orientated programming to expose values on a class or object. This chapter covers how properties work, how the user can best make use of them, and also how they are represented in the bytecode.

`Chapter 7`, *Null Safety, Reflection, and Annotations*, explains that null safety is one of the main features that Kotlin provides, and the first part of this chapter covers in depth the whys and hows of null safety in Kotlin. The second part of the chapter introduces reflection--run time introspection of code--and how it can be used for meta programming with annotations.

`Chapter 8`, *Generics*, explains that generics, or parameterized types, are a key component of any advanced type system, and the type system in Kotlin is substantially more advanced than that available in Java. This chapter covers variance, the type system including the Nothing type, and algebraic data types.

`Chapter 9`, *Data Classes*, shows that immutability and boiler-plate free domain classes are a current hot topic, due to the way they facilitate more robust code and simplify concurrent programming. Kotlin has many features focused on this area, which it calls data classes.

`Chapter 10`, *Collections*, explains that collections are one of the most commonly used aspects of any standard library, and Java collections are no different. This chapter describes the enhancements that Kotlin has made to the JDK collections, including functional operations such as map, fold, and filter.

`Chapter 11`, *Testing in Kotlin*, explains that one of the gateways into any new language is using it as a language for writing test code. This chapter shows how the exciting test framework KotlinTest can be used to write expressive, human-readable tests, with much more power than the standard jUnit tests allow.

`Chapter 12`, *Microservices in Kotlin*, shows that microservices have come to dominate server-side architecture in recent years, and Kotlin is an excellent choice for writing such services. This chapter introduces the Lagom microservice framework and shows how it can be used to great effect with Kotlin.

`Chapter 13`, *Concurrency*, explains that as multi-core aware programs are becoming more and more important in server-side platforms, This chapter is focused on a solid introduction to concurrent programming techniques that are vital in modern development, including threads, concurrency primitives, and futures.

What you need for this book

This book requires a computer running MacOS, Linux, or Windows, capable of running the latest versions of Java. It is recommended that the machine has enough memory to run a recent version of Jetbrains' Intellij IDEA.

Who this book is for

This book is aimed those who have little or no Kotlin experience and wish to learn the language quickly. The focus of the book is on server-side development in Kotlin and would be best suited to a developer who is currently a server-side developer or who wishes to learn. No prior knowledge of functional or object-orientated programming is required, but knowledge of some other programming language is recommended.

Some chapters contain brief sections comparing Java implementations to their Kotlin cousins, but these pages can be skipped by those who have no prior Java knowledge.

Conventions

In this book, you will find a number of text styles that distinguish between different kinds of information. Here are some examples of these styles and an explanation of their meaning.

Code words in text, database table names, folder names, filenames, file extensions, pathnames, dummy URLs, user input, and Twitter handles are shown as follows: "When using a data class, you get a `copy` method out of the box."

A block of code is set as follows:

```
public class Sensor {
  private final String id;
  private final double value;
  public Sensor(String id, double value) {
    this.id = id;
    this.value = value;
  }
```

When we wish to draw your attention to a particular part of a code block, the relevant lines or items are set in bold:

```
public class Sensor {
  private final String id;
  private final double value;
  public Sensor(String id, double value) {
```

```
        this.id = id;
        this.value = value;
    }
```

Any command-line input or output is written as follows:

```
$ sdk install gradle 3.0
```

New terms and **important words** are shown in bold. Words that you see on the screen, for example, in menus or dialog boxes, appear in the text like this: "In IntelliJ, choose **Code** | **Generate**."

Warnings or important notes appear in a box like this.

Tips and tricks appear like this.

Reader feedback

Feedback from our readers is always welcome. Let us know what you think about this book—what you liked or disliked. Reader feedback is important for us as it helps us develop titles that you will really get the most out of.

To send us general feedback, simply e-mail `feedback@packtpub.com`, and mention the book's title in the subject of your message.

If there is a topic that you have expertise in and you are interested in either writing or contributing to a book, see our author guide at `www.packtpub.com/authors`.

Customer support

Now that you are the proud owner of a Packt book, we have a number of things to help you to get the most from your purchase.

Downloading the example code

You can download the example code files for this book from your account at http://www.packtpub.com. If you purchased this book elsewhere, you can visit http://www.packtpub.com/support and register to have the files e-mailed directly to you.

You can download the code files by following these steps:

1. Log in or register to our website using your e-mail address and password.
2. Hover the mouse pointer on the **SUPPORT** tab at the top.
3. Click on **Code Downloads & Errata**.
4. Enter the name of the book in the **Search** box.
5. Select the book for which you're looking to download the code files.
6. Choose from the drop-down menu where you purchased this book from.
7. Click on **Code Download**.

You can also download the code files by clicking on the Code Files button on the book's webpage at the Packt Publishing website. This page can be accessed by entering the book's name in the Search box. Please note that you need to be logged in to your Packt account.

Once the file is downloaded, please make sure that you unzip or extract the folder using the latest version of:

- WinRAR / 7-Zip for Windows
- Zipeg / iZip / UnRarX for Mac
- 7-Zip / PeaZip for Linux

The code bundle for the book is also hosted on GitHub at https://github.com/PacktPublishing/Programming-Kotlin. We also have other code bundles from our rich catalog of books and videos available at https://github.com/PacktPublishing/. Check them out!

Downloading the color images of this book

We also provide you with a PDF file that has color images of the screenshots/diagrams used in this book. The color images will help you better understand the changes in the output. You can download this file from `https://www.packtpub.com/sites/default/files/downloads/ProgrammingKotlin_ColorImages.pdf`.

Errata

Although we have taken every care to ensure the accuracy of our content, mistakes do happen. If you find a mistake in one of our books—maybe a mistake in the text or the code—we would be grateful if you could report this to us. By doing so, you can save other readers from frustration and help us improve subsequent versions of this book. If you find any errata, please report them by visiting `http://www.packtpub.com/submit-errata`, selecting your book, clicking on the **Errata Submission Form** link, and entering the details of your errata. Once your errata are verified, your submission will be accepted and the errata will be uploaded to our website or added to any list of existing errata under the Errata section of that title.

To view the previously submitted errata, go to `https://www.packtpub.com/books/content/support`and enter the name of the book in the search field. The required information will appear under the **Errata** section.

Piracy

Piracy of copyrighted material on the Internet is an ongoing problem across all media. At Packt, we take the protection of our copyright and licenses very seriously. If you come across any illegal copies of our works in any form on the Internet, please provide us with the location address or website name immediately so that we can pursue a remedy.

Please contact us at `copyright@packtpub.com` with a link to the suspected pirated material.

We appreciate your help in protecting our authors and our ability to bring you valuable content.

Questions

If you have a problem with any aspect of this book, you can contact us at `questions@packtpub.com`, and we will do our best to address the problem.

1
Getting Started with Kotlin

It is time to write code. In this chapter, we will go over and write the typical entry code for every language: the famous *Hello World!* In order to do that, we will need to set up the initial environment required to develop software with Kotlin. We will provide a few examples using the compiler from the command line, and then we will move towards the typical way of programming using the IDEs and build tools available.

Kotlin is a JVM language, and so the compiler will emit Java bytecode. Because of this, of course, Kotlin code can call Java code, and vice versa! Therefore, you need to have the Java JDK installed on your machine. To be able to write code for Android, where the most recent supported Java version is 6, the compiler needs to translate your code to bytecode that is compatible at least with Java 6. For this book, however, all the code examples will be run with Java JDK 8. If you are new to the JVM world, you can get the latest version from `http://www.oracle.com/technetwork/java/javase/downloads/index.html`.

In this chapter you will learn how to:

- Use the command line to compile and execute code written in Kotlin
- Use the REPL and write Kotlin scripts
- Create a gradle project with Kotlin enabled
- Create a Maven project with Kotlin enabled
- Use IntelliJ to create a Kotlin project
- Use Eclipse IDE to create a Kotlin project
- Mix Kotlin and Java code in the same project

Using the command line to compile and run Kotlin code

To write and execute code written in Kotlin, you will need its runtime and the compiler. At the time of writing, version 1.1 milestone 4 is available (the stable release is 1.0.6). Every runtime release comes with its own compiler version. To get your hands on it, navigate to `https://github.com/JetBrains/kotlin/releases/tag/v1.1-M04`, scroll to the bottom of the page, and download and unpack the ZIP archive `kotlin-compiler-1.1-M04.zip` to a known location on your machine. The output folder will contain a subfolder `bin` with all the scripts required to compile and run Kotlin on Windows, Linux, or OS X. Now you need to make sure the `bin` folder location is part of your system PATH in order to call the `kotlinc` without having to specify the full path.

If your machine runs Linux or OS X, there is an even easier way to install the compiler by using `sdkman`. All you need to do is execute the following commands in a terminal:

```
$ curl -s https://get.sdkman.io | bash
$ bash
$ sdk install kotlin 1.1-M04
```

Alternatively, if you are using OS X and you have `homebrew` installed, you could run these commands to achieve the same thing:

$ brew update

```
$ brew install  kotlin@1.1-M04
```

Now that all of this is done, we can finally write our first Kotlin code. The application we will be writing does nothing else but display the text `Hello World!` on the console. Start by creating a new file named `HelloWorld.kt` and type the following:

```
fun main(args: Array<String>) {
  println("Hello, World!")
}
```

From the command line, invoke the compiler to produce the JAR assembly (`include-runtime` is a flag for the compiler to produce a self-contained and runnable JAR by including the Kotlin runtime into the resulting assembly):

```
kotlinc HelloWorld.kt -include-runtime -d HelloWorld.jar
```

Now you are ready to run your program by typing the following on your command line; it is assumed your `JAVA_HOME` is set and added to the system path:

```
$ java -jar HelloWorld.jar
```

The code is pretty straight forward. It defines the entry point function for your program, and in the first and only line of code, it prints the text to the console.

If you have been working with the Java or Scala languages, you might raise an eyebrow because you noticed the lack of the typical class that would normally define the standard `static` main program entry point. How does it work then? Let's have a look at what actually happens. First, let's just compile the preceding code by running the following command. This will create a `HelloWorld.class` in the same folder:

```
$ kotlinc HelloWorld.kt
```

Now that we have the bytecode generated, let's look at it by using the `javap` tool available with the JDK (please note that the file name contains a `suffix Kt`):

```
$ javap -c HelloWorldKt.class
```

Once the execution completes, you should see the following printed on your terminal:

```
    Compiled from "HelloWorld.kt"
    public final class HelloWorldKt {
      public static final void main(java.lang.String[]);
        Code:
          0: aload_0
          1: ldc           #9                  // String args
          3: invokestatic  #15                 // Method
kotlin/jvm/internal/Intrinsics.checkParameterIsNotNull:(Ljava/lang/Ob
ject;Ljava/lang/String;)V
          6: ldc           #17                 // String Hello, World!
          8: astore_1
          9: nop
          10: getstatic     #23                 // Field
java/lang/System.out:Ljava/io/PrintStream;
          13: aload_1
          14: invokevirtual #29                 // Method
java/io/PrintStream.println:(Ljava/lang/Object;)V
          17: return
    }
```

You don't have to be an expert in bytecode to understand what the compiler has actually done for us. As you can see on the snippet, a class has been generated for us, and it contains the program entry point with the instructions to print *Hello World!* to the console.

I would not expect you to work with the command line compiler on a daily basis; rather, you should use the tools at hand to delegate this, as we will see shortly.

Kotlin runtime

When we compiled `Hello World!` and produced the JAR, we instructed the compiler to bundle in the Kotlin runtime. Why is the runtime needed? Take a closer look at the bytecode generated, if you haven't already. To be more specific, look at line 3. It invokes a method to validate that the `args` variable is not null; thus, if you compile the code without asking for the runtime to be bundled in and try to run it, you will get an exception.

```
$ kotlinc HelloWorld.kt -d HelloWorld.jar
$ java -jar HelloWorld.jar
Exception in thread "main" java.lang.NoClassDefFoundError:
kotlin/jvm/internal/Intrinsics at HelloWorldKt.main(HelloWorld.kt)
Caused by: java.lang.ClassNotFoundException:
kotlin.jvm.internal.Intrinsics
```

The runtime footprint is very small; with ~800 K one can't argue otherwise. Kotlin comes with its own standard class library (`Kotlin runtime`), which is different from the Java library. As a result, you need to merge it into the resulting JAR, or provide it in the classpath:

```
$ java -cp $KOTLIN_HOME/lib/kotlin-runtime.jar:HelloWorld.jar  HelloWorldKt
```

If you develop a library for the exclusive use of other Kotlin libraries or applications, then you don't have to include the runtime. Alternatively there is a shorter path. This is done via a flag passed to the Kotlin compiler:

```
$kotlinc -include-runtime HelloWorld.kt -d HelloWorld
```

The REPL

These days, most languages provide an interactive shell, and Kotlin is no exception. If you want to quickly write some code that you won't use again, then the REPL is a good tool to have. Some prefer to quickly test their methods, but you should always write unit tests rather than using the REPL to validate that the output is correct.

You can start the REPL by adding dependencies to the classpath in order to make them available within the instance. To give an example, we will use the **Joda** library to deal with the date and time. First, we need to download the JAR. In a terminal window, use the following commands:

```
$ wget
https://github.com/JodaOrg/joda-time/releases/download/v2.9.4/joda-time-2.9
.4-dist.tar.gz
```

```
$ tar xvf joda-time-2.9.4-dist.tar.gz
```

Now you are ready to start the REPL, attach the Joda library to its running instance, and import and use the classes it provides:

```
$ kotlinc-jvm -cp joda-time-2.9.4/joda-time-2.9.4.jar
Welcome to Kotlin version 1.1-M04 (JRE 1.8.0_66-internal-b17)
Type :help for help, :quit for quit
>>> import org.joda.time.DateTime
>>> DateTime.now()
2016-08-25T22:53:41.017+01:00
```

Kotlin for scripting

Kotlin can also be run as a script. If `bash` or `Perl` is not for you, now you have an alternative.

Say you want to delete all the files older than N given days. The following code example does just that:

```
    import java.io.File
    val purgeTime = System.currentTimeMillis() - args[1].toLong() * 24  *
60 * 60 * 1000
    val folders = File(args[0]).listFiles { file -> file.isFile }
    folders ?.filter {
      file -> file.lastModified() < purgeTime }
    ?.forEach {
      file -> println("Deleting ${file.absolutePath}")
      file.delete()
    }
```

Create a file named `delete.kts` with the preceding content. Please note the predefined variable `args`, which contains all the incoming parameters passed when it is invoked. You might wonder what is the `?` character doing there. If you are familiar with the C# language and you know about nullable classes, you already have the answer. Even though you might not have come across it, I am sure you have a good idea of what it does. The character is called the safe call operator, and, as you will find out later in the book when the subject is discussed in greater length, it avoids the dreadful `NullPointerException` error.

The script takes two arguments: the target folder, and then the number of days threshold. For each file it finds in the target, it will check the last time it was modified; if it is less than the computed purge time, it will delete it. The preceding script has left out error handling; we leave this to the reader as an exercise.

Now the script is available, it can be invoked by running the following:

```
$ kotlinc -script delete.kts . 5
```

If you copy/create files in the current folder with a last modified timestamp older than five days, it will remove them.

Kotlin with Gradle

If you are familiar with the build tool landscape, you might be in one of three camps: Maven, Gradle, or SBT (more likely if you are a Scala dev). I am not going to go into the details, but we will present the basics of Gradle, t*he modern open source polyglot build automation system*, and leave it up to the curious to find out more from `http://gradle.org`. Before we continue, please make sure you have it installed and available in your classpath in order to be accessible from the terminal. If you have **SDKMAN**, you can install it using this command:

```
$ sdk install gradle 3.0
```

The build system comes with some baked-in templates, although limited, and in its latest 3.0 version Kotlin is not yet included. Hopefully, this shortfall will be dealt with sooner rather than later. However, it takes very little to configure support for it. First, let's see how you can interrogate for the available templates:

```
$ gradle help --task :init
```

You should see the following being printed out on the terminal:

```
Options
  --type  Set type of build to create.
   Available values are:
    basic
    groovy-library
    java-library
    pom
    scala-library
```

Let's go and use the Java template and create our project structure by executing this `bash` command:

```
$ gradle init --type java-library
```

This template will generate a bunch of files and folders; if you have been using Maven, you will see that this structure is similar:

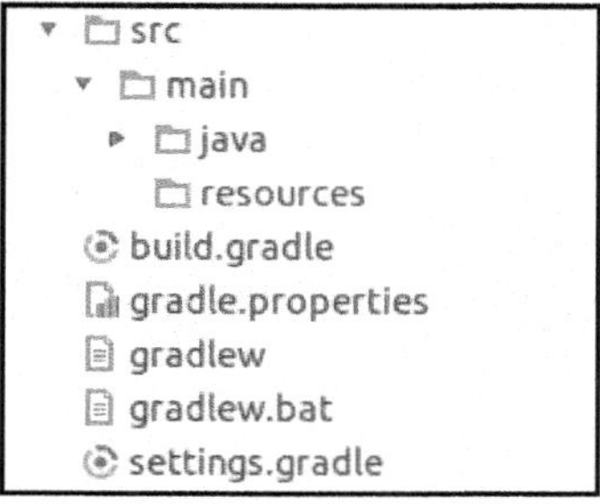

Project Folders layout

As it stands, the Gradle project is not ready for Kotlin. First, go ahead and delete `Library.java` and `LibraryTest.java`, and create a new folder named `kotlin`, a sibling of the java one. Then, using a text editor, open the `build.gradle` file. We need to add the plugin enabling the Gradle system to compile Kotlin code for us, so at the top of your file you have to add the following snippet:

```
buildscript {
  ext.kotlin_version = '1.1-M04'

  repositories {
    maven { url "https://dl.bintray.com/kotlin/kotlin-dev" }
    mavenCentral()
  }
  dependencies {
    classpath "org.jetbrains.kotlin:kotlin-gradle-
plugin:$kotlin_version"
  }
}
```

The preceding instructions tell Gradle to use the plugin for Kotlin, and set the dependency maven repository. Since Kotlin 1.1 is only at milestone 4, there is a specific repository to pick it from. See last entry in `repositories`. We are not done yet; we still need to enable the plugin. The template generated will already have an applied plugin: `java`. Replace it with the following:

```
apply plugin: 'kotlin'
apply plugin: 'application'
mainClassName = 'com.programming.kotlin.chapter01.ProgramKt'
```

Now Kotlin plugin support is enabled; you may have noticed that we have also added the application plugin, and set the class containing the program entry point. The reason for this is to allow the program to run directly, as we will see shortly.

We are not quite done. We still need to link to the Kotlin standard library. Replace the `repositories` and `dependencies` sections with the following:

```
repositories {
  maven { url "https://dl.bintray.com/kotlin/kotlin-dev" }
  mavenCentral()
}
dependencies {
  compile "org.jetbrains.kotlin:kotlin-stdlib:$kotlin_version"
  testCompile 'io.kotlintest:kotlintest:1.3.3'
}
```

Now let's create the file named `HelloWorld.Kt`. This time, we will set a namespace and thus avoid having our class as part of the default one. If you are not yet familiar with the term, don't worry; it will be covered in the next chapter.

From the terminal, run the following:

```
$ mkdir -p src/main/kotlin/com/programming/kotlin/chapter01
$ echo "" >> src/main/kotlin/com/programming/kotlin/chapter01/Program.kt
$ cat <<EOF >> src/main/kotlin/com/programming/kotlin/chapter01/Program.kt
package com.programming.kotlin.chapter01
fun main(args: Array<String>) {
  println("Hello World!")
}
```

We are now in a position to build and run the application:

```
$ gradle build
$ gradle run
```

Now we want to be able to run our program using `java -jar [artefact]`. Before we can do that, we need to adapt the `build.gradle`. First, we need to create a `manifest` file and set the main class; the JVM will look for the main function to start executing it:

```
jar {
  manifest {
    attributes(
      'Main-Class': 'com.programming.kotlin.chapter01.ProgramKt'
    )
  }
  from { configurations.compile.collect { it.isDirectory() ? it :
zipTree(it) } }
```

```
}
```

Furthermore, we also embed into the JAR the dependency for `kotlin-stdlib`, as well as `kotlin-runtime`. If we leave out these dependencies, we will need to add them to the classpath when we run the application. Now you are ready to build and run the code.

Kotlin with Maven

If you still prefer to stick with good old Maven, there is no problem. There is a plugin for it to support Kotlin as well. If you don't have Maven on your machine, you can follow the instructions at `https://maven.apache.org/install.html` to get it installed on your local machine.

Just as we did with Gradle, let's use the built-in templates to generate the project folder and file structure. From the terminal, within a brand new folder, you will have to run the following command:

```
$ mvn archetype:generate -DgroupId=com.programming.kotlin -
DartifactId=chapter01 -DarchetypeArtifactId=maven-archetype- quickstart -
DinteractiveMode=false
```

This will generate the `pom.xml` file and the `src` folder for Maven. But before we add the file containing the `kotlin` code, we need to enable the plugin. Just as before, start by deleting `App.java` and `AppTest.java` from `src/main/java/com/programming/kotlin` and `test/main/java/com/programming/kotlin/`, and create the `src/kotlin` folder (the subdirectory structure matches the namespace name):

```
$ mkdir -p src/main/kotlin/com/programming/kotlin/chapter01
$ mkdir -p src/test/kotlin/com/programming/kotlin/chapter01
```

In an editor of your choice, open up the generated `pom.xml` file and add the following:

```
<pluginRepositories>
  <pluginRepository>
    <snapshots>
      <enabled>true</enabled>
    </snapshots>
    <id>bintray-kotlin-kotlin-dev</id>
    <name>bintray</name>
    <url>http://dl.bintray.com/kotlin/kotlin-dev</url>
  </pluginRepository>
</pluginRepositories>

<repositories>
```

```
        <repository>
          <snapshots>
            <enabled>true</enabled>
          </snapshots>
          <id>bintray-kotlin-kotlin-dev</id>
          <name>bintray</name>
          <url>http://dl.bintray.com/kotlin/kotlin-dev</url>
        </repository>
      </repositories>
      <properties>
        <kotlin.version>1.1-M04</kotlin.version>
        <kotlin.test.version>1.3.3</kotlin.test.version>
      </properties>
      <build>
         <sourceDirectory>${project.basedir}/src/main/kotlin</sourceDirecto
ry>
         <testSourceDirectory>${project.basedir}/src/test/kotlin</testSourc
eDirectory>
        <plugins>
          <plugin>
            <artifactId>kotlin-maven-plugin</artifactId>
            <groupId>org.jetbrains.kotlin</groupId>
            <version>${kotlin.version}</version>

            <executions>
              <execution>
                <id>compile</id>
                <phase>process-sources</phase>
                <goals> <goal>compile</goal> </goals>
              </execution>

              <execution>
                <id>test-compile</id>
                <phase>process-test-sources</phase>
                <goals> <goal>test-compile</goal> </goals>
              </execution>
            </executions>
          </plugin>
        </plugins>
      </build>
```

All we have done so far is to enable the Kotlin plugin and make it run in the process-stages phase to allow the mixing of Java code as well. There are cases when you might have part of the source code written in good old Java. I am sure you also noticed the addition of source directory tags, allowing for the `kotlin` files to be included in the build.

The only thing left to do now is to add the library dependencies for the Kotlin runtime as well as the unit tests. We are not going to touch upon the testing framework until later in the book. Replace the entire `dependencies` section with the following:

```
<dependencies>
  <dependency>
     <groupId>org.jetbrains.kotlin</groupId>
     <artifactId>kotlin-stdlib</artifactId>
     <version>${kotlin.version}</version>
   </dependency>
   <dependency>
     <groupId>io.kotlintest</groupId>
     <artifactId>kotlintest</artifactId>
     <version>${kotlin.test.version}</version>
     <scope>test</scope>
   </dependency>
 </dependencies>
```

It is time now to add the `Hello World!` code; this step is similar to the one we took earlier when we discussed Gradle:

```
$ echo "" >> src/main/kotlin/com/programming/kotlin/chapter01/Program.kt
$cat <<EOF >> src/main/kotlin/com/programming/kotlin/chapter01/Program.kt
    package com.programming.kotlin.chapter01
    fun main(args: Array<String>) {
      println("Hello World!")
    }
```

We are now in a position to compile and build the JAR file for the sample program:

```
$ mvn package
$ mvn exec:java -
Dexec.mainClass="com.programming.kotlin.chapter01.ProgramKt"
```

The last instruction should end up printing the `Hello World!` text to the console. Of course we can run the program outside Maven by going back to executing Java, but we need to add the Kotlin runtime to the classpath:

```
$java -cp $KOTLIN_HOME/lib/kotlin-runtime.jar:target/chapter01-1.0-
SNAPSHOT.jar "com.programming.kotlin.chapter01.ProgramKt"
```

If you want to avoid the `Classpath` dependency setup when you run the application, there is an option to bundle all the dependencies in the resulted JAR and produce what is called a **fat jar**. For that, however, another plugin needs to be added:

```
<plugin>
  <groupId>org.apache.maven.plugins</groupId>
```

```
          <artifactId>maven-shade-plugin</artifactId>
          <version>2.4.3</version>
          <executions>
            <execution>
              <phase>package</phase>
              <goals>
                <goal>shade</goal>
              </goals>
               <configuration>
                <transformers>
                  <transformer
implementation="org.apache.maven.plugins.shade.resource.ManifestRe
sourceTransformer">
<mainClass>com.programming.kotlin.chapter01.ProgramKt</mainClass>
                  </transformer>
                </transformers>
              </configuration>
            </execution>
          </executions>
        </plugin>
```

We can execute the command to run our JAR without having to worry about setting the classpath since this has been taken care of by the plugin:

```
$ java -jar target/chapter01-1.0-SNAPSHOT.jar
```

IntelliJ and Kotlin

Coding using Vim/nano is not everyone's first choice; working without the help of an IDE with its code completion, intelli-sense, shortcuts for adding files, or refactoring code can prove challenging the more complex the project is.

For a while now, in the JVM world, people's first choice when it comes to their integrated development environment has been IntelliJ. The tool is made by the same company that created Kotlin: JetBrains. Given the integration between the two of them, it would be my first choice of IDE to use, but, as we will see in the next section it is not the only option.

IntelliJ comes in two versions: Ultimate and Community (free). For the code we will be using in the course of this book, the free version is enough. If you don't have it already installed, you can download it from `https://www.jetbrains.com/idea/download`.

From version 15.0, IntelliJ comes bundled with Kotlin, but if you have an older version you can still get support for the language by installing the plugin. Just go to **Settings | Plugins | Install IntelliJ plugins** and type Kotlin in the search.

We are going to use the IDE to create a Gradle project with Kotlin enabled, just as we did in the previous section. Once you have started IntelliJ, you will have to choose **Create new project**. You will get a dialog window from which you should select **Gradle** from the left-hand side section; check the **Kotlin(Java)** option from the right-hand side. As you can see here:

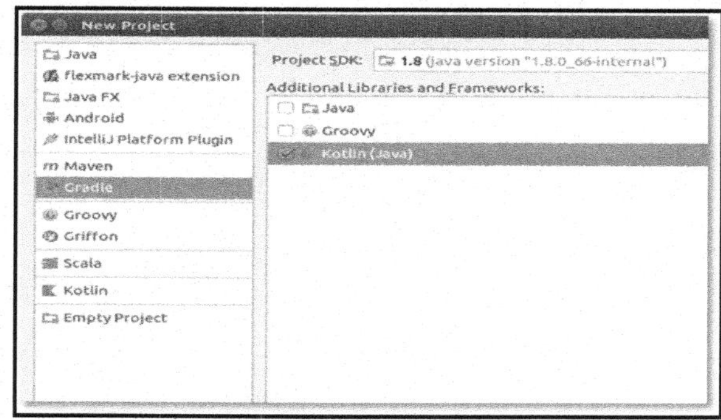

Selecting a project type

You should already have the system variable `JAVA_HOME` set up for the tool to pick it up automatically (see the **Project SDK** at the top of the screenshot). If this isn't the case, choose the **New** button and navigate to where your Java JDK is. Once you have selected it, you are ready to go to the next step by clicking on the **Next** button available on the bottom right-hand side of the screen.

The next window presented to you is asking you to provide the **Group Id** and **Artifact Id**. Let's go with `com.programming.kotlin` and `chapter01` respectively. Once you have completed the fields, you can move to the next step of the process where you tick the **Use auto-import flag** as well as **Create directories for empty directory roots automatically**. Now carry on to the next step, where you are asked where you wish to store the project on your machine. Set the project location, expand **More Settings**, type `chapter01` for the **Module name**, and hit the **Finish** button.

IntelliJ will go on and create the project, and you should have the outcome shown in the following screenshot:

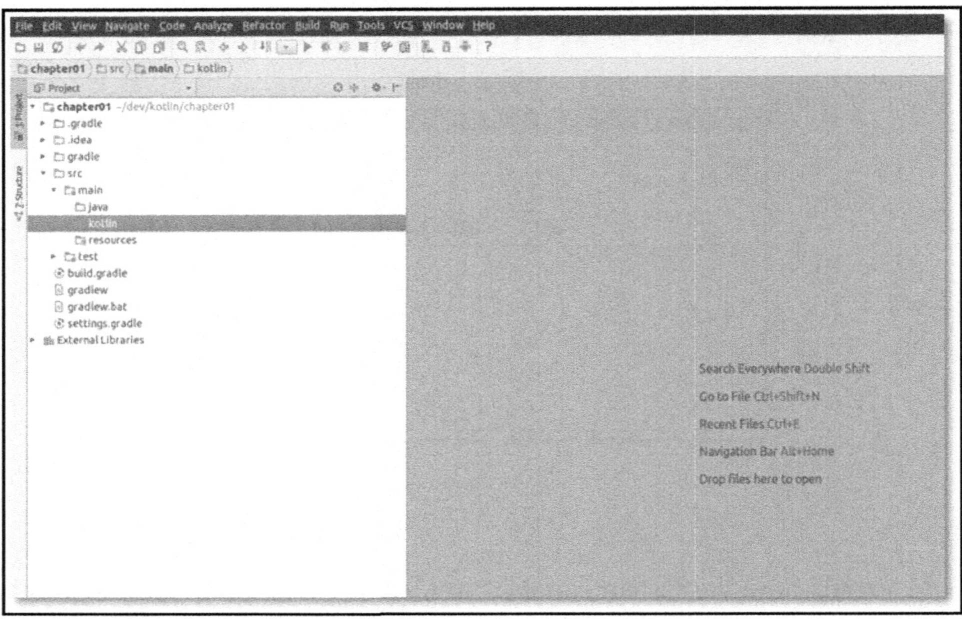

Hello World! basic project

On the selected `kotlin` folder, right-click and choose the **New** | **Package** option, and type `com.programming.kotlin.chapter01`:

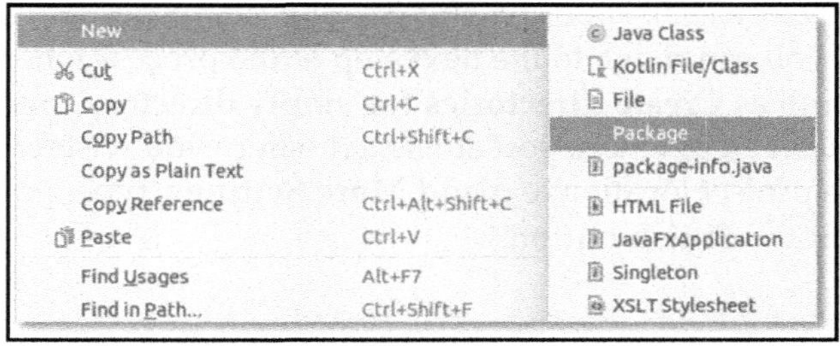

Setting up the package name

Below the `kotlin` folder, you should see a new one appear, matching what was typed earlier. Right click on that, choose **New** | **Kotlin File/Class**, and type `Program.kt`:

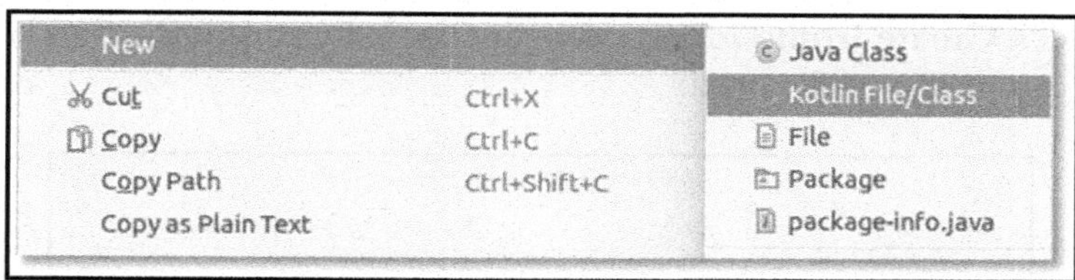

Creating Program.kt file

We are now ready to start typing our `Hello World!` Use the same code we created earlier in the chapter. You should notice the Kotlin brand icon on the left-hand side of the file editor. If you click on it, you will get the option to run the code, and if you look at the bottom of your IntelliJ window you should see the text `Hello World!` printed out:

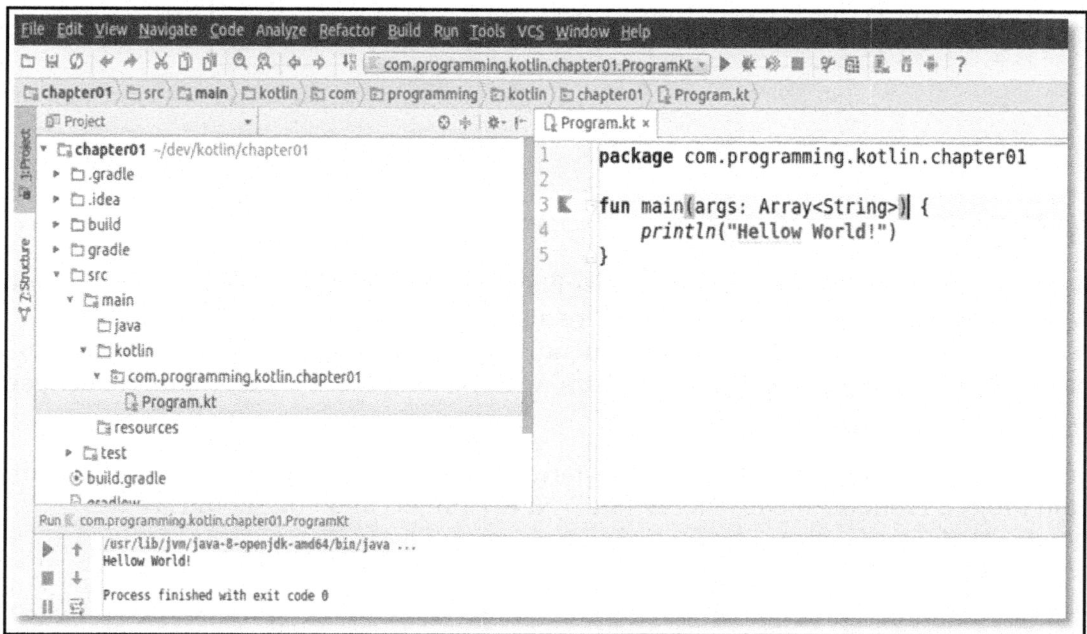

Hello World! program

Well done! You have written your first Kotlin program. It was easy and quick to set up the project and code, and to run the program. If you prefer, you can have a Maven rather than a Gradle project. When you choose **New** | **Project**, you have to select **Maven** from the left-hand side and check **Create from archetype** while choosing **org.jetbrains.kotlin:kotlin-archetype-jvm** from the list presented:

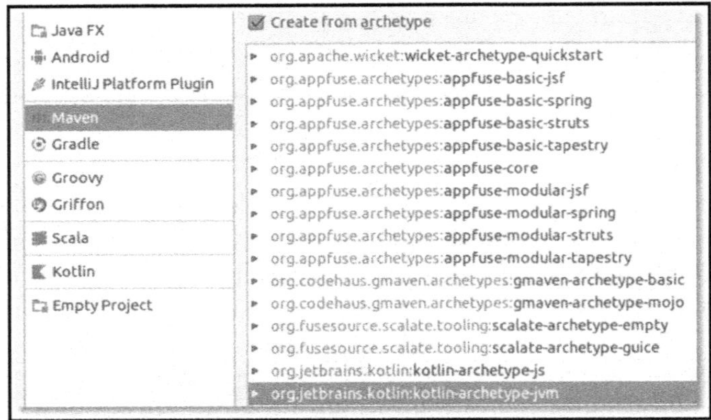

Maven project

Eclipse and Kotlin

There might be some of you who still prefer Eclipse IDE to IntelliJ; don't worry, you can still develop Kotlin code without having to move away from it. At this point, I assume you already have the tool installed. From the menu, navigate to **Help** | **Eclipse Marketplace**, look for the Kotlin plugin, and install it (I am working with the latest distribution: **Eclipse Neon**).

Once you have installed the plugin and restarted the IDE, you are ready to create your first Kotlin project. From the menu, choose **File** | **New** | **Project** and you should see the following dialog:

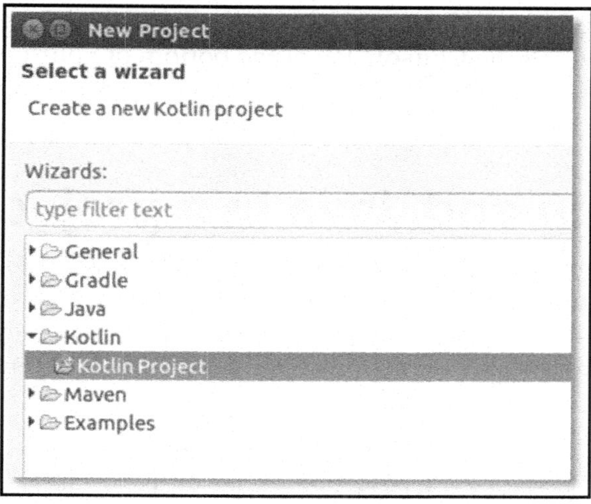

New Kotlin project

Click the **Next** button to move to the next step and, once you have chosen the source code location, click the **Finish** button. This is not a Gradle or Maven project! You can choose one of the two, but then you will have to manually modify the `build.gradle` or `pom.xml`, as we did manually in the Kotlin with Gradle and Kotlin with Maven sections of this chapter. Similar to the IntelliJ project, click on the `src` folder, choose **New package**, and name it `com.programming.kotlin.chapter01`. To add our `Program.kt`, you will need to right-click on the newly created package, select **New** | **Other**, and select **Kotlin** | **Kotlin File** from the list. Once the file has been created, type the simple lines of code to print out the text to the console. You should have the following result in your Eclipse IDE:

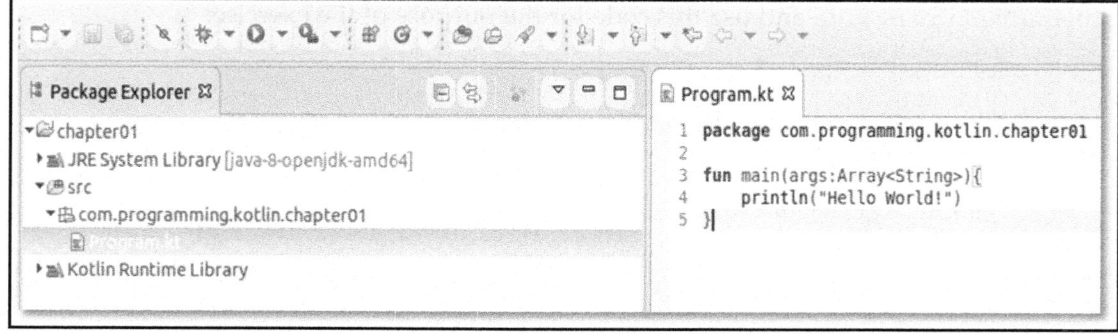

Hello World! with Eclipse

Now you are ready to run the code. From the menu select **Run** | **Run**. You should be able to trigger the execution, and in the **Console** tab at the bottom of your IDE you should see the **Hello World!** text printed out.

Mixing Kotlin and Java in a project

Using different languages within the same project is quite common; I came across projects where a mix of Java and Scala files formed the code base. Could we do the same with Kotlin? Absolutely. Let's work on the project created earlier, *Kotlin with Gradle*. You should see the following directory structure in your IntelliJ (the standard template for a Java/Kotlin project):

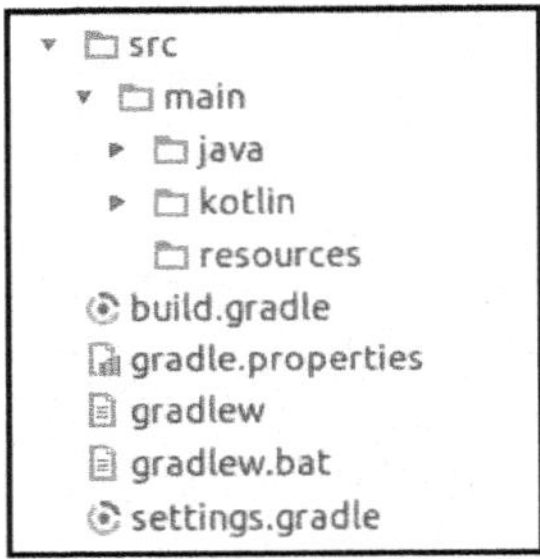

Project layout

You can place Java code within the `java` folder. Add a new package to the `java` folder with the same name as the one present in the `kotlin` folder: `com.programming.kotlin.chapter01`. Create a **New** | **Java class** named `CarManufacturer.java` and use this code for the purpose of the exercise:

```
public class CarManufacturer {
  private final String name;
  public CarManufacturer(String name) {
    this.name = name;
  }
  public String getName() {
    return name;
  }
}
```

What if you want to add a Java class under the `kotlin` subfolder? Let's create a `Student` class similar to the previous one and provide a field name for simplicity:

```
public class Student {
```

```
    private final String name;
    public Student(String name) {
      this.name = name;
    }
    public String getName() {
      return name;
    }
  }
```

In the `main` function, let's instantiate our classes:

```
fun main(args: Array<String>) {
  println("Hellow World!")
  val student = Student("Alexandra Miller")
  println("Sudent name:${student.name}")
  val carManufacturer = CarManufacturer("Mercedes")
  println("Car manufacturer:${carManufacturer.name}")
}
```

While the code compiles just fine, trying to run it will throw a runtime exception, saying that it can't find the `Student` class. We need to let the Java compiler look for code under the `src/main/kotlin` folder. In your `gradle.build`, add the following instruction:

```
sourceSets {
  main.java.srcDirs += 'src/main/kotlin'
}
```

Now we can compile and run the program:

```
$gradle jar
$ java -jar build/libs/chapter01-1.0-SNAPSHOT.jar
```

As your Kotlin code gets bigger, compilation will slow down since it will have to go and recompile each file. There is a way to speed it up, though: by only compiling files changed between builds. The easiest way to enable this is to create a file called `gradle.properties` alongside `build.gradle` and add `kotlin.incremental=true` to it. While the first build will not be incremental, the following ones will be, and you should see your compilation time cut down quite a bit.

Maven is still, probably, the most used build system on the JVM. So let's see how we can achieve our goal of mixing Kotlin and Java code in Maven. Starting with IntelliJ, choose **New | Project**, pick **Maven** as the option, and look for **kotlin-archetype-jvm** from the list of archetypes. We already covered this, so it should be a lot easier the second time around. We now have a project.

From the project tree, you will notice that there is no `java` folder source code created. Go ahead and create `src/main/java`, followed by the namespace folder `com.programming.kotlin` (this will be a subfolder of the `java` one). You will notice that right-clicking on the `java` folder won't give you the option to create a package. The project is not yet configured to include Java code. But first, what makes Maven handle Kotlin code? If you open the `pom.xml` file and go to the plugins section, you will notice the `kotlin` plugin:

```
<plugin>
  <groupId>org.jetbrains.kotlin</groupId>
  <artifactId>kotlin-maven-plugin</artifactId>
  <version>${kotlin.version}</version>
  <executions>
    <execution>
      <id>compile</id>
      <phase>compile</phase>
      <goals>
        <goal>compile</goal>
      </goals>
    </execution>
    <execution>
      <id>test-compile</id>
      <phase>test-compile</phase>
      <goals>
        <goal>test-compile</goal>
      </goals>
    </execution>
  </executions>
</plugin>
```

To add Java code to the mix, we need to set a new plugin that will be able to compile good old Java:

```
<plugin>
  <groupId>org.apache.maven.plugins</groupId>
  <artifactId>maven-compiler-plugin</artifactId>
  <version>3.5.1</version>
  <executions>
    <execution>
      <id>default-compile</id>
      <phase>none</phase>
    </execution>
    <execution>
      <id>default-testCompile</id>
      <phase>none</phase>
    </execution>
    <execution>
```

```
        <id>java-compile</id>
        <phase>compile</phase>
        <goals>
          <goal>compile</goal>
        </goals>
      </execution>
      <execution>
        <id>java-test-compile</id>
        <phase>test-compile</phase>
        <goals>
          <goal>testCompile</goal>
        </goals>
      </execution>
    </executions>
  </plugin>
```

The Kotlin compiler has to run before the Java compiler to get it all working, so we will need to amend the Kotlin plugin to do just that:

```
  <plugin>
    <artifactId>kotlin-maven-plugin</artifactId>
    <groupId>org.jetbrains.kotlin</groupId>
    <version>${kotlin.version}</version>
    <executions>
      <execution>
        <id>compile</id>
        <goals>
          <goal>compile</goal>
        </goals>
        <configuration>
          <sourceDirs>
            <sourceDir>${project.basedir}/src/main/kotlin</sourceDir>
            <sourceDir>${project.basedir}/src/main/java</sourceDir>
          </sourceDirs>
        </configuration>
      </execution>
      <execution>
        <id>test-compile</id>
        <goals>
          <goal>test-compile</goal>
        </goals>
        <configuration>
          <sourceDirs>
            <sourceDir>${project.basedir}/src/main/kotlin</sourceDir>
            <sourceDir>${project.basedir}/src/main/java</sourceDir>
          </sourceDirs>
        </configuration>
      </execution>
```

```
    </executions>
  </plugin>
```

To be able to produce the executable JAR for the code we are about to write, we need yet another Maven plugin:

```
  <plugin>
    <groupId>org.apache.maven.plugins</groupId>
    <artifactId>maven-jar-plugin</artifactId>
    <version>3.0.2</version>
    <configuration>
      <archive>
        <manifest>
          <addClasspath>true</addClasspath>
          <mainClass>com.programming.kotlin.HelloKt</mainClass>
        </manifest>
      </archive>
    </configuration>
  </plugin>
```

The preceding code will give you a JAR containing just your code; if you want to run it then you need the extra dependencies to the classpath:

```
  <plugin>
    <groupId>org.apache.maven.plugins</groupId>
    <artifactId>maven-assembly-plugin</artifactId>
    <version>2.6</version>
    <executions>
      <execution>
        <id>make-assembly</id>
        <phase>package</phase>
        <goals> <goal>single</goal> </goals>
        <configuration>
          <archive>
            <manifest>
              <mainClass>com.programming.kotlin.HelloKt</mainClass>
            </manifest>
          </archive>
          <descriptorRefs>
            <descriptorRef>jar-with-dependencies</descriptorRef>
          </descriptorRefs>
        </configuration>
      </execution>
    </executions>
  </plugin>
```

Now we are in a position to add the classes from the previous example (the `CarManufacturer` and `Student` classes) and change the `main` class to contain the following:

```
val student = Student("Jenny Wood")
println("Student:${student.name}")
val carManufacturer = CarManufacturer("Honda")
println("Car manufacture:${carManufacturer.name}")
```

This is not ready yet. While compiling will go well, trying to execute the JAR will yield an error at runtime about the `Student` class not being found. The Java compiler needs to know about the Java code sitting under the `kotlin` folder. For that, we bring in another plugin:

```
<plugin>
  <groupId>org.codehaus.mojo</groupId>
  <artifactId>build-helper-maven-plugin</artifactId>
  <executions>
    <execution>
      <phase>generate-sources</phase>
      <goals><goal>add-source</goal></goals>
      <configuration>
        <sources>
          <source>${project.basedir}/src/main/kotlin</source>
        </sources>
      </configuration>
    </execution>
  </executions>
</plugin>
```

Finally, we are in a position to compile and run the code. Executing the commands in a terminal will end up printing three lines in the output:

```
$ mvn package
$ java -jar target/chapter01-maven-mix-1.0-SNAPSHOT-jar-with-
dependencies.jar
```

Summary

This chapter has showed you how you can set up your development environment with the tools required to build and run Kotlin code. Now you are able to run and execute the examples created in the rest of the book, as well as experiment with your own Kotlin code.

In the next chapter you will delve into the basic constructs you will use daily when you code in Kotlin.

2
Kotlin Basics

It's time to discover the fundamental building blocks in Kotlin. For those coming from a Java background, this chapter will highlight some of the key similarities and differences between Kotlin and Java, and how Kotlin's language features compare to those in Java and on the JVM. For those who are not Java programmers, these differences can be safely skipped.

In this chapter we will cover the following topics:

- Variables and values
- Control flow and expressions
- Type inference
- Smart casting
- Basic types and the Kotlin type hierarchy

Vals and vars

Kotlin has two keywords for declaring variables, `val` and `var`. The `var` is a mutable variable, which is, a variable that can be changed to another value by reassigning it. This is equivalent to declaring a variable in Java:

```
val name = "kotlin"
```

In addition, the `var` can be initialized later:

```
var name: String
name = "kotlin"
```

Variables defined with `var` can be reassigned, since they are mutable:

```
var name = "kotlin"
name = "more kotlin"
```

The keyword `val` is used to declare a read-only variable. This is equivalent to declaring a final variable in Java. A `val` must be initialized when it is created, since it cannot be changed later:

```
val name = "kotlin"
```

A read only variable does not mean the instance itself is automatically immutable. The instance may still allow its member variables to be changed via functions or properties, but the variable itself cannot change its value or be reassigned to another value.

Type inference

Did you notice in the previous section that the type of the variable was not included when it was initialized? This is different to Java where the type of the variable must always accompany its declaration.

Even though Kotlin is a strongly typed language, we don't always need to declare types explicitly. The compiler attempts to figure out the type of an expression from the information included in the expression. A simple `val` is an easy case for the compiler because the type is clear from the right-hand side. This mechanism is called **type inference**. This reduces boilerplate whilst keeping the type safety we expect of a modern language.

Values and variables are not the only places where type inference can be used. It can also be used in closures where the type of the parameter(s) can be inferred from the function signature. It can also be used in single-line functions where the return value can be inferred from the expression in the function, as this example shows:

fun plusOne(x: Int) = x + 1

Sometimes it is helpful to explicitly annotate the :

```
val explicitType: Number = 12.3
```

Basic types

One of the big changes in Kotlin from Java is that in Kotlin everything is an object. If you come from a Java background, then you will already be aware that in Java there are special primitive types which are treated differently from objects. They cannot be used as generic types, do not support method/function calls, and cannot be assigned null. An example is the primitive type `boolean`.

Java introduced wrapper objects to offer a work around in which primitive types are wrapped in objects, so that `java.lang.Boolean` wraps a `boolean` in order to smooth over the distinctions. Kotlin removes this necessity entirely from the language by promoting the primitives to full objects.

Whenever possible, the Kotlin compiler will map basic types back to JVM primitives for performance reasons. However, sometimes the values must be boxed, such as when the type is nullable, or when it is used in generics. Boxing is the conversion from a primitive type to a wrapper type that types place whenever an object is required but a primitive is presented.

Two different values that are boxed might not use the same instance, so referential equality is not guaranteed on boxed values.

Numbers

The built-in number types are as follows:

Type	Width
Long	64
Int	32
Short	16
Byte	8
Double	64
Float	32

To create a number literal, use one of the following forms:

```
val int = 123
val long = 123456L
val double = 12.34
val float = 12.34F
val hexadecimal = 0xAB
val binary = 0b01010101
```

You will notice that a `long` value requires the suffix `L` and a `float`, the suffix `F`. The `double` is used as the default for floating point numbers, and `int` for integral numbers. The `hexadecimal` and `binary` use the prefixes `0x` and `0b` respectively.

Kotlin does not support automatic widening of numbers, so conversion must be invoked explicitly. Each number has a function that will convert the value to one of the other number types. For example to convert from an integer to a long we can do the following.

```
val int = 123
val long = int.toLong()
```

Similarly, to convert a float to a double, we use the `toDouble` function.

```
val float = 12.34F
val double = float.toDouble()
```

The full set of functions for conversions between types is `toByte()`, `toShort()`, `toInt()`, `toLong()`, `toFloat()`, `toDouble()`, `toChar()`.

The usual bitwise operators – left shift, right shift, unsigned right shift, logical and, logical or and exclusive logical or – are supported by Kotlin. Unlike Java, these are not built in operators but named functions instead but can still be invoked like operators:

```
val leftShift = 1 shl 2
val rightShift = 1 shr 2
val unsignedRightShift = 1 ushr 2

val and = 1 and 0x00001111
val or = 1 or0x00001111
val xor = 1 xor0x00001111
val inv = 1.inv()
```

Notice that inverse is not a binary operator, but a unary operator and so is invoked using the dot syntax on a number.

Booleans

Booleans are rather standard, and support the usual negation, conjunction, and disjunction operations. Conjunction and disjunction are lazily evaluated, so if the left-hand side satisfies the clause, then the right-hand side will not be evaluated:

```
val x = 1
val y = 2
val z = 2

val isTrue = x < y && x < z
val alsoTrue = x == y || y == z
```

Chars

Chars represent a single character. Character literals use single quotes such as A or Z. Chars also support escaping for the following characters: `\t`, `\b`, `\n`, `\r`, `'`, `"`, `\\`, and `\$`.

All unicode characters can be represented using the unicode number, for example, `\u1234`.

Note that the `char` type is not treated as a number, as used in Java.

Strings

Just as in Java, strings are immutable. String literals can be created using double quotes or triple quotes. Double quotes create an escaped string. In an escaped string, special characters, such as `new line`, must be escaped:

```
val string = "string with \n new line"
```

Triple quotes create a raw string. In a raw string, no escaping is necessary, and all characters can be included:

```
val rawString = """
raw string is super useful for strings that span many lines """
```

Strings also provide an iterator function which can be used in a `for` loop. This will be described later in the *For loop* section.

Arrays

In Kotlin, we can create an `array` by using the library function `arrayOf()`:

```
val array = arrayOf(1, 2, 3)
```

Alternatively, we can create an `Array` from an initial size and a function, which is used to generate each element:

```
val perfectSquares = Array(10, { k -> k * k })
```

Unlike Java, arrays are not treated as special by the language, and are regular collection classes. Instances of arrays provide an iterator function and a `size` function, as well as a `get` and a `set` function. The `get` and `set` functions are also available through bracket syntax like many C-style languages:

```
val element1 = array[0]
val element2 = array[1]
array[2] = 5
```

To avoid boxing types that will ultimately be represented as primitives in the JVM, Kotlin provides alternative array classes that are specialized for each of the primitive types. This allows performance-critical code to use arrays as efficiently as they would do in plain Java. The provided classes are `ByteArray`, `CharArray`, `ShortArray`, `IntArray`, `LongArray`, `BooleanArray`, `FloatArray`, and `DoubleArray`.

Comments

Comments in Kotlin will come as no surprise to most programmers as they are the same as Java, Javascript, and C, among other languages. Block comments and line comments are supported:

```
// line comment

/*
 A block comment
 can span many
 lines
*/
```

Packages

Packages allow us to split code into namespaces. Any file may begin with a package declaration:

```
package com.packt.myproject
class Foo
fun bar(): String = "bar"
```

The package name is used to give us the **fully qualified name** (**FQN**) for a class, object, interface, or function. In the preceding example, the class `Foo` has the fully qualified name `com.packt.myproject.Foo` and the top level function `bar` has the fully qualified name of `com.packt.myproject.bar`.

Imports

To enable classes, objects, interfaces, and functions to be used outside of the declared package we must import the required class, object, interface, or function:

```
import com.packt.myproject.Foo
```

Wildcard imports

If we have a bunch of imports from the same package, then to avoid specifying each import individually we can import the entire package at once using the `*` operator:

```
import com.packt.myproject.*
```

Wildcard imports are especially useful when a large number of helper functions or constants are defined at the top level, and we wish to refer to those without using the classname:

```
package com.packt.myproject.constants

val PI = 3.142
val E = 2.178

package com.packt.myproject
import com.packt.myproject.constants.*
fun add() = E + PI
```

Notice how the `add()` function does not need to refer to `E` and `PI` using the FQN, but can simply use them as if they were in scope. The wildcard import removes the repetition that would otherwise be needed when importing numerous constants.

Import renaming

If two different packages each use the same name, then we can use the `as` keyword to alias the name. This is especially useful when common names are used by multiple libraries, such as `java.io.Path` and `org.apache.hadoop.fs.Path`:

```
import com.packt.myproject.Foo
import com.packt.otherproject.Foo as Foo2

fun doubleFoo() {
  val foo1 = Foo()
  val foo2 = Foo2()
}
```

String templates

Java developers will be familiar with the usage of string concatenation to mix expressions with string literals:

```
val name = "Sam"
val concat = "hello " + name
```

String templates are a simple and effective way of embedding values, variables, or even expressions inside a string without the need for pattern replacement or string concatenation. Many languages now support this kind of feature, and Kotlin's designers also opted to include it (you might see the technique referred to in the Kotlin context as string interpolation).

String templates improve on the Java experience when using multiple variables in a single literal, as it keeps the string short and more readable.

Usage is extremely straightforward. A value or variable can be embedded simply by prefixing with a dollar (`$`) symbol:

```
val name = "Sam"
val str = "hello $name"
```

Arbitrary expressions can be embedded by prefixing with a dollar (`$`) and wrapping in braces `{}`:

```
val name = "Sam"
val str = "hello $name. Your name has ${name.length} characters"
```

Ranges

A range is defined as an interval that has a start value and an end value. Any types which are comparable can be used to create a range, which is done using the `..` operator:

```
val aToZ = "a".."z"
val oneToNine = 1..9
```

Once a range is created, the `in` operator can be used to test whether a given value is included in the range. This is why the types must be comparable. For a value to be included in a range, it must be greater than or equal to the start value and less than or equal to the end value:

```
val aToZ = "a".."z"
val isTrue = "c" in aToZ
val oneToNine = 1..9
val isFalse = 11 in oneToNine
```

Integer ranges (ints, longs, and chars) also have the ability to be used in a `for` loop. See the section on *For loops* for further details.

There are further library functions to create ranges not covered by the `..` operator; for example, `downTo()` will create a range counting down and `rangeTo()` will create a range up to a value. Both of these functions are defined as extension functions on numerical types:

```
val countingDown = 100.downTo(0)
val rangeTo = 10.rangeTo(20)
```

Once a range is created, you can modify the range, returning a new range. To modify the delta between each successive term in the range, we can use the `step()` function:

```
val oneToFifty = 1..50
val oddNumbers = oneToFifty.step(2)
```

You cannot use a negative value here to create a decreasing range. Finally, ranges can be reversed using the `reversed()` function. As the name implies, it returns a new range with the start and end values switched, and the step value negated:

```
val countingDownEvenNumbers = (2..100).step(2).reversed()
```

Loops

Kotlin supports the usual duo of loop constructs found in most languages – the `while` loop and the `for` loop. The syntax for `while` loops in Kotlin will be familiar to most developers, as it is exactly the same as most C-style languages:

```
while (true) {
  println("This will print out for a long time!")
}
```

The Kotlin `for` loop is used to iterate over any object that defines a function or extension function with the name iterator. All collections provide this function:

```
val list = listOf(1, 2, 3, 4)
for (k in list) {
  println(k)
}

val set = setOf(1, 2, 3, 4)
for (k in set) {
  println(k)
}
```

Note the syntax using the keyword `in`. The `in` operator is always used with `for` loops. In addition to collections, integral ranges are directly supported either inline or defined outside:

```
val oneToTen = 1..10
for (k in oneToTen) {
  for (j in 1..5) {
    println(k * j)
  }
}
```

Ranges are handled in a special way by the compiler, and are compiled into index-based `for` loops that are supported directly on the JVM, thus avoiding any performance penalty from creating iterator objects.

Any object can be used inside a `for` loop provided that it implements a function called `iterator` making this an extremely flexible construct. This function must return an instance of an object that provides the following two functions:

- operator `fun hasNext(): Boolean`
- operator `fun next(): T`

The compiler doesn't insist on any particular interface, as long as the object returned has those two functions present. For example, in the standard `String` class, Kotlin provides an `iterator` extension function that adheres to the required contract and so strings can be used in a `for` loop to iterate over the individual characters.

```
val string = "print my characters"
for (char in string) {
  println(char)
}
```

Arrays have an extension function called `indices`, which can be used to iterate over the index of an array.

```
for (index in array.indices) {
  println("Element $index is ${array[index]}")
}
```

The compiler also has special support for arrays, and will compile a loop over an array to a normal index based `for` loop avoiding any performance penalty just like for range loops.

Exception handling

Handling of exceptions is almost identical to the way Java handles exceptions with one key difference in Kotlin all exceptions are unchecked.

As a reminder, checked exceptions are those that must be declared as part of the method signature or handled inside the method. A typical example would be `IOException`, which is thrown by many `File` functions, and so ends up being declared in many places throughout the IO libraries.

Unchecked exceptions are those that do not need to be added to method signatures. A common example would be the all too familiar `NullPointerException`, which can be thrown anywhere. If this was a checked exception, literally every function would need to declare it!

In Kotlin, since all exceptions are unchecked, they never form part of function signatures.

The handling of an exception is identical to Java, with the use of `try`, `catch`, and `finally` blocks. Code that you wish to handle safely can be wrapped in a `try` block. Zero or more `catch` blocks can be added to handle different exceptions, and a `finally` block is always executed regardless of whether an exception was generated or not. The `finally` block is optional, but at least one `catch` or `finally` block must be present.

In this example, the `read()` function can throw an `IOException`, and so we may wish to handle this potential exception in our code. In this case, we assume the input stream must always be closed, regardless of whether the reading is successful or not, and so we wrap the `close()` function in a `finally` block:

```
fun readFile(path: Path): Unit {
  val input = Files.newInputStream(path)
  try {
    var byte = input.read()
    while (byte != -1) {
      println(byte)
      byte = input.read()
    }
  } catch (e: IOException) {
    println("Error reading from file. Error was ${e.message}")
  } finally {
    input.close()
  }
}
```

Instantiating classes

Creating an instance of a class will be familiar to readers who have experience of object-orientated programming. The syntax in many languages uses a `new` keyword followed by the name of the class to be created. The `new` keyword indicates to the compiler that the special constructor function should be invoked to initialize the new instance.

Kotlin, however, removes this ceremony. It treats calling a constructor function the same as a normal function, with the constructor function using the name of the class. This enables Kotlin to drop the `new` keyword entirely. Arguments are passed in as normal:

```
val file = File("/etc/nginx/nginx.conf")
val date = BigDecimal(100)
```

Referential equality and structural equality

When working with a language that supports object-oriented programming, there are two concepts of equality. The first is when two separate references point to the exact same instance in memory. The second is when two objects are separate instances in memory but have the same value. What same value means is specified by the developer of the class. For example, for two square instances to be the same we might just require they have the same length and width regardless of co-ordinate.

The former is called **referential equality**. To test whether two references point to the same instance, we use the `===` operator (triple equals) or `!==` for negation:

```
val a = File("/mobydick.doc")
val b = File("/mobydick.doc")
val sameRef = a === b
```

The value of the test `a === b` is false because, although `a` and `b` reference the same file on disk, they are two distinct instances of the `File` object.

The latter is called structural equality. To test whether two objects have the same value, we use the `==` operator or `!=` for negation. These function calls are translated into the use of the `equals` function that all classes must define. Note that this differs from how the `==` operator is used in Java – in Java the `==` operator is for referential equality and is usually avoided.

```
val a = File("/mobydick.doc")
val b = File("/mobydick.doc")
val structural = a == b
```

Note that, in the double equals check, the value was `true`. This is because the `File` object defines equality to be the value of the path. It is up to the creator of a class to determine what structural equality means for that class.

The == operator is null safe. That is, we don't need to worry if we are testing a null instance as the compiler will add the null check for us.

This expression

When inside a class or function, we often want to refer to the enclosing instance. For example, an instance may want to invoke a method passing itself as an argument. To do this, we use the keyword `this`:

```
class Person(name: String) {
  fun printMe() = println(this)
}
```

In Kotlin terminology, the reference referred to by the `this` keyword is called the current receiver. This is because it was the instance that received the invocation of the function. For example, if we have a string and invoke length, the string instance is the receiver.

In members of a class, `this` refers to the class instance. In extension functions, `this` refers to the instance that the extension function was applied to.

Scope

In nested scopes, we may wish to refer to an outer instance. To do that, we must qualify the usage of this, and we do that using labels. The label we use is typically the name of the outer class, but there are more complicated rules for functions and closures discussed in `Chapter 5`, *Higher Order Functions and Functional Programming*.

```
class Building(val address: String) {
  inner class Reception(telephone: String) {
    fun printAddress() = println(this@Building.address)
  }
}
```

Note the `print` function needed to qualify access to the `Building` outer instance. This is because `this` inside the `printAddress()` function would have referred to the closest containing class, which in this case is `Reception`. Do not worry about the `inner` keyword- that will be covered in `Chapter 3`, *Object Oriented Programming in Kotlin*.

Visibility modifiers

Usually not all functions or classes are designed to be part of your public API. Therefore, it is desirable to mark some parts of your code as internal and not accessible outside of the class or package. The keywords that are used to specify this are called visibility modifiers.

There are four visibility modifiers: Public, internal, protected, and private. If no modifier is given, then the default is used, which is public. This means they are fully visible to any code that wishes to use them.

Java developers will know that this contrasts to the Java default, which has package-level visibility.

Private

Any top-level function, class, or interface that is defined as `private` can only be accessed from the same file.

Inside a class, interface, or object, any `private` function or property is only visible to other members of the same class, interface, or object:

```
class Person {
  private fun age(): Int = 21
}
```

Here, the function `age()` would only be invokable by other functions in the `Person` class.

Protected

Top-level functions, classes, interfaces, and objects cannot be declared as protected. Any functions or properties declared as protected inside a class or interface are visible only to members of that class or interface, as well as subclasses.

Internal

Internal deals with the concept of a module. A module is defined as a Maven or Gradle module or an IntelliJ module. Any code that is marked as internal is visible from other classes and functions inside the same module. Effectively, internal acts as public to a module, rather than public to the universe:

```
internal class Person {
  fun age(): Int = 21
}
```

Control flow as expressions

An expression is a statement that evaluates to a value. The following expression evaluates to `true`:

```
"hello".startsWith("h")
```

A statement, on the other hand, has no resulting value returned. The following is a statement because it assigns a value to a variable, but does not evaluate to anything itself:

```
val a = 1
```

In Java, the common control flow blocks, such as `if...else` and `try..catch`, are statements. They do not evaluate to a value, so it is common in Java, when using these, to assign the results to a variable initialized outside the block:

```
public boolean isZero(int x) {
  boolean isZero;
  if (x == 0)
    isZero = true;
  else
    isZero = false;
  return isZero;
}
```

In Kotlin, the `if...else` and `try..catch` control flow blocks are expressions. This means the result can be directly assigned to a value, returned from a function, or passed as an argument to another function.

This small, yet powerful, feature allows boilerplate to be reduced, code made more readable, and the use of mutable variables avoided. The typical use case of declaring a variable outside of an `if` statement to then initialize it inside either branch can be avoided completely:

```
val date = Date()
val today = if (date.year == 2016) true else false

fun isZero(x: Int): Boolean {
  return if (x == 0) true else false
}
```

A similar technique can be used for `try..catch` blocks, which is as follows:

```
val success = try {
  readFile()
  true
} catch (e: IOException) {
  false
}
```

In that example, the success variable will contain the result of the `try` block only if it completes successfully; otherwise the `catch` clause return value will be used, in this case `false`.

Expressions need not be single lines. They can be blocks, of course, and in those cases the last line must be an expression, and that expression is the value that the block evaluates to.

When using `if` as an expression, you must include the `else` clause. Otherwise the compiler will not know what to do if the `if` did not evaluate to `true`. If you do not include the else clause, the compiler will display a compile time error.

Null syntax

Tony Hoare, the inventor of the quicksort algorithm, who introduced the concept of the null reference in 1965 called it his "billion dollar mistake". Unfortunately, we have to live with null references as they are present in the JVM, but Kotlin introduces some functionality to make it easier to avoid some common mistakes.

Kotlin requires that a variable that can assigned to null be declared with a `?`:

```
var str: String? = null
```

If this is not done, the code will not compile. This next example would result in a compile time error:

```
var str: String = null
```

Kotlin has much more than this to help in the fight against null pointer exceptions, and there is a full discussion of nulls and null safety in `Chapter 7`, *Null Safety, Reflection, and Annotations*.

Type checking and Casting: If a reference to an instance is declared as some general type A, but we want to test if we have a more specific type B, then Kotlin provides the `is` operator. This is equivalent to the `instanceof` operator in Java:

```
fun isString(any: Any): Boolean {
  return if (any is String) true else false
}
```

If the target type is invalid (a string was trying to be cast to a `File`), then a `ClassCastException` will be thrown at runtime.

Smart casts

If after type checking we want to refer to the variable as an instance of B, then the reference must be cast. In Java, this must be done explicitly, which results in duplication:

```
public void printStringLength(Object obj) {
  if (obj instanceof String) {
    String str = (String) obj
    System.out.print(str.length())
  }
}
```

The Kotlin compiler is more intelligent, and will remember type checks for us, implicitly casting the reference to the more specific type. This is referred to as a smart cast:

```
fun printStringLength(any: Any) {
  if (any is String) {
    println(any.length)
  }
}
```

The compiler knows that we can only be inside the code block if the variable was indeed an instance of string, and so the cast is performed for us, allowing us to access methods defined on the string instance.

Which variables can be used in a smart cast is restricted to those that the compiler can guarantee do not change between the time when the variable is checked and the time when it is used. This means that `var` fields and local vars that have been closed over and mutated (used in an anonymous function that assigns a new value) cannot be used in smart casts.

Smart casts even work on the right hand side of lazily evaluated Boolean operations if the left-hand side is a type check:

```
fun isEmptyString(any: Any): Boolean {
  return any is String && any.length == 0
}
```

The compiler knows that in this `&&` expression the right-hand side will not be evaluated unless the left-hand side was `true`, so the variable must be a string. The compiler, therefore, smart casts for us and allows us to access the `length` property on the right-hand side.

Similarly, in a `||` expression, we can test that a reference is not of a particular type on the left hand side, and if it is it not, then on the right-hand side it must be that type, so the compiler can smart cast the right-hand side:

```
fun isNotStringOrEmpty(any: Any): Boolean {
  return any !is String || any.length == 0
}
```

In this example, the function tests that we either don't have a string, or, if we do, then it must be empty.

Explicit casting

To cast a reference to a type explicitly, we use the `as` operator. Just as in Java, this operation will throw a `ClassCastException` if the cast cannot be performed legally:

```
fun length(any: Any): Int {
  val string = any as String
  return string.length
}
```

The null value cannot be cast to a type that is not defined as nullable. So the previous example would have thrown an exception if the value was null. To cast to a value that can be null, we simply declare the required type as nullable, as we would for a reference:

```
val string: String? = any as String
```

Remember that if a cast fails, then a `ClassCastException` will be thrown. If we want to avoid the exception, and instead have a null value if the cast fails, then we can use the safe cast operator `as?`. This operator will return the casted value if the target type is compatible, otherwise it will return null. In the next example, `string` would be a successful cast, but `file` would be null:

```
val any = "/home/users"
val string: String? = any as String
val file: File? = any as File
```

When expression

The classic `switch` statement has been supported in many languages, including C, C++, and Java, but is rather restrictive. At the same time, the functional programming concept of pattern matching has become more mainstream. Kotlin blends the two, and offers `when`, a more powerful alternative to `switch` while not going quite as far as full pattern matching.

There are two forms of `when`. The first is similar to `switch`, accepting an argument, and with a series of conditions, each of which is checked in turn against the value. The second is without an argument and used as a replacement for a series of `if...else` conditions.

When (value)

The simplest example of `when` is matching against different constants, which will be familiar as the typical usage of `switch` in a language like Java:

```
fun whatNumber(x: Int) {
  when (x) {
    0 -> println("x is zero")
    1 -> println("x is 1")
    else -> println("X is neither 0 or 1")
  }
}
```

Note that `when` must be exhaustive, and so the compile enforces that the final branch is an else.

If the compiler can infer that all possible conditions have been satisfied, then the else can be omitted. This is common with sealed classes or enums- more on those in future chapters.

Similar to `if...else` and `try..catch`, `when` can be used as an expression, and so the result of the evaluated branch is the result that is returned. In this example, the `when` expression is assigned to the `valisZero` before being returned:

```
fun isMinOrMax(x: Int): Boolean {
  val isZero = when (x) {
    Int.MIN_VALUE -> true
    Int.MAX_VALUE -> true
    else -> false
  }
  return isZero
}
```

Furthermore, constants can be combined together if the branch code is the same. To do this, we simply use a comma to separate constants:

```
fun isZeroOrOne(x: Int): Boolean {
  return when (x) {
    0, 1 -> true
    else -> false
  }
}
```

Note that, in this example, the 0 and 1 clauses were combined together and the return value was directly returned instead of being assigned to an intermediate variable.

We are not just restricted to matching on constants in each condition. We can use any function that returns the same type as the type being matched on. The function is invoked, and if the result matches the value, then that branch is evaluated:

```
fun isAbs(x: Int): Boolean {
  return when (x) {
    Math.abs(x) -> true
    else -> false
  }
}
```

In the example, the `Math.abs` function is invoked, and if the result is the same as the input value, then the value was already absolute, so `true` is returned. Otherwise, the result of `Math.abs` must have been different, and so the value was not absolute and `false` is returned.

Ranges are also supported. We can use the `in` operator to verify whether the value is included in the range, and if so, the condition is evaluated to `true`:

```
fun isSingleDigit(x: Int): Boolean {
```

```
    return when (x) {
      in -9..9 -> true
      else -> false
    }
  }
```

Note that if the value is contained in the interval (-9, 9), then it must be a single digit, and so `true` is returned, otherwise false is returned.

Along a similar line, we can use `in` to verify whether the value is contained in a collection:

```
fun isDieNumber(x: Int): Boolean {
  return when (x) {
    in listOf(1, 2, 3, 4, 5, 6) -> true
    else -> false
  }
}
```

Finally, `when` can also use smart casts. As discussed previously, smart casts allow the compiler to verify the runtime type of a variable, and expose it:

```
fun startsWithFoo(any: Any): Boolean {
  return when (any) {
    is String -> any.startsWith("Foo")
    else -> false
  }
}
```

In the previous example, the parameter is declared with a type of `Any`, so that there is no restriction on what type can be passed as an argument (analogous to Java's object type). Inside the `when` expression, we check if the type is a string, and if it is, we can then access functions declared on the string, such as the `startsWith` function.

There is no restriction on combining these different conditions types. You can happily mix smart casts, `in`, arbitrary functions, and constants, all in the same `when` expression.

When without argument

The second form of `when` is used without an argument, and is a drop-in replacement for `if...else` clauses. This can sometimes result in clearer code, especially if many of the conditions are simple comparisons. The following example shows two ways of writing the same code: The first with traditional `if...else` blocks, and the second using `when`:

```
fun whenWithoutArgs(x: Int, y: Int) {
  when {
```

```
        x < y -> println("x is less than y")
        x > y -> println("X is greater than y")
        else -> println("X must equal y")
    }
}
```

Function Return

To return a value from a function, we use the `return` keyword with the value or expression we want to return:

```
fun addTwoNumbers(a: Int, b: Int): Int {
  return a + b
}
```

Note that we specified the return value of the function. By default, `return` returns from the nearest enclosing function or anonymous function. So, in a nested function, this will return from the innermost function only:

```
fun largestNumber(a: Int, b: Int, c: Int): Int {
  fun largest(a: Int, b: Int): Int {
    if (a > b) return a
      else return b
  }
  return largest(largest(a, b), largest(b, c))
}
```

In this somewhat contrived example, the nested function `largest` returns only from itself. If the innermost function is an anonymous function, then that still counts for return purposes:

```
fun printLessThanTwo() {
  val list = listOf(1, 2, 3, 4)
  list.forEach(fun(x) {
    if (x < 2) println(x)
    else return
  })
  println("This line will still execute")
}
```

If we need to return a value from a closure, then we need to qualify the return with a label, otherwise the return would be for the outer function. A label is just a string that ends with an `@`:

```
fun printUntilStop() {
  val list = listOf("a", "b", "stop", "c")
```

```
    list.forEach stop@ {
      if (it == "stop") return@stop
      else println(it)
    }
}
```

We don't need to specify the label, in which case an implicit label can be used. Implicit labels are the name of the function that accepted the closure. If a label is defined, then the implicit label is not generated:

```
fun printUntilStop() {
  val list = listOf("a", "b", "stop", "c")
  list.forEach {
    if (it == "stop") return@forEach
    else println(it)
  }
}
```

Type hierarchy

In Kotlin, the uppermost type is called `Any`. This is analogous to Java's object type. The `Any` type defines the well-known `toString`, `hashCode`, and `equals` methods. It also defines the extension methods `apply`, `let`, and `to`, among others. These methods will be described in more detail in `Chapter 5`, *Higher Order Functions and Functional Programming*.

The Unit type is the equivalent of void in Java. Having a Unit type is common in a functional programming language, and the distinction between void and Unit is subtle. Void is not a type, but a special edge case that is used to indicate to the compiler that a function returns no value. Unit is a proper type, with a singleton instance, also referred to as `Unit` or `()`. When a function is defined as a returning Unit, then it will return the singleton unit instance.

This results in greater soundness of the type `system` as now all functions can be defined as having a return value, even if it's just the Unit type, and functions that have no arguments can be defined as accepting the Unit type.

Where Kotlin differs from Java most notably is the addition of a bottom type, `Nothing`, which is a type that has no instances. Similar to how `Any` is a superclass of all types, `Nothing` is the subclass of all types. For those who are new to the concept of a bottom type, it might seem strange to have such a type, but it has several use cases.

Firstly, `Nothing` can be used to inform the compiler that a function never completes normally; for example, it might loop forever, or always throw an exception. Another example is empty immutable collections. An empty list of `Nothing` could be assigned to a reference excepting a list of strings, and because the list is immutable, there is no danger of a string being added to such a list. Therefore, these empty values can be cached and reused. This is actually the basis of the implementation of the standard library functions `emptyList()`, `emptySet()`, and so on.

Summary

Kotlin has introduced many improvements over Java while at the same time keeping many of the features that made Java one of the most popular languages over the past two decades. After reading this chapter, you should feel comfortable delving into Kotlin programming and exploring some of the productivity enhancements Kotlin has to offer.

3
Object-Oriented Programming in Kotlin

Kotlin is an object-oriented programming (OOP) language with support for higher-order functions and lambdas. If you don't know what lambdas are, don't worry, there is a full chapter dedicated to them. If you have been using a functional language already, you will find functional language-like constructs supported in Kotlin.

Over time, software complexity has increased, and the OOP abstraction has allowed us to model the problem we have to solve in terms of *objects*. You can view each object as a minicomputer on its own: it has a state and can perform actions. An object through its available actions exhibits some sort of behavior; therefore, there is a clear analogy between objects/entities and real life.

The first characteristic of an object-oriented abstraction has been pinned down by Alan Key, one of the creators of the first successful OOP language: Smalltalk. In his book *The Early History Of Smalltalk*, he makes the following points:

- **Everything is an object**: An object is nothing but a block of memory allocated and configured according to a design/definition. From the problem space you have to solve, you take all the logical entities and translate them into objects in your program.
- **Objects communicate by sending and receiving messages (in terms of objects)**: Your program will be a set of objects performing different actions as a result of calling methods that each one expose.
- **Objects have their own memory (in terms of objects)**: This should be read as, *You can create an object by composing other objects*.
- **Every object is an instance of a class (which must be an object)**: Think of a class as a blueprint specifying what the type can do.

- **The class holds the shared behavior for its instances (in the form of objects in a program list)**: This means all the objects of a particular type can receive the same messages; in other words, they expose the same methods.

Kotlin provides full support for the points above but also supports fully the three pillars of any modern OOP language: encapsulation, inheritance, and polymorphism. Encapsulation means that a group of related fields and methods are treated as an object. Inheritance describes the capability of creating a new class from an existing one. Polymorphism means you can use different classes interchangeably despite the fact that each one implements its methods differently. Through the content of this chapter, we will get into a bit more detail about how language constructs support this.

The OOP abstraction is meant to help us alleviate the problems encountered with large code bases. This makes it easier for us to understand, maintain, and evolve code bases and keep them bug-free by providing us with the following:

- **Simplicity**: Program objects model the real world, thus reducing complexity and streamlining the program structure
- **Modularity**: Each object's internal workings are decoupled from other parts of the system
- **Modifiability**: Changes inside an object do not affect any other part of a program if you have done your design right
- **Extensibility**: An object's requirements change quite often, and you can quickly respond to them by adding new objects or modifying existing ones
- **Reusability**: The objects can be used in other programs

In this chapter you will learn:

- How to define and use classes and interfaces
- When to choose interfaces over abstract classes
- When to choose inheritance over composition

Classes

Classes are the main building blocks of any object-oriented programming language. The concept of a class was first studied by Aristotle. He was the first one to come up with the concept of a class of fishes and a class of birds. All objects, despite being unique, are part of a class and share common behavior.

A class enables you to create your own type by grouping together methods and variable of other types. Think of a class as a blueprint; it describes the data and the behavior of a type.

Classes are declared by using the class keyword, as shown in the following example:

```
class Deposit {
}
```

Compared to Java, you can define multiple classes within the same source file. The class keyword can be preceded by the access level. If it is not specified, it will default to public; this means anyone can create objects of this class. The name of the class follows the keyword and the curly braces contain the class body where the behavior and data are defined: fields, properties, and methods.

The class construct supports the first characteristic of an OOP language: encapsulation. The idea behind it is that you want to keep each class discreet and self-contained. This allows you to change its implementation without affecting any part of the code that uses it, as long as it continues to meet the terms of its contract.

So far, I have used the terms class and object interchangeably. As we move forward, we will make a clear distinction between the two. An object is a runtime instance of a class definition. In order to create an instance of a class, you need to call the constructor. In the preceding example, the class `Deposit` gets an empty constructor generated by the compiler automatically. But if you want to provide a constructor, you would need to write the following:

```
class Person constructor(val firstName: String, val lastName:  String,
val age: Int?) {}

fun main(args: Array<String>) {
  val person1 = Person("Alex", "Smith", 29)
  val person2 = Person("Jane", "Smith", null)
  println("${person1.firstName},${person1.lastName} is  ${person1.age}
years old")
  println("${person2.firstName},${person2.lastName} is
${person2.age?.toString() ?: "?"} years old")
}
```

If you have been a Java developer for years, you will most likely have noticed the lack of the `new` keyword. In Java, to create a new instance of a given class, you always use `new MyClass`. This is not the case in Kotlin though; you don't need to use it. If you do, you will actually get a compilation error since it is not a recognized keyword.

For a Scala developer, the preceding code would look very familiar, though you would probably ask why you have to use the constructor keyword. Doesn't the compiler know it is in the context of a constructor? The answer is that you don't, unless you specify access modifiers or annotations. The preceding constructor is called the primary constructor. I guess your next question will be, How can this primary constructor contain code; after all you want to validate that the incoming parameters are valid? The answer lies with the `init` block. To have any code run as part of your primary constructor, you would have to do this:

```
    class Person (val firstName: String, val lastName: String, val  age:
Int?){
      init{
        require(firstName.trim().length > 0) { "Invalid firstName
argument." }
        require(lastName.trim().length > 0) { "Invalid lastName  argument."
}
        if (age != null) {
          require(age >= 0 && age < 150) { "Invalid age argument." }
        }
      }
    }
```

Now the validation code will run as part of your primary constructor. The `require` method will throw `IllegalArgumentException` with the message you have provided if the expression given evaluates to `False`.

I am sure some of you would question how does it work with all the three arguments. Are they created as public fields of the class? The answer is, no. There are properties. If you are accustomed to the .NET world, you will immediately know what it is all about. There is a chapter later in the book where we will discuss in detail how properties work.

How does one create a new instance of `Person` and grab the values of all the three fields when using the class from Java code? This is done through the getter functions that any Java developer is accustomed to:

```
    Person p = new Person("Jack", "Miller", 21);
    System.out.println(String.format("%s, %s is %d age old",
p.getFirstName(), p.getLastName(), p.getAge()));
```

The third parameter of the constructor is a nullable integer; it would be good to have the option of not having to actually type null when instantiating an instance for which we don't have the age. Kotlin is a modern language that supports default value for a method parameter, but on this occasion let's just say it doesn't. So we want to have a second constructor for which we only pass the first and last name:

```
    constructor(firstName: String, lastName: String) :  this(firstName,
```

```
    lastName, null)
```

For any secondary constructor you need to call the primary constructor via `this`, and pass all the parameters required. Now you can create a new `Person` object like this:

```
val person2 = Person("Jane", "Smith")
```

If you don't want to have your constructor accessed directly, you should mark it private, protected, or internal. A typical singleton design consists of providing a private constructor and then having the `getInstance()` method give you that one instance of that class at runtime. When defining abstract classes you should flag your constructor visibility as protected; this way it can only be called by the derived classes. We will see this shortly as we cover inheritance. Given your module logic, you could expose classes whose instances can and should only be created within your module:

```
class Database internal constructor(connection:Connection) {
}
```

Prefixing your constructor arguments with `val` or `var` is not a must; if you don't want the getter (or setter if you use `var`) to be generated, you can always do the following:

```
class Person2(firstName: String, lastName: String, howOld:  Int?) {
  private val name: String
  private val age: Int?

  init {
    this.name = "$firstName,$lastName"
    this.age = howOld
  }

  fun getName(): String = this.name

  fun getAge(): Int? = this.age
}
```

Try creating a new instance of this class and then use the dot operator to prompt intellisense to display the available methods on your object. Unlike the first example, the three parameters are not translated into fields; the pop-up window will display two methods, named `getName` and `getAge`.

Access levels

All types and type members have accessibility levels, which constrains where they can be used. As mentioned earlier, not providing one would default to public. Kotlin comes with three different access levels, which are as follows:

- **Internal**: This means you can create a new instance of your class from anywhere within your module
- **Private**: This is more restrictive than the previous one because your class is only visible in the scope of the file defining it
- **Protected**: You can use this accessibility level only for subclasses; it is not available for the file-level type of declaration

The internal access level is the equivalent of private for classes when it comes to encapsulation, only this time it is at the module level. You could make it module-visible only if the code isn't accessed from outside the scope of the module. This reduces the API you exposed and makes it easier to understand. Furthermore, if a change is required in your module, you can assume that modifying the contract would only break the internal API of the assembly.

Nested classes

Working with Java, you may have come across the concept of creating a class within the body of another class, in other words, creating nested classes. You could do the same in Kotlin, and here is how you can do it:

```
class OuterClassName {

  class NestedClassName {

  }
}
```

You could, of course, provide the access level to the nested class. If you set it to private, you will be able to create an object of `NestedClassName` only from within the scope of `OuterClassName`. To allow for a code block within your module to be able to create an instance of the inner class, you will have to make use of the internal keyword. If you decide to set the access level as protected, any class that derives from `OuterClassName` would be able to create those instances. If the term deriving is not something you know about, don't worry; later in this chapter, we are going to address inheritance and it will all be clear.

In Java, nested classes come in two flavors: static and non-static. Nested classes declared using the `static` keyword are called static nested classes, whereas nested classes that are declared non-static are called inner classes. A nested class is considered a member of its enclosing class:

```
class Outer {
  static class StaticNested {}
  class Inner {}
}
```

There is a subtle difference between static and inner nested classes. The latter have access to the enclosing class members even if they are declared private, whereas the static nested classes can access the public members only. Furthermore, to create an instance of the inner class, you will first need an instance of an `Outer` class.

Kotlin, just like Java, supports the same construct. To create the equivalent of a static nested class, you could use this:

```
class BasicGraph(val name: String) {
  class Line(val x1: Int, val y1: Int, val x2: Int, val y2:  Int) {
    fun draw(): Unit {
      println("Drawing Line from ($x1:$y1) to ($x2, $y2)")
    }
  }
  fun draw(): Unit {
    println("Drawing the graph $name")
  }
}

val line = BasicGraph.Line(1, 0, -2, 0)
line.draw()
```

The example is pretty straightforward and shows you how it works. To allow the `Line` class to access a private member of the outer class `BasicGraph`, all you need to do is make the `Line` class inner; just prefix the class with the inner keyword:

```
class BasicGraphWithInner(graphName: String) {
  private val name: String

  init {
    name = graphName
  }

  inner class InnerLine(val x1: Int, val y1: Int, val x2: Int,  val y2:
Int) {
    fun draw(): Unit {
      println("Drawing Line from ($x1:$y1) to ($x2, $y2) for  graph
```

```
$name ")
          }
        }

        fun draw(): Unit {
          println("Drawing the graph $name")
        }
      }
```

Kotlin comes with a more powerful `this` expression than you may be accustomed with. You can refer the outer scope to this by using the label construct `this@label`. Here is an example:

```
class A {
  private val somefield: Int = 1
  inner class B {
    private val somefield: Int = 1
    fun foo(s: String) {
      println("Field <somefield> from B" + this.somefield)
      println("Field <somefield> from B" + this@B.somefield)
      println("Field <somefield> from A" + this@A.somefield)
    }
  }
}
```

In this case, both the outer and the inner classes contain a field sharing the same name; this expression helps with disambiguation.

Working on a UI code base, you will get into a situation where, for a control (listbox, button, and so on), you will have to provide an event handler for different events they raise. The most common example is the click event of a button on your screen. Typically, you will want to react to it and perform some action. The UI framework will expect you to provide an instance of a class; from this listener class, you will most likely want to access some state in the outer class scope. Therefore, you will end up providing an anonymous inner class, as in the following example where we count the number of clicks on a button:

```
class Controller {
  private var clicks:Int=0
  fun enableHook() {
    button.addMouseListener(object : MouseAdapter() {
      override fun mouseClicked(e: MouseEvent) {clicks++}
    })
  }
}
```

We assume there is a reference to a `UI` button and we attach the `enableHook` callback for its mouse events. Every time the button is clicked, it will increase the field clicks. All we have defined here in fact is an inner class, an anonymous one.

Data classes

It happens quite often we need to define classes for the sole purpose of holding data. If you have been coding in Scala, I'm sure case classes will come to your mind. Kotlin provides a similar concept, but the term is known as data classes. We will talk a bit more about this type of class in detail in a later chapter, but for now you can define such a class like this:

```
data class Customer(val id:Int, val name:String, var  address:String)
```

The compiler does a lot for us when we define a data class, but we will leave these details for later.

Enum classes

Enumeration is a specific type of class; a variable of a given `enum` type is limited to a set of predefined constants: the ones that have been defined by the type. To define an enumeration, you could use the `enum` class keywords, as in the following example where we create a type for all the days in a week:

```
    enum class Day {  MONDAY, TUESDAY, WEDNESDAY, THURSDAY,  FRIDAY,
SATURDAY, SUNDAY}
```

Enumeration, like all classes, can take a constructor parameter. We can define an `enum` class to represent the planets in our solar system, and for each planet we retain the total mass and radius:

```
    public enum class Planet(val mass: Double, val radius: Double) {
      MERCURY(3.303e+23, 2.4397e6), VENUS(4.869e+24, 6.0518e6),
EARTH(5.976e+24, 6.37814e6), MARS(6.421e+23, 3.3972e6),  JUPITER(1.9e+27,
7.1492e7), SATURN(5.688e+26, 6.0268e7),  URANUS(8.686e+25, 2.5559e7),
NEPTUNE(1.024e+26, 2.4746e7);
    }
```

I made the two parameters `val` to have them exposed as properties. All enumeration instances come with two properties predefined. One is *name* of type `String` and the second one is *ordinal* of type `int`. The former returns the name of the instance, and the latter gives you the position in the enumeration's type declaration.

Similar to Java, Kotlin provides you with helper methods to work with enumeration classes. To retrieve an `enum` value based on the name, you will need to use this:

```
Planet.valueOf("JUPITER")
```

To get all the values defined, you will need to write this:

```
Planet.values()
```

Just like any class, enumeration types can inherit an interface and implement it anonymously for each `enum` value. Here is an example of how you could achieve this:

```
interface Printable {
  fun print(): Unit
}

public enum class Word : Printable {
  HELLO {
    override fun print() {
      println("Word is HELLO")
    }
  },
  BYE {
    override fun print() {
      println("Word is BYE")
    }
  }
}

val w= Word.HELLO
w.print()
```

Static methods and companion objects

Unlike Java, Kotlin doesn't support static methods for a class. Most readers will know that static methods do not belong to the object instance but rather to the type itself. In Kotlin, it is advisable to define methods at the package level to achieve the functionality of static methods. Let's define a new Kotlin file and name it `Static`. Within this file, we will place the code for a function that will return the first character of the input string (if the input is empty, an exception will be raised), which is as follows:

```
fun showFirstCharacter(input:String):Char{
  if(input.isEmpty()) throw IllegalArgumentException()
  return input.first()
}
```

Then, in your code, you can simply call `showFirstCharacter("Kotlin is cool!")`. The compiler is here to do some of the work for you. Using `javap`, we can take a look at the byte code generated. Just run `javap -c StaticKt.class` to get the code produced by the compiler:

```
Compiled from "Static.kt"
public final class com.programming.kotlin.chapter03.StaticKt {
  public static final char showFirstCharacter(java.lang.String);
    Code:
      0: aload_0
      1: ldc           #9                  //String input
      3: invokestatic  #15                 //Method
kotlin/jvm/internal/Intrinsics.checkParameterIsNotNull:(Ljava/lang
/Object;Ljava/lang/String;)V
      ...
      40: aload_0
      41: checkcast     #17        //class java/lang/CharSequence
      44: invokestatic  #35                 //Method
kotlin/text/StringsKt.first:(Ljava/lang/CharSequence;)C
      47: ireturn
}
```

As you can see from the printout, the compiler has actually generated a class for us and has marked it as final; it can't be inherited, as you already know. Within this class, the compiler has added the function we defined. Let's call this method from the program entry point and again using the utility `javap` we can look at what the bytecode looks like:

```
fun main(args: Array<String>) {
  println("First lettter:" + showFirstCharacter("Kotlin is cool"))
}
Compiled from "Program.kt"
public final class com.programming.kotlin.chapter03.ProgramKt {
  public static final void main(java.lang.String[]);
    Code:
      0: aload_0
      ...
      18: ldc           #29                 //String Kotlin is  cool
      20: invokestatic  #35                 //Method
com/programming/kotlin/chapter03/StaticKt.showFirstCharacter:(Ljav
a/lang/String;)C
}
```

Most of the bytecode has been left out for the sake of simplicity, but at line 20 you can see there is a call to our method; in particular, the call is made via the `invokestatic` routine.

We can't talk about static methods and not bring singletons into the discussion. A singleton is a design pattern that limits the instantiation of a given class to one instance. Once created, it will live throughout the span of your program. Kotlin borrows the approach found in Scala. Here is how you can define a singleton in Kotlin:

```
object Singleton{
  private var count = 0
  fun doSomething():Unit {
    println("Calling a doSomething (${++count} call/-s in  total)")
  }
}
```

From any function, you can now call `Singleton.doSomething`, and each time, you will see the counter increasing. If you were to look at the bytecode produced, you will find out the compiler is doing some of the work for us once again:

```
public final class com.programming.kotlin.chapter03.Singleton {
  public static final com.programming.kotlin.chapter03.Singleton  INSTANCE;
  public final void doSomething();
    Code:
      0: new             #10       // class java/lang/StringBuilder
      43: return
      ...
      static {};
    Code:
       0: new             #2         //class
com/programming/kotlin/chapter03/Singleton
       3: invokespecial #61             //Method "<init>":()V
       6: return
}
```

I have left out the code produced for our `doSomething` method since it is not the focus of this topic. The compiler once again has created a class and marked it final. Furthermore, it has introduced a member called `INSTANCE` and has marked it static. The interesting part is at the end of the listing where you see the `static{};` entry. This is the class initializer, and it is called only once, JVM will make sure this happens, before:

- An instance of the class is created
- A static method of the class is invoked
- A static field of the class is assigned
- A non-constant static field is used
- An assert statement lexically nested within the class is executed for a top-level class

In this case, the code is called before the first call to `doSomething` because we access the static member `INSTANCE` (see the following `getstatic` bytecode routine). If we were to call this method twice, we would get the following bytecode:

```
public static final void main(java.lang.String[]);
  Code:
    0: aload_0
    1: ldc              #9                      // String args
    3: invokestatic     #15    //Method
kotlin/jvm/internal/Intrinsics.checkParameterIsNotNull:(Ljava/lang
/Object;Ljava/lang/String;)V
    6: getstatic      #21             //Field
com/programming/kotlin/chapter03/Singleton.INSTANCE:Lcom/programmi
ng/kotlin/chapter03/Singleton;
     9: invokevirtual #25          //Method
com/programming/kotlin/chapter03/Singleton.doSomething:()V
     12: getstatic      #21          //Field
com/programming/kotlin/chapter03/Singleton.INSTANCE:Lcom/programmi
ng/kotlin/chapter03/Singleton;
     15: invokevirtual #25          //Method
com/programming/kotlin/chapter03/Singleton.doSomething:()V
     18: return
```

You can see that in both occasions `doSomething` is called as a virtual method. The reason is you can create a singleton that inherits from a given class, as in the example here:

```
open class SingletonParent(var x:Int){
  fun something():Unit{
    println("X=$x")
  }
}
object SingletonDerive:SingletonParent(10){}
```

There is a way to call a static method as you would do in Java. To achieve this, you will have to place your object within a class and mark it as a companion object. This concept of a companion object will be familiar to someone with at least entry-level knowledge of Scala. The following example uses the factory design pattern to construct an instance of `Student`:

```
interface StudentFactory {
  fun create(name: String): Student
}
class Student private constructor(val name: String) {
  companion object : StudentFactory {
    override fun create(name: String): Student {
      return Student(name)
    }
  }
```

```
}
```

As you can see, the constructor for the `Student` type has been marked `private`. Thus, it can't be invoked from anywhere apart from inside the `Student` class or the `companion object`. The `companion` class has full visibility for all the methods and members of `Student`.

From the code, you will need to call `Student.create("Jack Wallace")` to create a new instance of `Student`. If you look in the build output, you will notice there are two classes generated for `Student`: one is `Student.class` and the other is `Student$Companion.class`. Let's see how the call to `Student.create` gets translated into bytecode:

```
public final class com.programming.kotlin.chapter03.ProgramKt {
  public static final void main(java.lang.String[]);
    Code:
      0: aload_0
      1: ldc           #9                 //String args
      3: invokestatic  #15                //Method
kotlin/jvm/internal/Intrinsics.checkParameterIsNotNull:(Ljava/lang
/Object;Ljava/lang/String;)V
      6: getstatic     #21                // Field
com/programming/kotlin/chapter03/Student.Companion:Lcom/programmin
g/kotlin/chapter03/Student$Companion;
      9: ldc           #23              //String Jack Wallace
      11: invokevirtual #29             //Method
com/programming/kotlin/chapter03/Student$Companion.create:(Ljava/l
ang/String;)Lcom/programming/kotlin/chapter03/Student;
      14: pop
      15: return
}
```

At line 6, you will notice there is a call for a static member `getstatic`. As you can probably imagine, there is a static field added to the `Student` class of the type `Student.Companion`:

```
public final class com.programming.kotlin.chapter03.Student {
  public static final  com.programming.kotlin.chapter03.Student$Companion
Companion;
  public final java.lang.String getName();
   static {};
   Code:
     0: new           #39   //class
com/programming/kotlin/chapter03/Student$Companion
     3: dup
     4: aconst_null
     5: invokespecial #42         //Method
```

```
com/programming/kotlin/chapter03/Student$Companion."<init>":(Lkotl
in/jvm/internal/DefaultConstructorMarker;)V
     8: putstatic     #44        //Field
Companion:Lcom/programming/kotlin/chapter03/Student$Companion;
     11: return

public
com.programming.kotlin.chapter03.Student(java.lang.String,kotlin.jvm.intern
al.DefaultConstructorMarker);
   Code:
     0: aload_0
     1: aload_1
     2: invokespecial #24        //Method  "<init>":(Ljava/lang/String;)V
     5: return
```

This code snippet proves the assumption is correct. You can see the `Companion` member being added to our class. And yet again, the class gets class initializer code generated to create an instance of our `companion` class. `Student.create` is shorthand for writing code such as `Student.Companion.create()`. If you were trying to create an instance of `Student.Companion` (that is, `val c = Sudent.Companion`), you would get a compilation error. A companion object follows all the inheritance rules.

Interfaces

An interface is nothing more than a contract; it contains definitions for a set of related functionalities. The implementer of the interface has to adhere to the interface the contract and implement the required methods. Just like Java 8, a Kotlin interface contains the declarations of abstract methods as well as method implementations. Unlike abstract classes, an interface cannot contain state; however, it can contain properties. For the Scala developer reading this book, you will find this similar to the Scala traits:

```
interface Document {
  val version: Long
  val size: Long

  val name: String
  get() = "NoName"

  fun save(input: InputStream)
  fun load(stream: OutputStream)
  fun getDescription(): String {
     return "Document $name has $size byte(-s)"}
}
```

This interface defines three properties and three methods; the *name* property and the `getDescription` methods provide the default implementation. How would you use the interface from a Java class? Let's see by implementing this interface:

```
public class MyDocument implements Document {

  public long getVersion() {
    return 0;
  }

  public long getSize() {
    return 0;
  }

  public void save(@NotNull InputStream input) {
  }

  public void load(@NotNull OutputStream stream) {
  }

  public String getName() {
    return null;
  }

  public String getDescription() {
    return null;
  }
}
```

You can see the properties have been translated into getters. Despite providing default implementations for `getDescription` along with the name, you still have to implement them. This is not the case when implementing the interface in a Kotlin class:

```
class DocumentImpl : Document {
  override val size: Long
  get() = 0

  override fun load(stream: OutputStream) {
  }

  override fun save(input: InputStream) {
  }
  override val version: Long
  get() = 0
}
```

Let's delve into the generated code and see what actually happens behind the scenes with the code for those two methods implemented at the interface level:

```
$ javap -c
build\classes\main\com\programming\kotlin\chapter03\DocumentImpl.class
Compiled from "KDocumentImpl.kt"
public final class com.programming.kotlin.chapter03.KDocumentImpl
implements com.programming.kotlin.chapter03.Document {
  public long getSize();
    Code:
      0: lconst_0
      1: lreturn
public void load(java.io.OutputStream);
  Code:
    0: aload_1
    1: ldc           #15                 //String stream
    3: invokestatic  #21                 //Method
kotlin/jvm/internal/Intrinsics.checkParameterIsNotNull:(Ljava/lang/Ob
ject;Ljava/lang/String;)V
    6: return
public void save(java.io.InputStream);
  Code:
    0: aload_1
    1: ldc           #26                 //String input
    3: invokestatic  #21          //Method
kotlin/jvm/internal/Intrinsics.checkParameterIsNotNull:(Ljava/lang/Ob
ject;Ljava/lang/String;)V
    6: return
public long getVersion();
   Code:
     0: lconst_0
     1: lreturn
public com.programming.kotlin.chapter03.KDocumentImpl();
   Code:
     0: aload_0
     1: invokespecial #32      //Method  java/lang/Object."<init>":()V
     4: return
public java.lang.String getName();
   Code:
     0: aload_0
     1: invokestatic  #39                //Method
com/programming/kotlin/chapter03/Document$DefaultImpls.getName:(Lcom/
programming/kotlin/chapter03/Document;)Ljava/lang/String;
     4: areturn
public java.lang.String getDescription();
   Code:
     0: aload_0
     1: invokestatic  #43                //Method
```

```
com/programming/kotlin/chapter03/Document$DefaultImpls.getDescription
:(Lcom/programming/kotlin/chapter03/Document;)Ljava/lang/String;
     4: areturn
}
```

You may have already spotted the calls to the `DefaultImpls` class in the code of `getDescription` and `getName`. If you look into the classes produced by the compiler (`build/main/com/ programming/kotlin/chapter03`), you will notice a file named `Document$DocumentImpls.class`. What is this class all about, I hear you ask? You haven't written such a class. We can find out what it contains by again turning to `javap`:

```
public final class com.programming.kotlin.chapter03.Document$DefaultImpls {
  public static java.lang.String
getName(com.programming.kotlin.chapter03.Document);
    Code:
      0: ldc           #9                    //String NoName
      2: areturn
public static java.lang.String
getDescription(com.programming.kotlin.chapter03.Document);
     Code:
       0: new           #14       //class java/lang/StringBuilder
       3: dup
       4: invokespecial #18                  //Method
java/lang/StringBuilder."<init>":()V
       7: ldc           #20             //String Document
       9: invokevirtual #24                 //Method
java/lang/StringBuilder.append:(Ljava/lang/String;)Ljava/lang/StringBuilder
;
       12: aload_0
       13: invokeinterface #29,  1        //InterfaceMethod
com/programming/kotlin/chapter03/Document.getName:()Ljava/lang/String ;
       40: invokevirtual #43            //Method
java/lang/StringBuilder.toString:()Ljava/lang/String;
       43: areturn
}
```

From the preceding code snippet (I left out some of the code for simplicity), you can clearly see the compiler has created a class for us containing two static methods that match the ones we have implemented in the interface.

While the code for `getName` is very simple, after all, we just return a string value, the one for `getDescription` is a bit more complex. The code makes use of `StringBuilder` to create the string for description purposes. The interesting part is how it goes back to `getSize` and `getName`. If you look at line 12, `aload_0` pushes the `Document` parameter (the method `getDescription` takes one parameter) to the stack. The next line makes the call by using `invokeinterface` to call a method defined by a Java interface. Discussing the details of the Java bytecode goes beyond the scope of this book. You can find quite a few details, if you are interested to know more, with a quick search on the Web.

Inheritance

Inheritance is fundamental to object-oriented programming. It allows us to create new classes that reuse, extend, and/or modify the behavior of the preexisting ones. The preexisting class is called the super (or base or parent) class, and the brand new class we are creating is called the derived class. There is a restriction on how many super classes we can inherit from; on a JVM, you can only have one base class. But you can inherit from multiple interfaces. Inheritance is transitive. If class C is derived from class B and that class B is derived from a given class A, then class C is a derived class of A.

A derived class will implicitly get all the parent classes (and the parent's parent class, if that is the case) fields, properties, and methods. The importance of inheritance lies in the ability to reuse code that has already been written and therefore avoid the scenario where we would have to reimplement the behavior exposed by the parent class. A derived class can add fields, properties, or new methods, thus extending the functionality available through the parent. We would say that class B, the derived one, specializes class A, the parent. A simpler example is to think of the animal kingdom chart. At the top, we have animal, followed by vertebrates and invertebrates; the former is further split into fish, reptile, mammals, and so on. If we take the yellow-fin tuna species, we can look at it as a specialized type of fish.

The next illustration shows a simple class hierarchy. Let's say you write a system to deal with payments. You will have a class called Payment that holds an amount and a **CardPayment** class to take such payments:

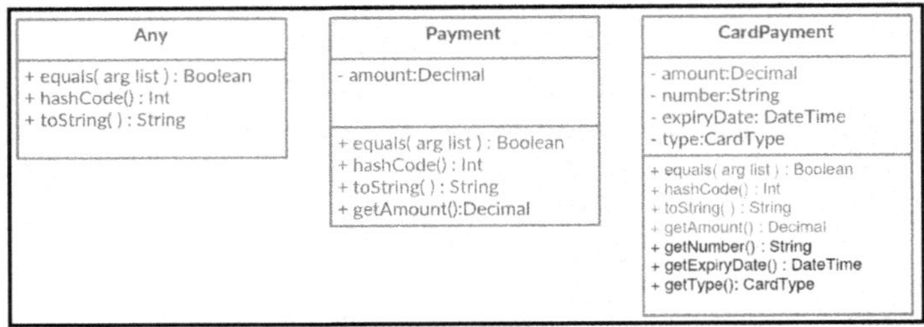

Simple inheritance

You must have noticed the presence of another entity called **Any** in the preceding screenshot. Every time you construct an entity that doesn't take any parent, it will automatically get this class as its parent. You will probably think **Any** is the `Object` class, the super/parent class of any class defined in Java. However, this is not the case. If you pay attention to the methods defined by the class `Any` you will notice it is a subset of those found for on the Java `Object` class. So how does Kotlin deal with Java object references? When the compiler sees such an object, it will translate it into **Any** and then it will make use of the extension methods to complete the method set.

Let's implement the preceding code and see how we actually define in Kotlin inheritance:

```
enum class CardType {
  VISA, MASTERCARD, AMEX
}

open class Payment(val amount: BigDecimal)
class CardPayment(amount: BigDecimal, val number: String, val
expiryDate: DateTime, val type: CardType) : Payment(amount)
```

We have created our classes based on the spec we just saw. `CardType` is an enumeration type, as hinted in the definition. The definition of Payment has introduced a new keyword, called `open`. Through this keyword, you are basically saying the class can be inherited from. The designers of Kotlin have decided the default behavior is to have the classes sealed for inheritance. If you have programmed in Java, you will have come across the `final` keyword, which does exactly the opposite of `open`. In Java, any class which hasn't been marked as `final` can be derived from. The definition of `CardPayment` marks the inheritance via a semicolon. The `: Payment` translates into: "`CardPayment` which extends from `Payment`". This is different to Java where you would use the `extends` keyword. Any developers with C++ or C# background will be very familiar with the construct.

In the preceding code, our `CardPayment` class has a primary constructor. Therefore, the parent one has to be called on the spot, hence `Payment(amount)`. But what if our new class doesn't define a primary constructor? Let's extend our class hierarchy to add a new type, named `ChequePayment`:

```
class ChequePayment : Payment {
  constructor(amount: BigDecimal, name: String, bankId: String) :
super(amount) {
    this.name = name
    this.bankId = bankId
  }
  var name: String
    get() = this.name
  var bankId: String
    get()  = this.bankId
}
```

Since we have chosen to avoid the primary constructor, the definition of a secondary constructor has to call the parent one. This call needs to be the first thing our constructor does. Hence, the body of our constructor is preceded by `super(args1,args2...)`. This is different from Java, where we would have moved this call as the first line in our constructor body.

In this example we inherit from one class only – as we said already we can't inherit from more than one class. However, we can inherit from multiple interfaces at the same time. Let's take a simple example of an amphibious car: it is a boat as well as a car. If you were to model this, we would consider having two interfaces: `Drivable` and `Sailable`. And we would have our amphibious car extend both of them:

```
interface Drivable {
  fun drive()
}
interface Sailable {
  fun saill()
}
class AmphibiousCar(val name: String) : Drivable, Sailable {
  override fun drive() {
    println("Driving...")
 }
  override fun saill() {
    println("Sailling...")
  }
}
```

Remember our class automatically derives from `Any`; it is as if we had written `class AmphibiousCar(val name:String):Any, Drivable, Sailable`. When we inherit an interface, we have to provide an implementation for all its methods and properties or we have to make the class abstract. We will talk shortly about abstract classes. There is no restriction on how many interfaces you can inherit from and the order in which you want to specify them. Unlike Java, if you inherit from a class and one or more interfaces, you don't need to list the class as the first entry in the list of parents:

```
interface IPersistable {
  fun save(stream: InputStream)
}

interface IPrintable {
  fun print()
}

abstract class Document(val title: String)

class TextDocument(title: String) : IPersistable, Document(title),
IPrintable {
  override fun save(stream: InputStream) {
      println("Saving to input stream")
    }

    override fun print() {
      println("Document name:$title")
    }
}
```

Visibility modifiers

When you define your class, the contained methods, properties, or fields can have various visibility levels. In Kotlin, there are four possible values:

- **Public**: This can be accessed from anywhere
- **Internal**: This can only be accessed from the module code
- **Protected**: This can only be accessed from the class defining it and any derived classes
- **Private**: This can only be accessed from the scope of the class defining it

If the parent class specifies that a given field is open for being redefined (overwritten), the derived class will be able to modify the visibility level. Here is an example:

```
open class Container {
  protected open val fieldA: String = "Some value"
}
class DerivedContainer : Container() {
  public override val fieldA: String = "Something else"
}
```

Now in the main class, you can create a new `DerivedContainer` instance and print out the value of `fieldA`. Yes, this field is now public to any code:

```
val derivedContainer =  DerivedContainer()
println("DerivedContainer.fieldA:${derivedContainer.fieldA}")
/*val container:Container =
derivedContainerprintln("fieldA:${container.fieldA}")*/
```

I commented out the code where we use `derivedContainer` as if it was an instance of `DerivedContainer`. If that is the case, trying to compile the commented code will yield an error because `fieldA` is not accessible.

Redefining the field doesn't mean it will replace the existing one when it comes to object allocation. Remember, a derived class inherits all the parent class fields. It takes just a little bit of code to prove this:

```
derivedContainer.javaClass.superclass.getDeclaredFields().forEach  {
  field->
  field.setAccessible(true)
  println("Field:${field.name},${Modifier.toString(field.modifiers)} ,
Value=${field.get(derivedContainer)}")
}
derivedContainer.javaClass.getDeclaredFields().forEach {
  field->
  field.setAccessible(true)
  println("Field:${field.name},${Modifier.toString(field.modifiers)} ,
Value=${field.get(derivedContainer)}")
}
```

Run the preceding code and it will print `fieldA` twice in the output; the first entry will come from the parent class and will be “Some Value”, and the latter will come from the derived class and will read “Something else”.

A typical use case would be to widen the access for a given field, method, and/or property. But you should be careful about using this since it might break the Liskov substitution principle. Following this principle, if a program is using a base class, then the reference to the base class can be replaced with a derived class without affecting the functionality of the program.

Abstract classes

Adding the `abstract` keyword in front of the class definition will mark the class as abstract. An abstract class is a partially defined class; properties and methods that have no implementation must be implemented in a derived class, unless the derived class is meant to be an `abstract` class as well. Here is how you would define an abstract class in Kotlin:

```
abstract class A {
  abstract fun doSomething()
}
```

Unlike interfaces, you have to mark the function abstract if you don't provide a body definition.

You cannot create an instance of an abstract class. The role of such a class is to provide a common set of methods that multiple derived classes share. The best example of such a case is the `InputStream` class. This will be very familiar to a developer who has already worked with Java. The JDK documentation says: "This abstract class is the superclass of all classes representing an input stream of bytes. Applications that need to define a subclass of `InputStream` must always provide a method that returns the next byte of input". If you look at the `java.io` package, you will find a few implementations for it: `AudioInputStream`, `ByteArrayInputStream`, `FileInputStream`, and many more. You could also provide an implementation of it.

You can inherit a class `A` with a function flagged as opened for being redefined (overridable, as we will see shortly) and marked it abstract in the derived class. This way the derived class will become abstract. Any class that inherits from the derived class will need to provide an implementation, and it won't be able to access the implementation defined in class `A`:

```
open class AParent protected constructor() {
  open fun someMethod(): Int = Random().nextInt()
}
abstract class DDerived : AParent() {
  abstract override fun someMethod(): Int
}
```

```
class AlwaysOne : DDerived() {
  override fun someMethod(): Int {
    return 1
  }
}
```

The example is pretty straightforward. We have a parent class that defines `someMethod`, returning a random integer. A `DDerived` class inherits this class (please note we have to invoke the empty constructor on the parent class) and marks the method abstract. Then, our `AlwaysOne` class will have to provide a function body for our method that always returns `1`.

Interface or abstract class

There is always a debate over using either an interface or an abstract class. Here are a few rules to follow when deciding which way to go:

- Is-a versus Can-Do: Any type can inherit from one parent class only and multiple interfaces. If for the derived class B you can't say B Is-an A (A is the base type), don't use an interface but rather an interface. Interfaces imply a Can-Do relationship. If the Can-do functionality is applicable to different object types, go with an interface implementation. For example, for both `FileOutputStream` and `ByteOutputpuStream` (and any of the other sibling implementations available), you can say they have an Is-a relationship with `java.io.OutputStream`. Hence you will see that `OutputStream` is an abstract class providing common implementations to all objects that represent a writable stream. However, `Autocloseable`, which represents an object holding a resource that can be released when the `close` method is invoked, provides a `Can-do` functionality and thus it makes sense to have it as an interface.
- Promote code reuse: I am sure you will agree it is easier to inherit a class rather than an interface, where you have to provide an implementation for all the methods defined. A parent class can provide a lot of common functionality; thus, the derived class has to only redefine or implement a small subset of the methods defined.
- Versioning: If you work with an interface and you add a new member to it, you force all the derived classes to change their code by adding the new implementation. The source code has to be changed and recompiled. The same is not applicable for an abstract class. You can add your new method and make use of it, and the user's source code doesn't even need to be recompiled.

Polymorphism

After encapsulation and inheritance, polymorphism is seen as the third pillar of object-oriented programming. It decouples the "what" from "how" at the type level. One of the advantages that polymorphism offers is improved code organization and readability; furthermore, it allows you to extend your programs at any point later, when new features are required to be implemented.

The word polymorphism originates from the Greek language: polys (πολύς), meaning many or much and morphē (μορφή), meaning form or shape. There are multiple forms of polymorphism, but in this chapter, we are going to talk about the one known as late-binding (or dynamic binding or runtime binding).

The power of polymorphism comes at runtime when objects of a derived class are treated as objects of the base class. This can happen for a method parameter or when it comes to storing a group of common elements in a collection or array. The peculiar thing here is that the object's declared type will not be identical with the actual runtime type when the code is executed. This sounds like there is some magic happening under the hood. All of this is happening through the use of virtual methods. Base classes may define and implement virtual methods, and derived classes can override them, thus providing their own implementation. This way, two distinct types behave differently when the same method is called. When the virtual method is called as your program is executed, the JVM looks up the runtime type of the instance and works out which method it should actually invoke. Later in the chapter, we will dedicate some space to discuss in a bit more detail how this is implemented under the bonnet.

Virtual methods unify how we work with a group of related types. Imagine you are working on the next big drawing application and it must support the rendering of a variety of different shapes on the screen. The program has to keep track of all the shapes the user will create and react to their input: changing the location on the screen, changing their properties (border color, size, or background color; you name it!), and so on. When you compile the code, you can't know in advance all the types of shapes you will support; the last thing you want to do is handle each one individually. This is where polymorphism steps in to help you. You want to treat all your graphical instances as a shape. The image reacting to the user clicking on the canvas and your code need to work out whether the mouse location is within the boundaries of one of the shapes drawn. What you should avoid is walking through all the shapes, and for each one calling a different method to do the hit check: calling `isWithinCircle` for a circle shape, `checkIsHit` for a rhombus shape, and so on.

Let's have a look at how you could implement this using a textbook approach. First, we will define a Shape class. This needs to be an abstract class and you shouldn't be able to create an instance of it. After all, how could it be drawn on the screen when it hasn't been specialized? Let's look at the code:

```
abstract class Shape protected constructor() {
  var XLocation: Int
    get() = this.XLocation
    set(value: Int) {
      this.XLocation = value
    }

  var YLocation: Int
    get() = this.XLocation
    set(value: Int) {
      this.XLocation = value
    }
  var Width: Double
    get() = this.Width
    set(value: Double) {
      this.Width = value
    }
  var Height: Double
    get() = this.Height
    set(value: Double) {
      this.Height = value
    }
  abstract fun isHit(x: Int, y: Int): Boolean
}
```

With this in place, we are going to implement two shapes: an ellipsis and a rectangle. A question for you: Does it make sense to implement a square type? Think about this. For now, let's implement the two shapes we just discussed:

```
class Ellipsis : Shape() {
  override fun isHit(x: Int, y: Int): Boolean {
    val xRadius = Width.toDouble / 2
    val yRadius = Height.toDouble / 2
    val centerX = XLocation + xRadius
    val centerY = YLocation + yRadius
    if (xRadius == 0.0 || yRadius == 0.0)
      return false
    val normalizedX = centerX - XLocation
    val normalizedY = centerY - YLocation
    return (normalizedX * normalizedX) / (xRadius * xRadius) +
(normalizedY * normalizedY) / (yRadius * yRadius) <= 1.0
  }
```

```
}

class Rectangle : Shape() {
  override fun isHit(x: Int, y: Int): Boolean {
    return x >= XLocation && x <= (XLocation + Width) && y >=
YLocation && y <= (YLocation  + Height)
  }
}
```

We consider that the top-left corner of the canvas is at point *(0,0)*. Given these types, we will create a few instances of them and see how polymorphism works. We will create two ellipses and one rectangle. We will then store their instances in a collection, and then for a given point, we will work out whether it is within any of the given shapes:

```
fun main(args: Array<String>) {
  val e1 = Ellipsis()
  e1.Height = 10
  e1.Width = 12
  val e2 = Ellipsis()
  e2.XLocation = 100
  e2.YLocation = 96
  e1.Height = 21
  e1.Width = 19
  val r1 = Rectangle()
  r1.XLocation = 49
  r1.YLocation = 45
  r1.Width = 10
  r1.Height = 10
  val shapes = listOf<Shape>(e1, e2, r1)
  val selected:Shape? = shapes.firstOrNull {shape ->  shape.isHit(50,
52)}
  if(selected == null){
    println("There is no shape at point(50,52)")
  }
  else{
    println("A shape of type ${selected.javaClass.simpleName} has  been
selected.")
  }
}
```

Running the code will print out an instance of a rectangle on the console at the given point. Using `javap`, look at the generated bytecode; the code should look similar to this (leaving out most of it for the sake of simplicity):

```
169: invokevirtual #69           // Method
com/programming/kotlin/chapter03/Shape.isHit:(II)Z
```

So, at the bytecode level, there is a method named `invokevirtual` to call a virtual function. It is because of this the code in `Rectangle` or `Ellipsis` gets invoked. But how does it know how and when to invoke it? Didn't I call the method on a `Shape` class?

Dynamic method resolution is handled via the `vtable` (that is, virtual table) mechanism. The actual approach might depend on the JVM implementation, but they will share the same logical implementation.

When any object instance is created, its memory allocation lives on the heap. The actual size of the memory being allocated is slightly bigger than the sum of all the allocated fields, including all the base classes, all the way to the `Any` class. The runtime footprint will get an extra space added at the top of the memory block to hold a reference to the type descriptor information. For each class type you define, there will be an object allocated at runtime. This entry has been added as the first entry to always guarantee the location, thus avoiding the need to compute it at runtime. This type descriptor holds the list of methods defined along with other information related to it. This list starts with the top class in the hierarchy and goes all the way to the actual type whose instance it belongs to. The order is deterministic; again, another example of optimization. This is known as the vtable structure and is nothing more than an array with each element pointing out (referencing) the actual native code implementation that will be executed. During the program execution, the JIT-er (the just-in time compiler) is responsible for translating the bytecode produced by your compiler into native/assembly code. If a derived class decides to override a virtual method, its vtable entry will point out to the new implementation rather than the last class in the hierarchy providing it.

Let's imagine we have a class **A** defining **fieldA**; it automatically derives from the **Any** class. Then, we derive it and add an extra field to the new class B. Once we do this, we name it **fieldB**:

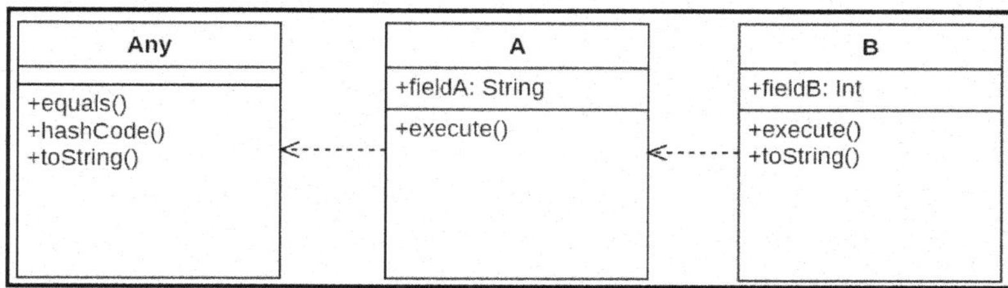

vtable class hierarchy

You can see from the preceding diagram that class **A** defines a method called execute, which the derived class overrides. Alongside this, **B** also overrides the `toString` method defined by **Any**. This is a very simple example; however, it shapes how the runtime memory allocation will look. Creating an instance of **B** at runtime should have the following memory footprint:

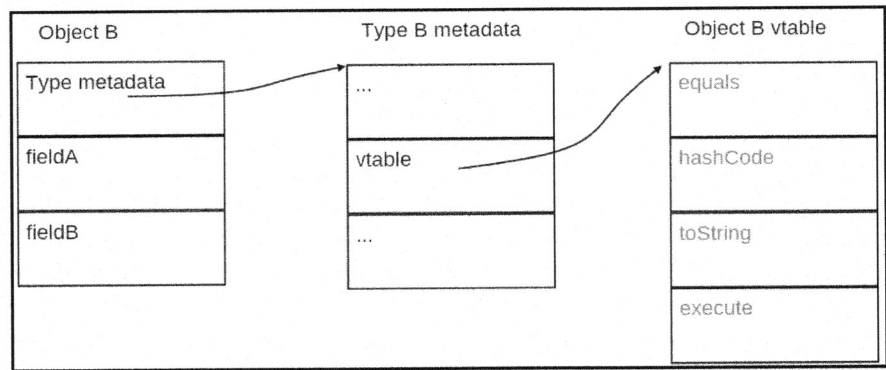

VTable structure

Your variable of type **B** is nothing but a reference to the memory block on the heap. Because the type information sits at the beginning of the block (as already discussed) with two indirections (or pointer dereferencing), the runtime can address it easily and quickly. The diagram is only referencing the **vtable** entries for the type `metadata`, for simplicity. I have highlighted the methods based on the class providing the implementation. The first two are defined and implemented by **Any**, and the next two are defined and implemented in the derived class **B**.

If you look at the bytecode generated when invoking the execute method via a reference of **A**, you will notice the presence of a special keyword: `invokevirtual`. This way, the runtime can execute its predefined procedure to discover which code it has to run. All this has been described earlier.

From what we just discussed, we can work out that a call to `invokevirtual` carries some runtime costs. The runtime has to first get the type `metadata`. From there, it identifies the **vtable** and then jumps to the beginning of the instruction set representing the assembly code for the method to be invoked. This is in contrast to a normal `invokestatic` routine, where executing such a method doesn't have to go through at least two levels of indirection. `Invokestatic` is the bytecode routine for calling a method non-virtually.

Any methods defined by an interface are virtual methods. When such a method is invoked for a derived class it gets special treatment . There is a specific method at the bytecode level to handle `this:invokeinterface`. Why can't it just be a simple `invokevirtual`? Well, such a call needs more involvement than just following the simple process of calling a virtual method. Every `invokeinterface` receiver is considered a simple object reference. Unlike `invokevirtual`, an assumption can't be made about the vtable's location. While a call to `invokevirtual` can be fulfilled by performing two or three levels of indirection to resolve the method, a call at the interface level needs to first check whether the class actually implements the interface and, if so, where these methods are recorded in the implementing class. There is no simple way to guarantee the methods order in the vtable for two different classes implementing the same interface. Therefore, at runtime, an assembly code routine has to walk through the list of all the implemented interfaces looking for the target. Once the interface is found, because of the itable (or interface method table), which is a list of methods whose entries' structure is always the same for each class implementing the interface, the runtime can proceed with invoking the method as a virtual function. There is a reason for this: we can have a class A that has implemented an interface X and a class B that is derived from A; this class B can override one of the methods declared at the interface level.

As you can see, virtual method calls are expensive. There are quite a few optimizations a JVM implementation would need to employ to short-circuit the call, but these details go beyond the scope of the current book. I will let you do your own research if your curiosity is at that level. However, this is not information you need to know. The rule of thumb is to avoid building a complex class hierarchy with many levels since that would hurt your program performance because of the reasons presented earlier.

Overriding rules

You decided your new class has to redefine one of the methods inherited from one of the parent classes. This is known as overriding; I have already used it in the previous chapter. If you have already programmed in Java, you will find Kotlin a more explicit language. In Java, every method is virtual by default; therefore, each method can be overridden by any derived class. In Kotlin, you would have to tag the function as being opened to redefine it. To do so, you need to add the `open` keyword as a prefix to the method definition, and when you redefine the method, you specifically have to mark it using the `override` keyword:

```
abstract class SingleEngineAirplane protected constructor() {
  abstract fun fly()
}

class CesnaAirplane : SingleEngineAirplane() {
```

```
    override fun fly() {
      println("Flying a cesna")
    }
  }
```

You can always disallow any derived classes from overriding the function by adding the `final` keyword in front of the method. Using the previous example, we don't want any of the Cesna models to redefine the method:

```
class CesnaAirplane : SingleEngineAirplane() {
  final override fun fly() {
    println("Flying a cesna")
  }
}
```

You are not limited to functions only. Since Kotlin borrows the concept of properties from C#, you can also mark properties as virtual:

```
open class Base {
  open val property1: String
    get() = "Base::value"
}
class Derived1 : Base() {
  override val property1: String
   get() = "Derived::value"
}
class Derived2(override val property1: String) : Base() {}
```

You can override a `val` property with `var` if your coding logic requires this, but the reverse is not possible:

```
open class BaseB(open val propertyFoo: String) {
}

class DerivedB : BaseB("") {
  private var _propFoo: String = ""
  override var propertyFoo: String
  get() = _propFoo
  set(value) {
    _propFoo = value
  }
}

fun main(args: Array<String>) {
  val baseB = BaseB("BaseB:value")
  val derivedB= DerivedB()
  derivedB.propertyFoo = "on the spot value"
  println("BaseB:${baseB.propertyFoo}")
```

```
    println("DerivedB:${derivedB.propertyFoo}")
  }
```

There are scenarios where you need to derive from one class and at least one interface and both define and implement a method with the same name and parameters. In such cases, the inheritance rule forces you to override the method. If you create a new instance of your object and call the method that is common to the immediate parent classes, which one should the compiler link to? Therefore, you need to remove ambiguity and provide the implementation; it could use any or both the parent classes' implementation. Imagine you have a class hierarchy for dealing with different image formats and you want to unify them with a third-party hierarchy. Since both class hierarchies come with a definition of the `save` function, you would need to override them:

```
open class Image {
  open fun save(output: OutputStream) {
    println("Some logic to save an image")
  }
}
interface VendorImage {
  fun save(output: OutputStream) {
    println("Vendor saving an image")
  }
}
class PNGImage : Image(), VendorImage {
  override fun save(output: OutputStream) {
    super<VendorImage>.save(output)
    super<Image>.save(output)
  }
}

fun main(args: Array<String>) {
  val pngImage = PNGImage()
  val os = ByteArrayOutputStream()
  pngImage.save(os)
}
```

The overriding is not enforced if the `VendorImage` interface would have not provided an implementation. Referencing the parent implementation is done via `super<PARENT>`, as you might have already noticed in the implementation earlier.

Inheritance versus composition

One of the compelling features of an OOPs language is code reuse. Once a class has been created and tested, it should represent a block of code/functionality ready to be used.

The simplest way to make use of an already defined class is to just create an instance of it, but you can also place an object of that class inside a new class. The new class can bundle in any number of other object types to create the functionality required. This concept of building up a brand new class by reusing existing ones is called association. This term is referred to as a has-a relationship. Imagine you have a class called **Desktop** to represent a typical PC; a desktop has a hard disk, motherboard, and so on. We have already used this concept in the previous code examples.

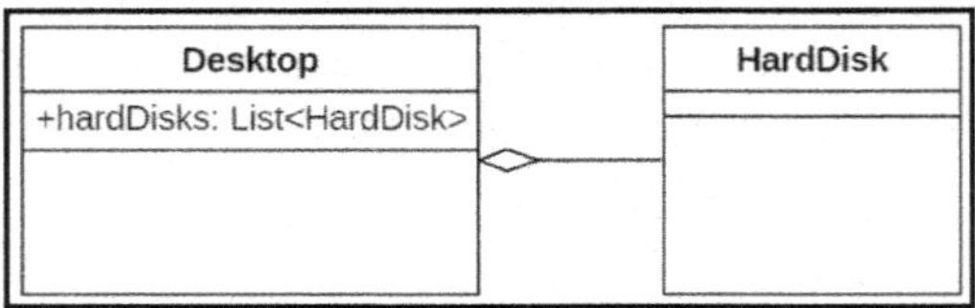

Aggregation example

Association comes in two flavors. This detail is most of the time overlooked. The first type of composition is called aggregation. An aggregation represents a relationship between two or more objects in which each object has its own life cycle, and there the notion of ownership is not applicable. Basically, the objects part of the relationship can be created and destroyed independently. Take the earlier example of **Desktop**. The computer can stop working through no fault of the hard drive. While the desktop can be thrown away, you can take the hard drive and put it in a different PC and it will still carry on working.

Composition is the next type of association. It is a specialized type of aggregation. In this case, once the container object is destroyed, the contained objects will cease to exist as well. In the case of composition, the container will be responsible for creating the object instances. You can think of composition in terms of "part of":

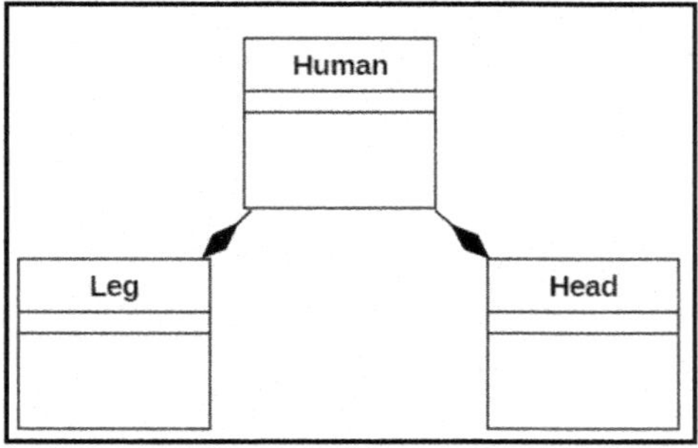

Composition example

Through composition, you can have a great deal of flexibility. Usually, your class member objects are private; a good encapsulation design would require you to do this. Since these objects are not accessible by the client of your class, you have the liberty of changing them, either by adding or removing them, without impacting the client code at all. You can even change the runtime types to provide different runtime behaviors if the requirements demand it. For example, the runtime instance for hard disks can be either a typical hard drive or the new standard: a solid state drive.

Typically, inheritance gets so much focus since it is so important in object-oriented programming, and a new developer uses it everywhere. This can result in awkward and over-complicated class hierarchies. You should first consider composition when you are about to create a new class, and only if applicable should you make use of inheritance.

Another term used frequently in the OOP world is *is-a*. This concept is based entirely on inheritance. We have already seen inheritance; it comes in two shapes: class or interface. Furthermore, it is unidirectional (a bicycle is a vehicle but a vehicle is not a bicycle; it could be a car, for example).

Of course, there are scenarios where mixing association (whatever form it takes) and inheritance is required. Imagine you build a class hierarchy for vehicles. You start with a **Vehicle** interface, and to provide a **Bicycle** type you will inherit the interface and will add, via composition, two references to the **Wheel** class as seen below:

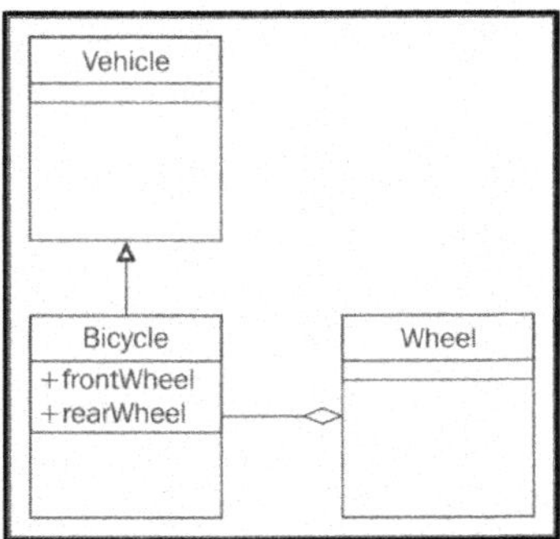

Mixing inheritance and association

Class delegation

You might have already heard about the delegation pattern or at least used it without even knowing it had a name. It allows a type to forward one or more of its methods call to a different type. Therefore, you need two types to achieve this: the delegate and the delegator.

This could easily sound like a proxy pattern, but it isn't. A proxy pattern is meant to provide a placeholder for an instance to get full control while accessing it. Let's say you are writing a UI framework and you start where your abstraction is **UIElement**. Each of the components define a **getHeight** and **getWidth**.

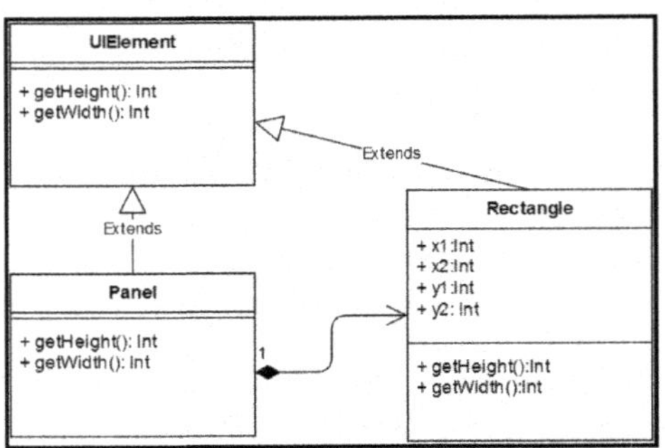

Class delegation via association

Below you see the UML translated into Kotlin. We defined the **UIElement** interface with both **Panel** and **Rectangle** classes inheriting from:

```
interface UIElement {
  fun getHeight(): Int
  fun getWidth(): Int
}
class Rectangle(val x1: Int, val x2: Int, val y1: Int, val y2: Int) :
UIElement {
  override fun getHeight() = y2 - y1
  override fun getWidth() = x2 - x1
}
class Panel(val rectangle: Rectangle) : UIElement by rectangle

val panel = Panel(Rectangle(10,100,30,100))
println("Panel height:"+panel.getHeight())
println("Panel witdh:" + panel.getWidth())
```

You have probably noticed the `by` keyword in the `Panel` class definition. It's basically a hint for the compiler to do the work for you: forwarding the calls for the methods exposed by the interface `UIElement` to the underlying `Rectangle` object.

Through this pattern, you replace inheritance with composition. You should always favor composition over inheritance for the sake of simplicity, reducing type coupling, and flexibility. Using this approach, you can chose and swap the type you put in the delegate position based on various requirements.

Sealed classes

A sealed class in Kotlin is an abstract class, which can be extended by subclasses defined as nested classes within the sealed class itself. In a way, this is a rather more powerful enumeration option. Just like Enum, a sealed class hierarchy contains a fixed set of possible choices. However, unlike Enum, where each option is represented by one instance, the derived classes of a sealed class can have many instances. Sealed classes are ideal for defining algebraic data types. Imagine you want to model a binary tree structure; you would do the following:

```
    sealed class IntBinaryTree {
      class EmptyNode : IntBinaryTree()
      class IntBinaryTreeNode(val left: IntBinaryTree, val value: Int, val
right: IntBinaryTree) : IntBinaryTree()
    }

    ...

    val tree = IntBinaryTree.IntBinaryTreeNode(
    IntBinaryTree.IntBinaryTreeNode(
      IntBinaryTree.EmptyNode(),
      1,
      IntBinaryTree.EmptyNode()),
      10,
      IntBinaryTree.EmptyNode())
```

Ideally, you won't hardcode the container value to be an integer, but make it generic in order to hold any type. But since we haven't introduced generics yet, we keep things a little bit simpler. In the preceding snippet, you may have noticed the presence of the `sealed` keyword. Trying to define a derived class outside the `IntBinaryTree` class scope will yield a compilation error.

The benefits of using such a class hierarchy come into play when you use them in a `when` expression. The compiler is able to infer a statement and cover all the possible cases; therefore, the check is exhaustive. For a Scala developer, this will sound familiar to pattern matching. Imagine we want to expose the elements of a tree to a list; for this, you would do the following:

```
    fun toCollection(tree: IntBinaryTree): Collection<Int> = when  (tree) {
      is IntBinaryTree.EmptyNode -> emptyList<Int>()
      is IntBinaryTree.IntBinaryTreeNode -> toCollection(tree.left) +
tree.value + toCollection(tree.right)
    }
```

If you leave one of the derived classes out of the when expression, you will get a compiler error: `Error:(12, 5) Kotlin: 'when' expression must be exhaustive, add necessary 'is EmptyNode' branch or 'else' branch instead.`

Summary

For a Java developer wanting to migrate to Kotlin, this chapter ended up reviewing well-known concepts. Regardless whether you have programmed in an OOP language before or not, you now know the key concepts of this software design approach, and you can write code that is object-orientated, using the new features available in Kotlin, and make it more structured and readable. I cannot over-emphasize how important it is to favor composition over inheritance. There is no standard recipe for getting it right. Your goal should always be to keep things simple, and you should do the same when building a class hierarchy.

In the next chapter you will get an in-depth view on functions in Kotlin. You will see how the language has borrowed from C# extension methods – special methods allowing you to add new functionality to existing classes.

4
Functions in Kotlin

he preceding code is compiled into the following equivalent code: In the previous chapters, we introduced the basics of Kotlin and how to write procedural and object-oriented code. The emphasis in this chapter will be on functions; how to take the first steps into functional programming; and the features that Kotlin supports, which makes programming with functions easier.

In this chapter, we will cover the following topics:

- Functions and function literals
- Extension functions
- Named parameters and default parameters
- Operator overloading
- Recursion and tail recursion

Defining functions

Functions are defined using the `fun` keyword with optional parameters and a return value. The parameter list must always be present, even if no parameters are defined. For example, this function has no parameters and it returns a `String` value:

```
fun hello() : String = "hello world"
```

Each parameter is in the form `name: type`. The following function accepts two parameters of the type `String` and also returns a `String` value:

```
fun hello(name: String, location: String): String =
  "hello to you  $name at $location"
```

If a function does not return any meaningful value, then it is defined to return `Unit`. As discussed in `Chapter 2`, *Kotlin Basics*, Unit is analogous to the Java and C void types. By using a class that is part of a type hierarchy-rather than a special type, such as void-the type system in Kotlin can be made more regular. Every function must return a value, and this value could be `Unit`.

Functions returning Unit can omit the return type for procedure-style syntax if the developer wishes so. The following two function declarations are equivalent:

```
fun print1(str: String): Unit {
  println(str)
}

fun print2(str: String) {
  println(str)
}
```

Single expression functions

Usually, a function must declare its return type; an exception exists only for functions that consist of a single expression. These are often referred to as **one line** or **single line** functions. Such functions can use a shortened syntax that omits the braces and uses the = symbol before the expression rather than the `return` keyword:

```
fun square(k: Int) = k * k
```

Notice how the function does not need to declare the return value of `Int`. This is inferred by the compiler. The rationale behind this feature is that very short functions are easy to read, and the return value is a bit of extra noise that doesn't add much to the overall process. However, you can always include the return value if you think it makes things clearer:

```
fun square2(k: Int): Int = k * k
```

Single expression functions can always be written in regular style if desired. For example, the following two functions are identical and compiled to the same bytecode:

```
fun concat1(a: String, b: String) = a + b
fun concat2(a: String, b: String): String {
  return a + b
}
```

The compiler enforces the rule that only a single expression function can omit the return type.

Member functions

The first type of functions is called **member functions**. These functions are defined inside a class, object, or interface. A member function is invoked using the name of the containing class or object instance with a dot, followed by the function name and the arguments in parentheses. For example, to invoke a function called take on an instance of a `string`, we do the following:

```
val string = "hello"
val length = string.take(5)
```

Member functions can refer to themselves and they don't need the instance name to do this. This is because function invocations operate on the current instance, and they are referred to as the following:

```
object Rectangle {

  fun printArea(width: Int, height: Int): Unit {
    val area = calculateArea(width, height)
    println("The area is $area")
  }

  fun calculateArea(width: Int, height: Int): Int {
    return width * height
  }
}
```

This code snippet shows two functions that calculate the area of a rectangle and output it to the console. The `printArea` function takes two parameters of `width` and `height` and uses the `calculateArea` function to do the math. The first function then outputs the result of the other function.

You will also notice that the `calculateArea` function uses `return`, as the value it computes is intended to be used by other functions. The `printArea` function does not have any meaningful value to return, so we define its return value as Unit.

Local functions

The idea behind functions is very simple: split up a large program into smaller chunks that can be reasoned more easily and allow the reuse of the code to avoid repetition. This second point is known as the **DRY** principle: **Don't Repeat Yourself**. The more the number of times you write the same code, the more the chances you create of a bug creeping in.

When this principle is taken to its logical conclusion, you would have created a program that consists of many small functions, each doing a single thing; this is similar to the Unix principle of small programs, where each program does a single job.

The same principle applies to the code inside a function. Typically, in say Java, a large function or method might be broken down by calling several support functions declared in either the same class or a helper class that contains static methods.

Kotlin allows us to take this a step further by supporting functions declared inside other functions. These are called *local* or *nested* functions. Functions can even be nested multiple times.

The earlier example of printing areas can be written in the following style:

```
fun printArea(width: Int, height: Int): Unit {
  fun calculateArea(width: Int, height: Int): Int = width * height
  val area = calculateArea(width, height)
  println("The area is $area")
}
```

As you can see, the `calculateArea` function is now inside `printArea` and thus not accessible to the code outside. This is useful when we want to hide functions that are just used as implementation details of a larger function. We could also achieve a similar effect by defining a member function as private. So do local functions have any other advantages? Yes, they do! Local functions can access the parameters and variables defined in the outer scope:

```
fun printArea2(width: Int, height: Int): Unit {
  fun calculateArea(): Int = width * height
  val area = calculateArea()
  println("The area is $area")
}
```

Notice that we've removed the parameters from the `calculateArea` function, and now it directly uses the parameters defined in the enclosing scope. This makes the nested function more readable and saves repeating the parameter definitions, which is very useful for functions with many parameters.

Let's work through an example of a function that could be broken down using local functions:

```
fun fizzbuzz(start: Int, end: Int): Unit {
  for (k in start..end) {
    if (k % 3 == 0 && k % 5 == 0)
      println("Fizz Buzz")
    else if (k % 3 == 0)
      println("Fizz")
    else if (k % 5 == 0)
      println("Buzz")
    else
      println(k)
  }
}
```

This is the well-known Fizz Buzz problem. The requirement asks you to print out the integers from the start to the end value. However, if the integer is a multiple of 3, you should print `Fizz`. If it is a multiple of 5, you should print `Buzz`. If it is a multiple of 3 and 5, then print `Fizz Buzz` together.

The first solution is short and readable, but it duplicates some code. The modulo checks are coded twice, which doubles the potential for a bug. Clearly, this example is extremely simple, so the chances of a typo are minimal; however, it serves to demonstrate the issue for larger problems.

We can declare a local function for each of the modulo checks, so that we only have to code it once. This brings us to the next iteration of our solution:

```
fun fizzbuzz2(start: Int, end: Int): Unit {

  fun isFizz(k: Int): Boolean = k % 3 == 0
  fun isBuzz(k: Int): Boolean = k % 5 == 0

  for (k in start..end) {
    if (isFizz(k) && isBuzz(k))
      println("Fizz Buzz")
    else if (isFizz(k))
      println("Fizz")
    else if (isBuzz(k))
      println("Buzz")
    else
      println(k)
  }
}
```

Here, our `if...else` branches now invoke the nested functions `isFizz` and `isBuzz`.

However, it is still a bit verbose to pass `k` to the function each time. Is there a way we can avoid this? Turns out, the answer is yes! We can define local functions not just directly inside other functions, but also in `for` loops, `while` loops, and other blocks:

```
fun fizzbuzz3(start: Int, end: Int): Unit {
  for (k in start..end) {

    fun isFizz(): Boolean = k % 3 == 0
    fun isBuzz(): Boolean = k % 5 == 0

    if (isFizz() && isBuzz())
       println("Fizz Buzz")
    else if (isFizz())
       println("Fizz")
    else if (isBuzz())
       println("Buzz")
    else
       println(k)
  }
}
```

In this third iteration of our function, we have moved the function definitions inside the `for` loop. So now, we can omit the parameter declarations and access `k` directly.

Finally, we could take advantage of the when statement introduced in `Chapter 2`, *Kotlin Basics*, to remove some of the noise of the `if...else` keywords:

```
fun fizzbuzz4(start: Int, end: Int): Unit {
  for (k in start..end) {

    fun isFizz(): Boolean = k % 3 == 0
    fun isBuzz(): Boolean = k % 5 == 0
    when {
      isFizz() && isBuzz() -> println("Fizz Buzz")
      isFizz() -> println("Fizz")
      isBuzz() -> println("Buzz")
      else -> println(k)
    }
  }
}
```

This gives us our final solution, which avoids repetition of code and is more readable than the initial iteration.

Top-level functions

In addition to member functions and local functions, Kotlin also supports declaring top-level functions. These are functions that exist outside of any class, object, or interface and are defined directly inside a file. The name top-level comes from the fact that functions are not nested inside any structure and so they are at the top of the hierarchy of classes and functions.

Top-level functions are especially useful for defining helper or utility functions. It does not necessarily make sense to group them with other functions or create them when the contained object adds no value. In Java, these kinds of functions exist as static functions inside helper classes. An example would be the functions of collections in the Java standard library.

However, some functions are so standalone that it makes little sense to take the trouble of creating a containing object. A good example would be `require`. This is a Kotlin standard library function that is used to ensure that parameters when invoked satisfy the invariant conditions. For example, if a parameter should always be greater than 10, we can write the following:

```
fun foo(k: Int) {
  require(k > 10, { "k should be greater than 10" })
}
```

This function and its siblings, namely `check`, `error`, and `requireNotNull`, could be placed inside an object called **Assertions** (or some name that means the same). But this adds no value, and by using top-level functions, we could define these functions directly in a file called `assertions.kt`.

Named parameters

Named parameters allow us to be explicit about naming arguments when passed to a function. This has the benefit that for functions with many parameters, explicit naming makes the intent of each argument clear. This makes the call site more readable.

In the following example, we check to see whether the first string contains a substring of the second:

```
val string = "a kindness of ravens"
string.regionMatches(14, "Red Ravens", 4, 6, true)
```

To use named parameters, we put the parameter name before the argument value. Here is the function call again, this time with named parameters:

```
    string.regionMatches(thisOffset = 14, other = "Red Ravens",
otherOffset = 4, length = 6, ignoreCase = true)
```

This second example is more readable at the cost of being more verbose, but it is now clear what each of the parameters is meant for. The final `Boolean`, which you might have guessed was case sensitivity, is now obvious. If you don't have named parameters, you must check the documentation or source code.

Another benefit is that for functions with multiple parameters of the same type, it makes errors less likely as the values can be associated with the name. In the next example, you will see how the function accepts multiple `Boolean` parameters. And without named parameters, it is easy to swap arguments erroneously:

```
    fun deleteFiles(filePattern: String, recursive: Boolean,  ignoreCase:
Boolean, deleteDirectories: Boolean): Unit
```

Compare the two different styles of calling this function:

```
    deleteFiles("*.jpg", true, true, false)
    deleteFiles("*.jpg", recursive = true, ignoreCase = true,
deleteDirectories = false)
```

Did you notice that the first parameter is not named, even when the others are? When calling a function, not all parameters need to be named. The rule is simple: once a parameter has been named, all the following parameters must be named too.

Named parameters also allow the parameter order to be changed to suit the caller. For example, the following two examples are equivalent:

```
    val string = "a kindness of ravens"
    string.endsWith(suffix = "ravens", ignoreCase = true)
    string.endsWith(ignoreCase = true, suffix = "ravens")
```

Why this is useful will be demonstrated in the next section on default parameters. Changing the order of parameters allows us to selectively choose which default parameters to override.

Named parameters can only be used on Kotlin-defined functions and not on Java-defined functions. This is because the Java code when compiled into bytecode does not always preserve the parameter names.

Default parameters

Sometimes, it is convenient to provide default values for parameters in a function. Let's say we want to create a thread pool. The parameter to set the number of threads could default to the number of CPU cores. This would be a sensible default, but the user might still want to use something different.

The way to achieve this in languages without default parameters is to offer overloaded versions of the same function:

```
fun createThreadPool(): ExecutorService {
  val threadCount = Runtime.getRuntime().availableProcessors()
  return createThreadPool(threadCount)
}

fun createThreadPool(threadCount: Int): ExecutorService {
  return Executors.newFixedThreadPool(threadCount)
}
```

Here, the user can now choose which version to invoke. However, sometimes the number of parameters means that we end up with many overloaded variations of the same function, resulting in needless boilerplate. For example, the Java standard library `BigDecimal` has the following functions:

```
    public BigDecimal divide(BigDecimal divisor)

    public BigDecimal divide(BigDecimal divisor, RoundingMode
roundingMode)
    public BigDecimal divide(BigDecimal divisor, int scale,  RoundingMode
roundingMode)
```

There are many other variations. Each function just delegates to the next one with a sensible default.

In Kotlin, a function can define one or more of its parameters to have default values, which are used if the arguments are not specified. This allows a single function to be defined for several use cases, thereby avoiding the need for multiple overloaded variants.

Here is the `divide` function again, but this time, by using default parameters, we can reduce the definition to a single function:

```
    fun divide(divisor: BigDecimal, scale: Int = 0, roundingMode:
RoundingMode = RoundingMode.UNNECESSARY): BigDecimal
```

When invoking this function, we can omit some or all of the parameters, but once a parameter is omitted, all the following parameters must be omitted as well. For instance, we could invoke this function in the following ways:

```
divide(BigDecimal(12.34))
divide(BigDecimal(12.34), 8)
divide(BigDecimal(12.34), 8, RoundingMode.HALF_DOWN)
```

But the following would not be legal:

```
divide(BigDecimal(12.34), RoundingMode.HALF_DOWN)
```

However, to solve this problem, we can mix named parameters and default parameters:

```
divide(BigDecimal(12.34), roundingMode = RoundingMode.HALF_DOWN)
```

In general, using named parameters in combination with default parameters is very powerful. It allows us to provide one function, and users can selectively override the defaults they wish.

When overriding a function that declares default parameters, we must keep the same function signature.

Default parameters can also be used in constructors to avoid the need for multiple secondary constructors. The following example shows multiple constructors:

```
    class Student(val name: String, val registered: Boolean, credits:  Int)
{
      constructor(name: String) : this(name, false, 0)
      constructor(name: String, registered: Boolean) : this(name,
registered, 0)
    }
```

These constructors can be rewritten as the following:

```
    class Student2(val name: String, val registered: Boolean = false,
credits: Int = 0)
```

Extension functions

Quite often, you come across a situation where a type that you don't have control over will benefit from an extra function. Maybe you've always wished `String` had a `reverse()` function or perhaps `list` had a drop function that would return a copy of `list` with the first `k` elements removed.

An object-orientated approach would be to extend the type, thereby creating a subtype that adds the required new functions:

```
abstract class DroppableList<E> : ArrayList<E>() {
  fun drop(k: Int): List<E> {
    val resultSize = size - k
    when {
      resultSize <= 0 -> return emptyList<E>()
      else -> {
        val list = ArrayList<E>(resultSize)
        for (index in k..size - 1) {
          list.add(this[index])
        }
        return list
      }
    }
  }
}
```

But this isn't always possible. A class may be defined as final, so you cannot extend it. It may also be the case that you may not control when instances are created, so you can't substitute your subtype for the existing type.

A typical solution in this case is to create a function in a separate class that accepts the instance as another argument. In Java, for example, it is quite common to see classes that consist entirely of helper functions for other instances. A good example of this is the `java.util.Collections` class. It contains dozens of static functions that offer the functionality for working with collections:

```
fun <E> drop(k: Int, list: List<E>): List<E> {
  val resultSize = list.size - k
  when {
    resultSize <= 0 -> return emptyList<E>()
    else -> {
      val newList = ArrayList<E>(resultSize)
      for (index in k..list.size - 1) {
        newList.add(list[index])
      }
      return newList
```

```
      }
    }
  }
```

The issue with this solution is two-fold. Firstly, we cannot use code completion in the IDE to see which function is available. This is because we write the function name first. Secondly, if we have many of these functions and we want to compose them, we end up with code that isn't particularly readable. For example, refer to the following:

```
reverse(take(3, drop(2, list)))
```

Wouldn't it be nice if we could access this function directly on the list instance so it could give us code that would compose like the following:

```
list.drop(2).take(3).reverse()
```

Extension functions allow us to achieve exactly this without having to create a new subtype, modify the original type, or wrap the class.

An extension function is declared by defining a top-level function as normal, but with the intended type prefixed before the function name. The type of the instance that the function will be used on is called the **receiver type**. The receiver type is said to be extended with the **extension function**. Here is our previous drop function again; this time, it is implemented as an extension function:

```
fun <E> List<E>.drop(k: Int): List<E> {
  val resultSize = size - k
  when {
    resultSize <= 0 -> return emptyList<E>()
    else -> {
      val list = ArrayList<E>(resultSize)
      for (index in k..size - 1) {
        list.add(this[index])
      }
      return list
    }
  }
}
```

Notice the use of the `this` keyword inside the function body. This is used to reference the receiver instance, that is, the object that the function was invoked on. Whenever we are inside an extension function, the `this` keyword always refers to the receiver instance, and the instances in the outer scope need to be qualified.

To use an extension function, we import it, as we would any other top-level function, using the name of the function and the package it lives in:

```
import com.packt.chapter4.drop
val list = listOf(1,2,3)
val droppedList = list.drop2(2)
```

Extension function precedence

Extension functions cannot override functions declared in a class or interface. If an extension function is defined with the exact same signature (the same name, parameters type and order, and return type), then the compiler will never invoke it.

During compilation, when the compiler finds a function invocation, it will first look for a match in the member functions defined in the instance type as well as any member functions defined in superclasses and interfaces. If a match is found, then that member function is the one that is bound.

Only if no matching member functions are found, the compiler will consider any extension imports in the scope. Consider the following definitions:

```
class Submarine {
  fun fire(): Unit {
    println("Firing torpedoes")
  }

  fun submerge(): Unit {
    println("Submerging")
  }
}

fun Submarine.fire(): Unit {
  println("Fire on board!")
}

fun Submarine.submerge(depth: Int): Unit {
  println("Submerging to a depth of $depth fathoms")
}
```

Here we have a type, `Submarine`, with two functions: `fire()` and `submerge()`. We also defined extension functions on `Submarine` with the same names. If we were to invoke these functions, we would use the following code:

```
val sub = Submarine()
sub.fire()
```

```
sub.submerge()
```

The output would be `FiringTorpedoes` and `Submerging`. The compiler will bind to the `fire()` function defined in the `submarine` class. In this example, the extension function can never be called as there is no way to disambiguate it from the function in the class proper.

However, the `submerge()` function has different function signatures, so the compiler is able to bind to either depending on the number of parameters used:

```
val sub = Submarine()
sub.submerge()
sub.submerge(10)
```

This would output `Submerging` and `Submerging to a depth of 10 fathoms.`

Extension functions on nulls

Kotlin even supports extension functions on null values. In those situations, the this reference will contain the null value, and so `Any` function that doesn't safely handle null references would throw a null pointer exception.

This functionality is how the equals function can be overloaded to provide safe usage to even null values:

```
fun Any?.safeEquals(other: Any?): Boolean {
  if (this == null && other == null) return true
  if (this == null) return false
  return this.equals(other)
}
```

Member extension functions

Extension functions are usually declared at the top level, but we can define them inside classes as members. This may be used if we want to limit the scope of an extension:

```
class Mappings {
  private val map = hashMapOf<Int, String>()
  private fun String.stringAdd(): Unit {
    map.put(hashCode(), this)
  }

  fun add(str: String): Unit = str.stringAdd()
```

```
}
```

In this example, we have defined an extension function that adds a string to `hashmap`. The second function just invokes this extension function. This round about way of adding to `hashmap` indicates how receivers work in member extension functions.

The hash code function is defined on **Any**, and so it exists on the `Mappings` class and `String` through inheritance. When `hashCode` is invoked in the extension function, there are two possible functions in scope that could be used. The first function in the `Mappings` instance is called the `dispatch` receiver. The second function on the instance of string is called the **extension receiver**.

When we have this kind of name shadowing, the compiler defaults to the extension receiver. So in the previous example, the hash code used will be the hash code of the string instance. To use the dispatch receiver, we must use a qualified this:

```
class Mappings {
  private val map = hashMapOf<Int, String>()

  private fun String.stringAdd(): Unit {
    map.put(this@Mappings.hashCode(), this)
  }
  fun add(str: String): Unit = str.stringAdd()
}
```

In this second example, the `hashCode` function will be invoked on the `Mappings` instance.

Overriding member extension functions

Member extension functions can be declared as open if you wish to allow them to be overridden in subclasses. In this case, the dispatcher receiver type will be virtual, that is, it will be the runtime instance. The extension receiver will always be resolved statically, however:

```
open class Element(val name: String) {

  open fun Particle.react(name: String): Unit {
    println("$name is reacting with a particle")
  }

  open fun Electron.react(name: String): Unit {
    println("$name is reacting with an electron to make an  isotope")
  }
```

```
    fun react(particle: Particle): Unit {
      particle.react(name)
    }
  }

  class NobleGas(name: String) : Element(name) {
    override fun Particle.react(name: String): Unit {
      println("$name is noble, it doesn't react with particles")
    }

    override fun Electron.react(name: String): Unit {
      println("$name is noble, it doesn't react with electrons")
    }

    fun react(particle: Electron): Unit {
      particle.react(name)
    }
  }
  fun main(args: Array<String>) {
    val selenium = Element("Selenium")
    selenium.react(Particle())
    selenium.react(Electron())
    val neon = NobleGas("Neon")
    neon.react(Particle())
    neon.react(Electron())
  }
```

The preceding code snippet outputs the following:

```
Selenium is reacting with a particle
Selenium is reacting with a particle
Neon is noble, and it doesn't react with particles
Neon is noble, and it doesn't react with electrons
```

This example shows how receivers work in overridden extension functions. We define two pairs of classes. The first pair comprises of `Element` and `NobleGas`, which extends `Element`. The second pair comprises of `Particle` and its subtype `Electron`.

In both these classes, we define two extension functions. The first functions are defined on `Particle` and the second on `Electron`.

We can see from the output that it doesn't matter which type of `Particle/Electron` we pass to the react function defined on `Element`. It will always invoke the extension function defined on `Particle`. This is because the receiver type is statically determined. This is the type that is determined by compile type and not by the runtime type. The `react` entry function was defined to accept a particle, so this is the type that was used to bind the extension function.

In `NobleGas`, we defined an extra function that accepts the subtype so the compiler can pick the function that is a more specific match. This kind of static dispatch is the same as in Java for static methods.

Companion object extensions

Extension functions can also be added to companion objects. They would then be invoked on the companion object rather than on instances of the class.

One example of where this might be useful is this: adding factory functions to a type. For example, we might wish to add a function to integers to return a different random value upon each invocation:

```
fun Int.Companion.random(): Int {
  val random = Random()
  return random.nextInt()
}
```

Then we can invoke the extension function as normal, without needing the companion keyword:

```
val int = Int.random()
```

This isn't as useful as regular extension functions. This is because we can always create a new object and put the function in there or create a top-level function. But it can be desirable to associate a function with some other type's namespace. As in the preceding example, a `random()` function invoked on the `Int` type is more intuitive than the same function on a class with a name like `IntFactory` or `RandomInts`.

Multiple return values

Let's say we wanted to calculate both the positive and negative square roots of an integer. We could approach this problem by writing two different functions:

```
fun positiveRoot(k: Int): Double {
  require(k >= 0)
  return Math.sqrt(k.toDouble())
}

fun negativeRoot(k: Int): Double {
  require(k >= 0)
  return -Math.sqrt(k.toDouble())
}
```

Another approach might be to return an array so we only have to invoke one function:

```
fun roots(k: Int): Array<Double> {
  require(k >= 0)
  val root = Math.sqrt(k.toDouble())
  return arrayOf(root, -root)
}
```

However, we do not know from the return type whether the positive root or negative root is at position 0. We will have to hope the documentation is correct; if not, inspect the source code. We could improve this further by using a class with two properties that wrap the return values:

```
class Roots(pos: Double, neg: Double)

fun roots2(k: Int): Roots {
  require(k >= 0)
  val root = Math.sqrt(k.toDouble())
  return Roots(root, -root)
}
```

This has the advantage of having named fields so we could be sure which is the positive root and which is the negative root. An alternative to a custom class is using the Kotlin standard library `Pair` type. This type simply wraps two values, which are accessed via the first and second fields:

```
fun roots3(k: Int): Pair<Double, Double> {
  require(k >= 0)
  val root = Math.sqrt(k.toDouble())
  return Pair(root, -root)
```

```
}
```

This is most often used when it is clear what each value means. For example, a function that returned a currency code and an amount would not necessarily need to have a custom class, as it would be obvious which was which. Furthermore, if the function were a local function, you might feel that creating a custom class would be unnecessary boilerplate for something that will not be visible outside of the member function. As always, the most appropriate choice will depend on the situation.

There exists a three-value version of `Pair`, which is appropriately named **Triple**.

We can improve this further by using destructuring declarations on the caller site. Destructuring declarations allow the values to be extracted into separate variables automatically:

```
val (pos, neg) = roots3(16)
```

Notice that the variables are contained in a parenthesis block; the first value will be assigned to the positive root, and the second value will be assigned to the negative root. This syntactic sugar works with any object that implements a special component interface. The built in `Pair` type, and all data classes, automatically implement this interface. There will be more on this mechanism in the chapter on data classes.

Infix functions

Infix notation is the notation where an operator or function is placed between the operands or arguments. An example in Kotlin is the `to` function, which is used to create a Pair instance:

```
val pair = "London" to "UK"
```

In Kotlin, member functions can be defined as an infix; this allows them to be used in the same style. Since an infix function is placed between two arguments, all infix functions must operate on two parameters. The first parameter is the instance that the function is invoked on. The second parameter is an explicit parameter to the function.

To define your own `infix` function, use the `infix` keyword before the `fun` keyword, remembering that `infix` functions have only one explicit parameter:

```
infix fun concat(other:String): String {
  return this + other
}
```

For instance, we may want to model a bank account class, which would contain balance. In this class, we would most likely want some kind of function that adds to the customer's balance:

```
class Account {
  var balance = 0.0

  fun add(amount: Double): Unit {
    this.balance = balance + amount
  }
}
```

To use this, we could invoke it using the regular `dot` syntax:

```
val account = Account()
account.add(100.00)
```

However, we could use this as an `infix` function if we wish to add the `infix` keyword to the function definition:

```
class InfixAccount {
  var balance = 0.0

  infix fun add(amount: Double): Unit {
    this.balance = balance + amount
  }
}
```

Then we could invoke it like an operator in infix style:

```
val account2 = InfixAccount()
account2 add 100.00
```

In this example, there is not much difference between the readability of either style. Therefore, one would likely settle on the standard `dot` notation. But there are occasions when infix functions can be a benefit.

An example of such a case is for short-named, frequently used functions, such as the to function that exists in the Kotlin standard library. The `to` function is an extension function on all types (defined on Any). It is used to create an instance of `Pair`. If you recall from the section on *Extension functions*, a `Pair` type is a simple wrapper for two values.

As useful as the `Pair` type is, when instantiated directly, it can add noise to the two values. Compare the following equivalent pieces of code and see what you think is more readable:

```
val pair1 = Pair("london", "paris")
val pair2 = "london" to "paris"
```

The second is less verbose, and in many cases, more readable. This particular function is very useful when creating map literals. Again, compare the following two styles:

```
val map1 = mapOf(Pair("London", "UK"), Pair("Bucharest",  "Romania"))
val map2 = mapOf("London" to "UK", "Bucharest" to "Romania")
```

Other good examples of infix functions include bitwise operations (see Basic Types in `Chapter 2`, *Kotlin Basics*) and custom DSLs.

One custom DSL that benefits from infix operations is in the **KotlinTest** testing framework. This framework uses infix functions so that assertions in tests can be written in a natural language way. For example, refer to the following:

```
myList should contain(x)
myString should startWith("foo")
```

KotlinTest and the testing DSL will be covered in depth in `Chapter 11`, *Testing in Kotlin.*

Operators

Operators are functions that use a symbolic name. In Kotlin, many built-in operators are actually function calls. For example, array access is a real function:

```
val array = arrayOf(1, 2, 3)
val element = array[0]
```

In this example, the `[0]` operation is translated into a call to the function `get(index: Int)` defined on the `Array class`.

Many operators are predefined in Kotlin, just like they are in most other languages, and most operators tend to be combined with the infix style. This is immediately familiar in the guise of binary operators on numbers.

Although Kotlin treats operations on basic types as functions, they are compiled to the appropriate byte code operations to avoid function overhead and ensure maximum performance.

Often operators are preferred over real names if the operators are already familiar to the users. In fields such as mathematics or physics, where operators are routinely used, it would be natural to also use operations in code where appropriate. For example, the case of matrices, using the + character for matrix addition, feels more natural than using the word `add` or `plus`. It is also easier to read when the parentheses are omitted:

```
val m1: Matrix =
val m2: Matrix =
val m3 = m1 + m2
```

Operator overloading

The ability to define functions that use operators is called **operator overloading**.

In general, programming languages lie somewhere between the scale of allowing no operator overloading right through to allowing almost any characters to be used. In Java, the set of operator functions is fixed by the language, and developers are unable to add their own. So Java sits at the far left side of this scale. Scala, on the other hand, is far more permissive and allows you to have virtually any combination; so, it sits on the opposite side of the scale.

What is better depends on your point of view. Allowing no operator overloading means developers would not be able to abuse operators to create obtuse function names. On the other hand, allowing many kinds of operators to be used would mean that powerful DSLs could be created for specific problems.

Kotlin's designers opted to sit somewhere in the middle and allow operator overloading in a fixed and controlled manner. There is a fixed list of operators that can be used as functions, but any arbitrary combinations are forbidden. To create such a function, the function must be prefixed with the `operator` keyword and defined using the English equivalent name of the operator.

All operators have a predefined English equivalent name that is used for overloading the operator. The compiler simply rewrites the usage of the operator to the invocations of the function.

Operators can only be defined as member functions or extension functions.

Using the earlier example of matrix addition, which we claimed would benefit from operator overloading, can be defined in the following way:

```
class Matrix(val a: Int, val b: Int, val c: Int, val d: Int) {
  operator fun plus(matrix: Matrix): Matrix {
    return Matrix(a + matrix.a, b + matrix.b, c + matrix.c, d +
matrix.d)
  }
}
```

This is a simple case that only allows two x matrices.

We defined a function called `plus`; this will implement matrix addition. Notice how this function is marked with the operator keyword before the `fun` keyword. Also, as mentioned in the previous chapter, the parameters must be marked with `val` to be used inside member functions.

Given such a class, we could execute code in the following way:

```
val m1 = Matrix(1, 2, 3, 4)
val m2 = Matrix(5, 6, 7, 8)
val m3 = m1 + m2
```

The preceding code is compiled into the following equivalent code:

```
val m1 = Matrix(1, 2, 3, 4)
val m2 = Matrix(5, 6, 7, 8)
val m3 = m1.plus(m2)
```

Although this is a limited example, it demonstrates how easy it is to use operator overloading.

The function can also be invoked in regular dot style if required, but it uses the actual function name rather than the operator symbol. Although this doesn't seem to make much sense in this example, there are times when it might be useful.

Operator functions are not limited to acting on the same type as the class they are defined in. For example, we could have defined a List class to which we could add elements using the + operator and removing elements using the - operator.

Basic operators

The list of basic operators and their English equivalent function names are given in this table:

Operation	Function name
a + b	`a.plus(b)`
A – b	`a.minus(b)`
A * b	`a.times(b)`
A / b	`a.div(b)`
A & b	`a.mod(b)`
a..b	`a.rangeTo(b)`
+a	`a.unaryPlus()`
-a	`a.unaryMinus()`
!a	`a.not()`

Kotlin has support for some other types of operators in addition to what's presented in the preceding table.

In/contains

The keyword `in`, which you are already familiar with from for loops or collection checking, can also be overloaded for use in your own classes. The mapped name is `contains`. The following example shows the code using both the styles:

```
val ints = arrayOf(1,2,3,4)

val a = 3 in ints
val b = ints.contains(3)

val c = 5 !in ints
val d = ints.contains(5)
```

Get/set

Familiar bracket access on arrays is mapped to functions called `get` and `set`. The number of arguments is arbitrary and are passed to the `get` and `set` functions in order. This is how bracket access works for classes such as list and collection:

```
private val list = listOf(1, 2, 3, 4)
val head =  list[0]
```

The next example uses get and set with more than one position argument:

```
enum class Piece {
  Empty, Pawn, Bishop, Knight, Rook, Queen, King
}

class ChessBoard() {
  private val board = Array<Piece>(64, { Piece.Empty })
  operator fun get(rank: Int, file: Int): Piece = board[file * 8 +
rank]

  operator fun set(rank: Int, file: Int, value: Piece): Unit {
    board[file * 8 + rank] = value
  }
}
```

Here we defined a class containing the pieces of a chess board. The `board` is defined as an array with 64 elements, and each element is empty to start with. We can `get` or `set` the piece at a given position using two coordinates, representing the rank and file of the chess board:

```
val board = ChessBoard()
board[0, 4] = Piece.Queen
println(board[0, 4])
```

Invoke

Parentheses can also be used as operators by naming your function invoke. In this case, we just invoke the function directly on the instance. This makes a class itself look like a function:

```
class RandomLongs(seed: Long) {
  private val random = Random(seed)
  operator fun invoke(): Long = random.nextLong()
}
```

In this example, we wrapped a `Random` with a custom seed and then allowed the user to invoke the class directly to provide the following usage:

```
fun newSeed(): Long = /// some secure seed
val random = RandomLongs(newSeed())
val longs = listOf(random(), random(), random())
```

There are no restrictions on the number of `invoke` functions, so you can overload them by the type and number of parameters:

```
object Min {
  operator fun invoke(a: Int, b: Int): Int = if (a <= b) a else b
  operator fun invoke(a: Int, b: Int, c: Int): Int = invoke(invoke(a,
b), c)
  operator fun invoke(a: Int, b: Int, c: Int, d: Int): Int =
invoke(invoke(a, b), invoke(c, d))

  operator fun invoke(a: Long, b: Long): Long = if (a <= b) a else b
  operator fun invoke(a: Long, b: Long, c: Long): Long =
invoke(invoke(a, b), c)
  operator fun invoke(a: Long, b: Long, c: Long, d: Long): Long =
invoke(invoke(a, b), invoke(c, d))
}
```

In this example, we've made multiple overloaded versions of min, and Kotlin will call any of these versions that match the given arguments, which could be invoked as follows:

```
min(1, 2, 3)
min(1L, 2L)
```

Comparison

The less-than, greater-than, less than equals, and greater than equals operators are all overloadable. All four of these operators require just a single function between them, called `compareTo`. This function must return an `Int` and must be consistent with the `Comparator` interface in Java. So, to indicate a is less than `b`, you must return a negative integer. When `b` is greater than `a`, you must return a positive integer. And for equality, return `0`:

```
class BingoNumber(val name: String, val age: Int) {
  operator fun compareTo(other: BingoNumber): Int {
    return when {
      age < other.age -> -1
      age > other.age -> 1
      else -> 0
    }
```

```
    }
}
```

Here we have defined `BingoNumber`, which is the number of a ball and the nickname a bingo caller shouts out for. Using the `compareTo` function, we can now compare bingo numbers using the <, >, <=, and >= operations:

```
val a = BingoNumber("Key to the Door", 21)
val b = BingoNumber("Jump and Jive", 35)
println(a < b) // true
println(b > a) // false
```

Assignment

For mutable variables, Kotlin supports overloading shorthand assignment operators, such as +=. You can use the standard operations in assignments as well. For example, the following definition works for both:

```
class Counter(val k: Int) {
  operator fun plus(j: Int): Counter = Counter(k + j)
}
var counter = Counter(1)
counter = counter + 3
counter += 2
```

However, if you wish to allow assignment operations and not basic operations, you can do so using the following code:

```
class Counter(var k: Int) {
  operator fun plusAssign(j: Int): Unit {
    k += j
  }
}

 var counter = Counter(1)
 counter += 2
```

In this case, the function should return Unit.

You cannot define both types of operations. For example, you can define either `plus` or `plusAssign`, but not both. The former can always be used for both assignments and non-assignments, but the latter can only be used for an assignment.

The method equivalent names are given in the following table:

Operation	Function name
a += b	`a.plusAssign(b)`
a -= b	`a.minusAssign(b)`
a *= b	`a.timesAssign(b)`
a /= b	`a.divAssign(b)`
a %= b	`a.modAssign(b)`

You may have noticed this is the same as for basic operations, just with assign added to the end of the name.

Java interop

Java does not support operator overloading at all, so there is no equivalent in Java of the Kotlin operator keyword. In order to work around this, Kotlin allows any Java method that has the correct signature to be used as an operator.

For example, take this Java method signature defined on a class called `Matrix`, which matches the name required for the + operator:

```
public Matrix plus(Matrix other) { }
```

Then this could be invoked in Kotlin as follows:

```
val matrix3 = matrix1 + matrix2
```

Function literals

Just like we define string literals, `hello`, or double literals (12.34), we can also define function literals. To do so, we simply enclose the code in braces:

```
{ println("I am a function literal") }
```

Function literals can be assigned to a variable just like other literals:

```
val printHello = { println("hello") }
printHello()
```

Notice in this example that once a function literal is defined, we can invoke it later using parentheses, like we do for a regular function. Of course, once defined, we can invoke the function multiple times.

Function literals can also accept parameters. For this, we write the parameters, along with types, before a thin arrow; this denotes the function body:

```
val printMessage = { message: String -> println(message) }
printMessage("hello")
printMessage("world")
```

As you can see, we pass in the parameter when invoking like a regular function. When a function literal is used in a place where the compiler can figure out the parameter type, we can omit the types:

```
{ message -> println(message) }
```

In fact, Kotlin has a neater trick. If there is only a single parameter and the type can be inferred, then the compiler will allow us to omit the parameter completely. In this case, it makes the implicit variable `it` available:

```
{ println(it) }
```

The use of function literals is primary as higher order functions. We will see this in the next chapter. They are also used in single abstract methods, which are covered later in this chapter.

Tail recursive functions

Recursion is a powerful functional programming tool that most programmers have come across before. A recursive function is one that, when certain conditions are held, invokes itself. An idiomatic example of a recursive function is often the Fibonacci sequence, which in English is defined as follows: the next value is the sum of the previous two values. In code, we can define Fibonacci as follows:

```
fun fib(k: Int): Int = when (k) {
  0 -> 1
  1 -> 1
  else -> fib(k - 1) + fib(k - 2)
}
```

Notice that for 0 and 1, we define the base case, which does not use recursion. However, for higher values, the function itself is called with the previous two values of `k`, and so on.

This is very succinct code, but it isn't the most efficient. Each time the `fib` function is invoked from within itself, the runtime must keep the existing stack frame so that the execution could continue once it returns. We can demonstrate this with the following pseudo code:

```
invoke fib with k:
  If k == 0 then return 1
  If k == 1 then return 1
  Let temp1 = invoke fib with k-1
  Let temp2 = invoke fib with k -2
  return temp1 + temp2
```

As you can see, after the recursive calls are completed, we add them together. So the compiler must keep this stack frame alive to store the variables `temp1` and `temp2`. If `fib` is invoked with a large number, then the number of recursive calls required before we get to the base cases would imply that we'd run out of stack space, leading to the famous stack overflow error.

This particular function could be improved by remembering the values of fib(k-1) instead of recalculating it each time. However, it demonstrates how recursion in general is problematic if the call depth is unbounded.

If an invocation of a recursive function is the last operation in a particular function and the result of the call is simply to return the value, then the system would not need to keep the previous stack frame in play. Since it does not need other variables for further operations, it could simply return the value from the recursive call. This technique is called **tail recursion**, and it allows us to write efficient recursive algorithms that would otherwise result in stack overflow errors.

To inform Kotlin that our function is expected to be a tail recursive function, we use the `tailrec` keyword when defining the function. Then the compiler will ensure that each use of recursion in the function is the last operation. If not, then a compile time error will occur.

Consider a function for calculating factorials in a recursive manner. Note that the factorial of `0` is defined as `1`:

```
fun fact(k: Int): Int {
  if (k == 0) return 1
  else return k * fact(k - 1)
}
```

The last operation is not the recursive call because the result from the recursive call is multiplied before it is returned. However, if we rewrite the function to carry the result with it, then we could return directly from the recursive call:

```
fun fact(k: Int): Int {
  fun factTail(m: Int, n: Int): Int {
    if (m == 0) return n
    else return factTail(m - 1, m * n)
  }
  return factTail(k, 1)
}
```

The inner `factTail` function is now tail recursive, so we can mark it as such and the compiler will confirm the following for us:

```
fun fact(k: Int): Int {
  tailrec fun factTail(m: Int, n: Int): Int {
    if (m == 0) return n
    else return factTail(m - 1, m * n)
  }
  return factTail(k, 1)
}
```

Varargs

Kotlin allows functions to be defined such that they would accept a variable number of arguments. Hence this feature is called **varargs**. Varargs allow users to pass in a comma-separated list of arguments, which the compiler will automatically wrap into an array. Java developers will already be familiar with the feature, which in Java looks like the following:

```
public void println(String.. args) { }
```

The Kotlin equivalent is to use the `vararg` keyword before the parameter name:

```
fun multiprint(vararg strings: String): Unit {
  for (string in strings)
  println(string)
}
```

This would be invoked in the following way:

```
multiprint("a", "b", "c")
```

Functions can have regular parameters, and at most one parameter marked as `vararg`:

```
fun multiprint(prefix: String, vararg strings: String): Unit {
  println(prefix)
  for (string in strings)
    println(string)
}
```

The `vararg` parameter is usually the last parameter, but it does not always have to be. If there are other parameters after `vararg`, then arguments must be passed in using named parameters:

```
    fun multiprint(prefix: String, vararg strings: String, suffix: String):
Unit {
      println(prefix)
      for (string in strings)
        println(string)
      println(suffix)
    }
```

The `vararg` parameter would be invoked using the following named parameter as a suffix:

```
multiprint("Start", "a", "b", "c", suffix = "End")
```

Spread operator

If a function is defined to accept a variable number of arguments using vararg, but you already have an array, then how do you pass it in? The answer lies in using the so-called spread operator `*`, which unwraps the elements of the array and passes them in as individual arguments.

Let's say we have an array of strings that we want to pass to the `multiprint` function we defined earlier. Then using the spread operator, the code will look like the following:

```
val strings = arrayOf("a", "b", "c", "d", "e")
multiprint("Start", *strings, suffix = "End")
```

Notice that we apply the spread operator before the variable name.

In current versions of Kotlin, the spread operator only works on Array types. This restriction will be lifted in future releases.

Standard library functions

Kotlin provides a standard library that is meant to augment, not replace, the standard Java library. There are many functions that adapt Java types and methods and allow them to be used as idiomatic Kotlin. In this chapter, we will cover some of the lower level functions that have far reaching use.

Apply

Apply is a Kotlin standard library extension function declared on Any, so it could be invoked on instances of all types. Apply accepts a lambda that is invoked with the receiver being the instance where `apply` was called on. Apply then returns the original instance.

It's primary use is to make the code that needs to initialize an instance more readable by allowing functions and properties to be called directly inside the function before returning the value itself. Refer to the following code:

```
val task = Runnable { println("Running") }
Thread(task).apply {  setDaemon(true) }.start()
```

Here we created a task, an instance of `Runnable`, and then created a new `Thread` instance to run this task. Inside the closure, we configure the thread instance to be a daemon thread.

Notice that the closure code is operating on the thread instance directly. The instance that apply was called on is the receiver for the closure. Further note that we can call `start()` on the return value because the original instance is always returned from `apply`, regardless of what the closure itself returns.

An alternative version of this code without apply looks as follows:

```
val task = Runnable { println("Running") }
val thread = Thread(task)
thread.setDaemon(true)
thread.start()
```

Let

Let is a Kotlin standard library extension function that is similar in vein to `apply`. The key difference is that it returns the value of the closure itself. It is useful when you wish to execute some code on an object before returning some different value and you don't need to keep a reference to the original:

```
val outputPath = Paths.get("/user/home").run {
  val path = it.resolve("output")
  path.toFile().createNewFile()
  path
}
```

Notice that it refers to the instance we invoked `run` on, the user's `home` folder. The advantage of writing code this way is that we don't need to assign the original path to an intermediate variable.

With

With is a top-level function designed for cases when you want to call multiple functions on an object and don't wish to repeat the receiver each time. The function `with` accepts a receiver and a closure to operate on such a receiver:

```
    val g2: Graphics2D = ...

    g2.stroke = BasicStroke(10F)
    g2.setRenderingHint(RenderingHints.KEY_ANTIALIASING,
RenderingHints.VALUE_ANTIALIAS_ON)g2.setRenderingHint(RenderingHints.KEY_DI
THERING,  RenderingHints.VALUE_DITHER_ENABLE)
    g2.background = Color.BLACK

    with(g2) {
      stroke = BasicStroke(10F)
      setRenderingHint(RenderingHints.KEY_ANTIALIASING,
RenderingHints.VALUE_ANTIALIAS_ON)
setRenderingHint(RenderingHints.KEY_DITHERING,
RenderingHints.VALUE_DITHER_ENABLE)
      background = Color.BLACK
    }
```

In this example, the first set of invocations operate on the `g2` reference directly. In the second set, the receiver is set to `g2`, so functions can be invoked on it directly.

Run

Run is an extension function that combines the use cases of `with` and `let`. This means a closure is passed to `run`, which has the instance as the receiver. The return value of the closure is used as the return value of `run` itself:

```
val outputPath = Paths.get("/user/home").run {
  val path = resolve("output")
  path.toFile().createNewFile()
  path
}
```

The key difference between `let` and `run` is that with `run`, the receiver is the instance, whereas in `let`, the argument to the closure is the instance.

Lazy

Lazy is another useful function that wraps an expensive function call to be invoked when first required:

```
fun readStringFromDatabase(): String = ... // expensive operation
val lazyString = lazy { readStringFromDatabase() }
```

The first time we require the result, we can access the value on the lazy reference. Only then will the wrapped function actually be invoked:

```
val string = lazyString.value
```

This is a common pattern seen in many languages and frameworks. The advantage of using this built-in function over rolling your own is that synchronization is taken care of for you. That is, if the value is requested twice, Kotlin will safely handle any race conditions by only executing the underlying function once.

Use

Use is similar to the try-with-resources statement that exists in Java 7. Use is defined as an extension on an instance of closeable and accepts a function literal that operates on this closeable. Use will safely invoke the function, closing down the resource after the function has completed whether an exception was raised or not:

```
val input = Files.newInputStream(Paths.get("input.txt"))
val byte = input.use({ input.read() })
```

Essentially, use is a more concise way of handling resources in simple cases, without needing the try/catch/finally block.

Repeat

As the name implies, repeat accepts a function literal and an integer `k`. The function literal will be invoked `k` number of times. This is a very simple function to avoid needing a for block for simple operations:

```
repeat(10, { println("Hello") })
```

Require/assert/check

Kotlin provides a triad of functions to enable us to add a limited amount of formal specifications to our program. A formal specification is an assertion that should always hold true or false at the location when the assertion is executed. These are also referred to as contracts or design by contract:

- Require throws an exception and it is used to ensure that arguments match the input conditions
- Assert throws an `AssertionException` exception and it is used to ensure that our internal state is consistent
- Check throws an `IllegalStateException` exception and it is also used for internal state consistency

These functions are all very similar. The key difference is in the type of exception that is raised. Assert can be disabled at runtime, but `require` and `check` cannot be disabled. Refer to the following example:

```
fun neverEmpty(str: String) {
  require(str.length > 0, { "String should not be empty" })
  println(str)
}
```

In this example, we always ensure we have not passed an empty String. The function literal that is passed as a message to the functions is lazily evaluated; it won't be invoked if the condition holds true.

Generic functions

Have you ever written a function for one type and then you had to write it again for another type? Perhaps you wrote a function that worked for strings and then had to write the same function again for integers.

To avoid such a case, functions can be generic in the types they use. This allows a function to be written that can work with any type, rather than a specific type only. To do this, we define the type parameters in the function signature:

```
fun <T> printRepeated(t: T, k: Int): Unit {
  for (x in 0..k) {
    println(t)
  }
}
```

In this example, we print the `t` element `k` number of times. You might be thinking that we could have defined this function using Any and it would still work, since `println` is defined to accept Any itself. That's correct! However, what you can't do with Any is ensure that multiple parameters are of the same type and that return values are the same as the input type. Let's say we want a function that returns a random element from three input instances:

```
fun <T> choose(t1: T, t2: T, t3: T): T {
  return when (Random().nextInt(3)) {
    0 -> t1
    1 -> t2
    else -> t3
  }
}
```

Now when we call this function, the compiler will enforce that the three elements are all of the same type. It doesn't matter which type, as long as they are all the same. In addition, the return value will be the same. So the following code all works with the `r` variable correctly being inferred as an integer:

```
val r = choose(5, 7, 9)
```

If we don't have generic functions, then our options would be to write a separate function for each different type we want to use or write a function that returns Any. The drawback to using Any here would be that the output type would have to be Any as well; therefore, the caller would have to resort to casting to get back to the original type.

Functions are not restricted to a single generic type, and they can also define the upper bounds on their type parameters. We will look at generics in more detail in `Chapter 10`, *Collections.*

Pure functions

In functional programming, the concept of a pure function is one that holds the following two properties:

- The function should always return the same output for the same input
- The function should not create any side effects

The first property means that when a function is invoked, the value returned should always be the same whenever the same input is used. A simple example is abs. The absolute value of an integer is always the same for the same input. A pure function can depend only on the input, but it does not have to necessarily use all the input types.

The second property is that a function should not cause any observable changes outside the function. So the function cannot depend on any external mutable state, change variables that exist outside the function, or write I/O.

If a function is said to be pure, then the function can be replaced at the call site with the result of the expression. Going back to the absolute function, any code that depends on abs(-4) can be replaced with 4 and the program will not change its meaning.

Consider the following function calls:

```
val x = impure(5) + impure(5)
val y = 2 * impure(5)
```

It might be tempting to think these two are the same; after all, $x + x$ is the same as $2 * x$. However, the implementation of the function is as follows:

```
val counter = AtomicInteger(1)
fun impure(k: Int): Int {
  return counter.incrementAndGet() + k
}
```

We can see that the function mutates a global state, so each invocation is different. This is a contrived example, but it indicates the difference between pure and impure.

The advantages of pure functions are several. The results of the functions can be cached, which is advantageous for slow functions. Pure functions can be easily parallelized since they don't write anything to a shared state. They can be tested in isolation since they depend on nothing but their input instances. The previous example would be hard to Unit test.

We'll cover pure functions and how they can help with testing in `Chapter 10`, *Collections*.

Java from Kotlin

One of the main selling points for Kotlin over other alternative JVM languages is the importance placed upon a high degree of interoperability between Kotlin and Java. Most Java code can be called without any special support, and some special cases are described here.

Getters and setters

The JavaBean convention in Java states that mutable fields have a getter and a setter, and immutable fields just have a getter. A getter is just a no-arg method named get followed by the name of the field. A setter is a single argument method named set followed by the name of the field, where the argument is the value you want to set the field to:

```
public class Named {
  private String name;

  public String getName() {
    return name;
  }

  public void setName(String name) {
    this.name = name;
  }
}
```

This pattern is standard across most of Java. In Kotlin, methods defined in this way can be accessed using property-style syntax:

```
val named = Named()
println("My name is " + named.name)
named.name = "new name"
```

Of course, the method names can be accessed as functions and that too normally if you wish.

If a Java field has a setter but not a getter, then this special syntax will not be available.

Single abstract methods

A common pattern in Java is interfaces that define a single method. You can see these all over the Java standard library, such as `Runnable`, `Callable`, `Closeable`, `Comparator`, and so on. They are often used in places where a single function would have been used had Java supported functions earlier. The name single abstract method, or SAMs, has been adopted to describe them.

Since they are so ubiquitous, Kotlin has support for converting a function literal directly into a SAM. If the conversion is unambiguous, you can simply pass the function literal where a SAM is expected:

```
val threadPool = Executors.newFixedThreadPool(4)
threadPool.submit {
  println("I don't have a lot of work to do")
}
```

In this example, the thread pool executor is defined to accept an instance of the type `Runnable`. So, the compiler will convert the function literal into an instance of `Runnable`, with the literal used as the implementation of the method `run`. The compiled code would be equivalent to the following snippet:

```
threadPool.submit(object : Runnable {
  override fun run() {
    println("I don't have a lot of work to do")
  }
})
```

This special support only works for interfaces and not abstract classes, even if the abstract class only has a single method.

What happens if the receiver defines an overload and it is ambiguous which SAM type to promote the function literal to? In this case, you can give the compiler a nudge by letting it know which type you intended:

```
threadPool.submit(Runnable {
  println("I don't have a lot of work to do")
})
```

Notice that this is very similar to the first example, except that we have simply prefixed the function literal with the name of the SAM type we want to use.

Kotlin will not perform this conversion on SAMs that are defined in Kotlin itself. This is because in Kotlin, you can define your function to accept another function, making this kind of pattern redundant.

Escaping Kotlin identifiers

Some Kotlin keywords are valid identifiers in Java, for example, `object`, `in`, and `when`. If you need to call a Java library method or field with one of these names, you can still do so by wrapping the name with backticks.

For example, consider that a Java library defines the following class and method:

```
public class Date {
  public void when(str:String) { .... }
}
```

If this happens, then it can be invoked like this:

```
date.`when`("2016")
Checked exceptions
```

As discussed previously, Kotlin does not have checked exceptions. So Java methods that have checked exceptions are treated in the same way as methods that do not.

For example, the method `createNewFile` is defined on file:

```
public boolean createNewFile() throws IOException
```

In Java, this means we would need a `try...catch...finally` block. In Kotlin, we do not.

Java void methods

We know by now that void in Java is analogous to Unit in Kotlin. Any void Java method is treated as a Unit returning function.

Kotlin from Java

Just as Java can be used seamlessly in Kotlin, Kotlin can just as easily be used from your Java programs.

Top-level functions

The JVM does not support top-level functions. Therefore, to make them work with Java, the Kotlin compiler creates a Java class with the name of the package. The functions are then defined as Java methods on this class, which must be instantiated before use.

For example, consider the following top-level function:

```
package com.packt.chapter4
fun cube(n: Int): Int = n * n * n
```

If this is given, the Kotlin compiler will generate a class called `com.packt.chapter4.Chapter4` with functions as static members. To use this from Java, we would access this function as we would access any other static method:

```
import com.packt.chapter4.Chapter4;
Chapter4.cube(3);
```

We can even change the name of the class the compiler creates by using an annotation:

```
@file:JvmName("MathUtils")
package com.packt.chapter4
fun cube(n: Int): Int = n * n * n
```

Top-level functions would cause the compiler to generate the methods in a class called `com.pact.chapter4.MathUtils` instead. Even better, we can tell the compiler to combine all the top-level functions from several Kotlin files with the same Java class. This uses another annotation:

```
@file:JvmMultifileClass
```

This is useful when top-level functions are spread in a package, but for use in Java, you want a simple, unified entry code.

Default parameters

JVM has no support for default parameters. Therefore, when a function is defined with defaults, the compiler must create a single function without the default parameters. However, we can instruct the compiler to create multiple overloads of the function for each default parameter. Then Java users can see the several functions and choose which one is most appropriate.

Consider we have the following function definition with defaults:

```
    @JvmOverloads fun join(array: Array<String>, prefix: String =  "",
separator: String = "", suffix: String = "")
```

If we have this, the annotation `@JvmOverloads` will cause the compiler to generate the following variants:

```
    public String join(String[] array) {
      return join(array, "");
    }

    public String join(String[] array, String prefix) {
      return join(array, prefix, "");
    }

    public String join(String[] array, String prefix, String separator) {
      return join(array, prefix, separator, "");
    }

    public String join(String[] array, String prefix, String separator,
String suffix) {
      //actual implementation
    }
```

Overloads will only be created for default parameters, dropping all the parameters to the right, and so on. This clever trick works for constructors and static methods.

Object and static methods

Named objects and companion objects are generated on a JVM as singleton instances of a particular class. For example, if you define an object called `Foo`, then the Kotlin compiler will create a class called `Foo`. `Foo` will contain a static field called `INSTANCE`, which will contain the only instance of `Foo`:

```
object Console {
  fun clear() : Unit { }
```

```
}
```

This Kotlin method can be called from Java as follows:

```
Console.INSTANCE.clear()
```

However, you can also inform the Kotlin compiler to generate this function as a Java static method. To do this, we mark the function with the annotation `@JvmStatic`:

```
object Console {
  @JvmStatic fun clear() : Unit { }
}
```

Now this method can be called from Java using `INSTANCE` as before, but also directly from the class:

```
Console.clear()
```

Erasure naming

JVM does not support generics in byte code. This means when you have a type such as list, which is generic, then `List<String>` and `List<Int>` are both compiled into the same underlying representation. This becomes an issue when there is a clash between function signatures after compilation.

For example, consider the following function declarations are given:

```
fun println(array: Array<String>): Unit {}
fun println(array: Array<Long>) : Unit {}
```

They will both result in the same signature.

Kotlin is able to differentiate between the two functions, so if we definitely want to use the same name, we can. We just need to indicate to the compiler what names it should use when compiling. We do this using the `@JvmName` annotation:

```
@JvmName("printlnStrings")
fun println(array: Array<String>): Unit  {}
@JvmName("printlnLongs")
fun println(array: Array<Long>) : Unit {}
```

These functions are accessible in Kotlin as before, with the original names. In Java, you would use the names passed to the annotation.

Checked exceptions

In Java, we can only catch checked exceptions if they are declared on the method, even if the method body throws that exception. Therefore, if we have a function that will be used from Java and we want to allow people to catch an exception, we must inform the compiler to add the exception to the method signature.

We can do this using the `@Throws` annotation:

```
@Throws(IOException::class)
fun createDirectory(file: File) {
  if (file.exists())
    throw IOException("Directory already exists")
  file.createNewFile()
}
```

In this example, the `createDirectory` function can now be used in a `try...catch...finally` block from Java:

```
try {
  Chapter4.createDirectory(new File("mobydick.txt"));
} catch (IOException e) {
  // handle exception here
}
```

Summary

Functions are the cornerstone of any modern language, and the full range of features Kotlin provides allows developers to be more expressive yet write less code. As we will see in the next chapter, functions are the key to unlocking powerful idioms known as higher ordered functions.

5

Higher Order Functions and Functional Programming

In the previous chapter, we introduced Kotlin's support for functions and the various features we can use while writing functions. In this chapter, we continue on that theme by discussing higher order functions and how we can use them to write cleaner and more expressive code.

In this chapter, we will cover:

- Higher order functions and closures
- Anonymous functions
- Function references
- Functional programming idioms
- Custom DSLs

Higher order functions

A higher order function is simply a function that either accepts another function as a parameter, returns a function as its return value, or both.

Let's consider the first example:

```
fun foo(str: String, fn: (String) -> String): Unit {
  val applied = fn(str)
  println(applied)
}
```

Here, we have defined a function `foo` with two parameters. The first is a string, and the second is a function from string to string. When we say from string to string, we mean the function accepts a string input and returns another string as the output. Also note the syntax used to define the function parameter. The input types are wrapped in parentheses and the output type is separated by a thin arrow.

To invoke this function, we can pass in a function literal (recall that function literals were introduced in `Chapter 4`, *Functions in Kotlin*):

```
foo("hello", { it.reversed() })
```

As you can see, the string we pass in is `hello`. This value is then passed as the input to the next function, which returns the reversed value. This is then printed out, so the result of this invocation would be to output `olleh`. Remember that a function literal that only has one argument can use `it` as a shortcut to avoid naming the argument explicitly.

At this stage you may wonder why this is useful. After all, we could have written code like the following:

```
fun foo2(str: String) {
  val reversed = str.reversed()
  println(reversed)
}
```

The result of this code would be the same. However, the advantages of first-order functions are clear when we want to write a function that can work for many scenarios. Let's consider an example of filtering elements from a list into odd and even elements. The imperative approach might be something like the following:

```
val ints = listOf(1, 2, 3, 4, 5, 6)

val evens = mutableListOf<Int>()
val odds = mutableListOf<Int>()
for (k in ints) {
  if (k % 2 == 0)
    evens.add(k)
  else
    odds.add(k)
}
```

Each value is added to another list as we iterate through, applying modulo operators to separate the values.

However, we can use higher order functions instead, as follows:

```
val ints = listOf(1, 2, 3, 4, 5, 6)
val odds = ints.filter { it % 2 == 1 }
val evens = ints.filter { it % 2 == 0 }
```

This kind of code has the rare property of being both quicker to write and easier to read. It also has the added benefit that the `evens` and `odds` results are immutable as they have been constructed for us.

Collections and the higher order functions available on them are covered in full in `Chapter 10`, *Collections*.

Returning a function

Let's now return to the definition of a higher order function. Remember that we said a function that returns another function is also considered a valid higher order function:

```
fun bar(): (String) -> String = { str -> str.reversed() }
```

In this example, invoking `bar()` will return a function from string to string. In this case, that particular string will be reversed. To return a function, we use an equals after the return type, and wrap the function in braces. Technically this is a one-line function, where the single expression after the equals is the function body.

We can invoke it as follows:

```
val reversi = bar()
reversi("hello")
reversi("world")
```

Here, we assign the function bar to a variable called `reversi`, before invoking it with two different values.

The usefulness of this technique can be seen when we have a function that accepts other values and then returns a function that uses the inputs to the original function. Lets return to the filter example from earlier and define a function for creating a `modulo`-based filter:

```
fun modulo(k: Int): (Int) -> Boolean = { it % k == 0 }
```

Note that the input value `k` is used in the returned function. This can now be combined with the higher order filter function available on the list class:

```
val ints = listOf(1, 2, 3, 4, 5, 6)
val odd = ints.filter(modulo(1))
val evens = ints.filter(modulo(2))
val mod3 = ints.filter(modulo(3))
```

We don't use braces here because, if we did, that would define another function, which would invoke the `modulo` function, giving us a function of a function.

Function assignment

Functions can also be assigned to variables to make it easier for them to be passed around:

```
val isEven: (Int) -> Boolean = modulo(2)

listOf(1, 2, 3, 4).filter(isEven)
listOf(5, 6, 7, 8).filter(isEven)
```

Here, using the `modulo` function defined earlier, we assign an instance of that function to a variable. In this example, the type has been explicitly added so that it is clear to the reader what the type being returned is, but this can usually be omitted. This same function instance is then used twice.

We can also assign function literals to variables. In those cases, we need to help the compiler with the parameter types in either of the following ways:

```
val isEven : (Int) -> Boolean = { it % 2 == 0 }
```

The following is another option:

```
val isEven = { k : Int -> k % 2 == 0 }
```

This can be useful if you need to set up a non-trivial or time-consuming function for use multiple times.

Languages that support higher order functions and function assignment are said to support *first class* functions.

Closures

In functional programming, a closure is a function that has access to variables and parameters defined in outer scopes. It is said that they "close over" these variables, hence the name *closure*.

Let's consider an example where we wish to load names from a database and filter them to only include those that match some search criteria. We will use our old friend, the filter method:

```
class Student(val firstName: String, val lastName: String)

fun loadStudents(): List = ...
   //  load from database

fun students(nameToMatch: String): List<Student> {
  return loadStudents().filter {
    it.lastName == nameToMatch
  }
}
```

Note that the function literal passed to the `filter` method uses the parameter to the outer function. This parameter is defined in an outer scope to the function, so the function is closing over the parameter.

Closures can access local variables as well:

```
val counter = AtomicInteger(0)
val cores = Runtime.getRuntime().availableProcessors()
val threadPool = Executors.newFixedThreadPool(cores)

threadPool.submit {
  println("I am task number ${counter.incrementAndGet()}")
}
```

In this example, we submit a number of tasks to a thread pool. As you can see, each task has access to a shared counter (using `AtomicInteger` for thread safety).

Closures can also mutate variables they have closed over:

```
var containsNegative = false

val ints = listOf(0, 1, 2, 3, 4, 5)
ints.forEach {
  if (it < 0)
    containsNegative = true
}
```

Very simply, this code closes over a local variable, `containsNegative`, setting it to `true` if a negative value is found in a list. In the real world, you'd use a built-in function for this rather than this function, but it indicates how vars can be updated from inside a function literal.

Anonymous functions

Often when using higher order functions we invoke them using function literals, especially if the function is short:

```
listOf(1, 2, 3).filter { it > 1 }
```

As you can see, there is no reason to define the passed function anywhere else. When using literals like this, we are unable to specify the return value. This is usually not a problem as the Kotlin compiler will infer the return type for us.

However, sometimes we may wish to be explicit about the return type. In those cases, we can use what is called an anonymous function. This is a function that looks similar to a normal function definition, except the name is omitted:

```
fun(a: String, b: String): String = a + b
```

This can be used in the following manner:

```
val ints = listOf(1, 2, 3)
val evens = ints.filter(fun(k: Int) = k % 2 == 0)
```

If the parameter type can also be inferred, then that can be omitted as well:

```
val evens = ints.filter(fun(k) = k % 2 == 0)
```

Function references

So far in this chapter, we have already seen how to pass functions as parameters. The ways we have done this so far are either by creating a function literal, or by using a function that returns another function.

Top-level function references

But what if we have a top-level function and we want to use that? We can wrap the function in another function, of course:

```
fun isEven(k: Int): Boolean = k % 2 == 0

val ints = listOf(1, 2, 3, 4, 5)
ints.filter { isEven(it) }
```

The alternative is to use what is called a function reference. Using the same definition for `isEven`, we can write it as follows:

```
val ints = listOf(1, 2, 3, 4, 5)
ints.filter(::isEven)
```

Note that the `::` syntax is used before the function name.

Member and extension function references

Function references can be used for extension and member functions by prefixing them with the name of the class. Let's define an extension function on integers called `isOdd`, as follows:

```
fun Int.isOdd(): Boolean = this % 1 == 0
```

We could use this inside a function literal as normal:

```
val ints = listOf(1, 2, 3, 4, 5)
ints.filter { it.isOdd() }
```

We can also use a reference to it instead:

```
val ints = listOf(1, 2, 3, 4, 5)
ints.filter(Int::isOdd)
```

A function reference to a member or extension function has an extra parameter-the instance or receiver that the function is invoked on.

Function references might seem just another way of doing basically the same thing, but consider a case where a function accepts multiple parameters:

```
fun foo(a: Double, b: Double, f: (Double, Double) -> Double) =  f(a, b)
```

Here, `foo` will invoke the function parameter with the inputs `a` and `b`. To invoke this, we can, of course, pass in a function literal:

```
foo(1.0, 2.0, { a, b -> Math.pow(a, b) })
```

`Math.pow` is a member function, and since we know it accepts two doubles and returns another double, we can use a function reference. This will have a matching function signature, and so reduces boilerplate:

```
foo(1.0, 2.0, Math::pow)
```

Bound references

In Kotlin 1.1, we are able to have function references that are bound to a particular instance. This means that we can place an expression before the `::` operator. The reference is then tied to that particular instance, meaning that, unlike unbound references, the arity of the returned function does not increase.

Compare the following two examples. The first uses unbound references:

```
    fun String.equalsIgnoreCase(other: String) = this.toLowerCase() ==
other.toLowerCase()

    listOf("foo", "moo", "boo").filter {
      (String::equalsIgnoreCase)("bar", it)
    }
```

We have a simple function for case insensitive equality, but when we make a function reference to it, it has the signature `(String, String) -> Boolean`. The first argument is the receiver. This means we can't simply pass in the reference to the `filter` function on the list, but instead have to wrap it again in another function literal.

Let's try again, this time using a bound reference:

```
    fun String.equalsIgnoreCase(other: String) = this.toLowerCase() ==
other.toLowerCase()

    listOf("foo", "baz", "BAR").filter("bar"::equalsIgnoreCase)
```

Using the same definition for `equalsIgnoreCase`, we can create a bound reference on the receiver, `bar`. This results in a function with the signature `(String) -> Boolean`. This reference has the correct shape to be passed in directly to the `filter` function.

Function-literal receivers

Recall from the previous chapter on functions that the receiver of a function is the instance that corresponds to the `this` keyword when inside the function body. In Kotlin, function parameters can be defined to accept a receiver when they are invoked. We do that using the following syntax:

```
fun foo(fn: String.() -> Boolean): Unit
```

Then, when we invoke the function `fn` in the `foo` function body, we are required to invoke it on an instance of string, as you can see if we complete the implementation of `foo`:

```
fun foo(fn: String.() -> Boolean): Unit {
  "string".fn()
}
```

This feature also works with anonymous functions:

```
val substring = fun String.(substr: String): Boolean =
this.contains(substr)
"hello".substring("ello")
```

You might prefer the anonymous function syntax if you wish to assign a function to a variable, as earlier. This is because a receiver cannot be specified with a function literal.

Function receivers are useful when writing custom DSLs. We'll cover this in detail in a later section.

Functions in the JVM

Prior to version 8 of the **Java Virtual Machine** (**JVM**), first class functions were not supported. Since Kotlin targets Java 6 for compatibility with Android devices, how are functions handled by the compiler?

It turns out that all functions in Kotlin are compiled into instances of classes called `Function0`, `Function1`, `Function2`, and so on. The number in the class name represents the number of inputs. If you look at the type inside an IDE, you will be able to see which class the function is being compiled into. For example, a function with the signature `(Int)->Boolean` would show the type as `Function1<Int, Boolean>`. Each of the function classes also has an invoke member function that is used to apply the body of the function.

Here is the definition of `Function0` from the Kotlin source code, which accepts no input parameters:

```
/** A function that takes 0 arguments. */
public interface Function0<out R> : Function<R> {
  /** Invokes the function. */
  public operator fun invoke(): R
}
```

Here is the definition of `Function1`, which accepts a single input parameter:

```
/** A function that takes 1 argument. */
public interface Function1<in P1, out R> : Function<R> {
  /** Invokes the function with the specified argument. */
  public operator fun invoke(p1: P1): R
}
```

All instances have a return type, and the return type is the rightmost type parameter. The other definitions of `FunctionN` follow logically from this.

Bytecode

As an example of the output that the Kotlin compiler will emit, we can view the bytecode generated for a simple function invocation. Let's use the integer filter functions from earlier.

Look at the following simple function:

```
val isEven: (Int) -> Boolean = { it % 2 == 0 }
```

This simple function will result in the following bytecode:

```
final class com.packt.chapter5._5_x_inlineKt$test$isEven$1 extends
kotlin.jvm.internal.Lambda implements
kotlin.jvm.functions.Function1<java.lang.Integer, java.lang.Boolean> {
public static final com.packt.chapter5._5_x_inlineKt$test$isEven$1
INSTANCE;
  public java.lang.Object invoke(java.lang.Object);
    Code:
      0: aload_0
      1: aload_1
      2: checkcast     #11                     // class java/lang/Number
      5: invokevirtual #15                     // Method
java/lang/Number.intValue:()I
      8: invokevirtual #18                     // Method invoke:(I)Z
      11: invokestatic  #24                     // Method
java/lang/Boolean.valueOf:(Z)Ljava/lang/Boolean;
      14: areturn
public final boolean invoke(int);
  Code:
    0: iload_1
    1: iconst_2
    2: irem
    3: ifne          10
    6: iconst_1
    7: goto          11
    10: iconst_0
    11: ireturn
com.packt.chapter5._5_x_inlineKt$test$isEven$1();
  Code:
    0: aload_0
    1: iconst_1
    2: invokespecial #33            // Method
kotlin/jvm/internal/Lambda."<init>":(I)V
    5: return
static {};
  Code:
    0: new           #2                    // class
com/packt/chapter5/_5_x_inlineKt$test$isEven$1
```

```
      3: dup
      4: invokespecial #53                  // Method "<init>":()V
      7: putstatic     #55                  // Field
INSTANCE:Lcom/packt/chapter5/_5_x_inlineKt$test$isEven$1;
      10: return
}
```

You can see in the first line that this class extends `kotlin.jvm.functions.Function1<java.lang.Integer, java.lang.Boolean>`.

This matches the function type we defined. You'll also notice that there is an invoke function, which contains the logic of the function, namely `iconst_2` and `irem`, which are performing the `modulo(2)` operation.

The rest of the bytecode is concerned with allowing the function to be invoked as a static method. Since functions have no state other than their inputs, they can be modeled as a singleton instance via a static method.

Closures are implemented by increasing the arity of the function to accept extra parameters, which are the closed-over variables. The compiler inserts this automatically.

Function composition

We have seen how we can extract a function value from an existing top-level or extension function. The logical next step would be functionality that allows us to combine multiple functions together in a concise way: function composition.

Unlike many other languages, Kotlin does not have any built-in support for function composition. However, it is very easy to add our own using the facilities we have seen so far for manipulation of functions.

We can start by defining a compose function that would accept two input functions, returning a new function that will invoke them in turn when applied. Of course, the output type from the first function must match up with the input type of the second:

```
fun <A, B, C> compose(fn1: (A) -> B, fn2: (B) -> C): (A) -> C = { a ->
  val b = fn1(a)
  val c = fn2(b)
  c
}
```

This example has been written in a fairly verbose way, assigning each step to its own variable, but this is so that it is clear to the reader what is going on. The returned function is the composed step of `A` to `C`, achieved by invoking `A` to `B`, then `B` to `C`.

We can call this function easily, as follows:

```
val f = String::length
val g = Any::hashCode
val fog = compose(f, g)
```

Here, we have derived two function references, the first to get the length of a string, and the second to get the hash of that length. Once combined together, we can invoke `fog` by applying a string:

```
fog("what is the hash of my length?")
```

This isn't function composition in the mathematical sense, which applies the right function first and then the left function to the result. Instead, we are applying the functions in a left to right order.

Recall that all the functions are compiled into instances of the built-in `FunctionN` classes. We can take advantage of this knowledge to create extension functions on these classes. Let's rework a function composition to use `infix` syntax along with an appropriate operator to make composition even easier to use.

Since we know that infix functions can only be defined as member functions or extension functions, we need to change `compose` to be defined as an extension function on the appropriate `FunctionN` instance:

```
infix fun <P1, R, R2> Function1<P1, R>.compose(fn: (R) -> R2):  (P1) ->
R2 = {
  fn(this(it))
}
```

This allows us to invoke code similar to the following:

```
val f = String::length
val g = Any::hashCode
val fog = f compose g
```

Now, let's update this to use an operator. At this stage, it is nothing more complicated than replacing the name with the operator-mapped name, and adding the `operator` keyword:

```
operator infix fun <P1, R, R2> Function1<P1, R>.times(fn: (R) ->  R2):
(P1) -> R2 = {
  fn(this(it))
}
```

This can be invoked as expected:

```
val f = String::length
val g = Any::hashCode
val fog = f * g
```

This is not much different from languages that have built-in support for this.

Inline functions

As we have seen from earlier sections, functions are instances of objects, and, of course, each instance requires an allocation in the heap. There are also method invocations required when invoking the function. Overall, using functions introduces an overhead.

Kotlin allows us to avoid this overhead by use of the `inline` keyword. This keyword indicates to the compiler that the function marked as inline, as well as function parameters, should be expanded and generated inline at the call site, hence the name.

What does this mean exactly? Let's consider a function that handles resources in a safe manner: that is, the resource will always be closed correctly, even if the code throws an exception:

```
fun <T : AutoCloseable, U> withResource(resource: T, fn: (T) -> U): U {
  try {
    return fn(resource)
  } finally {
    resource.close()
  }
}
```

As you can see, we are just wrapping the application of the function argument in a `try...finally` block. It's a very simple function, and acts simply to remove some boilerplate whenever we want to use a closeable resource. We can use it as follows:

```
fun characterCount(filename: String): Int {
  val input = Files.newInputStream(Paths.get(filename))
  return withResource(input) {
    input.buffered().reader().readText().length
  }
}
```

This function opens a file, reads in the text, and counts the number of characters. It uses `withResource` to ensure that the input stream is correctly closed if some exception was thrown.

When this code is compiled, we end up with the creation of the function argument as an instance. If code like this was being executed many times in a loop, those allocations would add up. Let's look at the bytecode generated by the compiler for the `characterCount` function:

```
0: aload_0
1: ldc           #37                 // String filename
3: invokestatic  #15                 // Method
kotlin/jvm/internal/Intrinsics.checkParameterIsNotNull:(Ljava/lang/Object;L
java/lang/String;)V
6: aload_0
7: iconst_0
8: anewarray     #39                 // class java/lang/String
11: invokestatic  #45                 // Method
java/nio/file/Paths.get:(Ljava/lang/String;[Ljava/lang/String;)Ljava/nio/fi
le/Path;
14: iconst_0
15: anewarray     #47                 // class java/nio/file/OpenOption
18: invokestatic  #53                 // Method
java/nio/file/Files.newInputStream:(Ljava/nio/file/Path;[Ljava/nio/file/Ope
nOption;)Ljava/io/InputStream;
21: astore_1
22: aload_1
23: checkcast     #25                 // class java/lang/AutoCloseable
26: new           #55                 // class
com/packt/chapter5/_5_x_inlineKt$first$1
29: dup
30: aload_1
31: invokespecial #59                 // Method
com/packt/chapter5/_5_x_inlineKt$first$1."<init>":(Ljava/io/InputStream;)V
34: checkcast     #19                 // class
kotlin/jvm/functions/Function1
```

```
37: invokestatic  #61                    // Method
withResource:(Ljava/lang/AutoCloseable;Lkotlin/jvm/functions/Function1;)Lja
va/lang/Object;
40: checkcast     #63                    // class java/lang/Number
43: invokevirtual #67                    // Method
java/lang/Number.intValue:()I
46: ireturn
```

For those unfamiliar with bytecode output, the key part we are interested in here is at 26. You can see that a new instance of the function literal is being created before being passed into the `withResource` function at 37. The class that contains the code of the function literal is called `com/packt/chapter5/_5_x_inlineKt$first$1`.

If we were to mark the `withResource` function as inline, then the Kotlin compiler would not generate this as an invocation on a new instance, but instead would generate the code at the call site.

Firstly, we annotate the function with the keyword:

```
    inline fun <T : AutoCloseable, U> withResource(resource: T, fn:  (T) ->
U): U {
      try {
        return fn(resource)
      } finally {
        resource.close()
      }
    }
```

The compiler would translate an invocation of `characterCount` into the following:

```
    fun characterCountExpanded(filename: String): Int {
      val input = Files.newInputStream(Paths.get(filename))
      try {
        return input.buffered().reader().readText().length
      } finally {
        input.close()
      }
    }
```

This is the original intent before we introduced the helper function. Now the output of the bytecode for `characterCount` has changed significantly:

```
0: aload_0
1: ldc            #48                    // String filename
3: invokestatic   #15                    // Method
kotlin/jvm/internal/Intrinsics.checkParameterIsNotNull:(Ljava/lang/Object;L
java/lang/String;)V
```

```
6: aload_0
7: iconst_0
8: anewarray     #50                  // class java/lang/String
11: invokestatic  #56                  // Method
java/nio/file/Paths.get:(Ljava/lang/String;[Ljava/lang/String;)Ljava/nio/fi
le/Path;
14: iconst_0
15: anewarray     #58                  // class java/nio/file/OpenOption
18: invokestatic  #64                  // Method
java/nio/file/Files.newInputStream:(Ljava/nio/file/Path;[Ljava/nio/file/Ope
nOption;)Ljava/io/InputStream;
21: astore_1
22: nop
23: nop
24: aload_1
25: checkcast     #31                  // class java/lang/AutoCloseable
28: checkcast     #66                  // class java/io/InputStream
31: astore_2
32: aload_1
33: invokevirtual #70                  // Method
java/io/InputStream.read:()I
36: istore        4
38: aload_1
39: checkcast     #31                  // class java/lang/AutoCloseable
42: invokeinterface #35,  1        // InterfaceMethod
java/lang/AutoCloseable.close:()V
47: iload         4
49: goto          66
52: astore        4
54: aload_1
55: checkcast     #31                  // class java/lang/AutoCloseable
58: invokeinterface #35,  1        // InterfaceMethod
java/lang/AutoCloseable.close:()V
63: aload         4
65: athrow
66: ireturn
```

The bytecode has expanded because the code that was previously generated inside the file called `com/packt/chapter5/_5_x_inlineKt$first$1` is now generated inline. In fact, the additional class does not exist at all, and you can see from the preceding bytecode that we are no longer allocating an instance of an object.

The use of this feature must be carefully weighed. The amount of code generated can increase, but if that means avoiding many allocations in a tight loop then the payoff may be worthwhile, especially on slower devices such as mobiles.

If the compiler believes that inlining will not result in much improvement, it will emit a warning. This warning can be disabled if required.

Noinline

Sometimes you may wish to only inline some functions. This is because a function marked as inline cannot be assigned to a variable inlined, we use the `noinline` annotation.

For example, let's change our `withResource` example to accept two functions. The first function will be applied as before, but the second will be applied after the resource has been closed:

```
inline fun <T : AutoCloseable, U, V> withResource(resource: T,  before:
(T) -> U, noinline after: (U) -> V): V {
  val u = try {
    before(resource)
  } finally {
    resource.close()
  }
  return after(u)
}
```

In the case of an exception, the second function will not be called.

Let's say, for whatever reason, that we didn't want the second function to be inlined. By adding the `noinline` annotation, the function will be wrapped in a `FunctionN` instance as normal. The first function, however, is not affected, and is still inlined.

Let's invoke this function using an updated character count that now returns the size in kilobytes:

```
fun characterCountInKilobytes(filename: String): Int {
  val input = Files.newInputStream(Paths.get(filename))
  return withResource( input, {
input.buffered().reader().readText().length }, { it * 1024 } )
}
fun characterCountInKilobytesExpanded(filename: String): Int {
  val input = Files.newInputStream(Paths.get(filename))
```

```
    val size = try {
      input.buffered().reader().readText().length
    } finally {
      input.close()
    }
    val fn: (Int) -> Int = { it * 1024 }
    return fn(size)
}
```

Since inlining can have major performance benefits, many of the standard library functions are defined with the inline annotation.

Currying and partial application

A common technique in functional programming is the concept of currying. Currying is the process of transforming a function that accepts multiple parameters into a series of functions, each of which accept a single function. Take the following definition of `foo`:

```
fun foo(a: String, b: Int) : Boolean
```

The curried form would look like the following:

```
fun foo(a: String): (Int) -> Boolean
```

Note that the curried `foo` returns a second function, which in turn, when invoked with an `Int`, would return the `Boolean` as before. Currying is a useful technique for allowing functions with multiple parameters to work with other functions that only accept single arguments.

Currying is related to the idea of partial application. *Partial application* is the process by which some, but not all, of the parameters of a function are specified in advance, returning a new function that accepts the missing parameters. The parameters that have been given are said to be fixed. In other words, partial application produces a specialized function from a more generic function.

Take the following function:

```
fun foo(a: Int, b: Boolean, c: Double): Long
```

In this instance, an example of partial application might be to apply the `Int` and `Double`, returning a new function of the form `(Boolean) -> Long`.

Partial application is useful for at least two reasons. Firstly, when some parameters are available in the current scope, but not every scope, we can partially apply those values, and then just pass a function of lower arity. This avoids the need to pass down all the parameters, as well as the function. Secondly, similar to currying, we can use partial application to reduce the arity of a function in order to match a lower arity input type of another function.

Currying in action

Let's show an example of the second case. Say we had a function that performed some logic, called `compute`. The `compute()` function accepts a logging function, which it can use to output progress:

```
fun compute(logger: (String) -> Unit): Unit
```

The logging function just accepts a string and does something with it. The `compute` function doesn't really care; it will just invoke it. Now let's assume we have a logging framework that provides the following logging function:

```
fun log(level: Level, appender: Appendable, msg: String): Unit
```

This might be invoked in a way similar to the following:

```
log(Level.Warn, System.out, "Starting execution")
```

Clearly, the log function signature isn't compatible with the function accepted by the `compute()` method. But if we could partially apply it to create a function of the form `(String) -> Unit`, then it would work.

We can do this manually by wrapping in a function literal:

```
fun compute {
  msg -> log(Level.Warn, Appender.Console, msg)
}
```

This works just fine. But wouldn't it be nice if we could do this automatically, especially if we were dealing with many parameters?

Unfortunately, Kotlin doesn't support partial application or currying out of the box. But the language is powerful, and provides enough features that we can create support ourselves.

Adding currying support

We'll show how easy it is to add support for currying by using the same logging example from earlier. The first step is to define extension functions on `FunctionN`, which will return the curried functions:

```
fun <P1, P2, R> Function2<P1, P2, R>.curried(): (P1) -> (P2) -> R  = {
  p1 -> {
    p2 -> this(p1, p2)
  }
}

fun <P1, P2, P3, R> Function3<P1, P2, P3, R>.curried(): (P1) ->  (P2)
-> (P3) -> R = {
  p1 -> {
    p2 -> {
      p3 -> this(p1, p2, p3)
    }
  }
}
```

Only support for `Function2` and `Function3` has been shown here. To add support for `Function4` and so on, it is a trivial case of copying and adding the other parameters. `Function1` doesn't need a curry function as it's already in its curried form.

You'll notice in the implementation that we simply return nested functions. Each time a function is applied, it returns another function with the arity reduced by one, and the parameter captured as a closure.

Now, given our earlier definition of a logging function:

```
fun logger(level: Level, appender: Appendable, msg: String)
```

We can curry this, and then partially apply it by invoking it for the first two values:

```
val logger = ::logger.curried()(Level.SEVERE)(System.out)
logger("my message")
```

Note that we need to first get a function reference using `::` before invoking the `curried()` function. Then we simply apply it twice. The verbose form would look like the following:

```
    val logger3: (Level) -> (Appendable) -> (String) -> Unit =
::logger.curried()
    val logger2: (Appendable) -> (String) -> Unit = logger3(Level.SEVERE)
    val logger1: (String) -> Unit = logger2(System.out)
    logger1("my message")
```

In the preceding example, the types have been explicitly added to make it clear to the reader the shape of the function at each step. As each parameter is applied, you can see that the arity of the returned function is reducing by one.

Memoization

Memoization is a technique for speeding up function calls by caching and reusing the output instead of recomputing for a given set of inputs. This technique offers a trade-off between memory and speed. The typical applications are for computationally expensive functions or for recursive functions, which branch out calling the recursive function many times with the same values, such as Fibonacci.

Let's use the latter to explore the effects of memoization. Fibonacci itself can be implemented recursively in the following manner:

```
fun fib(k: Int): Long = when (k) {
  0 -> 1
  1 -> 1
  else -> fib(k - 1) + fib(k - 2)
}
```

Note that when we invoke `fib(k)`, we need to invoke `fib(k-1)` and `fib(k-2)`. However, `fib(k-1)` will itself invoke `fib(k-2)` and `fib(k-3)`, and so on. The result is that we are making many duplicated calls with the same value. For example, for `fib(5)` we invoke `fib(1)` five separate times.

This diagram shows how the number of branches increases with each level of Fibonacci, yet most of the invocations are for the same input value.

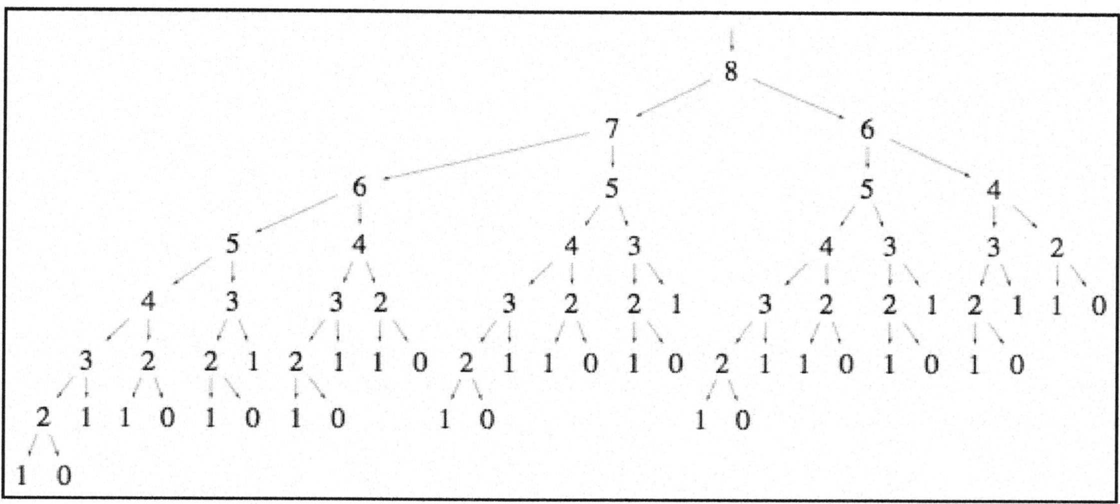

This explosion in recursive branches ends up slowing down the computation, as well as overflowing the stack for higher values. Here are some relative timings for invoking Fibonacci for various values:

fib(5)	**1 ms**
fib(10)	1 ms
fib(15)	1 ms
fib(20)	1 ms
fib(25)	2 ms
fib(30)	5 ms
fib(35)	54 ms
fib(40)	667 ms
fib(45)	6349 ms
fib(50)	69102 ms

As you can see, a basic Fibonacci is exponential in time complexity. Wouldn't it make sense if we could cache the results of fib for any particular value and reuse it each time it was called? It certainly would, and we can implement a simple cache ourselves using a map:

```
val map = mutableMapOf<Int, Long>()
fun memfib(k: Int): Long {
  return map.getOrPut(k) {
    when (k) {
      0 -> 1
      1 -> 1
      else -> memfib(k - 1) + memfib(k - 2)
    }
  }
}
```

Now, running the timings again gives us much improved results. In fact, the difference is so marked, `fib(k)` completes almost instantly for values of `k` up to many thousands (although we soon overflow even a `Long`).

Implementing memoization

The next question would be can we make this process automatic for any function? The answer is yes, we can, but only for functions that are not recursive. We can introduce a general purpose memoization function that uses the input values as keys in a cache to look up the stored result:

```
fun <A, R> memoize(fn: (A) -> R): (A) -> R {
   val map = ConcurrentHashMap<A, R>()
   return { a ->
     map.getOrPut(a) {
       fn(a)
     }
   }
}
```

To use this `memoize` function, we simply pass in the original function, and we receive back a wrapper function. This wrapper function will check the map for the result before computing it, if it hasn't yet been computed. We use a `ConcurrentHashMap` so that the memoized function is usable from multiple threads.

Say that we had an expensive operation, say, doing a long running query in a database, which we will call `query`. We can wrap this `query` function using the `memoize` function:

```
val memquery = memoize(::query)
```

To improve further, we can define memoize as an extension function on `Function1`, allowing us to invoke it using dot syntax:

```
fun <A, R> Function1<A, R>.memoized(): (A) -> R {
  val map = ConcurrentHashMap<A, R>()
  return {
    a -> map.getOrPut(a) {
      this.invoke(a)
    }
  }
}

val memquery = ::query.memoized()
```

We could add similar `memoized` functions on the other `FunctionN` classes if we wished.

Type alias

Kotlin 1.1 has introduced a new feature for referring to verbose types called type aliases. As the name suggests, a type alias allow us to declare a new type that is simply an alias of an existing type. We do this using the `typealias` keyword:

```
typealias Cache = HashMap<String, Boolean>
```

They are especially useful as a replacement for complex type signatures. Compare the following and see which you think is more readable:

```
fun process(exchange: Exchange<HttpRequest, HttpResponse>):
Exchange<HttpRequest, HttpResponse>
```

Or:

```
typealias HttpExchange = Exchange<HttpRequest, HttpResponse>
fun process2(exchange: HttpExchange): HttpExchange
```

A `typealias` carries no runtime overhead or benefit. The alias is simply replaced by the compiler. This means that new types are not created or allocated, so we suffer no performance penalty. It also means that two aliases that have the same right-hand side, can be used interchangeably. For example, these three definitions all reference a string:

```
typealias String1 = String
typealias String2 = String
fun printString(str: String1): Unit = println(str)

val a: String2 = "I am a String"
printString(a)
```

As you can see, we define the function to accept a `String1`, which is an alias of `String`. So we are able to pass in a `String2`, which is also a `String`.

This has the drawback that we cannot use type aliases to increase type safety on parameters of the same type. For example, consider a method called `volume`:

```
fun volume(width: Int, length: Int, height: Int): Int
```

If we change this to use type aliases for each of the dimensions, they can still be used interchangeably:

```
typealias Width = Int
typealias Length = Int
typealias Height = Int
fun volume(width: Width, length: Length, height: Height): Int
```

We are able to invoke this function in any of the following erroneous ways:

```
val width: Width = 2
val length: Length = 3
val height: Height = 4

volume(width, length, height)
volume(height, width, length)
volume(width, width, width)
```

At the time of writing, type aliases must be declared at the top level.

Either

In most functional programming languages, there is a type called **Either** (or a synonym). The `Either` type is used to represent a value that can have two possible types. It is common to see `Either` used to represent a success value or a failure value, although that doesn't have to be the case.

Although Kotlin doesn't come with an `Either` as part of the standard library, it's very easy to add one.

Let's start by defining a sealed abstract class with two implementations for each of the two possible types that `Either` will represent:

```
sealed class Either<out L, out R>

class Left<out L>(value: L) : Either<L, Nothing>()
class Right<out R>(value: R) : Either<Nothing, R>()
```

It is usual to call the two implementations `Left` and `Right`. By convention, when `Either` class is representing success or failure, the `Right` class is used for the success type.

Fold

The first function we'll add to `Either` is the `fold` operation. This will accept two functions. The first will be applied if the `Either` is an instance of the `Left` type, and the second will apply if the `Either` is the `Right` type. The return value from whichever function is applied will be returned:

```
sealed class Either<out L, out R> {
   fun <T> fold(lfn: (L) -> T, rfn: (R) -> T): T = when (this) {
     is Left -> lfn(this.value)
     is Right -> rfn(this.value)
   }
}
```

Let's see how it can be used. Firstly, let's create some basic classes that we will use for the rest of the examples in this section:

```
class User(val name: String, val admin: Boolean)
object ServiceAccount
class Address(val town: String, val postcode: String)
```

Then let's say we had a function that retrieved the current user, and another function that returns their addresses for a particular user:

```
fun getCurrentUser(): Either<ServiceAccount, User> = ...
fun getUserAddresses(user: User): List<Address> = ...
```

Note that the `getCurrentUser` function returns an `Either`, which contains two types of user. One is a regular user, and the other is a special `ServiceAccount`. We can then use that `Either` to get the addresses for the user:

```
    val addresses = getCurrentUser().fold({ emptyList<Address>() }, {
getUserAddresses(it) })
```

As you can see, we handle the lookup depending on the type we were given. In this case, the service account doesn't have any addresses, so we just return an empty list.

Projection

It is common to see functionality on an Either that allows us to map, filter, get the value, and so on. These functions are defined so that they apply to one of the types only, and are no-ops in the other case. The usual name for this is a left or right projection.

The user will decide whether they are interested in the left or right cases, and, by invoking a function, will receive a projection that contains the value they are interested in, or no value if the type they want is not the type the `Either` contains.

The way we will choose to implement this is to create two projection subclasses: A `ValueProjection`, and an `EmptyProjection`. The `ValueProjection` will implement the functions, and the `EmptyProjection` will implement no-ops. The `Either` class will then contain functions to get a projection for whichever side was requested.

Let's start by creating an abstract `Projection` class, which will define the functions we are interested in and be the supertype for both the implementing classes:

```
sealed class Projection<out T> {
  abstract fun <U> map(fn: (T) -> U): Projection<U>
  abstract fun getOrElse(or: () -> T): T
}
```

We're going to start with two functions for now: `map`, which will transform the value if the projection is one we are interested in, and `getOrElse`, which will return the value or apply a default function. The next step is to implement this for both the classes:

```
class ValueProjection<out T>(val value: T) : Projection<T>() {
  override fun <U> map(fn: (T) -> U): Projection<U> =
ValueProjection(fn(value))
  override fun getOrElse(or: () -> T): T = value
}

class EmptyProjection<out T> : Projection<T>() {
  override fun <U> map(fn: (T) -> U): Projection<U> =
EmptyProjection<U>()
  override fun getOrElse(or: () -> T): T = or()
}

fun <T> Projection<T>.getOrElse(or: () -> T): T = when (this) {
  is EmptyProjection -> or()
  is ValueProjection -> this.value
}
```

Note that the `EmptyProjection` just returns another instance of `EmptyProjection` without mapping anything. The `ValueProjection` actually performs the mapping.

`getOrElse` is implemented as an extension function on `Projection` itself because the function signature requires that `T` is an output in the `or` function. This breaks co-variance unless we use an extension function. Variance is covered in a later chapter.

The final step is to update our `Either` class to return these projections when asked for:

```
sealed class Either<out L, out R> {

  fun <T> fold(lfn: (L) -> T, rfn: (R) -> T): T = when (this) {
    is Left -> lfn(this.value)
    is Right -> rfn(this.value)
  }

  fun leftProjection(): Projection<L> = when (this) {
    is Left -> ValueProjection(this.value)
    is Right -> EmptyProjection<L>()
  }

  fun rightProjection(): Projection<R> = when (this) {
    is Left -> EmptyProjection<R>()
    is Right -> ValueProjection(this.value)
  }
```

```
}
```

Now, we can use this as follows:

```
val postcodes = getCurrentUser().rightProjection()
.map { getUserAddresses(it) }
.map { addresses.map { it.postcode } }
.getOrElse { emptyList() }
```

This is a similar method to the earlier example, but note how we can continue to map over the results, and then apply a default at the end. If the `Either` returned was not a `Right` value, then the maps would have no effect.

Further projection functions

We'll continue by adding more projection functions, namely, `exists`, `filter`, `toList`, and `orNull`.

The `exists` will accept a function, and if the projection has a value, it will apply the function and return the `Boolean` result. If the projection is empty then it will return `false`:

```
abstract fun exists(fn: (T) -> Boolean): Boolean
```

As the name suggests, `filter` will perform a filter operation on the projection. A value projection will apply the function and an empty projection will be returned if the filter function returns `false`:

```
abstract fun filter(fn: (T) -> Boolean): Projection<T>
```

The `toList` function will return a list of the values, or an empty list if the projection is empty:

```
abstract fun toList(): List<T>
```

Finally, `orNull` will return the value or null if the projection is empty:

```
abstract fun orNull(): T?
```

We'll round off our `Either` type with some more functions that allow us to inspect the type. So our final design for a basic `Either` type looks like the following:

```
sealed class Either<out L, out R> {
  fun <T> fold(lfn: (L) -> T, rfn: (R) -> T): T = when (this) {
    is Left -> lfn(this.value)
    is Right -> rfn(this.value)
```

```
    }

    fun leftProjection(): Projection<L> = when (this) {
     is Left -> ValueProjection(this.value)
     is Right -> EmptyProjection<L>()
    }

    fun isLeft() = when (this) {
      is Left -> true
      is Right -> false
    }

    fun rightProjection(): Projection<R> = when (this) {
     is Left -> EmptyProjection<R>()
     is Right -> ValueProjection(this.value)
    }

    fun isRight() = when (this) {
      is Left -> false
      is Right -> true
    }

}
```

With the following two subtypes implementing either case:

```
class Left<out L>(val value: L) : Either<L, Nothing>()
class Right<out R>(val value: R) : Either<Nothing, R>()
```

And the required extension functions:

```
fun <T> Projection<T>.getOrElse(or: () -> T): T = when (this) {
  is EmptyProjection -> or()
  is ValueProjection -> this.value
}

sealed class Projection<out T> {
  abstract fun <U> map(fn: (T) -> U): Projection<U>
  abstract fun exists(fn: (T) -> Boolean): Boolean
  abstract fun filter(fn: (T) -> Boolean): Projection<T>
  abstract fun toList(): List<T>
  abstract fun orNull(): T?
}

class EmptyProjection<out T> : Projection<T>() {
  override fun <U> map(fn: (T) -> U): Projection<U> =
EmptyProjection<U>()
```

```
        override fun exists(fn: (T) -> Boolean): Boolean = false
        override fun filter(fn: (T) -> Boolean): Projection<T> = this
        override fun toList(): List<T> = emptyList()
        override fun orNull(): T? = null
    }

    class ValueProjection<out T>(val value: T) : Projection<T>() {
        override fun <U> map(fn: (T) -> U): Projection<U> =
ValueProjection(fn(value))
        override fun exists(fn: (T) -> Boolean): Boolean = fn(value)
        override fun filter(fn: (T) -> Boolean): Projection<T> = when
(fn(value)) {
        true -> this
        false -> EmptyProjection()
    }

    override fun toList(): List<T> = listOf(value)
    override fun orNull(): T? = value
    }
```

Now we can execute code like the following:

```
    val service: ServiceAccount? =
getCurrentUser().leftProjection().orNull()
    val usersWithMultipleAddresses = getCurrentUser().rightProjection()
    .filter { getUserAddresses(it).size > 1 }
    val isAdmin = getCurrentUser().rightProjection().exists { it.admin }
```

Custom DSLs

A domain-specific language, or DSL, is a language that is specialized for one particular area. For example, online issue trackers, such as Jira, often come with a “little language” for querying, designed to make it easier to perform advanced searches. In programming, we most often see DSLs in the form of an API that has been tailored to make usage of the API easier.

Since Kotlin provides many features around the use of functions-named parameters, default parameters, operator overloading, and infix functions, to name a few-it makes Kotlin a powerful tool for creating your own custom DSL.

In this section, we will create a custom DSL used for assertions. This kind of functionality is often used in testing or behavior-driven development. In fact, we will devote a whole chapter to testing later in this book using the advanced `KotlinTest` library.

Infix functions as keywords

A simple assertion would be that a value is equal to another value. We could do this by having some kind of equal function:

```
fun equals(first: Any, second: Any): Unit {
  if (first != second)
    throw RuntimeException("$first was not equal to $second")
}
```

We could then use this function as follows:

```
equals("foobar", "foobaz")
```

This is fine, but not very domain-specific. The next step might be to make this an `infix` function:

```
infix fun Any.equals(other: Any): Unit {
  if (first != second)
    throw RuntimeException("$first was not equal to $second")
}
```

Note that this now becomes an extension function to allow the `infix` operator. We can use it as follows:

```
"foobar" equals "foobaz"
```

This is a little better. Perhaps we can rename the function to make it clearer to the reader what it is supposed to do:

```
fun Any.shouldEqual(other: Any): Unit {
  if (this != other)
    throw RuntimeException("$this was not equal to $other")
}
```

So now our assertion would read like this:

```
"foobar" shouldEqual "foobaz"
```

We can now build other assertions for cases that aren't straight equality. For example, we may wish to assert that a collection contains a particular element:

```
listOfNames.contains("george") shouldEqual true
```

But wouldn't it be nicer if we could have the assertion take care of the boilerplate so we could write something a little more readable? Ideally, we would be able to write the following:

```
listOfNames shouldContain "george"
```

We can do this by creating another keyword in the form of an extension function:

```
infix fun <E> Collection<E>.shouldContain(element: E): Unit {
  if (!this.contains(element))
    throw RuntimeException("Collection did not contain $element")
}
```

Note that this will work for any collection type. It also has the added benefit that the compiler will check that the element type is the same as the collection type, so we wouldn't be able to compile code like the following:

```
listOfNames shouldContain 10.0
```

Let's take this further by adding functionality to allow us to combine assertions. The initial aim is to be able to write code similar to the following:

```
listOfNames shouldContain "george" or listOfNames should beEmpty()
```

We know we're going to need an `infix` function `or`, which combines two assertions. It will have to be an extension or member function so we can use the `infix` modifier. The natural first thought is to define `or` on `Unit`:

```
infix fun Unit.or(other: Unit): Unit
```

However, since our assertions throw an exception, the left-hand side could have already thrown an exception before `or` is invoked, meaning we can't catch it. In which case, we need to invoke the assertions after they have been combined. At the same time, can we avoid duplicating the repeated left-hand side?

Let's introduce some type, `Matcher`, which will capture the assertion and allow for disjunction (`or`) and conjunction (`and`):

```
interface Matcher<T> {
  fun test(lhs: T): Unit
}
```

The idea here is that somehow we're going to create matches using keywords, and those matchers are going to be invoked to run the tests.

Firstly, we will need an implementation of `Matcher` for both `contains` and `empty`:

```
fun <T> contain(rhs: T) = object : Matcher<Collection<T>> {
  override fun test(lhs: Collection<T>): Unit {
    if (!lhs.contains(rhs))
     throw RuntimeException("Collection did not contain $rhs")
  }
}

fun <T> beEmpty() = object : Matcher<Collection<T>> {
  override fun test(lhs: Collection<T>) {
    if (lhs.isNotEmpty())
      throw RuntimeException("Collection should be empty")
  }
}
```

Now we need some way of invoking these on a receiver. Let's introduce a function called `should` that will do this for us:

```
infix fun <T> T.should(matcher: Matcher<T>) {
  matcher.test(this)
}
```

As you can see, the `should` function is just an enabler for the matchers. So now our earlier example can be rewritten like this:

```
listOfNames should contain("george")
```

Now it's time to add the `or` function to combine matchers. As we mentioned earlier, this needs to be an extension function, so we'll add it to the `Matcher` interface:

```
interface Matcher<T> {

  fun test(lhs: T): Unit

  infix fun or(other: Matcher<T>): Matcher<T> = object : Matcher<T> {
    override fun test(lhs: T) {
      try {
        this@Matcher.test(lhs)
      } catch (e: RuntimeException) {
        other.test(lhs)
      }
    }
  }
}
```

Note that we only require one of the matchers to be successful for `or` to be semantically correct, so any exception thrown by the first matcher must be caught to give the second matcher a chance to run. Conversely, if the first matcher is successful, there's no need to invoke the second at all.

Putting all this together allows us to create a syntax that fulfils our original goal:

```
listOfNames should (contain("george") or beEmpty())
```

Let's take advantage of Kotlin's function receivers to allow us to write a function that we can use to make many assertions at once:

```
listOfNames should {
  contain("george")
  beEmpty()
}
```

Using function receivers in a DSL

Function receivers can be used in a powerful way when writing DSLs. They allow us to introduce methods that can be used in function literals, but their use is restricted to the appropriate “section”.

For example, let's introduce some matchers that only work on collections, and allow several of them to be applied at the same time. The idea is to allow syntax like the following:

```
listOfNames should {
  contain("george")
  contain("harry")
  notContain("francois")
  haveSizeLessThan(4)
}
```

The assertions `contain`, `notContain`, and `haveSizeLessThan` are going to be defined on a class, which will be the receiver of the function literal block. This will allow those functions to be invoked without needing a prefix:

```
class CollectionMatchers<T>(val collection: Collection<T>) {

  fun contain(rhs: T): Unit {
    if (!collection.contains(rhs))
      throw RuntimeException("Collection did not contain $rhs")
  }

  fun notContain(rhs: T): Unit {
```

```
        if (collection.contains(rhs))
          throw RuntimeException("Collection should not contain $rhs")
      }

      fun haveSizeLessThan(size: Int): Unit {
        if (collection.size >= size)
          throw RuntimeException("Collection should have size less  than
$size")
      }
    }
```

Now that we have defined our assertions in the class called `CollectionMatchers`, we need to have a function that will use this as the receiver for a block of code. Let's make another `should` function to do this:

```
    infix fun <T> Collection<T>.should(fn: CollectionMatchers<T>.() ->
Unit) {
      val matchers = CollectionMatchers(this)
      matchers.fn()
    }
```

As you can see, it is marked infix again. The key part, though, is that the function has the receiver set. Inside the function body, we create an instance of `CollectionMatchers` and then invoke the supplied function on it. The end result is that the desired syntax is now supported. Because the `contains`, `notContains` and `haveSizeLessThan` functions are member functions of the `CollectionMatchers` class, we cannot invoke those functions in the wrong place.

Validation and error accumulation

To round up our introduction to functional programming, we'll cover another common pattern, that of error accumulation. This is also sometimes simply referred to as validation.

The idea is that we have a series of functions that individually error check a value. They can return some kind of success value if the input is good, and some kind of error value if the input is bad. These individual functions are then combined, retaining all the errors (if any). Finally, we can interrogate the accumulation to get the errors.

Let's start by modeling the good and bad values that we can use. We'll call these `Valid` and `Invalid`, respectively. They will both extend from a superclass called `Validation`:

```
sealed class Validation
object Valid : Validation()
class Invalid(val errors: List<String>) : Validation()
```

Note that the `Invalid` case contains a list of errors in the form of strings, and each successive error will be added to this. This is called **error accumulation**. The `Valid` implementation is just an object as it carries no state.

Our example will be checking that a `Student` instance is valid. Here is the `Student` class:

```
class Student(val name: String, val studentNumber: String, val  email:
String)
```

We're going to need some functions that check if the `name`, `studentNumber`, and `email` parameters are valid:

```
fun isValidName(name: String): Validation {
  return if (name.trim().length > 2)
    Valid
  else
    Invalid("Name $name is too short")
}

fun isValidStudentNumber(studentNumber: String): Validation {
  return if (studentNumber.all { Character.isDigit(it) })
    Valid)
  else
    Invalid("Student number must be only digits: $studentNumber")
}

fun isValidEmailAddress(email: String): Validation {
  return if (email.contains("@"))
    Valid
  else
    Invalid("Email must contain an '@' symbol")
}
```

Each of these functions is straightforward. The key point is that they are returning an instance of `Validation`: either `Valid` or `Invalid`, depending on the result of the error check. Of course, the `email` check is extremely basic, but this example is about error accumulation, not writing a production-ready `email` check.

We'll add a helper method to invalid's companion object so we can create an instance from a single string value, just to avoid some boilerplate:

```
class Invalid(val errors: List<String>) : Validation<Nothing>() {
  companion object {
    operator fun invoke(error: String) = Invalid(listOf(error))
  }
}
```

Now we need some way of accumulating the values and errors together. It would be nice if we could do this via some operator to keep the code readable, so let's overload the use of `plus`:

```
sealed class Validation {
  abstract infix operator fun plus(other: Validation): Validation
}
```

Each of the subclasses of `Validation` will need to implement this:

```
class Invalid(val errors: List<String>) : Validation() {

  override fun plus(other: Validation): Validation = when (other)  {
    is Invalid -> Invalid(this.errors + other.errors)
    is Valid -> this
  }
}
object Valid : Validation() {
  override fun plus(other: Validation): Validation = when (other)  {
    is Invalid -> other
    is Valid -> this
  }
}
```

Now we are able to combine instances of `Validation` together:

```
    val validation = isValidName(student.name) +
isValidStudentNumber(student.studentNumber) +
isValidEmailAddress(student.email)
```

Finally, we want to be able to do something useful with the errors. Of course, we could just access them directly as a field, but let's add a helper function to allow us to get a value, or apply some default.

The function will have the following signature:

```
abstract fun <T> getOrElse(t: T, or: (List<String>) -> T): T
```

This will be implemented in each of the subclasses as the following:

```
    class Invalid(val errors: List<String>) : Validation() {
      override fun <T> getOrElse(t: T, or: (List<String>) -> T): T =
or(errors)
    }

    object Valid : Validation() {
      override fun <T> getOrElse(t: T, or: (List<String>) -> T): T = t
    }
```

Now our use of the results of the validation step can be something like the following:

```
    fun validateStudent(student: Student): Student {

    val validation = isValidName(student.name) +
isValidStudentNumber(student.studentNumber) +
isValidEmailAddress(student.email)
    return validation.getOrElse(student, {
      throw  RuntimeException("Error creating student. The errors are $it")
}
    )
    }
```

There are many variations of this method. A common variation is to accumulate values along with errors, and then to use those values in a transform function to return the constructed final object.

Summary

During this chapter we discussed more advanced use cases of functions, especially higher order functions that underpin the collections library in most modern languages – Kotlin being no exception. We saw how the many features Kotlin provides around functions can be leveraged to write custom DSLs. Finally, we introduced common idioms in the functional programming space – eithers and validation.

In the next chapter, we'll discuss the complement of functions – properties – which are used to retrieve and update values in objects.

6
Properties

We touched upon properties briefly in `Chapter 3`, *Object Oriented Programming in Kotlin*. In this chapter, we will take a detailed look at them. You will learn about

- General properties
- Visibility
- Lazy and late initialized
- Delegated properties
- When to use properties instead of methods

Furthermore, we will see how to use a Kotlin property from Java and we'll take a peek at the bytecode produced to understand what the compiler does. If you are familiar with C#, the information presented here will be familiar, after all the concept of properties was brought in from the .NET world.

Why use properties?

Properties are nothing more than syntactic sugar that allows your source code to call a method using a simplified syntax. Kotlin comes with support for simple properties and delegated properties (we will see later in the chapter what they are).

How many times have you written a class containing state information, a state that can be either retrieved or changed? Usually, state information comes in the form of fields. Here is a typical class defining two fields:

```
class Student {
  private val name:String;
  private val age:Int;
}
```

Writing such a class in Java is quite repetitive (luckily IntelliJ is quite powerful when it comes to code generation and refactoring). You normally provide two methods for each field: a getter and a setter. The code will look similar to this:

```
public class Student {
  private String name;
  private intage;
  public Student(String name, intage){
    this.name= name;
    this.age= age;
  }
  public String getName() {
    return name;
  }
  public void setName(String name) {
    this.name= name;
  }
  public int getAge() {
    return age;
  }
  public void setAge(intage) {
    this.age= age;
  }
}
```

Now let's see how we can write the preceding code in Kotlin:

```
class Student(name: String, age: Int) {
  public var Name = ""
  set(value) {
    field = value
  }

  public var Age = 20
  set(value) {
    field = value
  }

  init {
    Name = name
    Age = age
  }
}
```

Pretty neat, I would say! Note the `init` block has to be defined after the property definitions. This is a limitation, and hopefully it will be addressed at some point in the future. If you don't write the `init` block after the properties definitions, you will get a compilation error. Here is how you could use the preceding class:

```
val student = Student("Jamie Fox", 20)
print("${student.Name} is ${student.Age} years old")
student.Age+=1
print("${student.Name} is ${student.Age} years old")
```

This looks easy, but let's see what actually happens under the hood. We turn again to the `javap` utility to get the bytecode produced. Running the command line, will get you something similar to the following:

```
public final class com.programming.kotlin.chapter06.Student {
  public final java.lang.String getName();
  Code:
    0: aload_0
    1: getfield #11 // Field Name:Ljava/lang/String;
    4: areturn

  public final void setName(java.lang.String);
  Code:
    ...
    6: aload_0
    7: aload_1
    8: putfield #11 // Field Name:Ljava/lang/String;
    11: return

    ...
  public com.programming.kotlin.chapter06.Student(java.lang.String, int);
  Code:
    ...
    24: invokevirtual #42 // Method setName:(Ljava/lang/String;)V
    27: aload_0
    28: iload_2
    29: invokevirtual #44 // Method setAge:(I)V
    32: return
}
```

For simplicity, I have left out part of the code. The code snippet makes it quite clear what the compiler did. It generated the get and the set methods as well as the backing field for both `name` and `age`. Noticed the usage of the `field` keyword inside the set block? It is an alias for the backing field generated for us. If you use the Kotlin code from Java, you will end up with the typical pattern of calling `get***` and `set***`:

```
    Student student = new Student("Alex Wood", 20);
    System.out.println("Student " + student.getName() + " is " +
student.getAge() + " years old");
    student.setAge(student.getAge() + 1);
```

We can make full use of the compiler capabilities when it comes to simple properties. If we define the `Student` constructor parameters as `val`, we let the compiler do all the work for us since it will generate the getter but not a setter. Typically, in the case of Student, you will want to provide a custom setter because you want to enforce some validation. Setting the age lower than 1 should throw an exception for example. But for the purpose of this exercise, we left that out:

```
class Student(var name: String, var age: Int)
```

If you look at the bytecode generated, you will notice it is almost the same. The difference is in the constructor body, where, instead of calling `invokevirtual #**` (`set***`), it will just use `putfield` to set the backing field value.

Syntax and variations

The syntax for declaring a property is as follows:

```
var/val<propertyName>:<PropertyType>[=<property_initializer>]
  [<getter>]
  [<setter>]
```

Both the initializer and the setter parts are optional. Furthermore, the property type can also be left out since the compiler can infer it, thus saving you keystrokes. However, for code clarity, it is advisable to add the property type.

If you define a read-only property by using the `val` keyword, you only have the getter and no setter. Imagine you have to define a class hierarchy for a drawing application. You would want a property for the area. Following is a typical implementation for such property when it comes to a `Rectangle` class:

```
interface Shape {
  val Area: Double
```

```
    get;
  }

  class Rectangle(val width: Double, val height: Double) : Shape {
    override val Area: Double
    get() = width * height

    val isSquare: Boolean = width == height
  }
```

The rectangle class implements the `Shape` interface and therefore has to define the `Area` property. Apart from that, it adds a new property to check if the rectangle is actually a square. You might believe we get a backing field for the `Area` property, however, it turns out we don't. This is what the bytecode reveals:

```
public final class com.programming.kotlin.chapter06.Rectangle implements
com.programming.kotlin.chapter06.Shape {
  public double getArea();
    Code:
     0: aload_0
     1: getfield      #12                 // Field width:D
     4: aload_0
     5: getfield      #15                 // Field height:D
     8: dmul
     9: dreturn
public final booleanisSquare();
    Code:
     0: aload_0
     1: getfield      #12                 // Field width:D
     4: aload_0
     5: getfield      #15                 // Field height:D
     16: iconst_0
     17: ireturn
public final double getWidth();
  Code:
    0: aload_0
    1: getfield      #12                 // Field width:D
    4: dreturn
public final double getHeight();
  Code:
    0: aload_0
    1: getfield      #15                 // Field height:D
    4: dreturn
publiccom.programming.kotlin.chapter06.Rectangle(double, double);
  Code:
    6: putfield      #12                 // Field width:D
    11: putfield      #15                 // Field height:D
    14: return
```

```
}
```

Sometimes, your property getter code is not as simple as returning the backing field. In such a case, you will need to provide the backing field yourself. You should follow best practices and avoid having complex logic in your getter. Imagine we have a class that provides a set of keywords. We want to lazily initialize the field only on its first usage. When we talk about delegated properties, we will see a different approach when we write idiomatic Kotlin code. Here is how you will implement the `keywords` cache for now:

```
class Lookup {
  private var _keywords: HashSet<String>? = null

  val keywords: Iterable<String>
  get() {
    if (_keywords == null) {
      _keywords = HashSet<String>()
    }
    return _keywords ?: throw RuntimeException("Invalid keywords")
  }
}
```

Visibility

The visibility access rules we have discussed for fields apply to properties as well. Therefore, you can have private, protected, or public (default) properties. Furthermore, the setter can have different, more restrictive visibility than the getter (the getter code is generated for you automatically in the following case):

```
class WithPrivateSetter(property: Int) {
  var SomeProperty: Int = 0
    private set(value) {
      field = value
    }

  init {
    SomeProperty = property
  }
}

val withPrivateSetter = WithPrivateSetter(10)
println("withPrivateSetter:${withPrivateSetter.SomeProperty}")
```

There are scenarios when properties are subject to class inheritance. If this happens, typically protected visibility, at least for the setter, is more appropriate:

```
open class WithInheritance {
  open var isAvailable: Boolean = false
    get() = field
    protected set(value) {
      field = value
    }
}

class WithInheritanceDerived(isAvailable: Boolean) :  WithInheritance()
{
  override var isAvailable: Boolean = isAvailable
    get() {
      //do something before returning the value
      return super.isAvailable
    }
    set(value) {
      //do something else before setting the value
      println("WithInhertianceDerived.isAvailable")
      field = value
    }

  fun doSomething() {
    isAvailable = false
  }
}

val withInheritance = WithInheritanceDerived(true)
withInheritance.doSomething()
println("withInheritance:${withInheritance.isAvailable}")
```

To adhere to the encapsulation rule, you the property `isAvailable` has been marked as open for overrides, but the setter has been made private.

Late initialization

Any non-null property has to be initialized in the constructor. What if you want to inject the property value via a dependency injection and you don't want to check for null every time you access it? Or, maybe you simply set the property value in one of the methods exposed by your type. Kotlin comes with support for delayed initialization. All you have to do is use the `lateinit` keyword:

```
class Container {
```

```
    lateinit var delayedInitProperty: DelayedInstance

    fun initProperty(instance: DelayedInstance): Unit {
      this.delayedInitProperty = instance
    }
  }

  class DelayedInstance (val number:Int)
  ...
  val container=  Container()
  container.initProperty(DelayedInstance(10))
  println("with delayed
initialization:Number=${container.delayedInitProperty.number}")
```

There are a few restrictions when using delayed properties. Firstly, the property type cannot be a primitive type. Secondly, your property cannot make use of custom getter or setter code. And last but not least, accessing your property before it has been initialized will end up in `kotlin.UninitializedPropertyAccessException`.

There is no magic happening under the hood when you use `lateinit`. Let's take a peek at the bytecode generated for the `Container` class:

```
public final class com.programming.kotlin.chapter06.Container {
  public com.programming.kotlin.chapter06.DelayedInstance
delayedInitProperty;
  public final com.programming.kotlin.chapter06.DelayedInstance
getDelayedInitProperty();
    Code:
      0: aload_0
      1: getfield      #11               // Field
delayedInitProperty:Lcom/programming/kotlin/chapter06/DelayedInstance ;
      4: dup
      5: ifnonnull     13
      8: ldc           #12                    // String  delayedInitProperty
      10: invokestatic  #18                   // Method
kotlin/jvm/internal/Intrinsics.throwUninitializedPropertyAccessExcept
ion:(Ljava/lang/String;)V
      13: areturn
```

Most of the code has been left out for simplicity. While the setter code is similar to the one generated for the `Student` class discussed earlier, the getter's instruction set is slightly different. The change is contained in line 10 where it will throw the exception if the field is set to null.

Delegated properties

Kotlin enhances the concept of properties to promote code reuse and make the developer coding task easier. There are many repetitive code snippets you and I could write. Ideally, we should have the following functionality out-of-the-box:

1. A property value should be computed lazily on its first ever access.
2. Notify the listeners of a change to one of the values of properties. Have you ever coded in C#? If yes, I am sure the `INotifyPropertyChange` interface will come to mind.
3. Use a map to store your fields rather than a materialized field.

Well, good news! Kotlin's delegate properties support all of these. We deal quite often with types for which we need an identifier:

```
interface WithId {
  val id: String
}

data class WithIdImpl(override val id: String) : WithId

class Record(id: String) : WithId by Record.identifier(id) {
  companion object Record {
    fun identifier(identifier: String) = WithIdImpl(identifier)
  }
}
...
val record = Record("111")
println(record.id)
```

We have seen in the chapter on object-oriented programming you can delegate methods. The same concept is applicable to properties as well. The syntax is similar: `val/var<property name>:<Type> by <expression>`. The expression that follows the `by` keyword is the actual delegate. In the preceding example, we provided a read-only property. The caller doesn't even know about `WithIdImpl`.

The delegates don't need to implement an interface. We could avoid inheritance and rely exclusively on composition. Imagine you are collecting data from a sensor device. Each measure produced will carry a `timestamp` of when the event was created. You will want to have a property that provides support for the `timestamp` while enforcing some validation. For simplicity, the validation part has been left out:

```
class TimestampValueDelegate {
```

```
    private var timestamp = 0L
    operator fun getValue(ref: Any?, property: KProperty<*>): Long {
      return timestamp;
    }

    operator fun setValue(ref: Any?, property: KProperty<*>, value: Long)
{
      timestamp = value
    }
  }

  class Measure {
    var writeTimestamp: Long by TimestampValueDelegate()
  }

  val measure = Measure()
  measure.writeTimestamp = System.currentTimeMillis()
  println("Current measure taken at:${measure.writeTimestamp}")
```

You might find the preceding code a bit unusual at the beginning. Probably, you are wondering what are those first two parameters for each method in `TimestampValueDelegate` methods. The `ref` parameter represents the instance on which you are accessing the property; in our case, it is an instance of `Measure`, variable `measure`. The second function parameter represents a property, such as a named `val` or `var` declaration. You can obtain the property information by using the `::` operator; in the preceding example, all you have to do is use `Measure::writeTimestamp`. If you are offering support to a read and write property, then you need to provide both get and set methods, just like we have done for `TimestampValueDelegate`. If your property is a read-only one, a `val`, then you only have to provide the `getValue` method. Both of these functions need to be prefixed by the `operator` keyword.

What is the magic that glues all of this together? A look at the generated bytecode will unveil the mechanism used. Let's use `javap` once again to get our hands on the code generated by the compiler:

```
public final class com.programming.kotlin.chapter06.Measure {
  public final long getWriteTimestamp();
    Code:
     0: aload_0
     1: getfield      #11                 // Field
writeTimestamp$delegate:Lcom/programming/kotlin/chapter06/TimestampValueDel
egate;
     4: aload_0
     5: getstatic     #15                 // Field
$$delegatedProperties:[Lkotlin/reflect/KProperty;
     8: iconst_0
```

```
     9: aaload
     10: invokevirtual #21                  // Method
com/programming/kotlin/chapter06/TimestampValueDelegate.getValue:(Lja
va/lang/Object;Lkotlin/reflect/KProperty;)J
     13: lreturn
public final void setWriteTimestamp(long);
   Code:
     0: aload_0
     1: getfield      #11                  // Field
writeTimestamp$delegate:Lcom/programming/kotlin/chapter06/TimestampValueDel
egate;
     4: aload_0
     5: getstatic     #15                  // Field
$$delegatedProperties:[Lkotlin/reflect/KProperty;
     8: iconst_0
     9: aaload
     10: lload_1
     11: invokevirtual #29                 // Method
com/programming/kotlin/chapter06/TimestampValueDelegate.setValue:(Lja
va/lang/Object;Lkotlin/reflect/KProperty;J)V
     14: return
public com.programming.kotlin.chapter06.Measure();
   Code:
    0: aload_0
    1: invokespecial #35                  // Method
java/lang/Object."<init>":()V
    4: aload_0
    5: new           #17                  // class
com/programming/kotlin/chapter06/TimestampValueDelegate
    8: dup
    9: invokespecial #36                  // Method
com/programming/kotlin/chapter06/TimestampValueDelegate."<init>":()V
    12: putfield      #11                 // Field
writeTimestamp$delegate:Lcom/programming/kotlin/chapter06/TimestampValueDel
egate;
    15: return
static {};
  Code:
    0: iconst_1
    1: anewarray     #51                  // class  kotlin/reflect/KProperty
    4: dup
    5: iconst_0
    6: new           #53                  // class
kotlin/jvm/internal/MutablePropertyReference1Impl
    9: dup
    10: ldc           #2                  // class
com/programming/kotlin/chapter06/Measure
    12: invokestatic  #59                 // Method
```

```
kotlin/jvm/internal/Reflection.getOrCreateKotlinClass:(Ljava/lang/Class;)Lk
otlin/reflect/KClass;
     15: ldc           #60                  // String writeTimestamp
     17: ldc           #62                  // String getWriteTimestamp()J
     19: invokespecial #65                  // Method
kotlin/jvm/internal/MutablePropertyReference1Impl."<init>":(Lkotlin/
reflect/KDeclarationContainer;Ljava/lang/String;Ljava/lang/String;)V
     22: invokestatic  #69                  // Method
kotlin/jvm/internal/Reflection.mutableProperty1:(Lkotlin/jvm/internal
/MutablePropertyReference1;)Lkotlin/reflect/KMutableProperty1;
     25: checkcast     #51                  // class
kotlin/reflect/KProperty
     28: aastore
     29: putstatic     #15                  // Field
$$delegatedProperties:[Lkotlin/reflect/KProperty;
      32: return
}
```

This is quite a bit of bytecode, but it is worth going over. We start with the last part of the code snippet . You notice the compiler has created a static constructor for us, which is responsible for initializing a static field named `$$delegatedProperties`: an array of `KProperty` (see the entry `static {}`). Line 1 is where this array is created and at line 29 it is stored into the static field `$$delegatedProperties`. Starting at line 6, it creates a `MutablePropertyReference1Impl` instance; it is a mutable implementation since we defined our field using `var`) and stores it as the first element of the array field (see line 5).

Moving on to the constructor-generated code, we can see there is a field of type `TimestampValueDelegate` created automatically (see line 12). Keep in mind we delegate the property to the `TimestampValueDelegate` class, hence the presence of this field.

Both the `getTimestamp` and `setTimestamp` methods are quite similar, therefore we will only discuss `getTimestamp`. At line 10, it's invoking the `getValue` method exposed by `TimestampValueDelegate`, passing the Measure object reference and the `KProperty` value obtained from the static field `$$delegatedProperties` (see line 5).

As you can see, there is no real magic used when using delegated properties; the compiler generates the boiler code for us.

There are cases when your type exposes a lot of fields and they might not always be initialized and used. Hence, you might be better off not having a backing field for each type to reduce the memory footprint. You would want to store the values of each property in a map, thus taking a small performance hit with a lookup. The next code example shows how you could write something like this:

```
class MapDelegate {
```

```
    private val map = mutableMapOf<String, Any?>()
    operator fun <T> getValue(ref: Any?, property: KProperty<*>): T  {
      return map[property.name] as T
    }
    operator fun <T> setValue(ref: Any?, property: KProperty<*>,  value: T?) {
      map.put(property.name, value)
    }
}

data class SomeData(val char: Char)

class PropsByMap() {
  private val mapDelegate = MapDelegate()
  var p1: Int by mapDelegate

  val p2: SomeData by mapDelegate

  init {
    mapDelegate.setValue(this, PropsByMap::p2, SomeData('K'))
    mapDelegate.setValue(this, PropsByMap::p1, 0)
  }
}

...

val propsByMap = PropsByMap()
println("Props with map: p1=${propsByMap.p1}")
println("Props with map: p2=${propsByMap.p2}")
propsByMap.p1 = 100
println("Props with map: p1=${propsByMap.p1}")
```

If you run the code, you should see `0`, `SomeData(char=K)`, and `100`.

Fortunately, we don't have to write code as in the preceding example since support for map-backed properties comes built in with Kotlin. If we have a class with read-only properties, we could write the following:

```
class Player(val map: Map<String, Any?>) {
  val name: String by map
  val age: Int     by map
  val height: Double by map
}

val player = Player(mapOf("name" to "Alex Jones", "age" to 28, "height" to 1.82))
println("Player ${player.name} is ${player.age} ages old and is ${player.height} cm tall")
```

If the class design requires a read and write property, we would need to make use of a mutable map class as opposed to the previous example where we used an immutable map.

```
class Player(val map: MutableMap<String, Any?>) {
  var name: String by map
  var age: Int by map
  var height: Double by map
}
```

The Kotlin library comes with an interface to help you with the methods signature required for delegated properties. If you deal with a read-only property, all you have to do is derive from the `ReadOnlyProperty` interface. There is a similar interface to support delegates for read and write properties; it is called the `ReadWriteProperty` interface. It is not required for you to make use of this interface; its presence in the framework will help you get the method signature right, rather than anything else:

```
    data class TrivialProperty(private val const: Int) :
ReadOnlyProperty<Trivial, Int> {
      override fun getValue(thisRef: Trivial, property: KProperty<*>):  Int
{
        return const;
      }
    }

    class Trivial {
      val flag: Int by TrivialProperty(999)
    }
    ...
    val trivial = Trivial()
    println("Trivial flag is :${trivial.flag}")
```

While this code doesn't do much other than return a value, and you should never use it like this, it does show the interface being used.

Lazy initializations

There are cases when you want to delay the creation of an instance of your object until its first usage. This technique is known as lazy initialization or lazy instantiation. The main purpose of lazy initialization is to boost performance and reduce your memory footprint. If instantiating an instance of your type carries a large computational cost and the program might end up not actually using it, you would want to delay or even avoid wasting CPU cycles. Imagine you are working on software for a health insurer.

For a customer, you will have a list of claims made. To get this list, you will need to go to the database and load the information. This is quite an expensive process and, if the user does not actually care about the information, it would be a waste of CPU cycles and memory. It is only when the user decides to list the claims that you will go and initialize the claims collection.

Of course, you can write your own code to handle initialization, but this work has been done for you by the makers of Kotlin. Initially, a lazy implementation could look trivial; after all, you just have to check whether the value has been set already. Right? But then, when you bring concurrency into the equation, the code for initializing your property is run simultaneously by different threads; you can see that the complexity is slightly different. I am sure the first implementation that comes to everyone's mind is to use a synchronization block to achieve this. While it is easy and fast to code, it will hurt your throughput. There are other ways to improve the code and avoid locking.

Concurrency is not for everyone; therefore, I recommend that you use the implementation provided rather than implement your own. Kotlin offers various implementations to suit all your needs.

To make use of the lazy initialized delegated property all you have to do is write `by lazy` and provide the logic for creating your instance. The rest is taken care of:

```
class WithLazyProperty {
  val foo: Int by lazy {
    println("Initializing foo")
    2
  }
}
...

val withLazyProperty= WithLazyProperty()
val total= withLazyProperty.foo + withLazyProperty.foo
println("Lazy property total:$total")
```

If you run the preceding code, you should see the number 4 being printed out on the console, but the text `Initializing foo` appears only once, even though you call the property twice.

The `lazy` function takes a lambda, the code responsible for creating the instance, and returns you an instance of `Lazy<T>`. The definition of the `Lazy` interface looks like this:

```
public interface Lazy<out T> {
  public val value: T
  public fun isInitialized(): Boolean
}
```

The framework provides you with three different `lazy` function definitions. They should cover any possible use cases. In the previous code example, we ended up using the following:

```
    fun <T> lazy(initializer: () -> T): Lazy<T> =
SynchronizedLazyImpl(initializer)
```

From the return class name, you can infer what it does. Without looking at the implementation, we know the initialization block will be run within a synchronized code block:

```
    private object UNINITIALIZED_VALUE

    private class SynchronizedLazyImpl<out T>(initializer: () -> T,  lock:
Any? = null) : Lazy<T>, Serializable {
      private var initializer: (() -> T)? = initializer
      @Volatile private var _value: Any? = UNINITIALIZED_VALUE
      private val lock = lock ?: this

      override val value: T
        get() {
            val _v1 = _value
            if (_v1 !== UNINITIALIZED_VALUE) {
                @Suppress("UNCHECKED_CAST")
                return _v1 as T
            }

            return synchronized(lock) {
                val _v2 = _value
                if (_v2 !== UNINITIALIZED_VALUE) {
                    @Suppress("UNCHECKED_CAST") (_v2 as T)
                }
                else {
                    val typedValue = initializer!!()
                    _value = typedValue
                    initializer = null
                    typedValue
                }
            }
        }
```

The class holds onto your lambda and uses a `lock` field to get synchronization support while initializing the `value` field. To improve the speed of your getter, the implementation sets an initial default value to the `value` field. This way, it can short-circuit the return without having to obtain the `lock`, thereby improving performance. You can supply your own instance for the lock if you want some more control. We can take the previous example and use the second overload of lazy:

```
    fun <T> lazy(lock: Any?, initializer: () -> T): Lazy<T> =
SynchronizedLazyImpl(initializer, lock)
    class WithLazyPropertyWithLocking{
      val lockingField = Any()

      val foo: Int by lazy(lockingField, {
        println("Initializing foo");
        2
      })
    }
```

The third and last overload of the `lazy` function gives you more control over what type of lazy implementation is created. Thus, this overloaded version is a factory method:

```
        fun <T> lazy(mode: LazyThreadSafetyMode, initializer: () -> T):
Lazy<T>
```

`LazyThreadSafteyMode` can take one of the following values (the description comes from the source code):

1. **SYNCHRONIZED**: This means locks are used to ensure that only a single thread can initialize the `[Lazy]` instance.
2. **PUBLICATION**: This means the initializer function can be called several times on concurrent access to uninitialized `[Lazy]` instance value, but only first returned value will be used as the value of `[Lazy]` instance.
3. **NONE**: This means no locks are used to synchronize the access to the `[Lazy]` instance value; if the instance is accessed from multiple threads, its behavior is undefined. This mode should be used only when high performance is crucial and it is guaranteed that the `[Lazy]` instance will never be initialized from more than one thread.

If you use the `Synchronized` mode, you basically end up with the same implementation we saw earlier. If you choose `Publication`, then the following `Lazy<T>` implementation is created for you:

```
    private class SafePublicationLazyImpl<out T>(initializer: () -> T) :
Lazy<T>, Serializable {
```

```
        private var initializer: (() -> T)? = initializer
        @Volatile private var _value: Any? = UNINITIALIZED_VALUE
        // this final field is required to enable safe publication of
constructed instance
        private val final: Any = UNINITIALIZED_VALUE

        override val value: T
        get() {
          if (_value === UNINITIALIZED_VALUE) {
            val initializerValue = initializer
            // if we see null in initializer here, it means that the value is
already set by another thread
            if (initializerValue != null) {
              val newValue = initializerValue()
              if (valueUpdater.compareAndSet(this, UNINITIALIZED_VALUE,
newValue)) {
                initializer = null
              }
            }
          }
          @Suppress("UNCHECKED_CAST")
          return _value as T
        }
        ...
        companion object {
          private val valueUpdater =
java.util.concurrent.atomic.AtomicReferenceFieldUpdater.newUpdater(
 SafePublicationLazyImpl::class.java,
          Any::class.java,
          "_value")
        }
      }
```

To ensure only the first call of the initializer is used, the implementation has to make use of `valueUpdater` to set the new value automatically; under the hood, it uses the compare and swap hardware instruction.

Finally, if you choose `NONE` for the synchronization mode, you will end up with an instance of `UnsafeLazyImpl`. This will yield the best throughput, but it needs to be used appropriately:

```
      internal class UnsafeLazyImpl<out T>(initializer: () -> T) : Lazy<T>,
Serializable {
        private var initializer: (() -> T)? = initializer
        private var _value: Any? = UNINITIALIZED_VALUE

        override val value: T
```

```
get() {
  if (_value === UNINITIALIZED_VALUE) {
    _value = initializer!!()
    initializer = null
  }
  @Suppress("UNCHECKED_CAST")
  return _value as T
}
```

As per the documentation, you should make sure the initialization happens on one thread, or for as long as it produces an instance with the same state and that state is immutable. You can have more than one thread calling the initialization block. The last value written will be kept, but the previous one will be left for the garbage collector.

The Kotlin standard library provides a lazy implementation for scenarios when the value is already known. All you have to do is call `lazyOf(Your_Value)0`.

Normally, you won't use this. There is no point in wrapping a known value into a lazy container. However, you might have a class hierarchy defining a field or a method as `Lazy<T>`. In this case, you can use the preceding construct to return the instance of `Lazy<T>` with the value already initialized.

Lateinit versus lazy

At first, `lateinit` var and by `lazy {...}` sound quite similar. However, there are significant differences between the two of them:

1. The `lazy {...}` delegate can only be used for val properties; `lateinit` can only be used for `var` properties.
2. A `lateinit` var property can't be compiled into a final field, hence you can't achieve immutability.
3. A `lateinit` var property has a backing field to store the value, whereas `lazy {...}` creates a delegate object that acts as a container for the value once created and provides a getter for the property. If you need the backing field to be present in the class, you will have to use `lateinit`.
4. The `lateinit` property cannot be used for nullable properties or Java primitive types. This is a restriction imposed by the usage of null for uninitialized values.

5. The `lateinit` var property is more flexible when it comes to where it can be initialized. You can set it up anywhere the object is visible from. For `lazy{}`, it defines the only initializer for the property, which can be altered only by overriding. The instantiation is thus known in advance, unlike a `lateinit` var property, where if you use a dependency injection, for example, it can end up providing different instances of derived classes.

Observables

What if you want to know when the delegated property is changed? You might need to react to the change and call some other code. The `Delegates` object comes with the following construct to allow you to achieve exactly that:

```
fun <T> observable(initialValue: T, crossinline onChange: (property:
KProperty<*>, oldValue: T, newValue: T) -> Unit):
    ReadWriteProperty<Any?, T>
```

We will see this at work with the following simple example. Every time the `value` property is changed, the `onValueChanged()` method is called and we print out the new value:

```
class WithObservableProp {
   var value: Int by Delegates.observable(0) { p, oldNew, newVal ->
onValueChanged()
   }

   private fun onValueChanged() {
     println("value has changed:$value")
   }
}
val onChange = WithObservableProp()
onChange.value = 10
onChange.value = -20
```

There is another observable implementation offered out of the box, one that allows us to reject the new value if the context enforces it:

```
class OnlyPositiveValues {
   var value: Int by Delegates.vetoable(0) { p, oldNew, newVal -> newVal
>= 0 }
}
val positiveVal= OnlyPositiveValues ()
positiveVal.value = 100
println("positiveVal value is ${positiveVal.value}")
```

```
positiveVal.value = -100
println("positiveVal value is ${positiveVal.value}")

positiveVal.value = 111
println("positiveVal value is ${positiveVal.value}")
```

If you run the preceding code, you will see that the value 100 will never be accepted; thus, it will print the value `100` twice.

A non-null property delegate

The Kotlin framework is quite rich; it provides support for a delegated property for non-null values. All you have to do is use `Delegates.nonNull`, like in this simple example:

```
class NonNullProp {
  var value: String by Delegates.notNull<String>()
}

val nonNull = NonNullProp()
nonNull.value = "Kotlin rocks"
println("Non null value is: ${nonNull.value}")

//this will not compile
nonNull.value = null
```

Trying to access the property value before it has been initialized would lead to an `IllegalStateException` being raised. Furthermore, if you try to set a null to it, you will get a compilation error.

Properties or methods?

Properties are very similar to methods; you end up with a getter/setter method under the hood as you have already seen. However, methods and properties have different usage patterns. You should view properties as fields on steroids. While they look like fields, the syntax for a property looks like we deal with a field; properties provide the flexibility of methods.

A class method represents an action, while a property represents data. Properties should be used like a field and not like an action or behavior. When you want to design your type and define one or more properties, follow these guidelines to decide whether it is suitable to do so:

1. Avoid having complex code in the getter code body. A caller expects a fast return. Definitely, do not connect to a database or do a rest call from the property's getter code base.
2. Getting a property should not cause any side-effects; avoid even throwing exceptions from the getter's code.
3. Mark your setter as private/protected if you don't want the caller to change the value, that is, you want to preserve your encapsulation. Remember, if the property type is a reference type, the caller can still change its state via the public methods/properties it might expose.
4. Make sure your properties can be set in any possible order, even if that means leaving your object in a temporally invalid state.
5. If a setter needs to throw an exception, make sure you retain the previous property value.

There are scenarios when you should be using a method over a property. While we can't cover all possible cases here, here are a few situations when you should use methods rather than properties:

1. If the code is considerably slower than the process of setting a field, then use a method. Think about scenarios where setting the value of a property involves a network connection or even accessing the file system. In these cases, you should definitely provide methods rather than properties.
2. If calling the property code yields different outcomes each time, you should use a method. Say you are returning the current time; you should create a method for it rather than providing a property.
3. If you want to convert your type to a different one, then make use of a method. A clear example is `toString()`. Any declaration where you see the pattern `to***` should be a method rather than a property.
4. If the result is a copy of the internal state of your object, it shouldn't be a property but a method. A typical example will be the `clone` method defined by the Java Object class.

Summary

You can say goodbye to having to write or generate getters and setters for your fields. Traditional techniques of encapsulation have relied exclusively on separate methods, but now properties allow you to access the object's state with field-like syntax while preserving encapsulation. You now know what properties are for and how they are used and can write better Kotlin idiomatic code.

In the next chapter, Null Safety, you will learn how Kotlin's new language features are working together to eliminate the null pointer exception. Furthermore you will see how Java null code integrates with these features.

7
Null Safety, Reflection, and Annotations

The dreaded null pointer exception is a familiar sight to anyone who has been a Java developer for any length of time. It is caused by a failure to handle null references correctly. Avoiding these errors has been the subject of many different ideas in many different programming languages. In this chapter, we'll review Kotlin's approach to null safety. Speaking at QCon, a conference organized by the developer blogging site InfoQ, Tony Hoare, the creator of the null pointer, said this:

> *"I call it my billion-dollar mistake. It was the invention of the null reference in 1965. At that time, I was designing the first comprehensive type system for references in an object oriented language (ALGOL W). My goal was to ensure that all use of references should be absolutely safe, with checking performed automatically by the compiler. But I couldn't resist the temptation to put in a null reference, simply because it was so easy to implement. This has led to innumerable errors, vulnerabilities, and system crashes, which have probably caused a billion dollars of pain and damage in the last forty years."*

There are several different approaches to solving this so-called billion dollar mistake.

In C, it was common for code that referenced a null pointer to simply crash. Java improved on this by having a `NullPointerException` that would not crash the JVM, but could be handled by a try/catch block; however, the burden was on the programming to remember to catch it. Groovy and C# introduced features designed to allow the compiler to catch potential nullable code and protect the developer. In Scala and Haskell and other Functional programming languages, there are the `Maybe` and `Option` monads.

Kotlin has null safety at the heart of its type system. That is, null safety is not represented by using a monadic null container, nor by forcing the programmer to catch exceptions, but instead support has been added directly into the type system and compiler.

The following features will be familiar to some readers, as languages such as groovy and C# have similar features already.

In this chapter, we will cover:

- Nullable and non-nullable types
- Null safe operators
- Reflection and runtime code inspection
- Annotations

Nullable types

Kotlin's type system is advanced enough that it can track the difference between nullable types and non-nullable types. When we define a variable in Kotlin, as we have been doing so far, we cannot assign a null to it. This code, for instance, would not compile:

```
val name: String = null // does not compile
```

Assigning null to a `var` will not compile either:

```
var name: String = "harry"
name = null // does not compile
```

To inform the Kotlin compiler that we will allow a variable to contain a null, we must suffix the type with a `?`:

```
val name: String? = null
var name: String? = "harry"
name = null
```

Both the preceding snippets will now compile.

Similarly, we can return nullable and non-nullable types from a function, use them as function parameters, and so on:

```
fun name1(): String = ...

fun name2(): String? = ...
```

The `name1` function cannot return a null reference. The `name2` function may or may not. If we were to write some code that used the result of `name1` then it is guaranteed that a null pointer exception will not be thrown. But if we were to try and write code that accessed the result of `name2` then no such guarantees can be made, so the compiler would not accept the code without extra handling.

Smart cast

We have just seen how nullable types are declared. So how do we use a nullable-type when we have one? The first option is to use smart casts. Briefly introduced in `Chapter 2`, *Kotlin Basics,* smart casts are a Kotlin feature whereby the compiler tracks conditions inside an if expression. As long as we perform a check that the variable is not null, then the compiler will allow us to access the variable as if it was declared as a non-nullable type:

```
fun getName(): String? = ...
val name = getName()
if (name != null) {
  println(name.length)
}
```

Note that we are able to invoke the length function on the name value inside the if expression. This is because the compiler has verified that we cannot be inside that block unless the name references a non-null value.

A null smart cast only works when the variable is either a member `val` without a backing field, a local `val`, or a local `var` that is not mutated between the check and the usage. Otherwise, the variable might be non-null when it's checked and then changed to null before we use it, thus throwing an exception. The compiler will enforce this restriction.

Safe null access

Smart casts are a very nice feature, and offer a readable way to do branching when dealing with nulls. However, when we have chained operations, and each step may produce a null, the code quickly becomes unreadable.

Consider the following snippet:

```
class Person(name: String, val address: Address?)
class Address(name: String, postcode: String, val city: City?)
class City(name: String, val country: Country?)
class Country(val name: String)

fun getCountryName(person: Person?): String? {
  var countryName: String? = null
  if (person != null) {
    val address = person.address
    if (address != null) {
      val city = address.city
      if (city != null) {
        val country = city.country
        if (country != null) {
          countryName = country.name
        }
      }
    }
  }
  return countryName
}
```

Look at the levels of nested if-not-null checks required! It's easy to imagine even more levels of nesting required in some scenarios. So can we do better?

With Kotlin we can. The alternative to smart casts is to use the safe null access operator. This is similar to the normal dot syntax for functions and properties, but uses `?.`. When using this operator, the compiler will automatically insert the null check for us to ensure that we don't access a null accidentally. So the previous example can be re-written as the following:

```
fun getCountryNameSafe(person: Person?): String? {
  return person?.address?.city?.country?.name
}
```

The difference is striking. If we examine the bytecode generated for this function, we can see that the compiler is indeed inserting the null checks:

```
public static final java.lang.String getCountryNameSafe(Person);
  Code:
    0: aload_0
    1: dup
    2: ifnull        32
    5: invokevirtual #15   // Method Person.getAddress:()LAddress;
    8: dup
    9: ifnull        32
```

```
    12: invokevirtual #21    // Method Address.getCity:()LCity;
    15: dup
    16: ifnull        32
    19: invokevirtual #27  // Method City.getCountry:()LCountry;
    22: dup
    23: ifnull        32
    26: invokevirtual #33         // Method
Country.getName:()Ljava/lang/String;
    29: goto          34
    32: pop
    33: aconst_null
    34: areturn
```

The key instructions here are 2, 9, 16, and 23, which show the compiler performing a null check and if-null jumping to instruction 32, before adding a null to the stack to be returned.

Force operator

Sometimes we might decide that we want to dispense with the compiler's checks and force a nullable type into a non-nullable type. This is useful in situations were we are dealing with Java code, which we know is never null, and we need to use a variable with a function that only accepts non-nullable values. To do this, we can use the `!!` operator:

```
val nullableName: String? = "george"
val name: String = nullableName!!
```

In the preceding example, you can see that the name has been declared as a non-nullable type, and so the `!!` is used to perform the conversion. We can do this for any expression that returns a nullable type. For example, in the following snippet the function returns a nullable type, but we have forced the compiler to allow us to treat it as a non-nullable type:

```
fun nullableAddress(): Address? = ...
val postcode: String = nullableAddress()!!.postcode
```

We can see that the !! operator is reverting to unsafe code if we check the bytecode:

```
public static final void forceFunction();
  Code:
    0: invokestatic  #62                    // Method
nullableAddress:()LAddress;
    3: dup
    4: ifnonnull     10
    7: invokestatic  #67    // Method
kotlin/jvm/internal/Intrinsics.throwNpe:()V
    10: invokevirtual #70     // Method
Address.getPostcode:()Ljava/lang/String;
    13: astore_0
    14: return
```

At instruction 7, a null pointer exception will be thrown if the variable was null.

Elvis operator

One of the most common scenarios when we have a nullable type is to use the value if it is not null, and a default if otherwise. For example, in Java we might usually write code like this:

```
String postcode = null
if (address == null) {
  postcode = "No Postcode"
}
else {
  if (address.getPostcode() == null) {
    postcode = "No Postcode"
  }
  else {
    postcode = address.getPostcode()
  }
}
```

What Kotlin offers us as a replacement is the so-called Elvis operator `?:`. Supposedly, if you turn your head sideways the operator looks like Elvis' hairstyle, but perhaps it would have been better with a different name. The usage of this is very similar to the ternary if statement in Java.

This infix operator can be placed in between a nullable expression and an expression to use if the nullable expression is indeed null. So the general usage resembles the following:

```
val nullableName: String? = ...
val name: String = nullableName ?: "default_name"
```

The right-hand side is an expression, so anything can be placed there that evaluates the value, such as a when expression or a function call. The operations can be chained too.

Another common method is to use the safe null access operator to chain nullable expressions together, before using the Elvis operator to return a default:

```
val nullableAddress: Address? = null
val postcode: String = nullableAddress?.postcode ?:  "default_postcode"
```

Safe casting

Recall that, in `Chapter 2`, *Kotlin Basics*, we introduced the `as` operator for casting a variable. If we want to safely cast to a type, or null if the cast would fail, then we can use the safe cast operator `as?`.

In the following example, we will cast a parameter that we know is a `String`, but the compiler doesn't know it is a `String` as we declared it as an `Any`:

```
val location: Any = "London"
val safeString: String? = location as? String
val safeInt: Int? = location as? Int
```

Optionals

Throughout the previous sections, we have discussed Kotlin's approach to null safety. But this is not the only approach. Languages such as Haskell have provided an alternative for many years. In Haskell's case, this is called the `Maybe` type. In Scala there is something similar called the `Option` type, and in the most recent version of Java (at the time of writing, Java 8) there is `Optional`.

All of these types-`Maybe`, `Option`, `Optional`-aim to do the same thing. That is, they use a type to indicate that a function or expression may or may not return a value.

In Functional programming. they are most often an algebraic data type with two values-one that represents a value and one that represents the lack of a value. In Haskell they are called `Just` and `Nothing`. In Scala they are called `Some` and `None`. In Java only a single type is used.

For the rest of this section, we will focus on the Java Optional. Remember, though, that this will not be available to you if you are not compiling on Java 8 or later.

Creating and returning an Optional

We can wrap a value in an `Optional` by simply calling the static method `of`:

```
val optionalName: Optional<String> = Optional.of("william")
```

If we wish to create an Optional for an empty value, then we can use the static method empty:

```
val empty: Optional<String> = Optional.empty()
```

If we wish to create an Optional that contains a value that may or may not be null, then we can use `ofNullable`. Usually, there is only one instance of empty that exists, since it is immutable and has no state.

So, if we had a function that could return null, we would define it to return `String?`. When using Optionals, we would define it to return an `Optional<String>`:

```
fun lookupAddress(postcode: String): String?
fun lookupAddress(postcode: String): Optional<String>
```

Those previous two snippets represent the same thing-that the `lookupAddress` function can possibly return no value for a given input.

Using an Optional

Optionals are very similar to Kotlin's null operators in terms of the operations they allow. When using Optionals, ultimately we need to extract the value from the Optional. To do this, we can use get or orElse. The former retrieves the value or throws an exception-this is the Optional equivalent of the force operator. The latter accepts a parameter that is used as a default if the Optional represents no value. See the following code:

```
fun lookupAddress(postcode: String): Optional<String> = ...

val address = lookupAddress("AB1 1BC").orElse("1600 Pennsylvania
Avenue")
```

In the preceding code, if the `lookupAddress` function has no address for the given `postcode`, the default value is used. This is the Optional equivalent of the `?:` operator.

Optionals also support map and `flatMap` operations to transform the contained value. The map operation accepts a function that will return a new Optional with the result of the function. If the Optional is empty, then the function will not be invoked.

The `flatMap` operation is similar, but will flatten nested optionals returned by the mapping function. Let's imagine another function that returns `Optional<Int>`:

```
fun lookupHousePrice(address: String): Optional<Int> = ...
```

Now we can chain this with `lookupAddress` to find the house price if the `address` exists. If the house price itself doesn't exist-say the house is not in the database-then `flatMap` will not return an `Optional<Optional<Int>>`, but will flatten the nested Optionals so the return type is `Optional<Int>`:

```
val price =
lookupAddress("AB11BC").flatMap(::lookupHousePrice).orElse(0)
```

Since after the `flatMap` we have an `Optional<Int>`, we can call `orElse` to return a default integer.

Reflection

Reflection is the name given to inspecting code at runtime instead of compile time. It can be used to create instances of classes, look up functions and invoke them, inspect annotations, find fields, and discover parameters and generics, all without knowing those details at compile time.

For example, we might want to persist types into a database, but we don't know, or don't want to have to know, in advance which types will be persisted. Reflection could be used to look up the fields of each type, creating the appropriate SQL code for each type.

Another example would be if we had a plugin system in our code, and at runtime we wanted to create instances of the plugin based on config or system properties. We could use reflection to instantiate classes based on the fully qualified name passed in.

For the rest of this chapter, we will cover the various reflection classes and functions that Kotlin has made available in its reflection package.

The Kotlin reflection classes are not part of the **kotlin-stdlib** library, but are instead part of an additional dependency called **kotlin-reflect**. This is to keep overall package sizes down for users of Android and other memory-restricted platforms.

KClass

`KClass` is the central type used in Kotlin reflection. Each type has a `KClass` instance at runtime that contains details of the functions, properties, annotations, and so on for that type. To get an instance of a `KClass` for any type, we use the special `::class` syntax on an instance of that type:

```
val name = "George"
val kclass: KClass<String> = name::class
```

Note that a `KClass` instance is parameterized by the type it represents. We can also get a reference to a `KClass` for a type by using the same syntax on the type itself:

```
val kclass2: KClass<String> = String::class
```

For each class loader there is only one `KClass` for any given type. So in the same class loader, invoking `::class` on any particular instance would return the same `KClass` as would be returned when invoking it on any other instance of that type, or the type itself:

```
val kclass1: KClass<String> = "harry"::class
val kclass2: KClass<String> = "victoria"::class
val kclass3: KClass<String> = String::class
```

In the preceding example, all three `kclass` variables reference the same instance.

Aside from retrieving a handle to a `KClass` via instances and types, we can also get one from the fully qualified name of a class. To do this, we must first get a reference to the Java reflection API's equivalent of the `KClass`, which is called simply `Class`. Then we access the property labeled `kotlin`, as the following example shows:

```
val kclass = Class.forName("com.packt.MyClass").kotlin
```

The `Class.forName` static method is the Java reflection API's way of retrieving a handle to an instance of `Class`. In fact, many of the functions in `KClass` are named/inspired by the methods available on `Class`, but are updated to support the advanced features of Kotlin.

Instantiation using reflection

As mentioned earlier, one of the most common uses of reflection is to create instances of types without knowing those types at compile time. The simplest way of doing this is to use the `createInstance` function on a `KClass` reference:

```
class PositiveInteger(value: Int = 0)

fun createInteger(kclass: KClass<PositiveInteger>): PositiveInteger {
  return kclass.createInstance()
}
```

As you can see, our createInteger function uses the KClass parameter to create a new instance of PositiveInteger. This contrived example isn't much use as you know the type in advance, but the point of reflection is for those times when you don't.

The drawback with `createInstance` is that it will only work for classes with no parameters, or where all parameters are optional. A parameter is considered optional if it has a default value supplied.

Let's consider a typical use case of this kind of instantiation. In a data processing application we may have an import step, which imports or ingests data from CSV files into our database. Our application is going to ingest data from many different sources, and we want to be able to add new ingesters at runtime without requiring a rebuild of the core code.

We would start by defining some .config file, which contains a list of ingesters. Each ingester would be referenced by its fully qualified name (**FQN**: the name of the class prefixed with its package name). It might look like this:

```
ingesters.props
ingesters=com.packt.ingester.AmazonIngester,com.packt.ingester.Goo
gleIngester
```

In some Bootstrap class, we would load this property file, break apart the Strings to get the ingester names, and then, using reflection, instantiate them. Once we have a reference to each of the ingesters, we could invoke each of them in turn. This would require that they all implement some common interface with an entry point function:

```
interface Ingester {
  fun ingest(): Unit
}

val props = Properties()
props.load(Files.newInputStream(Paths.get("/some/path/ingesters.pr
ops")))
val classNames = (props.getProperty("ingesters") ?: "").split(',')

val ingesters = classNames.map {
  Class.forName(it).kotlin.createInstance() as Ingester
}

ingesters.forEach { it.ingest() }
```

Note that we first defined the Ingester interface that each implementation of ingester would extend. When we reflectively instantiate each ingester, we are required to cast to the type that we know it is. This operation would throw an exception if a class in the config was not actually of the type `Ingester`. Obviously, the compiler is unable to assert this for us based on a string alone.

The benefit to this kind of approach is that, should we need to add another ingester, say a `com.packt.ingester.FacebookIngester` implementation, then we don't need to touch the core code of the application. We could deploy the new ingester in a separate JAR file, adding that jar to the classpath and simply updating the config to include the new FQN.

This kind of technique is common for systems that rely on plugins where the developers of the core system cannot possibly know in advance what implementations will exist when their library is used.

Remember that createInstance doesn't allow parameters. It might not seem very useful to reflectively create instances without parameters, but in use cases like the previous example, we can't possibly hope to support all variations of constructors that plugin authors would want to use. So we might restrict them to no parameters, and require that they create delegates as required.

Constructors

Sometimes we may want to inspect the available constructors on a type. Perhaps we need to create a type that has a constructor that requires values. Or perhaps we want to determine which fields are needed to create an instance of a type at runtime. Or, similarly, perhaps we want to see if a class can be created from the parameters we have available.

We can return a list of all the constructors declared on a given type by using the `constructors` property available on the `KClass` type. This property returns a list of `KFunction` reflective instances, since `constructors` are themselves functions, just functions defined in a special way:

```
fun <T : Any> printConstructors(kclass: KClass<T>) {
  kclass.constructors.forEach {
    println(it.parameters)
  }
}
```

The preceding example simply iterates over each constructor, printing out the parameters it accepts. For example, look at the following defined class:

```
class Kingdom(name: String, ruler: String, peaceful: Boolean) {
  constructor(name: String, ruler: String) : this(name, ruler,  false)
}
```

If we invoked `printConstructors` for this type:

```
fun main(args: Array<String>) {
  printConstructors(Kingdom::class)
}
```

Then the output would be the following:

```
[parameter #0 name of fun <init>(kotlin.String, kotlin.String): Kingdom,
parameter #1 ruler of fun <init>(kotlin.String, kotlin.String): Kingdom]
[parameter #0 name of fun <init>(kotlin.String, kotlin.String,
kotlin.Boolean): Kingdom, parameter #1 ruler of fun <init>(kotlin.String,
kotlin.String, kotlin.Boolean): Kingdom, parameter #2 peaceful of fun
<init>(kotlin.String, kotlin.String, kotlin.Boolean): Kingdom]
```

Given a reference to a constructor, we can invoke it using the `call` and `callBy` functions available. There are two versions. The first simply accepts a `varargs` list of parameters and expects them to be in the order as declared by the `constructor`. The second accepts a map of parameters and uses the parameter names to match them up:

```
    fun createKingdom(name: String, ruler: String, peaceful: Boolean):
Kingdom {
      val constructor = Kingdom::class.constructors.find {
        it.parameters.size == 3
      } ?: throw RuntimeException("No compatible constructor")
      return constructor.call(name, ruler, peaceful)
    }
```

In the earlier code, we used the first variant, which passes the arguments in order.

When reflectively creating instances, we must ensure the types are compatible. If, for example, the first parameter expected a `java.lang.String` and we pass in a `java.math.BigDecimal`, the JVM would throw a `java.lang.IllegalArgumentException`.

Instantiation with callBy

The callBy variant, which uses a map, is useful if we wish to reflectively build the appropriate arguments themselves. To build this map, we can use the information about parameters that the constructors provided to us through the property named parameters.

This property returns a collection of KParameter instances-one for each parameter in the constructor. These parameter reflection instances can be used to determine the name and type of the parameter, and whether it is varargs, inline, or Optional.

Let's show this by creating an instance of `Plugin`, a type we will define that can accept either a JDBC connection, a properties instance, or a `FileSystem`. At compile time, we won't know which of these parameters our constructor will need, so we will use reflection to find out.

We will define the `Plugin` interface, as well as our mock implementation called `OraclePlugin`:

```
interface Plugin {
  fun configure(): Unit
}

class OraclePlugin(conn: Connection) {
  fun configure(): Unit = ... // run queries on the connection
}
```

Note that the `OracePlugin` accepts a `Connection` instance. The real meat of this example will be in the reflection code that creates these plugins:

```
    fun createPlugin(className: String): Plugin {
       val kclass = Class.forName(className).kotlin
       assert(kclass.constructors.size == 1, { "Only supply plugins with a
single constructor" })
       val constructor = kclass.constructors.first()

      assert(constructor.parameters.size == 1, { "Only supply plugins with
one parameter" })
      val parameter: KParameter = constructor.parameters.first()

      val map = when (parameter.type.jvmErasure) {
        java.sql.Connection::class -> {
          val conn =
DriverManager.getConnection("some_jdbc_connection_url")
          mapOf(parameter to conn)
        }
        java.util.Properties::class -> {
          val props = Properties()
          mapOf(parameter to props)
        }
        java.nio.file.FileSystem::class -> {
          val fs = FileSystems.getDefault()
          mapOf(parameter to fs)
        }
        else -> throw RuntimeException("Unsupported type")
      }

      return constructor.callBy(map) as Plugin
```

```
    }
```

Firstly, we use `Class.forName` as before to get a reference to a `KClass` instance for the `className` argument. Then, using this, we retrieve the first constructor and the first parameter for that constructor. In this particular case, we are expecting our plugin implementations to have only a single constructor with a single parameter, and we've added assertions to that effect.

Next, we inspect the type that the KParameter represents. Depending on what that type is, we build a map that contains a value for one of the three supported types: Connection, Properties, and FileSystem.

Finally, that map is passed to callBy in order to instantiate an instance, with a cast to get us to the required type.

Objects and companions

We can even get a reference to objects or `companion` objects through reflection. For example, take the following definition of a class and a `companion` object:

```
    class Aircraft(name: String, manufacturer: String, capacity: Int)  {
      companion object {
        fun boeing(name: String, capacity: Int) = Aircraft(name,  "Boeing",
capacity)
      }
    }
```

Given this, we can retrieve a reference to the `companion` object using the appropriately named `companionObject` property defined on the KClass type:

```
    val kclass = Aircraft::class
    val companionKClass = kclass.companionObject
```

From then on, we have another KClass instance, this one modeling the functions and members of the companion object.

In fact, using the `companionObjectInstance` property, we can even get a handle to the instance of the `companion` object. Then, we could invoke functions or access properties on it directly if we cast to the appropriate type:

```
    val kclass = Aircraft::class
    val companion = kclass.companionObjectInstance as  Aircraft.Companion
    companion.boeing("747", 999)
```

Note that the type of the companion object we casted to is `Aircraft.Companion` as it was an unnamed companion object.

Analogously, if we have a KClass that represents an object singleton, then we can use the `objectInstance` property to retrieve the actual instance:

```
object PizzaOven {
  fun cook(name: String): Pizza = Pizza(name)
}

val kclass = PizzaOven::class
val oven: PizzaOven = kclass.objectInstance as PizzaOven
```

As you can see, the final oven variable is the instance of the `PizzaOven` object.

Useful KClass properties

A KClass fully describes a particular class including its type parameters, superclasses, functions, constructors, annotations, and properties. Let's define a toy class:

```
class Sandwich<F1, F2>()
```

Now we can inspect the KClass for this and find out the types of parameters it declares. We do this using the `typeParameters` property available on the KClass instance:

```
val types = Sandwich::class.typeParameters
```

From here, we can get the label of the type parameter, and the upper bounds, if any have been defined (otherwise `Any`):

```
types.forEach {
  println("Type ${it.name} has upper bound ${it.upperBounds}")
}
```

In the case of `Sandwich`, this would output the following:

```
Type F1 has upper bound [kotlin.Any?]
Type F2 has upper bound [kotlin.Any?]
```

Next, let's show the superclasses for a given type. Firstly, we need a type that has many parents:

```
class ManyParents : Serializable, Closeable, java.lang.AutoCloseable
```

Then, on the KClass of this, we access the property `superclasses` to get a list of the superclasses and interfaces, but not the actual class itself:

```
val superclasses = ManyParents::class.superclasses
```

If we were to output the preceding list, we would see the following:

```
class java.io.Serializable
class java.io.Closeable
class java.lang.AutoCloseable
```

This, of course, is what we expect. But what about `Any`? Don't all classes extend from that? So why isn't it listed? It is because superclasses only includes immediate parents; for that we need the `allSuperclasses` property:

```
val allSuperclasses = ManyParents::class.allSuperclasses
```

If outputted, this gives us the full list:

```
class java.io.Serializable
class kotlin.Any
class java.io.Closeable
class java.lang.AutoCloseable
```

Reflective functions and properties

Reflection doesn't stop with classes and objects. Most of the Kotlin system can be accessed, and that includes functions and properties. Let's start with a class that contains some member functions, an extension function for `Double`, and a couple of properties:

```
class Rocket() {
  var lat: Double = 0
  var long: Double = 0

  fun explode() {
    println("Boom")
  }

  fun setCourse(lat: Double, long: Double) {
    require(lat.isValid())
```

```
        require(long.isValid())
        this.lat = lat
        this.long = long
    }

    fun Double.isValid() = Math.abs(this) <= 180
}
```

The extension function is used to check that the `Double` parameter is a valid latitude or longitude whenever we invoke `setCourse`.

The next function is similar to the function for printing constructors from earlier, and prints out the names of each function defined in this class. The appropriately named property `memberFunctions` is used on `KClass` to get references to each function in the class. In the reflection API, functions are represented by instances of `KFunction`:

```
fun <T : Any> printFunctions(kclass: KClass<T>) {
  kclass.functions.forEach {
    println(it.name)
  }
}
```

If we invoke this function, we'll get an output like the following:

```
explode
setCourse
equals
hashCode
toString
```

As expected, this contains both the member functions we defined, as well as the functions declared in `Any`: the ultimate supertype of all classes. Note, however, that the extension function `Double.isValid()` does not appear in the list. In order to get a reference to a KFunction for an extension function, we need to use another property named `memberExtensionFunctions`.

There is a third property, simply named functions, which returns both non-extension and extension functions in the same list. It is the same as combining the output of the previous two properties. KFunction instances themselves have many useful functions and properties, and are used to discover details such as whether the function is inline, an operator, infix, its return type, parameter types, and so on.

When it comes to properties, there are analogous properties named memberProperties and memberExtensionProperties, which are used in the same way as for the functions. In the reflection API, properties are represented by instances of KProperty.

Let's use those to find the properties we declared on the Rocket class:

```
fun <T : Any> printProperties(kclass: KClass<T>) {
  kclass.memberProperties.forEach {
    println(it.name)
  }
}
```

This function, when invoked, would output lat, long as we would expect.

Invoking a function reflectively

The real utility in reflective access to functions lies in the ability to invoke them. KFunction defines a function named call that accepts a vararg list of parameters, and uses those to invoke the function on an instance of the type that the function is declared on.

Given that the KFunction instance itself is not tied to any particular instance, we need to also provide the receiver that the function should be invoked on. This is always the first argument to call.

Using the Rocket example from earlier, we will invoke a function dynamically, without reference to it at compile time:

```
val function = kclass.functions.find { it.name == "explode" }
val rocket = Rocket()
function?.call(rocket)
```

Note that we look up all functions locating the one with the explode name. The explode function doesn't actually declare any parameters itself, so the only argument to call is the instance to use as the function receiver. In this case, that happens to be a freshly instantiated rocket.

Declared and undeclared

At this point it is worth pointing out the difference between declared and undeclared functions and properties. Each of the properties that can be used to get member functions, member properties, constructors, and so on, come in declared and undeclared variants.

The undeclared variants, which are the ones we've covered so far, include functions and properties declared in the type referenced by the `KClass`, as well as parent classes and interfaces.

The declared variants, which are named `declaredMemberExtensionFunctions`, `declaredMemberFunctions`, and so on, only include functions and properties declared in the type itself. Any functions and properties declared in parent classes or interfaces are not returned by these functions.

Annotations

Annotations allow developers to add extra meaning to classes, interfaces, parameters, and so on at compile time. They are a form of meta-programming in that respect. Annotations can then be used by the compiler or by your own code via reflection at runtime. Depending on the annotation value, the meaning of the program or data can change.

Annotations are present in Java as well as Kotlin, and so the most common annotations are those that are provided as part of the Kotlin or Java standard libraries. Some annotations you may be familiar with already are `@SuppressWarnings` and `@tailrec`.

To define your own annotation, simply prefix a class with the keyword `annotation`:

```
annotation class Foo
```

This annotation can then be used in classes, functions, parameters, and so on. In fact, annotations can pretty much be used anywhere, as the following table shows:

Target	Example
Class	`@Foo class MyClass`
Interface	`@Foo interface MyInterface`
Object	`@Foo object MyObject`
Parameter	`fun bar(@Foo param: Int): Int = param`
Function	`@Foo fun foo(): Int = 0`
Type Alias	`@Foo typealias MYC = MyClass`
Property	`class PropertyClass { @Foo var name: String? = null}`
Constructor	`class Bar @Foo constructor(name: String)`
Expressions	`val str = @Foo "hello foo"`

Return Values	`fun expressionAnnotation(): Int { return (@Foo 123)}`
Function Literals	`@Foo { it.size > 0 }`

Note that annotations begin with an `@` when they are used. Before they can be used, however, we must specify the allowed targets using a meta-annotation named `@Target`. For example, to allow an annotation only on a constructor, we could define it as follows:

```
@Target(AnnotationTarget.CONSTRUCTOR)
annotation class Woo
```

We can specify as many targets as we want for any particular annotation.

There are several other meta-annotations available for use when defining custom annotations. These are described in the following table:

Annotation Name	**Usage**
`@Retention`	Determines how the annotation is stored in the resultant class files. The options are: • Source: The annotation is removed at compile time. • Binary: The annotation is included in the class files, but is not visible by reflection. • Runtime: The annotation is stored in the class files and is visible by reflection.
`@Repeatable`	If present, then allows that annotation to be included more than once in any particular target.
`@MustBeDocumented`	If present, then the annotation is included when generating documents via Dokka.

Annotation parameters

Annotations can, of course, have parameters as you have already seen with `@AnnotationTarget`. Custom annotations can specify their own constructors with whatever parameters they wish. To do this, we declare a constructor as we would for a regular class by just listing the parameters after the class name. For example:

```
annotation class Ipsum(val text: String)
```

Annotation parameters must always be declared as `val`.

Then, when we use such an annotation, we simply pass in the value required:

```
@Ipsum("Lorem") class Zoo
```

The types of parameters are limited to a certain subset. Allowed types are Int, Double, Long, Float, Boolean, String, KClass, enum, and other annotations themselves. Arrays of allowed types are also allowed. So, for example, we could have an array of Strings or an array of annotations.

Standard annotations

The Kotlin standard library includes several annotations that affect the output of the compiler. Some we have seen already and others are introduced here for the first time.

@JvmName

Due to erasure in the JVM, it is impossible to declare two functions with the same name and the same erased signature. For example, the following declarations in Java would result in a compile error:

```
public void foo(list: List<String>)
public void foo(list: List<Int>)
```

Erasure is caused by the fact that the JVM does not retain type parameters. This means, among other examples, that variables of `List<String>` and `List<Int>` both compile to `List<Any>`.

The most commonly used solution to this problem is to name the methods differently. But sometimes that isn't desirable. In Kotlin, we can retain the same names as long as we provide alternative names for when they are compiled. To do this we annotate the functions using `@JvmName` with a supplied alternative, as the following examples show:

```
@JvmName("filterStrings")
fun filter(list: List<String>): Unit

@JvmName("filterInts")
fun filter(list: List<Int>): Unit
```

At compile time the name supplied to the annotation will be used. We can see this by inspecting the generated bytecode:

```
public static final void filterStrings(java.util.List<java.lang.String>);
  Code:
    [ ... ]
public static final void filterInts(java.util.List<java.lang.Integer>);
  Code:
    [ ... ]
```

When using these functions from Kotlin, we continue to use the original names. The `@JvmName` annotation is invisible to Kotlin users. The compiler will do the necessary translation for us, but when invoking these functions from Java we use the alternative name.

@JvmStatic

The `@JvmStatic` annotation informs the compiler that you wish the function or property annotated to have a Java static method generated in the compiled output. This annotation can only be used on objects or companion objects.

By default an object or companion object is compiled into a class that has a single instance. This instance is then stored in a static field named `INSTANCE`. To access functions on these objects in Java, you are required to first resolve the singleton. For example:

```
HasStaticFuncs.INSTANCE.foo();
```

However, the annotation will result in the function being a static method rather than an instance method, so we can invoke it directly on the type:

```
HasStaticFuncs.foo();
```

@Throws

Since all exceptions in Kotlin are unchecked exceptions, there is no need to add a list of possible exceptions to method signatures like there is in Java. However, we may wish to inform Java users that our API throws exceptions in certain situations. We can do this using the @Throws annotation, which is used to instruct the compiler to generate throw clauses on generated methods.

For example, let's define a simple class in Kotlin that contains a function that can throw an exception:

```
class File(val path: String) {
  fun exists(): Boolean {
    if (!Paths.get(path).toFile().exists())
    throw FileNotFoundException("$path does not exist")
    return true
  }
}
```

This can be called directly from Java in the following way:

```
public void throwsExample() {
  boolean exists = new File("somefile.txt").exists();
  System.out.println("File exists");
}
```

Note that the method signature does not include throws. This is perfectly compilable code so far. However, should we decide that we want Java users to be informed that the `exists()` function throws an exception, we can add this to the method signature in the compiled class file:

```
class File(val path: String) {
  @Throws(FileNotFoundException::class)
  fun exists(): Boolean {
    if (!Paths.get(path).toFile().exists())
  throw FileNotFoundException("$path does not exist")
    return true
  }
}
```

As you can see, we've added the `@Throws` annotation. This annotation accepts an argument, which is the exception classes we want to be included in the method signature. Now the previous Java example would no longer compile, and must be updated to handle the exception:

```
public void throwsExample() throws FileNotFoundException {
```

```
    boolean exists = new File("somefile.txt").exists();
    System.out.println("File exists");
  }
```

Finally, the difference can be seen in the generated bytecode to show that the Kotlin compiler is definitely adding the exceptions to the method signature.

The first exists function has the following bytecode header:

```
public final boolean exists();
  descriptor: ()Z
  flags: ACC_PUBLIC, ACC_FINAL
```

The second has the following bytecode header:

```
public final boolean exists() throws  java.io.FileNotFoundException;
  descriptor: ()Z
  flags: ACC_PUBLIC, ACC_FINAL
```

@JvmOverloads

`@JvmOverloads` has already been covered, but we'll recap it here with more implementation detail. Given a function with default parameters, `@JvmOverloads` will result in the compiler creating multiple, overloaded, methods for each default parameter.

For example, take the following function:

```
fun foo(name: String = "Harry", location: String = "Cardiff"):  Unit
```

The compiler will emit three methods in the compiled class file-one with no parameters that will use both defaults, a second which will use the default for location, and a third which uses no defaults. We can verify this by viewing the generated bytecode:

```
public static void foo$default(com.packt.SomeClass, java.lang.String,
java.lang.String, int, java.lang.Object);
descriptor:
(Lcom/packt/SomeClass;Ljava/lang/String;Ljava/lang/String;ILjava/lang
/Object;)V
flags: ACC_PUBLIC, ACC_STATIC, ACC_BRIDGE, ACC_SYNTHETIC
  Code:
    [ ... ]
public final void foo(java.lang.String, java.lang.String);
  descriptor: (Ljava/lang/String;Ljava/lang/String;)V
  flags: ACC_PUBLIC, ACC_FINAL
    Code:
      [ ... ]
```

```
public void foo(java.lang.String);
  descriptor: (Ljava/lang/String;)V
  flags: ACC_PUBLIC
    Code:
      [ ... ]
public void foo();
  Code:
    0: aload_0
    1: aconst_null
    2: aconst_null
    3: iconst_3
    4: aconst_null
    5: invokestatic  #41
    8: return
```

This verifies that three overloaded versions of foo have been defined. The implementations for all but the last variant have been omitted here as they run into the hundreds of instructions. The general idea can be seen from the implementation of the final function. Each version of foo delegates to a fourth `foo$default` function using nulls as arguments where appropriate. This fourth foo function then checks each argument, replacing them with the default values if they are null.

Runtime annotation discovery

Custom annotations are only useful if they can be discovered and used. The standard annotations mostly exist for the benefit of the compiler, but custom annotations are commonly used as runtime metadata.

To find the annotations declared on a class, function, or other construct, we can use the `annotation` property available on `KClass`, `KFunction`, `KParameter`, and `KProperty`. This property returns a collection that has an instance for each of the defined annotations.

For example, let's create an annotation called `Description`, which accepts a single parameter of String. This String is used to add a description to a class, which might be used to generate documentation in a web service:

```
annotation class Description(val summary: String)
```

Then we'll use this to describe a class:

```
@Description("This class creates Executor instances") class  Executors
```

Now, at runtime, we could look up this annotation and use the value:

```
val desc = Executors::class.annotations.first() as Description
val summary = desc.summary
```

Clearly, in this example we haven't added any defensive programming that would be needed in the real world, such as programming that would check that the class actually contains the annotations, or that it really is the correct type of annotation.

Remember that in order for custom annotations to be discoverable by reflection, they must have a `@Retention` value of `RUNTIME`.

Summary

During this chapter we have seen how Kotlin handles null safety in a safe way, and how reflection can be used to inspect code at runtime. Several useful Kotlin annotations have been introduced and their effect on the compiler.

In the next chapter, we will begin a discussion on Kotlin's advanced type system and how we can write generic code.

8
Generics

Generics, or generic programming, is a technique whereby functions can be written in terms of types that are not specified when the function is written, and then later used for many different types. Generics is the term used in Java and Kotlin, but other names, such as parametric polymorphism and templates, are used in other languages for similar features.

In this chapter we will cover:

- Type parameterization
- Type bounds and recursive type bounds
- Invariance, covariance and contravariance
- Algebraic data types

Parameterised functions

Consider a function called `random()` that, when given some elements, returns one element randomly. We don't need to know what the types of the elements are when we write this function, as we will not be using the elements ourselves. We just need to be able to select one to return. When we use a type in this way – abstracting over the type, we use the term **type parameter**. So, our random function would have a single type parameter: the type of the elements we are selecting from.

If we want to write a generic function, like the `random()` function just mentioned, we might decide to start with something like this:

```
fun random(one: Any, two: Any, three: Any): Any
```

This would work as we can pass in any instances we choose. However, no matter what types we choose to pass in as arguments, our returned type would be inferred as `Any`. We'd then be forced to cast back to the original type, and this is error prone, not to mention ugly.

We can do better with a type parameter that will fix the types and allow the compiler to correctly infer the return value. To define a function with a type parameter, we use angle bracket (< . . . >) syntax, giving the type parameter a name, before the function name.

```
fun <T> random(one: T, two: T, three: T): T
```

In this definition, we have defined a single type parameter-`T`-which we then use for all three parameters and the return type. We are informing the compiler that whatever type we fix `T` to be, we will return that same type. This allows the compiler to correctly infer the return type.

To invoke this function, we don't need to do anything other than pass in instances, respecting the relationship between them:

```
val randomGreeting: String = random("hello", "willkommen",  "bonjour")
```

You can see the variable `randomGreeting` is annotated with `String`. This is just to show that the return value is indeed a string. In reality this can be inferred as normal.

What did we mean by respecting the relationship between the types? Simply that each time a particular type parameter is used, it must refer to the same type. In our example, we had a single type parameter and it was set to `String`. Therefore, the function also returns a string.

Of course, in this example, we could have passed in any values we wanted, and it would still have compiled. The inferred type would be the lowest common supertype. For example, the following code compiles fine:

```
val any: Any = random("a", 1, false)
```

This is because all types have the top level `Any` type, and so the compiler can infer `T` to be `Any` and the constraints would still be satisfied.

However, for other examples, this may not work, for example, accepting a list of `T` and another element `T` to add to the list. In that case, the list and element must be compatible. We'll see a concrete example of this in the *Bounded Polymorphism* section when we talk about upper bounds.

Functions can, of course, have more than one type parameter. We could write a function that accepts two different types and puts them into a cache. The first element could be used for a key, and the second for the value:

```
fun <K, V>put(key: K, value: V): Unit
```

This kind of signature will be familiar to anyone who has used generics before in collections.

Parameterized types

It is not just functions that can be parameterized types themselves can be parameterized as well. Such types are sometimes referred to as *container* types because of the close association with collections and the fact that they contain one or more type parameters.

To declare a parameterized type, we again use the angle bracket syntax, this time on the right-hand side of the type name. For example, to declare a `Sequence` of an element `T`, we would write the following:

```
class Sequence<T>
```

Again, we can declare more than one type parameter:

```
class Dictionary<K, V>
```

The most commonly used parameterized types are collections, and these are covered in more detail in `Chapter 10`, *Collections*.

When a type has been declared with a type parameter, we must "fill in" that type when we instantiate it by replacing the parameters with *concrete* or *proper* types. So, to create an instance of our `Sequence` class for `Boolean`, we would write the following:

```
val seq = Sequence<Boolean>()
```

For `Dictionary`, we could do something like the following:

```
val dict = Dictionary<String, String>()
```

Note that there's no reason the different type parameters cannot actually refer to the same concrete type. They don't have to, that's the point of allowing them to be different types, but the choice is up to the user.

Bounded polymorphism

Functions that are generic for any type are useful, but somewhat limited. Often we will find ourselves wanting to write functions that are generic for *some* types that share a common characteristic. For instance, we might want to define a function to return the minimum of two values, for any values that support some notion of comparability.

We'd start by writing a function that has a type parameter representing the types of the two values being compared. But how can we compare these values, since they could be instances of anything, including `Any` itself? Since `Any` has no comparison function, we wouldn't have a way to compare the two values.

The solution is to restrict the types to those that support the functions we need to invoke; this way, the compiler knows that no matter what the runtime type of the arguments is, those functions must be available. Therefore, it allows us to invoke those functions. This is called **bounded polymorphism**.

Upper bounds

Kotlin supports one such type of bound known as an **upper bound**. As the name implies, an upper bound restricts the types to those that are subclasses of the bound. To use an upper bound, we simply declare it alongside the type parameter:

```
fun <T : Comparable<T>>min(first: T, second: T): T {
  val k = first.compareTo(second)
  return if (k <= 0) first else second
}
```

`Comparable` is the standard library type that defines `compareTo`, which returns less than zero if the first element is smaller, greater than zero if the second element is smaller, and zero if they are equal. We defined our type parameter with the upper bound of `Comparable<T>`, so any time this function is called, the value of `T` must extend from this type:

```
val a: Int = min(4, 5)
val b: String = min("e", "c")
```

As you can see, we can invoke integers and strings, receiving the correct type back, since both `Int` and `String` extend `Comparable`. However, if we tried this for a type such as `Pair`, which doesn't, the compiler would emit an error.

Whenever a type parameter is used without an explicit upper bound, the compiler will use `Any` as an implicit upper bound for us.

Also of interest is that we cannot necessarily invoke this function with two different types as we could before for `random`. Recall that if we invoked `random` with arguments of `String`, `Int`, and `Boolean`, the compiler could infer `Any` as that still satisfies the constraints of the default upper bound.

However, if we were to invoke `min` with say a `String` and an `Int`, the upper bound of `String` would be `Comparable<String>` and the upper bound of `Int` would be `Comparable<Int>`. Because neither of those types are a supertype of the other (see the discussion of variance in the next section) the only common supertype the compiler can pick from is `Any`. Since `Any` does not implement `Comparable`, `Any` cannot be used as the concrete type for the type parameter as it does not satisfy the declared bound. Therefore, the compiler has no choice but to emit an error.

Multiple bounds

Sometimes we may wish to declare multiple upper bounds. For example, we may wish to expand our `min()` function example to only work on values that are also serializable. To do this, we move the upper bound declaration out of the type parameter and into a separate `where` clause:

```
fun <T>minSerializable(first: T, second: T): T
where T : Comparable<T>,T : Serializable {
  val k = first.compareTo(second)
  return if (k <= 0) first else second
}
```

Note that all the upper bounds are listed as separate clauses of the `where` statement and form an upper bound union.

Now, if we were to have a type that only implemented one of the upper bounds, the compiler would throw an error if we tried to use this in the `minSerializable` function:

```
class Year(valvalue: Year) : Comparable<Year> {
  override fun compareTo(other: Year): Int =
  this.value.compareTo(other.value)
}
```

The next line would fail to compile:

```
val a = minSerializable(Year(1969), Year(2001))
```

But if we extend the type so that it also implements `Serializable`, then we can use it just fine:

```
    class SerializableYear(valvalue: Int) : Comparable<SerializableYear>,
Serializable {
      override fun compareTo(other: SerializableYear): Int =
      this.value.compareTo(other.value)
}

    val b = minSerializable(SerializableYear(1969), SerializableYear(1802))
```

Classes can also define multiple upper bounds:

```
class MultipleBoundedClass<T>where T : Comparable<T>, T :  Serializable
```

Note that the syntax is similar, with the `where` clause written after the type parameter.

Type variance

Type variance refers to the techniques by which we can allow, or not allow, subtyping in our parameterized types. If we consider a class `Apple`, which is a subtype of `Fruit`, then is a `Crate<Apple>` a subtype of a `Crate<Fruit>`? The first instinct is to think 'of course', since an `Apple` can be used where a `Fruit` is required, but generally speaking the answer is no.

In fact, a `Crate<Apple>` can be a subtype of `Crate<Fruit>`, a supertype of it, or neither depending on which type of *variance* is used.

Invariance

Firstly, let's discuss why a `Crate<Apple>` might not be a subtype of `Crate<Fruit>` by default. Let's start by creating some classes:

```
class Fruit
class Apple : Fruit()
class Orange : Fruit()

class Crate<T>(val elements: MutableList<T>) {
  fun add(t: T) = elements.add(t)
```

```
    fun last(): T = elements.last()
}
```

As you can see, `Crate` is just a wrapper around a `MutableList`. If a function was defined that accepts a parameter of type `Crate<Fruit>`, the function may decide to add a new element to our mutable `crate`:

```
fun foo(crate: Crate<Fruit>): Unit {
  crate.add(Apple()) // does not compile
}
```

This seems fine so far; we have a crate, and it contains fruit. `Apple` is a fruit, so why can't we add it to the `crate`? The reason lies in code that could call this function, and what happens after. Let's imagine we were able to write the following code:

```
val oranges = Crate(mutableListOf(Orange(), Orange()))
foo(oranges)
val orange: Orange = oranges.last()
```

This seems fine on the surface, since the method is asking for a crate of fruit, and oranges are fruit. Therefore, our crate of oranges should satisfy. However, by now the error in this thinking is clear – `foo` only knows it has a crate of fruit, and thinks it can add an apple to what is really a crate of oranges. Therefore, if this code was allowed, we'd have a runtime `ClassCastException` when accessing the last element because it wouldn't actually be an orange.

The simplest solution to this problem is the approach taken in Kotlin, which is to make type parameters invariant by default. When type parameters are invariant, there is no subtype relationship between the types. That is to say, a type `M<T>` is neither a subtype nor a supertype of `M<U>`, regardless of the relationship between `T` and `U`. So to the complier a `Crate<Apple>` and a `Crate<Fruit>` are as related as a `Crate<Apple>` and a `Crate<BigDecimal>`.

Covariance

So we've looked at what it means to be invariant, but that comes with some problems. Let's return to our crate example and imagine another function, which we'll call `verify`. This function will check that if we have a crate of fruit, then that each fruit is safe to eat. If they were not, we'd have to throw away all the fruit or risk some serious illness. Let's add that function to the `Fruit` class:

```
open class Fruit {
  fun isSafeToEat(): Boolean = ...
```

```
}
```

Now, if we wanted to implement `verify`, we would define it in terms of a crate of fruit. After all, we don't care what fruit is in the box, as long as it's safe to eat:

```
fun isSafe(crate: Crate<Fruit>): Boolean = crate.elements.all{
  it.isSafeToEat()
}
```

Now, we already know the following code won't compile:

```
val oranges = Crate(mutableListOf(Orange(), Orange()))
isSafe(oranges)
```

This time, however, there is no reason why it shouldn't compile. The logic is sound, we simply want to invoke the `isSafeToEat()` function on each instance, which we know they all have since that function is defined on the `Fruit` class itself.

The answer lies in changing what is known as the variance of the crate class. We want to allow a crate of oranges when we are asked for a crate of fruit, but safely. This means we want a crate of oranges to be considered a subtype of a crate of fruit. We already know that this is unsafe when we mutate the crate by adding in a different subtype, such as an apple or a pear. So is there a way to get this to work? The answer is yes and it's called **covariance**.

When defining a class, we can mark a type parameter as covariant, which means that the class will maintain the subtyping relationship of the concrete type parameters. To do that, we prefix the type parameter with the keyword `out`:

```
class CovariantCrate<out T>(val elements: List<T>)
```

Remember that it was a mutation of the instance that caused us issues before. Therefore, in order to allow covariance, the compiler insists that we do not allow an instance to be modified. How can it enforce this? It does this by checking that a covariant type parameter is never used as an input to a function. If it is not used as input, then an apple cannot be used where only an orange was expected.

The opposite case is fine, however; we can still use `T` as the return value. This is because any code that expects the crate to return a fruit is happy to have an apple, because an apple is a fruit.

Therefore, our `CovariantCrate` cannot have `T` as an input parameter, and the `add` function that was present on `Create` must be removed. The `last` function can remain, as that function only uses `T` as the return type:

```
class CovariantCrate<out T>(val elements: List<T>) {
```

```
    fun last(): T = elements.last()
}
```

Now we can check for edible food, and the compiler is happy to accept a crate of oranges.

```
val oranges = CovariantCrate(listOf(Orange(), Orange()))
isSafe(oranges)
```

Covariance is incredibly powerful and used by many immutable collection types: Sets, lists, maps, iterators, and collections all define type parameters as covariant, in addition to `Pair`, `Triple`, `Lazy`, and many more.

Covariant return

The return type of a function can also be covariant. This is the default, and so, if a subtype wishes to return a type that is more specific, it can do so. It simply needs to override the definition:

```
open class Animal
class Sheep : Animal()
class Frog : Animal()

abstract class Farm {
  abstract fun get(): Animal
}

abstract class SheepFarm() : Farm() {
  abstract override fun get(): Sheep
}
```

You can see we have a type hierarchy of animals, and our generic `Farm` just returns an `Animal`. The more specific `SheepFarm()` wants to return a `Sheep`, and this is legal in Kotlin. When the function is invoked, the type the compiler will infer for the return value will depend on the type of the farm variable itself:

```
val farm: Farm = SheepFarm()
val animal1 = farm.get()

val sheepFarm = SheepFarm()
val animal2 = sheepFarm.get()
```

The `animal1` variable is only of type `Animal`, whereas the `animal2` variable is of type `Sheep`.

Contravariance

The opposite of covariant is contravariant. When a type parameter is marked as contravariant, then the relationship between the type parameters is reversed in the types themselves. That is, `String` is a subtype of `Any`, but a `Box<String>` would be a supertype of a `Box<Any>` if `Box` had its type parameter marked as contravariant.

To mark a type parameter as contravariant, we mark the type parameter with the keyword `in`.

This might seem a little strange at first; why would we want to invert the relationship? As usual, it's best seen through the lens of an example.

Imagine we had a class called `EventStream` that produced events of type `T`. Our `EventStream` class also accepts a listener, which is invoked each time an event is generated:

```
interface Listener<T> {
  fun onNext(t: T): Unit
}

class EventStream<T>(val listener: Listener<T>) {
  fun start(): Unit = ...
  fun stop(): Unit = ...
}
```

Now, if we created an `EventStream` of strings, we could pass in a `stringlistener`, like so:

```
val stringListener = object : Listener<String> {
  override fun onNext(t: String) = println(t)
}
val stringStream = EventStream<String>(stringListener)
stringStream.start()
```

All seems good so far. Let's make another stream, this time for `Date`:

```
val dateListener = object : Listener<Date> {
  override fun onNext(t: Date) = println(t)
}
val dateStream = EventStream<Date>(dateListener)
stringStream.start()
```

Something should seem amiss here. We have written the exact same listener twice, just varying the type parameters. Could we not instead just write a single logginglistener and use that for any stream? After all, the only function we need to access is toString, and that is defined on Any. String and Date are certainly subtypes of Any:

```
val loggingListener = object : Listener<Any> {
  override fun onNext(t: Any) = println(t)
}
```

If we tried that approach then the compiler would reject using this listener as an argument to the EventStream. This is because, if the compiler is expecting a Listener<String>, then it must receive either a listener of that type, or a listener of a subtype. This is just basic object-orientated principles at play: A function can be invoked with a type or a subtype of the required type.

This is where contravariance comes to the rescue. By marking the type parameter as contravariant, then, for a given type M, M<T> is a subtype of M<U> if U is a subtype of T. In our case, this means that a Listener<Any> is now considered a subtype of Listener<String> because String is a subtype of Any, and we're able to use it as we wanted.

Let's update the Listener and EventStream classes to be contravariant.:

```
interface Listener<in T> {
  fun onNext(t: T): Unit
}

class EventStream<in T>(val listener: Listener<T>) {
  fun start(): Unit = TODO()
  fun stop(): Unit = TODO()
}
```

Now we can use this for any type we want:

```
EventStream<Double>(loggingListener).start()
EventStream<BigDecimal>(loggingListener).start()
```

Recall that when we marked a type parameter as covariant the compiler then restricted the use of the type parameter to return values only. In contrast, when using contravariance, we can only use the type parameters as input parameters and not as return types. The reason is essentially the inverse of the fruit and oranges problem we started this chapter with.

If we had a function that returned a `T` and we allowed that `T` to be contravariant, then a particular instance may be expecting to receive values of `Orange`, but instead could be given a `Fruit`. Trying to peel the orange would fail if the fruit was actually a `Tomato`.

We can demonstrate this through a quick example:

```
interface Generator<in T> {
  fun generate(): T
}

class OrangePicker(val generator: Generator<Orange>) {

  fun pick() {
    val orange = generator.generate()
    peel(orange)
  }
  fun peel(orange: Orange): Unit = // peel the orange
}
```

Our `generator` class is marked as contravariant and has the type parameter in the return position. When we instantiate an `OrangePicker`, we pass in a `generator`. Say that we invoked it like this, with a generic `Fruit` generator:

```
val generator = object : Generator<Fruit> {
  override fun generate(): Fruit = Tomato() // random fruit
}

val picker = OrangePicker(generator)
picker.pick()
```

Since `generator` is contravariant, a `generator` of fruit is considered a subtype of a `generator` of oranges and so can be passed into the constructor. However, the `pick` function only expects instances of `Orange`, and so we would end up with a runtime exception. For this reason, contravariance is restricted to input positions only.

Variance overview

To make clear the different variances and the relationships between classes, the following handy chart gives us a visualization. Recall that, if an **Orange** is a subtype of **Fruit**, then the default invariant state is that a **Crate** of oranges has no relationship to a **Crate** of fruit. With covariance, a **Crate** of oranges is a subtype of a **Crate** of fruit. And finally, with contravariance, a **Crate** of oranges is a supertype of a **Crate** of fruit.

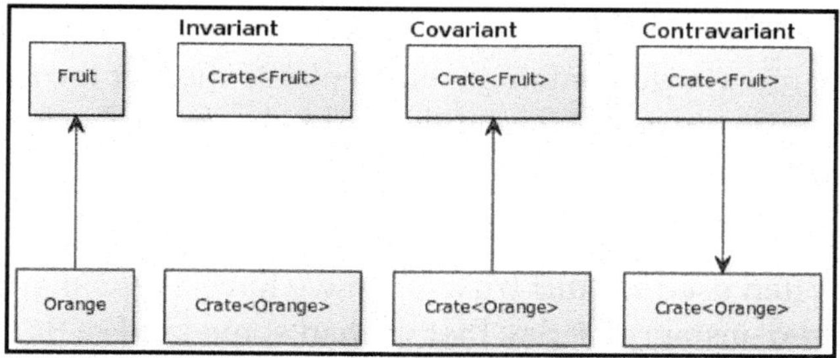

Nothing type

In `Chapter 2`, *Kotlin Basics* we briefly touched on the Kotlin type hierarchy. The notion of a `Nothing` type was mentioned: A type that is the subtype of all other types, in a similar vein to how `Any` is a superclass of all types. The idea of a `Nothing` type is nothing new (pun intended) for those who have used a functional language, such as Scala. For those who are new to the idea, we will cover why such a type is useful.

The first use case is to indicate that a function would never complete normally. What we mean by normally is that it is not expected to return a value. It may intentionally perform an infinite loop, only ending when the process or thread is killed, or it may only return by throwing an exception. For example, the `error` function defined in the Kotlin standard library has the following implementation:

```
    inline fun error(message: Any): Nothing = throw
IllegalStateException(message.toString())
```

The main use, however, is as a type parameter in variant types. If we have a covariant type, and we want to create an instance that is compatible with all supertypes, we can use `Nothing` as the type parameter. For example, look at the following type:

```
class Box<out T>
```

The following instance would be compatible with this:

```
Box<Nothing>()
```

It might seem useless to have a `Box` of `Nothing`, but it would serve perfectly well as an empty `Box`. An empty box would contain no elements, so the fact the functions on it would return the `Nothing` type is not a problem. If the empty box was also immutable, then we would only need a single instance. This is how, for example, the empty list is defined in Kotlin as a shared single object implementing `List<Nothing>`.

`Nothing` as a type is often used for this trick when we have a type that we might wish to have an empty, or no-op, instance of. Say that we had some kind of `Marshaller`, which was parameterized by the type of message it returns. Something like this:

```
interface Marshaller<out T> {
  fun marshall(json: String): T?
}
```

We could easily create a single no-op instance that could be used anywhere a `Marshaller` was expected:

```
object NoopMarshaller : Marshaller<Nothing> {
  override fun marshall(json: String) = null
}
```

Finally, it was worth noting that there are no instances of `Nothing`. `Nothing` is defined as a type, but it cannot ever be instantiated.

Type projection

In the *Type variance* section, we worked through examples of covariance and contravariance, and how each of these restricts type parameters to be used as input types or return types respectively. This is usually not an issue when we are defining our own interfaces and classes as we can come up with the correct abstractions required.

But what about the case where someone else has defined a class to be invariant and you require it to be used in a covariant or contravariant way? Kotlin addresses this by introducing a powerful addition called **type projections**.

When using type parameters, there is a distinction between use site and declaration site variance. Use site variance is the term used when the variance of type parameters is set by the variable itself, as in Java. Declaration site variance is the term used when the type or function determines the variance, as in Kotlin.

Type projections allow us to specify variance at the use site instead. Let's revisit our earlier example of a mutable crate of fruit:

```
class Crate<T>(val elements: MutableList<T>) {
  fun add(t: T) = elements.add(t)
  fun last(): T = elements.last()
}
```

If you recall, the reason this crate was restrictive was because we could not pass a crate of oranges to a function that required a crate of fruit. We worked around this by creating a new class, `CovariantCrate`, which marked `T` as covariant, and removed the `add` function because it used `T` as an input parameter type.

This was fine because we were the authors of the `Crate` class and so could adapt it to our will. If, however, the class was coming from some library, we wouldn't be able to redefine it. Our options are to create a new class and copy the elements, or to use a type projection.

A type projection allows us to restrict the functions available on a type so that it fulfills the criteria necessary to be considered covariant or contravariant. If we could inform the compiler that we have no desire to call `add` on the `Crate` type, then there is no reason why we couldn't use it in a covariant way.

To do this, we use the `out` and `in` keywords when we define the function that is going to accept the parameterized type. For example, to create a function that accepts a `Crate` projected as covariant, we could define the following:

```
fun isSafe(crate: Crate<out Fruit>): Boolean = crate.elements.all{
  it.isSafeToEat()
}
```

This can now be invoked with our original invariant `crate` type:

```
val oranges = Crate(mutableListOf(Orange(), Orange()))
isSafe(oranges)
```

If you recall, the last line failed originally, before we knew about type projections.

The same trick works for contravariant projections too. If we use the event stream example from earlier, we could have used an invariant listener by adapting the `EventSteam` class to project the `Listener` type:

```
interface Listener<T> {
  fun onNext(t: T): Unit
}

class EventStream<in T>(val listener: Listener<in T>) {
```

```
        fun start(): Unit = TODO()
        fun stop(): Unit = TODO()
    }
```

Note the `in` keyword added to the `listener` parameter in the constructor.

When using a type projection, the compiler restricts us to only invoking functions where the type parameter is in the allowed position. So, if we project as covariant, we can only invoke functions that return `T` (or don't use `T` at all), and if we project as contravariant, we can only invoke functions that accept `T` (or again don't use `T`).

Type erasure

Kotlin is designed primarily as a language for the **Java Virtual Machine (JVM)**, and when the JVM was first designed, generics were not included as a feature. Over time it became apparent that this was a major flaw of the language, and so in Java 1.5 (or Java SDK 5), released in 2004, generics were added as a feature to the compiler.

However, because of a desire to stay backwards compatible with previous versions of Java, the designers of Java decided that generics would be implemented using a technique called **erasure**. Erasure is the name given to the process by which the compiler removes type parameters during compilation.

In Java, a class defined as `List<T>` in the source code would be compiled simply as `List`, or `List<Object>`, if you like. This poses problems, some of which have already been introduced:

- Functions with the same names and same erased parameters will clash. The `fun print(list: List<String>)` and `fun print(list: List<Int>)` will have the same function signature after erasure.
- At runtime, it is not possible to see what type parameters were used when instantiating an object.
- You cannot test whether an instance is of type `T`.
- You cannot test whether an instance is of a parameterized type.
- The class `literal` cannot be accessed for `T`.
- The classes that use a type parameter have the type parameter replaced with an object or the upper bound.

Since Kotlin targets the JVM, Kotlin is also restricted by these issues. We can see this from looking at the bytecode when creating two functions, each accepting a different type of `List`, but otherwise identical:

```
fun printInts(list: Set<Int>): Unit {
  for (int in list) println(string)
}

fun printStrings(list: Set<String>): Unit {
  for (string in list) println(string)
}
```

The bytecode generated for the first function is as follows:

```
0: aload_0
1: ldc           #9                   //String list
3: invokestatic  #15
6: aload_0
7: invokeinterface #21,  1          //InterfaceMethod
java/util/Set.iterator:()Ljava/util/Iterator;
12: astore_2
13: aload_2
14: invokeinterface #27,  1          //InterfaceMethod
java/util/Iterator.hasNext:()Z
19: ifeq           46
22: aload_2
23: invokeinterface #31,  1           //InterfaceMethod
java/util/Iterator.next:()Ljava/lang/Object;
28: checkcast      #33                 //class java/lang/Number
31: invokevirtual #37                  //Method
java/lang/Number.intValue:()I
34: istore_1
35: nop
36: getstatic      #43             //Field
java/lang/System.out:Ljava/io/PrintStream;
39: iload_1
40: invokevirtual #49     //Method java/io/PrintStream.println:(I)V
43: goto           13
46: return
```

Here is the almost identical bytecode for the second function:

```
0: aload_0
1: ldc           #9                   //String list
3: invokestatic  #15
6: aload_0
7: invokeinterface #21,  1           //InterfaceMethod
java/util/Set.iterator:()Ljava/util/Iterator;
```

```
12: astore_2
13: aload_2
14: invokeinterface #27,  1          //InterfaceMethod
java/util/Iterator.hasNext:()Z
19: ifeq          43
22: aload_2
23: invokeinterface #31,  1          //InterfaceMethod
java/util/Iterator.next:()Ljava/lang/Object;
28: checkcast     #55                //class java/lang/String
31: astore_1
32: nop
33: getstatic     #43    //Field
java/lang/System.out:Ljava/io/PrintStream;
36: aload_1
37: invokevirtual #58      //Method
java/io/PrintStream.println:(Ljava/lang/Object;)V
40: goto          13
43: return
```

Note that the opcodes emitted by the compiler are identical, except for instruction 28, which is the cast operation. The compiler is inserting a cast from the runtime type of object down to the compile time type. The only difference is the type in the cast, which is stored in the constant pool and referenced by the number after the cast op.

The generated bytecode is equivalent to the following source code:

```
fun printInts(list: Set<Any>): Unit {
  for (obj in list) {
    println(obj as Int)
  }
}

fun printStrings(list: Set<Any>): Unit {
  for (obj in list) {
    println(obj as String)
  }
}
```

Functions are not the only issue. If we have a class that uses a type parameter in function signatures, then that type parameter will be replaced with either `java.lang.Object`, or the upper bound if the type parameter is bounded. Take the following function as an example:

```
fun <T : Comparable<T>>max(list: List<T>): T {
  var max = list.first()
  for (t in list) {
    if (t >max)
```

```
        max = t
    }
    return max
}
```

When viewing the bytecode, you will notice that the function body must cast the elements of the list:

```
0: aload_0
1: ldc              #9                    //String list
3: invokestatic  #15                           6: aload_0
7: invokestatic  #68
10: checkcast      #70                  //class java/lang/Comparable
13: astore_1
14: aload_0
15: invokeinterface #73,  1           //InterfaceMethod
java/util/List.iterator:()Ljava/util/Iterator;
20: astore_3
21: aload_3
22: invokeinterface #27,  1           //InterfaceMethod
java/util/Iterator.hasNext:()Z
27: ifeq            56
30: aload_3
31: invokeinterface #31,  1             //InterfaceMethod
java/util/Iterator.next:()Ljava/lang/Object;
36: checkcast      #70                //class java/lang/Comparable
39: astore_2
40: aload_2
41: aload_1
42: invokeinterface #77,  2
47: iconst_0
48: if_icmple      53
51: aload_2
52: astore_1
53: goto            21
56: aload_1
57: areturn
```

There are a couple of ways of working around some of these issues. Firstly, as covered in the chapter on annotations, we can mark functions that have the same erased signature with a different name when compiled. Remember that we do this by using the `@JvmName` annotation.

The other approach is a limited form of reification.

Type reification

A reifiable type is the name given to a type when its type information can be inspected at runtime. Examples of types that are considered reified are non-generic types, such as `String` or `BigDecimal`. On the JVM, primitives such as boolean or double are also considered to be reified.

A non-reifiable type is one that has suffered the effect of type erasure so that some, or all, of its type information has been lost at runtime. Examples of this are parameterized types, such as `List<String>` and `List<Boolean>`, which look the same at runtime.

We've seen how erasure removes types at runtime and the issues this can cause. Now we will look at a way that we can work around some of those issues. Kotlin has introduced a feature called **type reification** that enables type information to be kept at runtime for inline functions.

To use this feature, we add the keyword `reified` before the type parameter, as shown in the following snippet. Then we are able to perform operations on `T`:

```
inline fun <reified T>runtimeType(): Unit {
  println("My type parameter is " + T::class.qualifiedName)
}
```

Note how we are able to get the runtime type of `T` as a `KClass`. We can also use `T` for type checking:

```
inline fun <reified T>List<Any>.collect(): List<T> {
  return this.filter { it is T }.map { it as T }
}
```

In that example, we filter out elements of a `List`, only returning those that match the type parameter. We do this by checking each element to see if it is an instance of `T`. We could only do this if we had access to the type parameter at runtime because it is impossible to know in advance what elements the `List` might contain.

We could use it in the following way:

```
val list = listOf("green", false, 100, "blue")
val strings = list.collect<String>()
```

So how does Kotlin perform this trick? The answer lies in the fact that reified functions must be defined as `inline`. In all places that the function is invoked, the body will be copied into the call site. Since at the call site the compiler knows the type parameter used, it is able to replace references to `T` with references to the proper type.

We can see this by examining the bytecode for a reified function. Let's define a shorter example, so we have less bytecode to look through:

```
inline fun <reified T>printT(any: Any): Unit {
  if (any is T)
  println("I am a tee: $any")
}
```

This function simply checks that the input parameter is of type `T` and, if so, prints it out. We will invoke it with the following code:

```
printT<Int>(123)
```

The generated bytecode looks like the following:

```
0: aload_0
1: ldc              #159                    //String args
3: invokestatic     #163
6: bipush           123
8: invokestatic     #125                    //Method
java/lang/Integer.valueOf:(I)Ljava/lang/Integer;
11: astore_1
12: nop
13: aload_1
14: instanceof      #122                    //class java/lang/Integer
17: ifeq            48
20: new         #8                      //class java/lang/StringBuilder
23: dup
24: invokespecial #11   //Method java/lang/StringBuilder."<init>":()V
27: ldc             #150                    //String I am a tee:
29: invokevirtual #17
32: aload_1
33: invokevirtual #153
36: invokevirtual #40               //Method
java/lang/StringBuilder.toString:()Ljava/lang/String;
39: astore_2
40: nop
41: getstatic       #46         //Field
```

```
java/lang/System.out:Ljava/io/PrintStream;
44: aload_2
45: invokevirtual #52                //Method
java/io/PrintStream.println:(Ljava/lang/Object;)V
48: return
```

Instruction `14` is the important point here. That is the line where the compiler has inserted a check for the reified type parameter. `#122` refers to `java.lang.Integer` in the constant pool, which was the proper type we had used when invoking the function.

Recursive type bounds

Recursive type bounds has a catchy name and sounds rather complicated, but it is actually intuitive once explained. It is an extension of bounded polymorphism, and describes a type that includes one or more type parameters, where at least one of the type parameters uses the type itself.

All will become clearer with an example. Let's say we are writing an API for accounts in a financial system. We want to define an `Account` object, and we want to be able to sort all types of account, but with the restriction that we only want to be able to sort accounts of the same type. The first step is defining the interface for our accounts, and a couple of concrete implementations:

```
interface Account {
  val balance: BigDecimal
}

data class SavingsAccount(override val balance: BigDecimal,val
interestRate: BigDecimal) : Account,  Comparable<SavingsAccount> {
  override fun compareTo(other: SavingsAccount): Int =
  balance.compareTo(other.balance)
}

data class TradingAccount(override val balance: BigDecimal, val
margin: Boolean) : Account, Comparable<TradingAccount> {
  override fun compareTo(other: TradingAccount): Int =
  balance.compareTo(other.balance)
}
```

There is nothing new in the preceding code. Both implementations extend the `Account` interface, and both extend `Comparable` so they can be used by the standard library sorting functions. For instance, we can now compare a savings account to another, and similarly for a tradings account:

```
val savings1 = SavingsAccount(BigDecimal(105), BigDecimal(0.04))
val savings2 = SavingsAccount(BigDecimal(396), BigDecimal(0.05))
savings1.compareTo(savings2)

val trading1 = TradingAccount(BigDecimal(211), true)
val trading2 = TradingAccount(BigDecimal(853), false)
trading1.compareTo(trading2)
```

Even better, the following would fail to compile:

```
savings.compareTo(trading) compile error
```

This is what we want, in this case. Part of our original brief was to only allow sorting between accounts of the same type.

Note that we are duplicating code in the `compareTo` functions. In fact, they are identical. As they stand, they are fairly simple, so this isn't too much of a problem, but in a real system they might stretch over many lines. Can we improve this by bringing the `compareTo` function into the interface?

```
interface Account2 : Comparable<Account2> {
  val balance: BigDecimal
  override fun compareTo(other: Account2): Int =
  balance.compareTo(other.balance)
}

class SavingsAccount2(override val balance: BigDecimal) : Account2

class TradingAccount2(override val balance: BigDecimal) : Account2
```

However, the issue has now become that we can compare instance of `Account2` to any other instance. For example, the following code compiles fine:

```
val savings = SavingsAccount2(BigDecimal(105), BigDecimal(0.04))
val trading = TradingAccount2(BigDecimal(210), true)
savings.compareTo(trading)
```

Now, this could cause issues if we don't want to be able to compare different types of accounts. This is a side effect of the fact that we have defined `Account` to implement `Comparable<Account>`. How can we share the implementation of `compareTo`, but at the same time avoid comparing different types? We might consider introducing a type parameter, and using that in the `extends` clause for `Comparable`:

```
interface Account3<E> : Comparable<E> {
  val balance: BigDecimal
  override fun compareTo(other: E): Int =
  balance.compareTo(other.balance)
}

data class SavingsAccount3(override val balance: BigDecimal, val
interestRate: BigDecimal) : Account3<SavingsAccount3>
data class TradingAccount3(override val balance: BigDecimal, val
margin: Boolean) : Account3<TradingAccount3>
```

At a glance, this looks perfect. Each concrete type will only be comparable with itself, and the logic has been kept in the interface. However, there is an issue in that the compiler does not recognize `other.balance` in the comparison code.

Since `Account3` defines its type parameter with no bound, we could create an account that uses `String`, `Foo`, or anything we liked. And since the property `balance` is not defined on `String` or `Foo`, the compiler is right to throw an error when we try to access it.

So how can we keep the good progress and make this work? The answer is to introduce an upper bound on the type parameter for `Account` so that when we create an instance of `Account` the `Comparable` interface is passed our type as that contains the `balance` property. We can do this by using what is known as a **recursive type bound**:

```
interface Account4<E : Account4<E>> : Comparable<E> {
  val balance: BigDecimal
  override fun compareTo(other: E): Int =
  balance.compareTo(other.balance)
}

data class SavingsAccount4(override val balance: BigDecimal, val
interestRate: BigDecimal) : Account4<SavingsAccount4>

data class TradingAccount4(override val balance: BigDecimal, val
margin: Boolean) : Account4<TradingAccount4>
```

Note how `E` is now declared as extending `Account<E>`. This gives us the shared `compareTo` code, and allows accounts to only be compared with themselves:

```
val savings1 = SavingsAccount4(BigDecimal(105), BigDecimal(0.04))
```

```
val savings2 = SavingsAccount4(BigDecimal(396), BigDecimal(0.05))
savings1.compareTo(savings2)

val trading1 = TradingAccount4(BigDecimal(211), true)
val trading2 = TradingAccount4(BigDecimal(853), false)
trading1.compareTo(trading2)
```

And, as per our original design, we are back to having a compile error if we try the following:

```
savings.compareTo(trading) compile error
```

There is a final flaw, in that we cannot stop accounts being defined with a type parameter of another account, for example, `class BettingAccount : Account<ShareAccount>`. This is a restriction that Java also shares.

Algebraic data types

Algebraic data types is another of those functional programming concepts that sounds complicated when you first stumble across it, but, after seeing an example or two, the mystery disappears. The term itself refers to the fact that algebra is defined as a set of *things* and the *operations* that are allowed to be performed on those things. For example, in mathematics the + operator is defined on integers to return the sum, and thus is an algebraic concept.

Therefore, an algebra for a type defines operations or functions on that type, hence the term algebraic data type. In computing languages, the term is generally applied to a closed set of composite types where those types implement the required functions. In Kotlin, we achieve the closed property by using the keyword `sealed`, which restricts the allowed types to only those defined in the same file.

Algebraic data types should not be confused with the similarly named abstract data types. Despite sharing the same acronym, these are distinct concepts.

Let's move on from these abstract descriptions to a concrete example; we will use the very common example of a linked list. The general structure of a linked list is that each element in the list is held in a *node*, and each node contains a link to the next node. A link to the initial node allows us to navigate the entire list by iterating over the links.

We can start by defining a sealed class that will contain our operations. Note that `sealed` cannot be used on an interface:

```
sealed class List<out T>
```

Next, we will define two implementations. The first will represent a node that contains a value, and the second will represent an empty node:

```
class Node<T>(val value: T, val next: List<T>) : List<T>()
object Empty : List<Nothing>()
```

A list can be thought of as a sequence of nodes that always terminate with an empty node. Therefore, an empty list is nothing more than just the empty node itself. The data nodes have two properties, one for the value they contain and one to point to the next element in the list.

For example, a list of two elements would look like this:

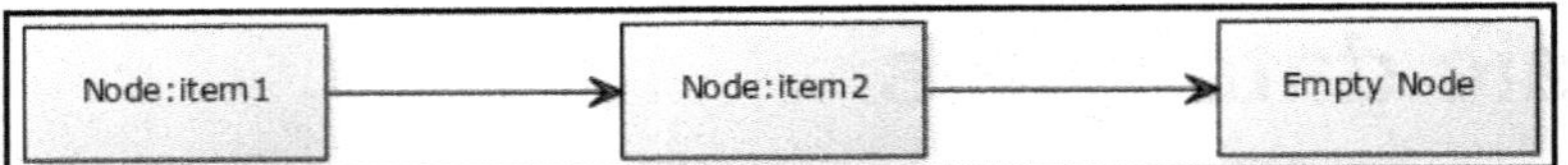

Note that the empty node is actually defined as an object. This is because it has no state, and so we don't need more than a single instance of it. Since we are using a single empty node, we must fix the type parameter with `Nothing` for the reasons described in the section on the `Nothing` type.

Let's begin to fill in the functions that a typical list would require. We can start with the easiest: Is the list empty or not?

```
sealed class List<out T> {
  fun isEmpty() = when (this) {
    is Node -> false
    is Empty -> true
  }
}
```

Note that we are just type checking, and, depending on what type our list is, we know if the list is empty or not. We don't even need to look at any of the properties.

This is also where the `sealed` keyword comes into play. When a class is `sealed`, the compiler knows that all implementations must live in the same file, and so knows the full set of concrete types. Therefore, when a `sealed` class is used in a `when` expression, the compiler is able to emit an error if we do not cover all cases. If, for example, we had an algebraic data type that consisted of six types, and we only covered five in the `when` expression, we would need to either add the final type or add an `else` clause.

Next up is adding a `size()` function. We'll define this recursively, which, in the real world, wouldn't be efficient, but we're demonstrating the concept of algebraic data types and not efficiency:

```
fun size(): Int= when (this) {
  is Node -> 1 + this.next.size()
  is Empty -> 0
}
```

Similar to the `isEmpty` function, we type check, that if the node is empty we return zero. Otherwise, we just add one to the size of the tail.

Many functions are similar in implementation. For example, the `head` function, which returns the first element of the list, looks like this:

```
fun head(): T = when (this) {
  is Node<T> -> this.value
  is Empty -> throw RuntimeException("Empty list")
}
```

The empty node has no element, and so must throw an exception (or we could define the function to be nullable). A data node would just return its value; notice the smart cast in operation on the right-hand side to access the `value` property. Other data access functions follow along the same lines.

An interesting function is `append`. When we append to a list, we are creating a new list, with the element added to the end in a new node. To do this, we would define a function which accepts an element `T`, and returns `List<T>`. However, the type parameter on `List` is defined as covariant, which, if you recall, means we cannot use `T` as an input parameter.

In some other languages, the solution is to introduce a new type parameter, `U`, and then use that as the return type of the new list. To do this, we would require that `U` is a supertype of `T` so that all the existing elements are compatible with the new list. For example, if we had a list of integers, we could append a double to then have a list of numbers.

Unfortunately, Kotlin doesn't support the functionality to say that `U` must be a supertype of `T`. This would be an example of a lower bound, and only upper bounds are supported at the time of writing. However, we can work around this in a couple of ways.

Firstly, we can allow `T` as in input parameter even though we told the compiler earlier that it shouldn't allow it, by overriding the variance checks for this function:

```
fun append(t: @UnsafeVariance T): List<T> = when (this) {
  is Node<T> -> Node(this.value, this.next.append(t))
  is Empty -> Node(t, Empty)
}
```

Note the annotation, `UnsafeVariance`, which disables the compiler error. In this example, we know this will be okay because our `List` implementation is immutable. As such, we can't cause errors by adding invalid values to an existing list.

The other alternative is to declare `append` as an extension function, whereby the type parameter is invariant:

```
fun <T>List<T>.append(t: T): List<T> = when (this) {
  is Node<T> -> Node(this.value, this.next.append(t))
  is Empty -> Node(t, Empty)
}
```

We can wrap up our example by making the concrete types private. There is no reason for those to be exposed, and we can add a companion object method so that instances of `List` can be created directly through the `List` type itself. The final listing looks like the following:

```
sealed class List<out T> {

  fun isEmpty() = when (this) {
    is Empty -> true
    is Node -> false
  }

  fun size(): Int= when (this) {
    is Empty -> 0
    is Node -> 1 + this.next.size()
  }

  fun tail(): List<T> = when (this) {
    is Node -> this.next
    is Empty -> this
  }
```

```
    fun head(): T = when (this) {
      is Node<T> ->this.value
      is Empty -> throw RuntimeException("Empty list")
    }

    operator fun get(pos: Int): T {
      require(pos>= 0, { "Position must be >=0" })
      return when (this) {
        is Node<T> -> if (pos == 0) head() else this.next.get(pos - 1)
        is Empty -> throw IndexOutOfBoundsException()
      }
    }

    fun append(t: @UnsafeVarianceT): List<T> = when (this) {
      is Node<T> -> Node(this.value, this.next.append(t))
      is Empty -> Node(t, Empty)
    }

    companion object {
      operator fun <T>invoke(vararg values: T): List<T> {
        var temp: List<T> = Empty
        for (value in values) {
          temp = temp.append(value)
        }
        return temp
      }
    }
  }

  private class Node<out T>(val value: T, val next: List<T>) :  List<T>()
  private object Empty : List<Nothing>()
```

Examples of using this `List` are as follows:

```
  val list = List("this").append("is").append("my").append("list")

  println(list.size()) // prints 4
  println(list.head()) // prints "this"
  println(list[1]) // prints "is"
  println(list.drop(2).head()) // prints "my"
```

Algebraic data types are very common in functional programming, and can be used for all manner of abstractions. Data structures, such as trees, in addition to monads, such as `Either`, `Try`, and `Option`, are often implemented in this manner. In fact, any type that lends itself to a union or product type is often conveniently implemented using this approach.

Summary

This chapter has shown how the power of the advanced Kotlin type system can be used to improve the robustness of our code, and increase re-usability of generic functions. The type system is one of the biggest improvements over Java that Kotlin offers. In later chapters the examples will use type parameterization in the real world, showing how useful it really can be.

9
Data Classes

We came across the term data class in `Chapter 3`, *Object Oriented Programming in Kotlin;* however, we didn't go into much detail of what it could bring to the table. This chapter will cover the process of annotating classes, which will allow you to have boilerplate-free code. We will dig deep to see what the compiler does for us behind the scenes when we use a data class. In this chapter, you will learn:

- What destructuring is and how data classes are automatically eligible for destructuring operations
- How you get copy, toString, hashCode, and equals methods implemented for you
- Rules to obey when defining data classes
- Limitations of data classes

Data classes are intended for types that are meant to be data containers and nothing more. Code readability is important to me and most likely to anyone who reads this book. When you open a source file, you would really want to be able to quickly grasp what the code does. When it comes to a **POJO** (**Plain Old Java Object**), I am sure you would very much like to avoid having to write the code for setters and getters if all they do is return a value. Furthermore, the constructor's code body is bold in almost every case; it just takes the incoming parameters and assigns them to the concerned fields after it performs any validation that is required. This is where data classes could help you. If you have coded in Scala, you will already be accustomed with the case class construct, and I am pretty sure the idea of even having to press a shortcut key to let IntelliJ build your getter and setter might be far from ideal.

A modern compiler should take the burden of boilerplate code away from you. Why Java hasn't supported this until now is still an enigma. This can be achieved quite easily with the addition of an annotation, which can be picked up by the compiler, thus not breaking any existing code. The sad thing is that such a functionality is not even on the horizon. But luckily, we have Kotlin!

Imagine we have the following class in Java to represent a blog entry:

```
public class BlogEntryJ {
  private final String title;
  private final String description;
  private final DateTime publishTime;
  private final Boolean approved;
  private final DateTime lastUpdated;
  private final URI url;
  private final Integer comments;
  private final List<String> tags;
  private final String email;

  public BlogEntryJ(String title, String description, DateTime
publishTime, Boolean approved, DateTime lastUpdated, URI url,  Integer
comments, List<String> tags, String email) {
    this.title = title;
    this.description = description;
    this.publishTime = publishTime;
    this.approved = approved;
    this.lastUpdated = lastUpdated;
    this.url = url;
    this.commentCount = commentCount;
    this.tags = tags;
    this.email = email;
  }

  public String getTitle() {
    return title;
  }

  public String getDescription() {
    return description;
  }
}
```

Most of the getters have been left out for the sake of simplicity. In this example, all the fields have been made read only. If you wish to have a mutable data structure, you would need to add setters (you would have to return a copy of the `tags` field to maintain immutability; otherwise, the caller would be able to add/remove items, thus breaking your encapsulation). Let's discuss how you can achieve this, and more as you will see later, in Kotlin. For the code in Kotlin, I have chosen to make some of the fields writable in order to discuss the setters code as well. In the following code snippet, you will notice that a writable field is marked as `var`, whereas a read-only field is marked as val. It would be nice if the compiler would default to val, the Scala compiler already does this for the case classes:

```
data class BlogEntry(var title: String, var description: String,  val
```

```
publishTime: DateTime,val approved: Boolean?, val lastUpdated:  DateTime,
val url: URI, val commentCount: Int?, val topTags:  List<String>, val
email: String?)

    val blogEntry = BlogEntry("Data Classes are here", "Because Kotlin
rulz!", DateTime.now(), true, DateTime.now(),
URI("http://packt.com/blog/programming_kotlin/data_classes"), 0,
emptyList(), null)
```

There is no comparison between the two; the Kotlin approach is a lot cleaner since all of the boilerplate code is removed.

You might think, for now, you just got a few keystrokes saved. But there is a lot more happening behind the scenes, which I am sure you will end up appreciating. To see all of the work the Kotlin compiler has actually done for us, we need to look at the bytecode generated.

Automatic creation of getters and setters

For a given `var` declaration in the constructor, the compiler will create the getters and setters automatically. Considering the title field, the compiler has actually created a `getTitle` and `setTitle` method. This means interacting with Java would now translate to calling these two methods:

```
public final java.lang.String getTitle();
  Code:
    0: aload_0
    1: getfield      #11                 // Field title:Ljava/lang/String;
    4: areturn
public final void setTitle(java.lang.String);
  Code:
    0: aload_1
    1: ldc           #17                 // String <set-?>
    3: invokestatic  #23                 // Method
kotlin/jvm/internal/Intrinsics.checkParameterIsNotNull:(Ljava/lang/Object;L
java/lang/String;)V
    6: aload_0
    7: aload_1
    8: putfield      #11                 // Field title:Ljava/lang/String;
    11: return
```

The code is pretty straightforward. In the setter code body, see line 3, we have an implicit check for null values via the standard library method, `checkParameterIsNotNull`. In Kotlin, the type system distinguishes between references that can hold null values and those that cannot. In the case of title, the type definition indicates it doesn't allow any null value. In contrast to this, the email field allows null values, and this is reflected in the code generated for it:

```
public final void setEmail(java.lang.String);
  Code:
    0: aload_0
    1: aload_1
    2: putfield      #72                 // Field email:Ljava/lang/String;
    5: return
```

As you can see, the implicit check for null is omitted in this case.

If you declare your field as val, the compiler will generate only the getter method for you. This is the case with the `lastUpdated` field. I won't go through the bytecode generated for it since it is similar to the one for the `title` field.

The copy method

When using a data class, you get a `copy` method out of the box. This method allows you to create a new instance of your type while cherry-picking the fields you want to change. For example, you may decide that you want to get a new `BlogEntry` instance from an existing instance of which you just want to change the title and description `fields`:

```
    blogEntry.copy(title = "Properties in Kotlin", description =
"Properties are awesome in Kotlin")
```

If you are familiar with Java, you will notice a similarity with the clone method. However, the copy method is more powerful; it allows you to change any of the fields in your new copied instance.

If you look at the parameter information of the copy method (*CTRL+ P* is the default keyboard shortcut), you should see the following:

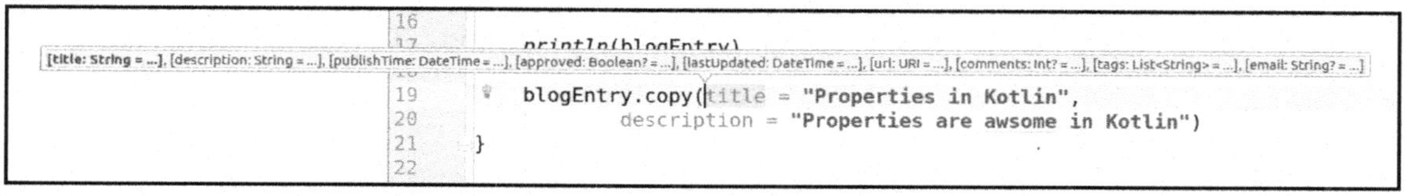

```
[title: String = ...], [description: String = ...], [publishTime: DateTime = ...], [approved: Boolean? = ...], [lastUpdated: DateTime = ...], [url: URI = ...], [comments: Int? = ...], [tags: List<String> = ...], [email: String? = ...]

        println(blogEntry)

        blogEntry.copy(title = "Properties in Kotlin",
                description = "Properties are awsome in Kotlin")
}
```

Copy method parameters

In the screenshot, you can see that each field is contained within `[]`, thus marking it optional. To make this work, the compiler generates two methods for us. Here is the byte-level code snippet (once again, some of the code has been left out for clarity):

```
public final com.programming.kotlin.chapter09.BlogEntry
copy(java.lang.String, java.lang.String, org.joda.time.DateTime,
java.lang.Boolean, org.joda.time.DateTime, java.net.URI,
java.lang.Integer, java.util.List<java.lang.String>,  java.lang.String);
  Code:
    0: aload_1
    1: ldc           #76                 // String title
    3: invokestatic  #23                 // Method
kotlin/jvm/internal/Intrinsics.checkParameterIsNotNull:(Ljava/lang/Ob
ject;Ljava/lang/String;)V
     34: ldc           #81                 // String tags
     36: invokestatic  #23                 // Method
kotlin/jvm/internal/Intrinsics.checkParameterIsNotNull:(Ljava/lang/Ob
ject;Ljava/lang/String;)V
     39: new           #2          // class
com/programming/kotlin/chapter09/BlogEntry
     42: dup
     43: aload_1
     44: aload_2
     45: aload_3
     46: aload         4
     48: aload         5
     50: aload         6
     52: aload         7
     54: aload         8
     56: aload         9
     58: invokespecial #97                 // Method
"<init>":(Ljava/lang/String;Ljava/lang/String;Lorg/joda/time/DateTime
;Ljava/lang/Boolean;Lorg/joda/time/DateTime;Ljava/net/URI;Ljava/lang/
Integer;Ljava/util/List;Ljava/lang/String;)V
     61: areturn
```

```
public static com.programming.kotlin.chapter09.BlogEntry
 copy$default(com.programming.kotlin.chapter09.BlogEntry,
java.lang.String, java.lang.String, org.joda.time.DateTime,
java.lang.Boolean, org.joda.time.DateTime, java.net.URI,
java.lang.Integer, java.util.List, java.lang.String, int,
java.lang.Object);
  Code:
    0: aload         11
    2: ifnull        15
    5: new           #101        // class
java/lang/UnsupportedOperationException
    8: dup
    9: ldc           #103       // String Super calls with  default
arguments not supported in this target, function: copy
    11: invokespecial #105             // Method
java/lang/UnsupportedOperationException."<init>":(Ljava/lang/String;) V
    14: athrow
    15: aload_0
    16: iload         10
    18: iconst_1
    19: iand
    20: ifeq          28
    23: aload_0
    24: getfield      #11                      // Field
title:Ljava/lang/String;
    27: astore_1
    28: aload_1
    29: iload         10
    31: iconst_2
    32: iand
    33: ifeq          41
    36: aload_0
    37: getfield      #27                      // Field
description:Ljava/lang/String;
    40: astore_2
    41: aload_2
    42: iload         10
    44: iconst_4
    45: iand
    46: ifeq          54
    145: aload_0
    146: getfield      #72                      // Field
email:Ljava/lang/String;
    149: astore        9
    151: aload         9
    153: invokevirtual #107                     // Method
copy:(Ljava/lang/String;Ljava/lang/String;Lorg/joda/time/DateTime;Lja
va/lang/Boolean;Lorg/joda/time/DateTime;Ljava/net/URI;Ljava/lang/Inte
```

```
ger;Ljava/util/List;Ljava/lang/String;)Lcom/programming/kotlin/chapte
r09/BlogEntry;
     156: areturn
```

The first method generated is an instance method; it takes a list of parameters that represent all the fields declared for the data class. After all the parameters null checks, the code at line 58 calls the constructor for `BlogEntry:58: invokespecial #97 // Method "<init>":(Ljava/lang/....` The curious part is the presence of the second method, `copy$default;` this method is static and takes an instance of `BlogEntry` as the first parameter, followed by a parameter for each field that is defined. The interesting part comes next. Let's consider the title field. You are not expected to know the bytecode at this level, but you might work out what is happening. The key lies in these two lines: `18: iconst_1` and `20: ifeq 28`. Here's the code snippet for this:

```
15: aload_0
16: iload          10
18: iconst_1
19: iand
20: ifeq           28
23: aload_0
24: getfield       #11                  // Field title:Ljava/lang/String;
27: astore_1
28: aload_1
```

Let me translate what happens. If the parameter title is equal to a constant value, then it will go and retrieve the value for the title from the instance; see line `24: getfield #11`. Otherwise, it uses the value passed to the copy method. You might wonder, like I did, where are these constants coming from? The hint lies in `iconst_1`, `iconst_2`, and so on. Let's look at the code generated when we call the copy function. This will help us answer the question. Here is the Kotlin code used:

```
    fun main(args: Array<String>) {
      val blogEntry = BlogEntry("Data Classes are here","Because  Kotlin
rulz!", DateTime.now(),true, DateTime.now(),
URI("http://packt.com/blog/programming_kotlin/data_classes"),0,
emptyList(),"")
      println(blogEntry)
      blogEntry.copy(title = "Properties in Kotlin",
      description = "Properties are awesome in Kotlin",
      approved = true,
      tags = listOf("tag1"))
    }
```

This is the bytecode generated for the last method call:

```
69: ldc #76 // String Properties in Kotlin
71: ldc #78 // String Properties are awesome in Kotlin
73: aconst_null
74: iconst_1
75: invokestatic #38 // Method
java/lang/Boolean.valueOf:(Z)Ljava/lang/Boolean;
78: aconst_null
79: aconst_null
80: aconst_null
81: ldc #80 // String tag1
83: invokestatic #84 // Method
kotlin/collections/CollectionsKt.listOf:(Ljava/lang/Object;)Ljava/util/List
;
86: aconst_null
87: sipush 372
90: aconst_null
91: invokestatic  #88                    // Method
com/programming/kotlin/chapter09/BlogEntry.copy$default:(Lcom/programming/k
otlin/chapter09/BlogEntry;Ljava/lang/String;Ljava/lang/String;Lorg/joda/tim
e/DateTime;Ljava/lang/Boolean;Lorg/joda/time/DateTime;Ljava/net/URI;Ljava/l
ang/Integer;Ljava/util/List;Ljava/lang/String;ILjava/lang/Object;)Lcom/prog
ramming/kotlin/chapter09/BlogEntry;
```

Starting at line 69, the code starts pushing the variables on the stack. It follows the order of the properties defined in the `data` class. For example, we overwrite `title` and `description` values and then we jump to the `approve` field. For all the non provided values we get a null via the `aconst_null` bytecode routine. Although you call the `copy` method on the object `blogEntry`, the bytecode actually calls the static copy$default method and not the instance method as one would have expected.

Since a static method has been defined in the `BlogEntry` class, you would expect this method to be available in the auto-completion dropdown. This is not the case, however. This method doesn't even exist.

You might wonder whether you can achieve the same while calling the `copy` method from a piece of Java code. Well, I will have to disappoint you. In this case, the call to the copy method will end up calling the instance method and not the static one. This means you won't get the benefit of overwriting a subset of the instance fields.

From within the Java source code, ask IntelliJ to display the parameter information. You should get the following result:

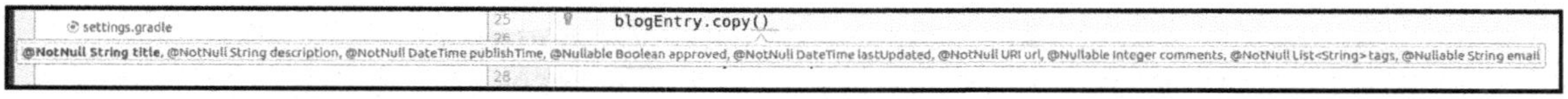

```
settings.gradle        25        blogEntry.copy()
@NotNull String title, @NotNull String description, @NotNull DateTime publishTime, @Nullable Boolean approved, @NotNull DateTime lastUpdated, @NotNull URI url, @Nullable Integer comments, @NotNull List<String> tags, @Nullable String email
                       28
```

Calling the copy method from Java

You will have to provide all the parameters when you call this function, and they must be non-null. Here is how the code will look:

```
    blogEntry.copy("Properties in Kotlin","Properties are awesome in
Kotlin", blogEntry.getPublishTime(), blogEntry.getApproved(),
blogEntry.getLastUpdated(), blogEntry.getUrl(), blogEntry.getComments(),
blogEntry.getTags(), blogEntry.getEmail());
```

toString out of the box

When you define a new type, best practices dictate that you should provide an override for the `toString` method. This method should return a string describing the instance. Let's consider the `BlogEntry` class we defined at the beginning of this chapter. There is quite a bit of typing you will have to do to implement this method. But why do it when you can get it out of the box? Let the compiler do it for you. If you add or remove a new field, it will automatically update the code for you. The likelihood of you leaving out the change to the `toString` code body when a field is added/renamed/removed is quite high:

```
public java.lang.String toString();
  Code:
    0: new             #122                  // class  java/lang/StringBuilder
    3: dup
    4: invokespecial #123                  // Method
java/lang/StringBuilder."<init>":()V
    7: ldc             #125                  // String BlogEntry(title=
    9: invokevirtual #129                  // Method
java/lang/StringBuilder.append:(Ljava/lang/String;)Ljava/lang/StringB
uilder;
    12: aload_0
    13: getfield      #11                   // Field
title:Ljava/lang/String;
    16: invokevirtual #129                 // Method
java/lang/StringBuilder.append:(Ljava/lang/String;)Ljava/lang/StringB
uilder;
    108: aload_0
    109: getfield      #72                  // Field
```

```
email:Ljava/lang/String;
    112: invokevirtual #129                  // Method
java/lang/StringBuilder.append:(Ljava/lang/String;)Ljava/lang/StringB
uilder;
    115: ldc           #150                  // String )
    117: invokevirtual #129                  // Method
java/lang/StringBuilder.append:(Ljava/lang/String;)Ljava/lang/StringB
uilder;
    120: invokevirtual #152        // Method
java/lang/StringBuilder.toString:()Ljava/lang/String;
    123: areturn
```

The code is quite simple to understand. It creates a new instance of the `StringBuilder` type, and for each field that is declared, it appends the text `FIELD=VALUE`. At the end of the function, it will return the value accumulated.

hashCode and equals methods generated for you

Every type is derived from `Any`, which comes with a `hashCode` method declaration. This is the equivalent of a Java Object class `hashCode` method. This method is important when you want to place your instances in collections, such as a map.

An object's hash code allows algorithms and data structures to place the instances in buckets. Imagine you implement a phone book. You'll place any name that starts with A in the A section, any name that starts with B in the B section, and so on. This simple approach allows you to have faster lookups when searching for someone. This is how hash-based collections, such as `HashMap` and `HashSet`, are implemented.

When implementing the method, you need to adhere to a contract:

1. When invoked on the same object more than once during the runtime, the `hashCode` method must consistently return the same value, given the object was not modified.
2. If for two objects the `equals` method returns true, then calling the `hashCode` method on each of them should return the same integer value.
3. If two objects are not equal – that means the `equals` method returns false for the pair-it is not a requirement to have each object `hashCode` method return distinct values. However, producing a distinct integer for unequal objects could improve the performance of hash-based collections.

The other method you would get out of the box is the equals method. This indicates whether the other object is structurally equal to the current one.

Of course, IntelliJ can generate the two methods mentioned. Leaving aside the wizard screen that asks you for the fields selection and which fields are non-null, why not have the compiler handle all of that for you out of the box. Again, this is the boilerplate code that you won't have to modify in most scenarios. Because the Kotlin-type system distinguishes between null and non-null types, we don't need to be prompted with a selection of non-null fields; the compiler has all of the information required.

Let's generate the methods for the Java class `BlogEntryJ`. In IntelliJ, choose **Code | Generate** and pick the `equals()` and `hashCode()` methods. The Java code generated for you would look something similar to this:

```
    @Override
    public boolean equals(Object o) {
      if (this == o)
        return true;
      if (o == null || getClass() != o.getClass())
        return false;

      BlogEntryJ that = (BlogEntryJ) o;
      if (!title.equals(that.title))
        return false;
      if (!description.equals(that.description))
        return false;
      if (!publishTime.equals(that.publishTime))
        return false;
      if (approved != null ? !approved.equals(that.approved) :
that.approved != null)
        return false;
      if (!lastUpdated.equals(that.lastUpdated))
        return false;
      if (!url.equals(that.url))
        return false;
      if (comments != null ? !comments.equals(that.comments) :
that.comments != null)
        return false;
      if (tags != null ? !tags.equals(that.tags) : that.tags != null)
        return false;
      return email != null ? email.equals(that.email) : that.email == null;
    }

    @Override
    public int hashCode() {
      int result = title.hashCode();
      result = 31 * result + description.hashCode();
```

```
        result = 31 * result + publishTime.hashCode();
        result = 31 * result + (approved != null ? approved.hashCode() : 0);
        result = 31 * result + lastUpdated.hashCode();
        result = 31 * result + url.hashCode();
        result = 31 * result + (comments != null ? comments.hashCode() : 0);
        result = 31 * result + (tags != null ? tags.hashCode() : 0);
        result = 31 * result + (email != null ? email.hashCode() : 0);
        return result;
    }
```

This is all good and very handy; however, in Kotlin's case, there are no clicks and no selection. Most important of all, you don't have to regenerate the two methods every time you change the type structure by either renaming the field or changing the type, or adding/removing a field entirely.

For the bytecode hungry reader, here is a trimmed-down version of the code generated. We will focus at the `hashCode` method only and will leave it up to you to go and look at equals in your own time. You will see it does the same code as the Java code earlier. See line 16 where the 31 prime number is going to be multiplied with the hashCode of the title retrieved at line 8. And then adds the hashCode value for the `description` field. This temporarily value is then multiplied by 31 and gets the `publishTime` hashCode added. And it goes like this until the `email` field. If a field is null, it will be left out; see, for example, line 164 where it jumps at line 173 in case `email` holds a null value:

```
public int hashCode();
  Code:
    0: aload_0
    1: getfield      #11                 // Field title:Ljava/lang/String;
    4: dup
    5: ifnull        14
    8: invokevirtual #156                // Method
java/lang/Object.hashCode:()I
    11: goto          16
    14: pop
    15: iconst_0
    16: bipush        31
    18: imul
    19: aload_0
    20: getfield      #27                 // Field
description:Ljava/lang/String;
    159: aload_0
    160: getfield      #72                 // Field
email:Ljava/lang/String;
    163: dup
    164: ifnull        173
    167: invokevirtual #156                // Method
```

```
java/lang/Object.hashCode:()I
    170: goto          175
    173: pop
    174: iconst_0
    175: iadd
    176: ireturn
```

Destructed declarations

If you create an instance of `BlogEntry` and then get the autocompletion dialog and navigate through the available methods, you will notice nine methods; these methods start with a series of components: `component1()`, `component2()`,... `component9()`. Each of these methods correspond to each of the fields defined by the type. Their return type will therefore match their respective field type. Here is the snippet for `component6()`, corresponding to the `url` field:

```
public final java.net.URI component6();
  Code:
    0: aload_0
    1: getfield      #51                 // Field url:Ljava/net/URI;
    4: areturn
```

The Scala developer reading this will most likely think of the Product class and pattern matching. Kotlin is not as powerful when it comes to pattern matching, but still gives you a flavor of it.

You might find it quite useful to break the object into a tuple of variables. Given the preceding instance of `blogEntry`, we can actually write the following:

```
    val (title, description, publishTime,approved, lastUpdated, url,
comments, tags, email) = blogEntry

    println("Here are the values for each
    field in the entry:
      title=$title description=$description publishTime=$publishTime
      approved=$approved lastUpdated=$lastUpdated, url=$url
comments=$comments tags=$tags email=$email")
```

If you run this code, you will get a nice printout of each field value. But how does it work? Yet again, the bytecode will provide the answer. Here is the code snippet for the first line in the previous code example:

```
61: astore        11
63: aload         11
```

```
65: invokevirtual #66                   // Method
com/programming/kotlin/chapter09/BlogEntry.component1:()Ljava/lang/St ring;
68: astore_2
69: aload         11
71: invokevirtual #69                   // Method
com/programming/kotlin/chapter09/BlogEntry.component2:()Ljava/lang/St ring;
74: astore_3
117: aload         11
119: invokevirtual #93                   // Method
com/programming/kotlin/chapter09/BlogEntry.component9:()Ljava/lang/St ring;
122: astore        10
124: aconst_null
```

All the compiler has done is translate that Kotlin code into calls to the *componentN* method. This approach will not work from Java source code; after all, it is nothing more than syntax sugar. Once again, the compiler does a lot of work for us.

Destructing types

With the data type, you get the destruction out of the box. But, can we achieve the same thing without a data class? The answer is yes. All you have to do is provide the componentN methods. The only requirement is to prefix each method definition with the keyword operator. Let's say we have a class `Vector3` that represents the coordinates in a 3D space. For the sake of an argument, we will not make this class a data class:

```
    class Vector3(val x:Double, val y:Double, val z:Double){
      operator fun component1()=x
      operator fun component2()=y
      operator funcomponent3()=z
    }

    for ((x,y,z) in listOf(Vector3(0.2,0.1,0.5), Vector3(-12.0, 3.145,
5.100))){
      println("Coordinates: x=$x, y=$y, z=$z")
    }
```

As you can see, for each member field, we created the equivalent *componentN* method. Because of this, the compiler can apply the destruction during a `for` loop construct.

What if you are dealing with a library for which you don't control the source code, but you would like to have the option of destructing the type? In this case too, you can provide componentN through extension methods. Let's say you are working on an Internet of Things app and you are using a library that gives you readings from your sensors. Here is the Java-defined class for your Sensor data:

```
public class Sensor {
  private final String id;
  private final double value;
  public Sensor(String id, double value) {
    this.id = id;this.value = value;
  }
  public String getId() {
    return id;
  }
  public double getValue() {
    return value;
  }
}
...
//Kotlin code
operator fun Sensor.component1()= this.id
operator fun Sensor.component2()=this.value

for((sensorId, value) in listOf(Sensor("DS18B20", 29.2),
Sensor("DS18B21", 32.1))){
  println("Sensor $sensorId reading is $value degrees Celsius")
}
```

If you run the code, you will get a nice text with the sensor reading. Pretty awesome! The code is quite easy to understand. The Java type has two fields exposed via the get methods. Using the Kotlin extension methods, we provide the equivalent componentN methods, thus allowing the compiler to call them during a for loop block.

Data class definition rules

If any of the methods that were just presented are present in your class already, the compiler won't overwrite them with its own version. You can, therefore, take full control if the requirements are as such. When you define a data class, you need to follow the following rules:

- The primary constructor needs to have at least one parameter
- All primary constructor parameters need to be marked as val or var

- Data classes cannot be abstract, open, sealed, or inner
- Data classes cannot extend other classes (but may implement interfaces)

Many Java frameworks require your class to provide a default parameter less constructor. Imagine you are writing an e-mail application and you model the `Email` type like this (is the way it is for the sake of simplicity):

```
data class Email(var to:String = "",
                 var subject:String= "",
                 var content:String= "")
```

The key to having the empty constructor option is to provide a default value for each parameter. Once you have this, you'd be able to write `Email email = new Email();` from Java.

If you look at the bytecode generated, you will notice three constructors were actually created:

```
public com.programming.kotlin.chapter09.Email(java.lang.String,
java.lang.String, java.lang.String);
  Code:
    0: aload_1
    1: ldc           #36                 // String to
    3: invokestatic  #23                 // Method
kotlin/jvm/internal/Intrinsics.checkParameterIsNotNull:(Ljava/lang/Ob
ject;Ljava/lang/String;)V
    6: aload_2
    7: ldc           #37                 // String subject
    9: invokestatic  #23                 // Method
kotlin/jvm/internal/Intrinsics.checkParameterIsNotNull:(Ljava/lang/Ob
ject;Ljava/lang/String;)V
    18: aload_0
    19: invokespecial #41                 // Method
java/lang/Object."<init>":()V
    22: aload_0
    23: aload_1
    24: putfield      #11                 // Field  to:Ljava/lang/String;
    34: putfield      #32                 // Field
content:Ljava/lang/String;
    37: return
public com.programming.kotlin.chapter09.Email(java.lang.String,
java.lang.String, java.lang.String, int,
kotlin.jvm.internal.DefaultConstructorMarker);
  Code:
    0: aload_0
    1: iload         4
    3: iconst_1
```

```
     4: iand
     5: ifeq          11
     8: ldc           #44                  // String
     10: astore_1
     11: aload_1
     12: iload         4
     14: iconst_2
     15: iand
     16: ifeq          22
     19: ldc           #44                  // String
     21: astore_2
     22: aload_2
     34: invokespecial #46                  // Method
"<init>":(Ljava/lang/String;Ljava/lang/String;Ljava/lang/String;)V
     37: return
public com.programming.kotlin.chapter09.Email();
  Code:
     0: aload_0
     1: aconst_null
     2: aconst_null
     3: aconst_null
     7: invokespecial #52                  // Method
"<init>":(Ljava/lang/String;Ljava/lang/String;Ljava/lang/String;ILkot
lin/jvm/internal/DefaultConstructorMarker;)V
     10: return
```

The logic behind this is similar to the `copy` method. If you provide a default value, the empty constructor will store three nulls. Then, the second constructor listed will compare with the stored nulls, and if it is the case, it will use the default value provided in the method declaration (see line `19: ldc #44 // String`).

The Kotlin standard library comes with two backed-in data classes, namely Pair and Triple:

```
    public data class Pair<out A, out B>(public val first: A,public  val
second: B) : Serializable
```

Here is how you would use these classes:

```
    val countriesAndCaptial = listOf( Pair("UK", "London"),  Pair("France",
"Paris"), Pair("Australia", "Canberra"))
    for ((country, capital) in countriesAndCaptial) {
      println("The capital of $country is $capital")
    }
    val colours = listOf( Triple("#ff0000", "rgb(255, 0, 0)", "hsl(0, 100%,
50%)"), Triple("#ff4000", "rgb(255, 64, 0)", "hsl(15, 100%, 50%)"))
    for((hex, rgb, hsl) in colours){
      println("hex=$hex; rgb=$rgb;hsl=$hsl")
    }
```

While they are present in the library, you should always favor building your own by providing proper naming for the classes, thus making the code more readable.

Limitations

For now, you cannot inherit another class when defining a data class. To avoid delaying the 1.0 release, the makers of Kotlin have decided to have this restriction to avoid the problems that would be caused by this. Imagine a data class, Derived, inherits from a data class, Base; if this happens, then these questions need to be answered:

1. Should an instance of Base be equal to an instance of Derived if they have the same values for all the shared fields?
2. What if I copy an instance of Derived through a reference of the type Base?

I am sure, in the future, all the limitations will be addressed and we would be able to write code similar to this (the Scala developer would be familiar with the construct of `Either`):

```
sealed abstract class Either<out L, out R> {
  data class Left<out L, out R>(val value: L) : Either<L, R>()
  data class Right<out L, out R>(val value: R) : Either<L, R>()
}
```

Summary

Kotlin is quite powerful, and the data classes are just proving that. You have learned how the language and the compiler work together to provide you with boilerplate-free constructs. We get to extend our keyboard's lifetime while focusing more on the problem to solve. You have also seen how destructing an object in a number of variables can prove to be quite handy, promoting code that is a lot more readable.

In the next chapter, we will cover the Kotlin extensions to the Java collections library. It introduces mutable versus immutable state, and why the latter can be useful. It shows the Kotlin additions, which make using collections easier than Java.

10
Collections

Most of us developers write a lot of code which ends up processing a collection of items, such as lists, maps, sets. Getting familiar with, and understanding the Kotlin standard library for collections is key to any aspiring Kotlin developer. If you have been working with Scala collections, you will find quite a few similarities. However, if your development background is Java only, you will find a new and improved way of dealing with your collections of objects, and will probably appreciate how easy it is to achieve a lot with very little code.

This chapter covers the Kotlin standard library for collections, and you will learn how it extends the Java collections library to make your daily coding a lot easier. It will present the two flavors of collections: mutable and immutable. You will learn how this is achieved, and how it works when interacting with Java code. The chapter will finish with an introduction to the streaming API.

Class hierarchy

Like Scala, Kotlin distinguishes between mutable and immutable collections. A mutable collection can be updated in place by adding, removing or replacing an element, and it will be reflected in its state. On the other side, an immutable collection, while it provides the same operations-addition, removal, or replacement-via the operator functions will end up producing a brand-new collection, leaving the initial one untouched. You will see later in this chapter how immutability is achieved through interface definition; at runtime, the implementations relies on Java's mutable collections.

Unlike Scala, Kotlin's makers have decided to avoid having two separate namespaces for each collection mode. You will find all the collections in the `kotlin.collections` namespace.

In the following figure, you will see the Kotlin collections class diagram. All mutable types can be easily identified since they carry the prefix `Mutable`. All of following types are parameterized. One thing to notice, which is not described by the following diagram, is that all read-only interfaces are covariant (**Array** is the only class in the diagram and the parameter type T is the only invariant). Covariant is a term referring to the ability to change the generic type argument from a class to one of its parents. This means that you can take a `List<String>` and assign it to `List<Any>` because the `Any` class is a parent of `String`. In Kotlin, you indicate covariant generic type parameters with the `out` keyword-interface `Iterable<out T>`. Covariance has been talked about in a lot more detail in `Chapter 8`, *Generics*. You can always revisit the chapter to refresh your knowledge.

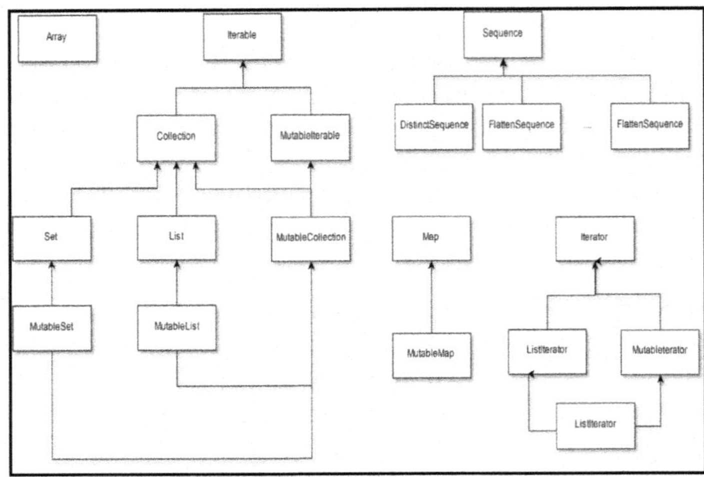

Collections class hierarchy

At the top of the class hierarchy sits the `Iterable` interface. Its definition is simple, as you can see in this code snippet:

```
public interface Iterable<out T> {
  public abstract operator fun iterator(): Iterator<T>
}
```

The `Collection` interface extends `Iterable`, and defines methods for determining the presence of elements in the collection, as well as the collection size and the check for the zero size container. You can think of this method as the query operators for a given collection:

```
public interface Collection<out E> : Iterable<E> {
  public val size: Int
  public fun isEmpty(): Boolean
```

```
    public operator fun contains(element: @UnsafeVariance E):  Boolean
    override fun iterator(): Iterator<E>
    public fun containsAll(elements: Collection<@UnsafeVariance E>):
Boolean
  }
```

A sibling of `Collection` is the `MutableIterable` interface. All this does is redefine the parent `iterator()` method to return a mutable iterator rather than an immutable one:

```
    public interface MutableIterable<out T> : Iterable<T> {
     override fun iterator(): MutableIterator<T>
    }
```

From the `Collection` class derives probably the most used type, `List`. A list is an ordered collection of elements. Methods in this interface support read-only access to the collection. The most noticeable function is `get`; it allows the retrieval of an element based on its position index:

```
    public interface List<out E> : Collection<E> {
      //Query Operations
      override val size: Int
      override fun isEmpty(): Boolean
      override fun contains(element:
      override fun iterator(): Iterator<E>
      override fun containsAll(elements: Collection<@UnsafeVariance  E>):
Boolean
      public operator fun get(index: Int): E
      public fun indexOf(element: @UnsafeVariance E): Int
      public fun lastIndexOf(element: @UnsafeVariance E): Int

      //List Iterators
      public fun listIterator(): ListIterator<E>
      public fun listIterator(index: Int): ListIterator<E>
      //View
      public fun subList(fromIndex: Int, toIndex: Int): List<E>
    }
```

The next interface deriving from `Collection` is `Set`. A set is an unordered collection of elements that does not allow duplicates to be present. Functions in this interface support read-only access to the set:

```
    public interface Set<out E> : Collection<E> {
      //Query Operations
      override val size: Int
      override fun isEmpty(): Boolean
      override fun contains(element: @UnsafeVariance E): Boolean
      override fun iterator(): Iterator<E>
```

```
        //Bulk Operations
        override fun containsAll(elements: Collection<@UnsafeVariance  E>):
Boolean
    }
```

So far, we have seen only the types for read-only/immutable collections. The support for collections allowing the addition or removal of elements comes via the `MutableCollection` interface. The next code snippet presents all the methods defined by this interface:

```
    public interface MutableCollection<E> : Collection<E>,
MutableIterable<E> {
        //Query Operations
        override fun iterator(): MutableIterator<E>

        //Modification Operations
        public fun add(element: E): Boolean
        public fun remove(element: E): Boolean

        //Bulk Modification Operations
        public fun addAll(elements: Collection<E>): Boolean
        public fun removeAll(elements: Collection<E>): Boolean
        public fun retainAll(elements: Collection<E>): Boolean
        public fun clear(): Unit
    }
```

The `MutableCollection` interface is specialized further by `MutableList`. This one extends the the parent methods by adding new ones, allowing the replacement or retrieval of an item based on its position order:

```
    public interface MutableList<E> : List<E>, MutableCollection<E> {
        //Modification Operations
        override fun add(element: E): Boolean
        override fun remove(element: E): Boolean

        //Bulk Modification Operations
        override fun addAll(elements: Collection<E>): Boolean
        public fun addAll(index: Int, elements: Collection<E>): Boolean
        override fun removeAll(elements: Collection<E>): Boolean
        override fun retainAll(elements: Collection<E>): Boolean
        override fun clear(): Unit

        //Positional Access Operations
        public operator fun set(index: Int, element: E): E
        public fun add(index: Int, element: E): Unit
        public fun removeAt(index: Int): E
```

```
    //List Iterators
    override fun listIterator(): MutableListIterator<E>
    override fun listIterator(index: Int): MutableListIterator<E>
    //View
    override fun subList(fromIndex: Int, toIndex: Int):  MutableList<E>
  }
```

Similarly, we have the equivalent of a mutable set via the `MutableSet` interface:

```
  public interface MutableSet<E> : Set<E>, MutableCollection<E> {
    //Query Operations
    override fun iterator(): MutableIterator<E>

    //Modification Operations
    override fun add(element: E): Boolean
    override fun remove(element: E): Boolean

    //Bulk Modification Operations
    override fun addAll(elements: Collection<E>): Boolean
    override fun removeAll(elements: Collection<E>): Boolean
    override fun retainAll(elements: Collection<E>): Boolean
    override fun clear(): Unit
  }
```

You will notice both `Map` and `MutableMap` are not inheriting any of the previously discussed interfaces. You might wonder how can we iterate over them. If you remember, in `Chapter 9`, *Data Classes*, we discussed destructuring a map, and we mentioned the two extension methods-iterator, `component1`, and `component2`. So, we can iterate over a map thanks to the iterator extension method. A map is a collection that stores pairs of objects, keys and values, and supports the efficient retrieval of the value corresponding to a given key. The map keys are unique, and a map can store only one value for each key. Methods defined in the `Map` interface provide the contract for a read-only collection:

```
  public interface Map<K, out V> {
    //Query Operations
    public val size: Int
    public fun isEmpty(): Boolean
    public fun containsKey(key: K): Boolean
    public fun containsValue(value: @UnsafeVariance V): Boolean
    public operator fun get(key: K): V?


    public fun getOrDefault(key: K, defaultValue: @UnsafeVariance  V): V
{
      //See default implementation in JDK sources
      return null as V
    }
```

```
    //Views
    public val keys: Set<K>
    public val values: Collection<V>
    public val entries: Set<Map.Entry<K, V>>
    public interface Entry<out K, out V> {
      public val key: K
      public val value: V
    }
}
```

In order to support mutability, the class hierarchy has been enriched with the `MutableMap` type. In the following code, you will find its definition, and there you will see the methods `remove`, `put`, `putAll`, or `clear`:

```
public interface MutableMap<K, V> : Map<K, V> {
  //Modification Operations
  public fun put(key: K, value: V): V?
  public fun remove(key: K): V?
  //Bulk Modification Operations
  public fun putAll(from: Map<out K, V>): Unit
  public fun clear(): Unit

  //Views
  override val keys: MutableSet<K>
  override val values: MutableCollection<V>
  override val entries: MutableSet<MutableMap.MutableEntry<K, V>>
  public interface MutableEntry<K,V>: Map.Entry<K, V> {
    public fun setValue(newValue: V): V
  }
}
```

Sitting on its own in the class diagram is the `Array` class. An array is just a container for holding a fixed number of values of a given type. Its length is established at creation time and can't change:

```
public class Array<T> : Cloneable {
  public inline constructor(size: Int, init: (Int) ->T)
  public operator fun get(index: Int): T
  public operator fun set(index: Int, value: T): Unit
  public val size: Int
  public operator fun iterator(): Iterator<T>
  public override fun clone(): Array<T>
}
```

On the bottom-right side of the class hierarchy diagram you can see the iterators group. An iterator over a collection can be represented as a sequence of elements. Kotlin provides support for both immutable and mutable iterators. Each collection type will, therefore, return the corresponding iterator implementation. For example, a `List` will return an implementation of `Iterator`, while `MutableList` will return an instance of `MutableIterator`:

```
public interface Iterator<out T> {
  public operator fun next(): T
  public operator fun hasNext(): Boolean
}

public interface MutableIterator<out T> : Iterator<T> {
  public fun remove(): Unit
}
```

Typically, an `Iterator` is forward reading only. That means you can't go back to the previously visited element. To support this functionality, the library contains the `ListIterator`, thus the caller can go back and forth over the underlying collection. This too comes in two flavors: immutable and mutable. The mutable version allows the addition, removal, or replacement of items as you go over the underlying collection:

```
public interface ListIterator<out T> : Iterator<T> {
  //Query Operations
  override fun next(): T
  override fun hasNext(): Boolean
  public fun hasPrevious(): Boolean
  public fun previous(): T
  public fun nextIndex(): Int
  public fun previousIndex(): Int
}

public interface MutableListIterator<T> : ListIterator<T>,
MutableIterator<T> {
  //Query Operations
  override fun next(): T
  override fun hasNext(): Boolean

  //Modification Operations
  override fun remove(): Unit
  public fun set(element: T): Unit
  public fun add(element: T): Unit
}
```

The remaining group of interfaces are related to sequences (see the top right side of the diagram). A sequence returns values through an iterator. All the sequence values are evaluated lazily, and it could happen for such a sequence to never end thus being infinite. Most of the sequences can be iterated multiple times, but there are some implementations that constrain you to one iteration only; a flattening sequence is one of those exceptions. The Sequence interface contains only one method:

```
public interface Sequence<out T> {
  public operator fun iterator(): Iterator<T>
}
```

All the collections presented earlier can be translated to a sequence via the asSequence extension methods; iterables and arrays provide their own implementation as you will see later.

One important thing to understand is that Kotlin does not provide its own implementation for its collection types, but rather taps into the existing Java collections. If you were to search the Kotlin source code for an implementation of the List interface, for example, you would be wasting your time. There isn't any. The magic happens at compile time. Kotlin deals with some of the Java collection classes in a special way: it maps the Java type to a Kotlin type. This mapping is not extended into the runtime. The Java types remain unchanged at runtime. The following is a table detailing the mapping between the Java collection types and their Kotlin equivalent immutable and mutable types:

Java Type	**Kotlin Immutable Type**	**Kotlin Mutable Type**	**Platform Type**
Iterator<T>	Iterator<T>	MutableIterator<T>	(Mutable)Iterator<T>!
Iterable<T>	Iterable<T>	MutableIterable<T>	(Mutable)Iterable<T>!
Collection<T>	Collection<T>	MutableCollection<T>	(Mutable)Collection<T>!
Set<T>	Set<T>	MutableSet<T>	(Mutable) Set<T>!
List<T>	List<T>	MutableList<T>	(Mutable) List<T>!
ListIterator<T>	ListIterator<T>	MutableListIterator<T>	(Mutable) ListIterator<T>!
Map<K, V>	Map<K, V>	MutableMap<K, V>	(Mutable) Map<K, V>!

Kotlin is a null safe language by design. Because of Java interoperability, the Kotlin team had to relax the type system a little bit. Therefore, the term of platform type was introduced. A platform type is nothing but a type coming from the underlying JVM platform, and it will get special treatment:

- The Kotlin compiler will not enforce null safety for them; therefore, you can end up with a NullPointerExcepiont for variables coming from Java.

- You cannot name platform types in your Kotlin code, but you will see IntelliJ displaying them with an exclamation mark at the end: `String!`, `ArrayList<Int!>!`, and so on.
- When storing a platform type, you would have to pick a Kotlin type. The compiler will do that for you, but you can fine tune it. Say you have the following Java code: `String getName()`.You can write the following in Kotlin: `val name=getName` (the IDE will display `String!` as the type) or `val name:String?= getName()` or `val name:String = getName()`.
- Like the previous point, when you override a method defined in Java, you would need to provide a Kotlin type. Let's say we have a method in Java defined as `void addFlag(String flag)`. If you were to override this method in Kotlin, you would need to pick one of the two options: `override fun addFlag(flag:String):Unit` or `override fun addFlag(flag:String?)`.

This type mapping happening at compile type allows for the following code to compile and run:

```
fun <T> itWorks(list: List<T>): Unit {
  println("Java Class Type:${list.javaClass.canonicalName}")
}

val jlist = ArrayList<String>()
jlist.add("sample")
itWorks(jlist)
itWorks(Collections.singletonList(1))
```

The code is declaring a method taking a Kotlin `list` parameter, and then it calls it twice, providing two different parameters: `java.util.ArrayList` and `java.util.Collections.SingletonList`. In the first case, the compiler has interpreted the type as `List<String>`. If you hover the mouse over the `singletonList`, you will see the hint as to the platform type, `(Mutable)List<Int!>!`.

Arrays

We have already addressed what an array is in the previous section: *Class* Hierarchy. Now it is time to have a look at how you work with arrays in a bit more detail.

Declaring and initializing arrays can be done like this:

```
val intArray = arrayOf(1, 2, 3, 4)
println("Int array:${intArray.joinToString(",")}")
println("Element at index 1 is:${intArray[1]}")
```

```
val stringArray = kotlin.arrayOfNulls<String>(3)
stringArray[0] = "a"
stringArray[1] = "b"
stringArray[2] = "c"
//stringArrays[3]="d" --throws index out of bounds exception
println("String array:${stringArray.joinToString(",")}")

val studentArray = Array<Student>(2) { index ->
  when (index) {
    0 -> Student(1, "Alexandra", "Brook")
    1 -> Student(2, "James", "Smith")
    else ->throw IllegalArgumentException("Too many")
  }
}
println("Student array:${studentArray.joinToString(",")}")
println("Student at index 0:${studentArray[0]}")

val longArray = emptyArray<Long>()
println("Long array:${longArray.joinToString(",")}")
```

Here you can see four ways of initializing your array collection. The first approach is to make use of the `arrayOf` method to initialize an array of integers. The second method is to use the `arrayOfNulls` to return an array of a given size where each element is set to null. To retrieve an item of your array, you make use of the `get` operators: see `studentArray[0]` as an example. The third initialization option makes use of the `Array` class constructor; it provides the array size and the lambda function, allowing you to construct each element. The last example shows how you can create an empty array in a Kotlin-idiomatic way.

Arrays on the JVM get quite a special treatment, so a Kotlin array should end up being translated to similar bytecode, otherwise the interoperability is broken. Looking at the bytecode generated will provide us with the answers:

```
Compiled from "ArraysCollection.kt"
public final class  com.programming.kotlin.chapter10.ArraysCollectionKt {
  public static final void arrays();
    Code:
      0: iconst_4
      1: anewarray     #8                    // class java/lang/Integer
      4: dup
      5: iconst_0
      6: iconst_1
      7: invokestatic  #12  // Method
java/lang/Integer.valueOf:(I)Ljava/lang/Integer;
      10: aastore
      35: checkcast     #14                   // class "[Ljava/lang/Object;"
```

```
38: checkcast      #16                  // class "[Ljava/lang/Integer;"
41: astore_0
```

The key lies with the `anewarray` instruction. The bytecode instruction definition reads: `anewarray <type>`, where `<type>` is either the name of a class or interface, for example, `java/lang/String`. The byte code routine allocates a new array for holding object references. It pops an `int` off the stack representing the array size. Using this, it constructs the new array to hold references for the type indicated by `<type>`:

```
anewarray      #8              // class
com/programming/kotlin/chapter10/Student
```

The reference to the new array is pushed onto the stack via the `astore_0` bytecode-level instruction. The rather strange thing is that you can't see any trace of the actual class `Array` and its constructor! You might rightfully ask yourself what is going on? More on this in a moment.

The Kotlin standard library provides out-of-the-box support for primitive arrays: `intArrayOf`, `longArrayOf`, `charArrayOf`, `doubleArrayOf`, and so on. For each one, you will get an instance of their equivalent Kotlin class: `IntArray`, `LongArray`, `CharArray`, `DoubleArray`, and so on. The important and interesting part is that none of these classes derive from or are related to the `Array` type presented earlier. Let's look at an example of constructing a primitive array of integers:

```
val ints = intArrayOf(1,2,3, 4, 5, 6, 7, 8, 9, 10)
println("Built in int array:${ints.joinToString(",")}")
```

This time, the type will be `IntArray` as opposed to `Array<Int>`, as defined previously. Looking at the bytecode generated, we will see it has changed compared to the previous example:

```
0: iconst_3
1: newarray         int
3: dup
4: iconst_0
5: bipush          100
7: iastore
20: astore_0
```

The bytecode routine used for creating an array has changed. This time, the `newarray` instruction is used. Unlike `anewarray`, this one is used to allocate single-dimension arrays of primitive types: booleans, chars, floats, doubles, bytes, shorts, ints, or longs. This is an optimization at the JVM level to avoid boxing and unboxing operations, and it has been done in order to improve performance.

With this in place, you should make sure you always use ***ArrayOf when dealing with primitive types instead of arrayOf. If you don't, your program will pay a performance cost associated with boxing/unboxing operations.

The reason we don't see any trace of our Kotlin Array class in the generated bytecode is because they are an alias for the Java type. This type mapping happens only at compile time. For performance reasons, they compile straight to Java arrays. Please keep in mind that a Java int[] maps to IntArray (this is valid for the other primitive types mentioned), and String[] or T[] are mapped to Array<out String/T>.

The compiler gives arrays special treatment. When compiling to JVM bytecodes, it will optimize the bytecode generated to avoid any overhead:

```
val countries = arrayOf("UK", "Germany", "Italy")
for (country in countries) {
  print("$country;")
}
```

You would probably expect the for construct to make use of the iterator to move one by one over the array. However, this is not the case; no iterator is used:

```
val numbers = intArrayOf(10, 20, 30)
for (i in numbers.indices) {
  numbers[i] *= 10
}
```

The same principle is being applied while iterating with an index over the array. Additionally, retrieving and setting the value is not making use of the actual get and set methods available on the array. Once again, this was done to improve performance.

Another optimization the compiler employs happens when you have an if block like the following:

```
val index=Random().nextInt(10)
if (index in numbers.indices) {
  numbers[index]=index
}
```

In this case, the if statement behaves as if you had written it like this:

```
if (index >=0 && index < numbers.size) {}
```

The power of the standard library comes through the richness of the API allowing us to manipulate an array. In the Kotlin standard library under `kotlin.collections` there is a class named `ArraysKt`. Within this, you will find a lot of helper functions (extension methods), covering `Array<T>` and the primitive types arrays `IntArray`, `FloatArray`, `ByteArray`, and so on. We will not go through each and every one, but will cover some of them. You should go and study the rest of the methods on your own:

```
    println("First element in the IntArray:${ints.first()}")
    println("Last element in the IntArray:${ints.last()}")
    println("Take first 3 elements of the
IntArray:${ints.take(3).joinToString(",")}")
    println("Take last 3 elements of the
IntArray:${ints.takeLast(3).joinToString(",")}")
    println("Take elements smaller than 5 of the  IntArray:${
      ints.takeWhile {
        it <5
      }
      .joinToString(",")
    }")
    println("Take every 3rd element in IntArray: ${ints.filterIndexed  {
      index, element -> index % 3 == 0
    }
    .joinToString(",")}")
```

Let's go through each of the previously mentioned examples individually. The `first()` is an extension method that does what it says on the tin. It returns the first element in the collection. This is almost as if you were writing `ints[0]`. The reason I say almost is because, in the case of an empty array, you will get a `NoSuchElementException` as opposed to `IndexOutOfBoundsException`. Run the preceding code and you should see the output containing the number `1`.

The next example uses the method `last()` to retrieve, you guessed it (good method naming is always important), the last element in the collection. This is a fast operation, since it takes the array length, subtracts `1`, and then uses the `get` operator to retrieve the element.

The `take(n)` extension method returns to the caller the first `N` elements of the target collection. It applies to all operations that are returning a subset of the initial collection, but the interesting part is that the return type is not an `IntArray`, but rather a `List<Int>`. You can see in the following code snippet that the actual implementation relies on a Java `ArrayList` implementation:

```
public fun IntArray.take(n: Int): List<Int> {
  require(n >= 0) { "Requested element count $n is less than zero." }
  if (n == 0) return emptyList()
  if (n >= size) return toList()
```

```
        if (n == 1) return listOf(this[0])
        var count = 0
        val list = ArrayList<Int>(n)
        for (item in this) {
          if (count++ == n)
            break;
          list.add(item)
        }
        return list
      }
```

The next line of code does something similar: it takes three elements from the array, not from the beginning, but from the end of the collection. Executing the code will end up printing the number `8`, `9`, and `10` on the console.

There are scenarios where you might want to return elements from an array when they fulfill a criteria/predicate. In the sample code provided earlier, the predicate is a function that checks whether the element is smaller than five. The output for this line of code will contain the numbers one to four.

Returning every nth element (every third element, in the example provided) couldn't have been easier, since we can use the `filterIndexed` extension method. This method takes a lambda function with two parameters, one being the current position in the array and the second the actual element. The output for the code will print the numbers `1`, `4`, `7`, and `10` to the console.

My favorite extension methods are `map` and `flatMap`. These sound very familiar to any Scala developer reading this book, but remember that Kotlin is not a functional language, and, therefore, the notion of monads is not applicable. I am not going to expand on the concept of monads since it goes beyond the purpose of this book into the realm of functional programming. Instead, I will encourage you to go and read about the topic, even if you are not even considering making the transition to a functional language.

The `map` function allows you to translate the underlying element type to a different one, if you have such requirements. The simplest example is to translate the `IntArray` to a collection of strings:

```
      val strings = ints.map { element ->"Item " + element.toString() }
      println("Transform each element IntArray into a
  string:${strings.joinToString(",")}")
```

If you execute this code, you should see the following output: `Transform each...: Item 1, Item 2, Item 3,..., Item 10`. Let's see how this is implemented. The following snippet contains the actual standard library code:

```
    public inline fun <R> IntArray.map(transform: (Int) ->R): List<R> {
      return mapTo(ArrayList<R>(size), transform)
    }

    public inline fun <R, C : MutableCollection<in R>>
IntArray.mapTo(destination: C, transform: (Int) ->R): C {
      for (item in this)
        destination.add(transform(item))
      return destination
    }
```

The same map extension method is defined for `LongArrays`, `DoubleArrays`, `ByteArray`, and so on, as well as the `Array<T>` class. This way, you can work with the API collections in a uniform manner despite the lack of any type relation. All the map method does is forward the call to another extension method, `mapTo`, while passing a Java `ArrayList` as the first argument and your lambda expression as the second argument. The `mapTo` method iterates through the target collection and applies the transformation method to each element. The result of each transformation is then added to the destination collection, in this case, a Java `ArrayList`.

You might still wonder how the `mapTo` works when providing a Java `ArrayList`. After all, the extension method requires the target collection to inherit from `MutableCollection`. As discussed earlier, there is no magic to this. During compilation, the Java collection type is aliased to a Kotlin collection. In this case, the compiler will treat the `ArrayList` reference as a Kotlin `MutableCollection` instance. At runtime, therefore, you are still dealing with the Java collection.

The extension method `flatMap` returns a merged list of all the collections returned by your transformation lambda. In this case, it is expected that your lambda function return type is an `Iterable<T>`. In other words, `flatMap` flattens the sequence of `Iterable` instances. Here is an example where for each element of the array we will create three replicas:

```
    val charArray = charArrayOf('a', 'b', 'c')
    val tripleCharArray = charArray.flatMap { c ->charArrayOf(c, c,
c).asIterable() }
    println("Triple each element in the
charArray:${tripleCharArray.joinToString(",")}}")
```

The result is a list (yes, we change the container type) with the following character items: `a,a,a,b,b,b,c,c,c`. The implementation is very similar to the `map` method presented earlier; this is the source code taken from the Kotlin standard library:

```
    public inline fun <R> CharArray.flatMap(transform: (Char) ->
Iterable<R>): List<R> {
      return flatMapTo(ArrayList<R>(), transform)
    }

    public inline fun <R, C : MutableCollection<in R>>
CharArray.flatMapTo(destination: C, transform: (Char) ->  Iterable<R>): C {
      for (element in this) {
        val list = transform(element)
        destination.addAll(list)
      }
      return destination
    }
```

The code iterates through the target array of chars invoking the `transform()` method. All the items returned from it are added to the `destination` collection. You might have noticed already, but the `destination` needs to derive from `MutableCollection` since it needs to append elements.

The standard library API provides quite a few methods that allow you to convert an array to a different collection type. These methods are extension methods covering all the array type classes. Here are a few examples of how you would convert your array collection to a different collection:

```
    val longs = longArrayOf(1, 2, 1, 2, 3, 4, 5)
    val hashSet: HashSet<Long> = longs.toHashSet()
    println("Java HashSet:${hashSet.joinToString(",")}")
    val sortedSet: SortedSet<Long> = longs.toSortedSet()
    println("Sorted
Set[${sortedSet.javaClass.canonicalName}]:${sortedSet.joinToString (",")}")
    val set: Set<Long> = longs.toSet()
    println("Set[${set.javaClass.canonicalName}]:${set.joinToString(",
")}")
    val mutableSet = longs.toMutableSet()
    mutableSet.add(10)
    println("MutableSet[${mutableSet.javaClass.canonicalName}]:${
mutableSet.joinToString(",")}")
    val list: List<Long> = longs.toList()
    println("List[${list.javaClass.canonicalName}]:${list.joinToString
(",")}")
    val mutableList: MutableList<Long> = longs.toMutableList()
    println("MutableList[${mutableList.javaClass.canonicalName}]:${
mutableList.joinToString}")
```

I don't usually use the in place variable type (that is, `val set: Set<Long>`), but if you are a novice to Kotlin then I would recommend you to do it at the beginning. The code defines a simple array of longs and converts it to different sets (a few variations of a set and list). For each variable, apart from the Java `HashSet`, the actual collection type name is written to the console. Here is what the code earlier ends up printing:

```
Java HashSet:1,2,3,4,5
Sorted Set[java.util.TreeSet]:1,2,3,4,5
Set[java.util.LinkedHashSet]:1,2,3,4,5
MutableSet[java.util.LinkedHashSet]:1,2,3,4,5,10
List[java.util.ArrayList]:1,2,1,2,3,4,5
MutableList[java.util.ArrayList]:1,2,1,2,3,4,5
```

Although you are dealing with Kotlin immutable types, the Java collection used under the bonnet is mutable. So once again, the immutability in Kotlin is achieved via the interface definition.

What do you think will happen if I cast my list to a Java `ArrayList` and then I add an element? For example:

```
val hackedList = (list as ArrayList<Long>)
hackedList.add(100)
println("List[${list.javaClass.canonicalName}]:${list.joinToString
(",")}")
```

It is not a trick question; the code earlier compiles and runs fine; after all, we are in the JVM world. So, once we have our hands on the `ArrayList` instance, we can change its elements, and this will be reflected automatically by our Kotlin list instance. Now why is this dangerous? Look at the next Java method:

```
public static void dangerous(Collection<Long> l) {
  l.add(1000L);
}
```

Say you have such a library method, which you call from your Kotlin code `Arrays.dangerous(list)`. Because of the compile time type aliasing (we touched upon this subject at the beginning of the chapter), no compiler error is raised. The problem is that you are dealing with an immutable collection in your Kotlin code; however, once it has been handed over to the Java code, that immutability is broken. Therefore, if you want to preserve your collection state, you will have to provide a copy of your collection. For that, use the `.toList` extension.

Dealing with collections is quite easy, thanks to the rich API provided by the standard library. However, you will need to pay a bit more attention at the beginning before you get familiar with it. For example, for the `mutableSet`, the code complete dialog will list you two methods: `plus` and `plusAssign`. If you call any of the `plus` methods, the source mutable set will actually remain unchanged. The return value is a new collection, this time of the type `Set<Long>`, which is immutable. This is a little bit counterintuitive. You can argue that `plus` for a mutable collection should reflect the change, but this is not the case. To apply the change to the source collection, you have to use the `plusAssign`; this time, the return type is `Unit`. The reason these `plus` methods behave like this is because the extension method is defined for the `Set` type, which is immutable.

One last thing on arrays and we can move over to the next collection type. Do you remember that Kotlin supports object destruction (you need to provide an iterator method alongside *componentN* methods)? This still holds true for arrays. We saw at the start of the chapter that the `Array` class defines an `iterator` method. The *componentN* methods are provided as extension methods:

```
public inline operator fun IntArray.component1(): Int {
  return get(0)
}
```

For each array type (`IntArray`, `CharArray`, `...`, `Array<T>`), you will find these methods. The Kotlin team has decided to provide `component1` to `component5`. This means that you can deconstruct only the first five elements. There is always the option for you to write one or more extra `componentN`, thus allowing a greater number of elements to be retrieved via deconstruction:

```
val integers = intArrayOf(1, 2, 3, 4, 5, 6)
val (i1, i2, i3, i4, i5) = integers
println("i1:$i1; i2:$i2;..;i5=$i5")
```

Executing this code will print you the first five elements of the integers array. What would happen, though, if you deconstruct and your array length does not match the number of elements used in the deconstruction? For example:

```
val integers = intArrayOf(1, 2, 3)
val (i1, i2, i3, i4, i5) = integers
```

In this case, you will end up with a `java.lang.ArrayIndexOutOfBoundsException` being thrown. Therefore, always make sure you check the array length before you deconstruct it.

Lists

Lists are ordered collections. With a list, you can insert an element at a very specific location, as well as retrieve elements by the position in the collection. Kotlin provides a couple of pre-built methods for constructing immutable and mutable lists. Remember, immutability is achieved via interface. Here is how you would create lists in idiomatic Kotlin:

```
    val intList: List<Int> = listOf
    println("Int
list[${intList.javaClass.canonicalName}]:${intList.joinToString(", ")}")

    val emptyList: List<String> = emptyList<String>()
    println("Empty
list[${emptyList.javaClass.canonicalName}]:${emptyList.joinToStrin
g(",")}")

    val nonNulls: List<String> = listOfNotNull<String>(null, "a", "b",
"c")
    println("Non-Null string
lists[${nonNulls.javaClass.canonicalName}]:${nonNulls.joinToString (",")}")

    val doubleList: ArrayList<Double> = arrayListOf(84.88, 100.25,  999.99)
    println("Double list:${doubleList.joinToString(",")}")

    val cartoonsList: MutableList<String> = mutableListOf("Tom&Jerry",
"Dexter's Laboratory", "Johnny Bravo", "Cow&Chicken")
    println("Cartoons list[${cartoonsList.javaClass.canonicalName}]:
${cartoonsList.joinToString(",")}")

    cartoonsList.addAll(arrayOf("Ed, Edd n Eddy","Courage the Cowardly
Dog"))
    println("Cartoons list[${cartoonsList.javaClass.canonicalName}]:
${cartoonsList.joinToString(",")}")
```

The first three lists (`intList`, `emptyList`, and `nonNulls`) are read-only instances, whereas the last two are mutable. Apart from the `ListOf` array, all the other ones return a Kotlin type. For all the Kotlin types, the code prints out the name of the actual class used at runtime. The output for the preceding code is this:

```
    Int list[java.util.Arrays.ArrayList]:20,29,40,10
    Empty list[kotlin.collections.EmptyList]:
    Non-Null string lists[java.util.ArrayList]:a,b,c
    Double list:84.88,100.25,999.99
    Cartoons list[java.util.ArrayList]: Tom&Jerry,Dexter's
Laboratory,Johnny  Bravo,Cow&Chicken
```

```
    Cartoons list[java.util.ArrayList]: Tom&Jerry,Dexter's
Laboratory,Johnny Bravo,Cow&Chicken,Ed, Edd n Eddy,Courage the  Cowardly
Dog
```

It might come as a surprise to you that, despite working with immutable types, the actual implementation is using a mutable collection: `ArrayList`. Even more interesting is that `listOf` actually returns `Arrays.ArrayList`. This class is different to `java.util.ArrayList`. The former, although it derives from the `Collection` class, can't be changed by adding/removing items. Both the `add` and `remove` methods end up throwing a `UnsupportedOperationException`. However, it is not a truly immutable collection because you can still replace an item at a specific position within your collection. So the Kotlin type system achieves immutability through interface definition, but nothing is stopping you from doing the following:

```
    (intList as AbstractList<Int>).set(0, 999999)
    println("Int
list[${intList.javaClass.canonicalName}]:${intList.joinToString(", ")}")

    (nonNulls as java.util.ArrayList).addAll(arrayOf("x", "y"))
    println("countries
list[${nonNulls.javaClass.canonicalName}]:${nonNulls.joinToString( ",")}")

    val hacked: List<Int>= listOfNotNull(0,1)
    CollectionsJ.dangerousCall(hacked)
    println("Hacked
list[${hacked.javaClass.canonicalName}]:${hacked.joinToString(",") }")

    //Java code
    public class CollectionsJ {

      public static void dangerousCall(Collection<Integer> l) {
        l.add(1000);
      }
    }
```

In the first example, the collection is converted to the `Arrays.ArrayList` parent class: `AbstractList`; you can't cast to the `Arrays.ArrayList` since that class is marked private in the JDK. Once we have changed the type, we can use the `set` method and simply replace the first integer with a new one: *999999*. In the second example, the variable is casted to the the Java `ArrayList` and then uses the methods exposed to modify the collection. The last example is the typical unforeseen problem. Working within the context of JVM, you are bound to use third-party libraries. If you hand over your immutable Kotlin collection reference to it, the immutability guarantee can't hold anymore. If your requirements are such that you must not change your collection, you should pass a snapshot. Therefore, just use `hacked.toList` and this problem goes away.

You have seen how to construct lists (remember you can also convert other collections to lists via the `.toList` method), but now let's have a look at a few simple examples to showcase some of the extension methods provided in the library:

```
data class Planet(val name: String, val distance: Long)

val planets = listOf( Planet("Mercury", 57910000), Planet("Venus",
108200000), Planet("Earth", 149600000), Planet("Mars", 227940000),
Planet("Jupiter", 778330000), Planet("Saturn", 1424600000),
Planet("Uranus", 2873550000), Planet("Neptune", 4501000000),
Planet("Pluto", 5945900000))

println(planets.last())          //Pluto
println(planets.first())         //Mercury
println(planets.get(4))          //Jupiter
println(planets.isEmpty())       //false
println(planets.isNotEmpty())    //true

println(planets.asReversed())        //"Pluto", "Neptune"
println(planets.elementAtOrNull(10)) //Null
```

This code snippet defines the list of planets in our solar system and their distance from the sun. Using this list as a target, you can see the basic methods in action. I will not go through each one individually since their name provides more than enough description of what they do.

Let's move on to slightly more complex operations on a list. Say you want to join one collection with another one. The library provides support for such functionality via the `.zip` method. In the following example, the planets list is joined to the array containing each planet's diameter:

```
planets.zip(arrayOf(4800, 12100, 12750, 6800, 142800, 120660,  51800,
49500, 3300))
.forEach {
  val (planet, diameter) = it
  println("${planet.name}'s diameter is $diameter km")
}
```

Run the code and it will print each planet's diameter. I bet you are asking yourself, what happens if the two collections are of a different size? Let's say we omitted the diameter for `Pluto`. In this case, the join operation will drop the planet `Pluto`.

The collection library has been inspired quite a bit by the Scala collection library, I would say. It comes with support for `foldLeft` and `foldRight`, methods that should be quite familiar to any Scala developer reading this. These methods are accumulators; they take an initial value and iterate (from left to right or from right to left) the target collection, and then execute the lambda function for each element, returning the new revised accumulator value. Say we want to list the planets from the furthest to the closest to the sun. Here is one way to achieve this via `foldRight`:

```
val reversePlanetName = planets.foldRight(StringBuilder()) {
  planet, builder -> builder.append(planet.name)
  builder.append(";")
}
println(reversePlanetName)    //Pluto, Neptune..Earth;Venus;Mercury
```

To showcase the `foldLeft`, let's move to a different domain problem. Say you have an electronic cart and you want to calculate the price of all the items in a shopping cart. For that, `foldLeft` could provide you with the means to calculate the total price:

```
    data class ShoppingItem(val id: String, val name: String, val  price:
BigDecimal, val quantity: Int)

    val amount = listOf( ShoppingItem("1", "Intel i7-950 Quad-Core
Processor", BigDecimal("319.76"), 1), ShoppingItem("2", "Samsung  750 EVO
250 GB 2.5 inch SDD", BigDecimal("71.21"), 1))
    .foldRight(BigDecimal.ZERO) {
      item, total -> total + BigDecimal(item.quantity) * item.price
    }
    println(amount)    //390.97
```

All the list types are getting the support for the `map` and `flatMap` extension methods. They are the most expressive functions in the whole of the standard library API when it comes to manipulating a collection:

```
planets.map { it.distance }    //List(57910000, ...,5945900000)

val list = listOf(listOf(10, 20), listOf(14, 18), emptyList())
val increment = { x: Int -> x + 1 }
list.flatMap { it.map(increment) }    //11,21,15,10
```

The first line in the example extracts another collection (a `List<Long>` to be precise) from the planets collection. This new collection contains the distance from the sun for each of the planets in our solar system. Pretty easy!

The second part of the example is a bit more evolved. It starts with a list of integers and then it defines a lambda function to increase an integer parameter by one. The last line of code applies the lambda to each element of each of the three lists and then flattens the resulting collection. The list of lists of integers becomes a list of integers.

Object deconstruction applies to lists as well. As with arrays, you get out-of-the-box support for deconstructing the first five elements of a list. The code is similar to the one used for arrays:

```
val chars = listOf('a', 'd', 'c', 'd', 'a')
val (c1,c2,c3,c4,c5) = chars
println("$c1$c2$c3$c4$c5")//adcda
```

I will conclude this section on lists by showing how you can convert a list to a different collection type:

```
val array: Array<Char> = chars.toTypedArray()
val arrayBetter: CharArray = chars.toCharArray()
val set: Set<Char> = chars.toSet()                    //[a,d,c]
val charsMutable: MutableList<Char> = chars.toMutableList()
```

The sample provides two options for converting a list to an array. In the arrays section, you learned about the difference between `Array<T>` and `IntArray`, `DoubleArray`, and so on, and why it is better to use the primitive types implementation. The same logic applies for this conversion as well. Therefore, it is better to use the `to***Array` when dealing with primitive types.

Maps

A map collection, as the name implies, allows you to associated an object (key) to another object (value). A map dictates that your collection can't contain duplicate keys, and each key is mapped to at most one value. The interesting part about a map is that its interface provides three collection views: the set of keys, the collection of all the values, and the set of key-value mappings.

When using a map, you need to pay attention to the keys you are using. When adding an item to the map, first thing it does is to locate which bucket it should go into. To do so, it will use the `hashCode` method, and after that, depending on the implementation, it will use the `equals` method. Therefore, your keys need to be immutable, otherwise the behavior of the map can't be specified.

We know already that Kotlin provides support for immutable and mutable maps at the interface level. This is reflected in the collection API since there are specific methods for each flavor of map:

```
    data class Customer(val firstName: String, val lastName: String,  val
id: Int)

    val carsMap: Map<String, String> = mapOf("a" to "aston martin",  "b" to
"bmw", "m" to "mercedes", "f" to "ferrari")
    println("cars[${carsMap.javaClass.canonicalName}:$carsMap]")
    println("car maker starting with 'f':${carsMap.get("f")}")    //Ferrari
    println("car maker starting with 'X':${carsMap.get("X")}")  //null

    val states: MutableMap<String, String>= mutableMapOf("AL" to
"Alabama", "AK" to "Alaska", "AZ" to "Arizona")
    states += ("CA" to "California")
    println("States [${states.javaClass.canonicalName}:$states")
    println("States keys:${states.keys}")//AL, AK, AZ,CA
    println("States values:${states.values}")//Alabama, Alaska,  Arizona,
California

    val customers: java.util.HashMap<Int, Customer> = hashMapOf(1 to
Customer("Dina", "Kreps", 1),  2 to Customer("Andy", "Smith", 2))

    val linkedHashMap: java.util.LinkedHashMap<String, String> =
linkedMapOf("red" to "#FF0000","azure" to "#F0FFFF","white" to  "#FFFFFF")

    val sortedMap: java.util.SortedMap<Int, String> = sortedMapOf(4 to
"d", 1 to "a", 3 to "c", 2 to "b")
    println("Sorted
map[${sortedMap.javaClass.canonicalName}]:${sortedMap}")
```

First two constructs return you a Kotlin type, whereas the last three are returning Java util map implementations. If you run the code, you will get the output for the Kotlin map types and the Java class used as the implementation. In both scenarios, that class is `LinkedHashMap`. I am sure most of you reading the lines know the difference between the three types of map, but revisiting their definitions won't hurt anyone:

- `HashMap` A table-based implementation for the map interface. While it allows nulls as either key or values the class makes no guarantees on the items' order or the fact it will remain constant over time. This implementation has constant-time cost for the `get` and `put` methods, assuming the hash function distributes the elements properly among the buckets. The class retains a load factor as a measure of how full the map can be before its capacity is increased. When the number of entries in the hash table exceeds the product of the load factor and the current capacity, the map table is rehashed (that is, internal data structures are rebuilt) so that the hash table has approximately twice the number of buckets.

- `LinkedHashMap`: A combination of `HashMap` and linked-list implementation for the map interface, with a predictable iteration order. This implementation differs from `HashMap` in that it maintains a doubly-linked list running through all of its entries. This linked list defines the iteration ordering, which is normally the order in which the keys were inserted into the map. The insertion order is not changed when a key is re-inserted into the map.
- `TreeMap`: A map implementation based on a **red-black tree** implementation. The map is sorted based on the default ordering of its keys, or by a comparator provided at the map's creation time, depending on which constructor is used. This implementation provides a guaranteed *log(n)* time cost for the `containsKey`, `get`, `put`, and `remove` operations. A red-black tree is a special case of a binary search tree, where each node has one color (red or black) associated with it (in addition to its key and left and right children). The tree structure is governed by the following rules: the root node is black; the descendants of a red node are black; each leaf node is black, the number of black nodes on the path from the root to the null child are the same.

Since this book does not focus on data structures, I think this is enough information on these map implementations. You can always go and do a bit more research to familiarize yourself with (or refresh your knowledge on) these implementations and the pros and cons of using one over the other.

We already mentioned, for lists, that once you pass your reference to a Java library, immutability is off the table. The same applies to any of the Kotlin map types. In the following code, you can see a simple example of a Java function taking a map of string to string. All it does is add a new entry (it can very easily remove one or clear the entire map). When calling the code from Kotlin, you will see the IDE showing you the platform type `(Mutable)Map<String!,String!>`, so always check what the calling code does:

```
public static void dangerousCallMap(Map<String,String> map){
  map.put("newKey!", "newValue!");
}

CollectionsJ.dangerousCallMap(carsMap)
println("Cars:$carsMap")   //Cars:a=aston martin, b=bmw, m=mercedes,
f=ferrari, newKey!=newValue!
```

If you want to avoid changing your map collection, then you need to take a snapshot of your map and hand it over to the Java method. While it is not the nicest code, it does the job: `carsMap.toList().toMap()`.

Now let's look at some of the extension methods available for the map type:

```
    customers.mapKeys { it.toString() }   // "1" =
Customer("Dina","Kreps",1),
    customers.map { it.key * 10 to it.value.id }         // 10= 1, 20  =2
    customers.mapValues { it.value.lastName }  // 1=Kreps, 2="Smith
    customers.flatMap { (it.value.firstName +  it.value.lastName).toSet()
}.toSet() //D, i, n, a, K, r, e, p, s,  A, d, y, S, m, t, h]
    linkedHashMap.filterKeys { it.contains("r") }  //red=#FF0000,
    states.filterNot { it.value.startsWith("C") } //AL=Alabama,  AK=Alaska,
AZ=Arizona
```

The first example allows you to change the key type. While the `it` points to the entire `Map.Entry` instance, this method won't change the values type. If your lambda function ends up returning the same value more than once, you will lose elements; only the last value is kept. Imagine if we returned a constant value from the function; then the resulting map will have one item. The second example allows the caller to change both the keys and the values type. The third example unlike the first example, you can return the same value without affecting the collection size. You will just end up with a values collection where some elements appear more than once. Remember, any `flatMap` function in the standard library will return a `List<T>`. In the sample code earlier determines all the characters used in the customers in names. The last two methods show how you can cherry pick the elements of a map based on a filter. In both cases, you will end up with a new map instance containing the items meeting your criteria.

Sets

A set is a collection that contains no duplicate items. This means you can't have `i1` and `i2` in the collection if `i1==i2` (which translates to `i1.equals(i2) == true`). The same reasoning applies for a null reference - you can't have more than one null item stored in your set.

To create instances of sets, you can use any of the methods in the following code example:

```
    data class Book(val author: String, val title: String, val year:  Int,
val isbn: String)

    val intSet: Set<Int> = setOf(1, 21, 21, 2, 6, 3, 2)  //1,21,2,6,3
    println("Set of  integers[${intSet.javaClass.canonicalName}]:$intSet")

    val hashSet: java.util.HashSet<Book> = hashSetOf(
      Book("Jules Verne", "Around the World in 80 Days Paperback",  2014,
"978-1503215153"),
```

```
        Book("George R.R. Martin", "Series: Game of Thrones: The Graphic
Novel (Book 1)", 2012, "978-0440423218"),
        Book("J.K. Rowling", "Harry Potter And The Goblet Of Fire (Book  4)
Hardcover", 2000, "978-0439139595"),
        Book("Jules Verne", "Around the World in 80 Days Paperback",  2014,
"978-1503215153")
    ) //Jules Verne,  J.K. Rowling,George R.R. Martin
    println("Set of books:${hashSet}")

    val sortedIntegers: java.util.TreeSet<Int> = sortedSetOf(11, 0, 9,  11,
9, 8)  //0,8,9,11
    println("Sorted set of integer:${sortedIntegers}")

    val charSet: java.util.LinkedHashSet<Char> = linkedSetOf('a', 'x',
'a', 'z', 'a')    //a,x,z
    println("Set of characters:$charSet")

    val longSet: MutableSet<Long> = mutableSetOf( 20161028141216,
20161029121211, 20161029121211) //20161028141216, 20161029121211
    println("Set of longs[${longMutableSet.javaClass.canonicalName}]
:$longSet")
```

You can see the result of each set in the comments. Only `setOf` and `mutableSetOf extensions` are returning a Kotlin type; the other three methods used give you back a Java type. If you run the code, you will see that the Kotlin immutable and mutable set implementations are materialized by `LinkedHashSet`, which is, of course, mutable. To understand the difference between the various implementations, let's see what the JDK says on each one:

- `LinkedHashSet`: The hash table and linked list implementation of the set interface, with predictable iteration order. This implementation differs from `HashSet` in that it maintains a doubly-linked list running through all of its entries. This linked list defines the iteration ordering, which is the order in which elements were inserted into the collection. The implementation spares its clients from chaotic ordering provided by `HashSet`, without incurring the increased cost associated with `TreeSet`.
- `HashSet`: It implements the set interface, backed by a hash table (actually a `HashMap` instance). It makes no guarantees as to the iteration order of the set; it does not guarantee that the order will remain constant over time. This class offers constant time performance for the basic operations (add, remove, contains, and size), assuming the hash function disperses the elements properly among the map buckets.

- `TreeSet`: A set implementation based on a `TreeMap`. The elements are ordered using their natural ordering, or by a comparator provided at set creation time, depending on which constructor is used. This implementation provides guaranteed *log(n)* time cost for the basic operations (add, remove, and contains).

Covering each method available on the set interface goes beyond the scope of this chapter. However, we will showcase some of the methods available. You can always pick up the documentation and learn about the entire set of methods exposed:

```
    println(intSet.contains(9999))    //false
    println(intSet.contains(1))     //true
    println(books.contains(Book("Jules Verne", "Around the World in 80
Days Paperback", 2014, "978-1503215153"))) //true
    println(intSet.first())           //1
    println(sortedIntegers.last())    // 11
    println(charSet.drop(2))          // z
    println(intSet.plus(10))          // 1,21,2,6,3,10
    println(intSet.minus(21))          // 1,2,6,3
    println(intSet.minus(-1))          // 1,21,2,6,3
    println(intSet.average())          // 6.6
    println(longSet.plus(11))      // 20161028141216, 20161029121211
    println(longSet)          //20161028141216, 20161029121211
```

You can see the output in the comments. The methods' names should be descriptive enough to give an impression of the actions they perform. One thing to notice is that the `plus` and `minus` methods don't alter the collection. Those extension methods are defined at the immutable `Set` interface, and, therefore, will end up generating a new immutable collection.

We can't talk about a collection type without highlighting the two extensions: `map` and `flatMap`. In the first sample, the code extracts an author-title pair from the set of books while the second example gets all the characters used for all the book titles in the map:

```
    println(books.map{Pair(it.author,it.title)})     // Jules Verne- Around
the World in 80 Days Paperback,
    println(books
      .flatMap { it.title.asIterable() }
      .toSortedSet()
    )    //[ , (, ), 0, 1, 4, 8, :, A, B, D, F, G, H, N, O, P, S, T,  W, a,
b, c, d, e, f, h, i, k, l, m, n, o, p, r, s, t, u, v, y]
```

As we have seen with the other collections, the standard library provides extension methods to convert a set to another collection type. There are quite a few extension methods to take that pain away from you, as shown in the following code:

```
    val longsList: List<Long> =longSet.toList()
```

```
val longsMutableList = longSet.toMutableList()
val donot= longSet.toLongArray()
val rightArray = longSet.toTypedArray()
```

This code example has been purposefully chosen to reiterate the conversion to arrays. While there are two options for primitive types, make sure you always pick the `to***Array` to get the best performance out of it.

Read-only views

When working with Kotlin, you will come across the concept of a read-only view of a mutable collection. You will probably wonder what is the difference between this and an immutable collection. It is easier to understand using an example. In this case, let's create a mutable list of strings. This applies to all the collections we have covered:

```
    val carManufacturers: MutableList<String> =  mutableListOf("Masserati",
"Aston  Martin","McLaren","Ferrari","Koenigsegg")
    val carsView: List<String> = carManufacturers

    carManufacturers.add("Lamborghini")
    println("Cars View:$carsView")  //Cars View: Masserati, Aston Martin,
McLaren,  Ferrari, Koenigsegg, Lamborghini
```

The code initializes a mutable list of car manufacturers and then provides a view on it via the `carsView` variable. If, going forward, we only keep a reference to the latter variable, we could actually consider the collection to be fully immutable, hence the read-only view term. However, if that is not the case, any changes made to the underlying collection would be reflected in the view automatically. The view is achieved by casting the collection to the immutable interface `List`. Keep in mind that the actual runtime implementations are not immutable.

Indexed access

Kotlin makes it easier to access the elements of a list or return the values for a key when it comes to a map. There is no need for you to employ the Java-style syntax `get(index)` or `get(key)`, but you can simply use array-style indexing to retrieve your items:

```
val capitals = listOf("London", "Tokyo", "Instambul", "Bucharest")
capitals[2]   //Tokyo
//capitals[100] java.lang.ArrayIndexOutOfBoundException

val countries = mapOf("BRA" to "Brazil", "ARG" to "Argentina",  "ITA"
```

```
to "Italy")
    countries["BRA"]    //Brazil
    countries["UK"]     //null
```

While it saves you a few keystrokes, I find this construct a lot clearer to read. But nothing is stopping you from falling back to the `.get` method.

The preceding syntax is only available in Kotlin, and the reason it works lies in the interface declaration for `List` and `Map`. They were listed at the beginning of this chapter. There you can find the following definition:

```
//list
public operator fun get(index: Int): E

//map
public operator fun get(key: K): V?
```

Since the methods have been declared as operators, we can use array like indexing as a shortcut to typing `.get`.

Sequences

We defined what a sequence is and what it does at the start of this chapter. Sequences are great for scenarios when the size of the collection is not known in advance. Think about reading a table from a database, where you wouldn't know how many records you will get back; or reading a local .csv file, where you don't know how many lines it contains. You can think of a sequence as a list that goes on and on. A sequence is evaluated on a need-to-know basis, and only to the point needed. Think of the Fibonacci series; there is no point in constructing the collection in advance. How many items do you need to compute? The caller determines that.

If you have worked with Scala or Java 8, you will see the sequences as the Kotlin equivalent of `Stream` types. Since Kotlin supports Java 6 and it doesn't support a streaming library, they had to come with their own version. To avoid the confusion with Java 8, the Kotlin team has chosen this term. Unfortunately, the Kotlin library doesn't come with support for parallel sequence processing.

Before going further with a few examples, here are several ways to create a sequence:

```
    val charSequence: Sequence<Char> =
charArrayOf('a','b','c').asSequence()   //a,b,c
    println("Char
sequence:[${charSequence.javaClass.canonicalName}]:${charSequence.
```

```
joinToString(",")}")
    println("Char
sequence:[${charSequence.javaClass.name}]:${charSequence.joinToStr
ing(",")}")

    val longsSequence: Sequence<Long> = listOf(12000L, 11L, -
1999L).asSequence()  // 1200,11,-1999
    println("Long
sequence:[${longsSequence.javaClass.canonicalName}]:${longsSequenc
e.joinToString(",")}")
    println("Long
sequence:[${longsSequence.javaClass.name}]:${longsSequence.joinToS
tring(",")}")

    val mapSequence: Sequence<Map.Entry<Int, String>> =  mapOf(1 to  "A", 2
to "B", 3 to "C").asSequence() //1=A,2=B,3=C
    println("Long
sequence:[${mapSequence.javaClass.canonicalName}]:${mapSequence.jo
inToString(",")}")
    println("Long
sequence:[${mapSequence.javaClass.name}]:${mapSequence.joinToStrin
g(",")}")

    val setSequence: Sequence<String> = setOf("Anna","Andrew", "Jack",
"Laura","Anna").asSequence()
    println("String
sequence:[${setSequence.javaClass.canonicalName}]:${setSequence.jo
inToString(",")}")  //Anna, Andrew,Jack, Laura

    val intSeq = sequenceOf(1, 2, 3, 4, 5)
    println("Sequence of
integers[${intSeq.javaClass.canonicalName}]:$intSeq")

    val emptySeq: Sequence<Int> = emptySequence<Int>()
    println("Empty
sequence[${emptySeq.javaClass.canonicalName}]:$emptySeq")

    var nextItem = 0
    val sequence = generateSequence {
      nextItem += 1
      nextItem
    }
    //    sequence.joinToString(",") -> don't! Out of memory will be
thrown
    println("Unbound int
sequence[${sequence.javaClass.canonicalName}]:${sequence.takeWhile  {
      it <100
     }.joinToString(",")}") //1,2,3...99
```

```
    // println("Unbound int
sequence[${sequence.javaClass.canonicalName}]:${sequence.takeWhile  {
      it < 100
    }.joinToString(",")}")  //java.lang.IllegalStateException: This
sequence can be consumed  only once.

    val secondSequence = generateSequence(100) { if ((it + 1) % 2 ==  0) it
+ 1 else it + 2 }

    println("Unbound int
sequence[${secondSequence.javaClass.canonicalName}]:${secondSequen
ce.takeWhile {
      it <110
    }.toList()}") //100, 102, 104, 106, 108]
```

All the collection types we have seen so far can be converted to a sequence. The interesting part is the output for the class name. Run the code and you will see the console output is `null` when it comes to the class `canonical` name. However, when we print the name, you will see
`kotlin.collections.ArraysKt___ArraysKt$asSequence$$inlined$Sequence$9`.Why is that? Looking at the source code will clear all of this. Here is what actually gets executed when `asSequence` is called:

```
    public fun <T> Iterable<T>.asSequence(): Sequence<T> {
      return Sequence { this.iterator() } }

    public inline fun <T> Sequence(crossinline iterator: () ->
Iterator<T>): Sequence<T> = object : Sequence<T> {
      override fun iterator(): Iterator<T> = iterator()
    }
```

We have the `Sequence` interface, but we also have the `Sequence` extension method with one parameter-a function returning an `iterator`. All types derived from `Iterable`, by contrast, provide such a method: `iterator()`. Thus, the `asSequence` makes use of it. The `Sequence` method creates an instance of an anonymous class inheriting from the `Sequence` interface, and uses the `iterator` argument to return the iterator. There are special extension methods for arrays, since they don't derive from `Iterable`. Because we are using a `CharArray`, the following standard library code covers this type only, but there are equivalent implementations for the other array types:

```
    public fun CharArray.asSequence(): Sequence<Char> {
      if (isEmpty()) return emptySequence()
      return Sequence {
        this.iterator()
      }
    }
```

To create a fixed-length sequence, you can always rely on the `sequenceOf` extension. Because the method takes a variable length list of arguments, it uses the `Array<T>.asSequence` code. For scenarios where your sequence's upper limit is not known, you can use the `generateSequence` method. The first example returns all the integer numbers smaller than 100. As you can see in the code snippet, not adding a limit, will end up throwing an `OutOfMemoryError` if you want to build a string listing all the numbers in the sequence. The `joinToString` method will create a `StringBuffer` and keep appending the items to it; since there is no upper limit, eventually it will end up filling the runtime heap space and the error will be thrown. The same outcome will happen if you convert to a list or set. Therefore, avoid storing an unbounded sequence into a collection. Leaving aside the details of the Java garbage collector and its various implementations, the memory footprint for these `genearateSequence` methods is resumed to the parameter type `T` you are returning. The last part of the code example generates a sequence using a starting seed in order to return all the odd numbers from 100 to 110.

There is a fundamental difference between the two overloaded `generateSequence` extension methods. Iterating a second time over the sequence variable will end up in an exception: `IllegalStateException`. The reason for this lies with the code implementation for `generateSequence(nextFunction: ()->T?)`:

```
    public fun <T : Any> generateSequence(nextFunction: () ->T?):
Sequence<T> {
      return GeneratorSequence(nextFunction, { nextFunction()
}).constrainOnce()
    }

    public fun <T> Sequence<T>.constrainOnce(): Sequence<T> {
      return if (this is ConstrainedOnceSequence<T>) this else
ConstrainedOnceSequence(this)
    }

    private class ConstrainedOnceSequence<T>(sequence: Sequence<T>) :
Sequence<T> {
      private val sequenceRef =
java.util.concurrent.atomic.AtomicReference(sequence)

      override fun iterator(): Iterator<T> {
        val sequence = sequenceRef.getAndSet(null) ?: throw
IllegalStateException("This sequence can be consumed only once.")
        return sequence.iterator()
      }
    }
```

In this case, as you can see in the preceding snippet, the standard library will hand you back an instance of `ConstrainedOnceSequence`. Any attempt to get the iterator a second time will yield the exception mentioned earlier. The API documentation is quite good, and will let you know if the result is a sequence that can only be iterated once.

Let's see how we can use the API sequence to read a file. The next code example looks for a resource file, and uses the Java I/O library to open and read it line by line until null is returned:

```
    val stream =
Thread.currentThread().javaClass.getResourceAsStream("/afile.txt")
    val br = BufferedReader(InputStreamReader(stream))
    val fileContent = generateSequence { br.readLine() }.takeWhile {  it !=
null }
    println("File content:${fileContent.joinToString(" ")}")
```

For simplicity, all the error handling code has been left out. The output for this code will read: `Kotlin is awesome!`.

When talking about sequences, generating the Fibonacci series is almost a must, for some reason. So, let's follow the pattern and see how you can write that in Kotlin:

```
var prevNumber: Int = 0
val fibonacci1 = generateSequence(1) {
  val tmp = prevNumber
  prevNumber = it
  it + tmp
}
println("Fibonacci sequence: ${fibonacci1.take(12).joinToString(",")}")
```

The Fibonacci series is driven by the following rule: that every number after the first two is the sum of the two preceding ones: 1,1,2,3,5,8,13,21,34,55,89,144, and so on. In this first run of implementing such a sequence, we keep a reference of the previous number. Run the code and you should see the numbers mentioned earlier. This implementation, however, is not ideal. Can we create the sequence without having to close on the `prevNumber` variable? It turns out we can:

```
val fibonacc2 = generateSequence(1 to 1) {
  it.second to it.first + it.second
}.map { it.first }
println("Fibonacci sequence: ${fibonacc2.take(12).joinToString(",")}")
```

This second attempt is slightly more complex. It will produce a sequence of pairs (integer-integer) containing the current and next Fibonacci number, so 1-1, 1-2,2-3,3-5,5-8,8-13, and so on. Then, via the mapping function, it selects the first item of each pair. The result matches the previous one.

Summary

You have seen how to use the Kotlin collection API in great detail. You have learned how the standard library provides you with the distinction between immutable and mutable collection types, and how immutability is achieved at the interface level. You know now that Kotlin doesn't add any new collection, but rather relies on the existing Java large-collection library. Type aliasing done by the Kotlin compiler is not a mystery anymore. Now you can go and use the arrays properly because you leaned to use the specific implementations over the generic one when it comes to primitive types.

The Kotlin standard library provides you with the building blocks to express complex computations via a few simple extension methods, hopefully giving you a different perspective when it comes to choosing your next project language.

This chapter covers unit and integration testing using Kotlin using unit test frameworks. Unit testing is often a gateway into a new language, and this is no different.

11
Testing in Kotlin

One of the first things developers often do when adopting or evaluating a new language is that they roll it out gradually, starting with unit tests. The advantage of using this approach is that since your tests are not going into production, any issues with the language or bugs in the language library won't impact the real code. It gives the developers a chance to evaluate whether the language is a good fit for their needs, without worrying about the need to rewrite critical parts of their main code base if they decide to reject the new language.

In this chapter, we will introduce a powerful Kotlin testing library known as KotlinTest. This open source library is available on GitHub. By leveraging the powerful features of Kotlin, it provides useful testing features beyond what the typical Java test frameworks, such as JUnit or TestNG, currently offer.

Getting started

Writing your first test with KotlinTest is very straightforward. Firstly, the KotlinTest dependency will need to be added to your build. The easiest way to do this if you are using Gradle or Maven is to search Maven central for `io.kotlintest`– just visit `http://search.maven.org` and grab the latest version. You will need to add this to your Gradle build using the following:

```
testCompile 'io.kotlintest:kotlintest:2.0.0'
```

Alternatively, for Maven, use the following code:

```
<dependency>
  <groupId>io.kotlintest</groupId>
  <artifactId>kotlintest</artifactId>
  <version>2.0.0</version>
```

```
    <scope>test</scope>
  </dependency>
```

Next, create the test source folder, usually `src/test/kotlin`, if it doesn't exist already. We are going to write a unit test for the standard library String class. So create a file called `StringTest.kt`. Inside this file, create a single class called `StringTest`, which should extend `FunSpec`. The contents of the file should look something like the following:

```
import io.kotlintest.specs.FunSpec
class StringTest : FunSpec()
```

To write a unit test, we invoke a function called `test`, which takes two parameters. The first is a description of the test, and the second is a function literal that contains the body of the test. The description, or name, of the test will appear in the output so we know which tests have failed and which have passed.

For our first test, we'll assert that the `startsWith` function defined on the String should return `true` for valid prefixes. Each individual test is just placed inside an `init {}` block in the body of the class:

```
class StringTest : FunSpec() {
  init {
    test("String.startsWith should be true for a prefix") {
      "helloworld".startsWith("hello") shouldBe true
    }
  }
}
```

Notice the use of `shouldBe true`. This is an infix function that accepts a value and performs an equality check. If the values don't match, then the test will fail. KotlinTest refers to functions such as these as assertions.

Choosing a spec

In the first test that we wrote, we extended a class called `FunSpec`, which is just one example of what KotlinTest calls a *spec*. A spec, or style, is just the manner in which the tests are laid out in the class files. There are several different specs available, and which one you use is simply a matter of personal preference. The `FunSpec` class is the style most similar to the old preannotation JUnit style, which readers from a Java background may be familiar with.

The rest of this section will cover the various specs that are available for you to choose from. The first alternative style to the `FunSpec` class is `FlatSpec`. This forces the user to use the word `should` in the test names. This might appeal to developers who like uniformity in the testing names:

```
class MyTests : FlatSpec() {
  init {
    "String.length" should "return the length of the string" {
      "hello".length shouldBe 5
      "".length shouldBe 0
    }
  }
}
```

Very similar to `FlatSpec`, we have `WordSpec`, which again uses the word `should`. However, with `WordSpec`, instead of writing the test names on the same flat (flattened), you nest them:

```
class MyTests : WordSpec() {
  init {
    "String.length" should {
      "return the length of the string" {
        "hello".length shouldBe 5
        "".length shouldBe 0
      }
    }
  }
}
```

The next style is `ShouldSpec`, which is almost the same as the `FunSpec` class. There is one difference though, that is, the function name is `should` instead of `test`:

```
class MyTests : ShouldSpec() {
  init {
    should("return the length of the string") {
      "hello".length shouldBe 5
      "".length shouldBe 0
    }
  }
}
```

With `ShouldSpec`, the tests can actually be nested inside Strings if you wish to have multiple tests share the same parent namespace. What we mean by parent namespace is that these tests will be grouped together in a hierarchy inside the IDE:

```
class MyShouldSpec : ShouldSpec() {
  init {
    "String.length" {
      should("return the length of the string") {
        "hello".length shouldBe 5
      }
      should("support empty strings") {
        "".length shouldBe 0
      }
    }
  }
}
```

Moving on, we have `BehaviorSpec`. This is aimed at people who like to structure their tests in the style of specifications often seen in behavior-driven development. The tests are nested in three blocks, named `given`, `when`, and `then`. When combined, these blocks read like a natural language sentence. In addition, when looking at a report of executed tests, the behavior spec style can be read very nicely even by non-developers.

In Kotlin, `when` is a keyword, so we must stop using it with backticks. Alternatively, we can use the title case equivalents, namely `Given`, `When`, and `Then`, which are also provided:

```
class MyBehaviorSpec : BehaviorSpec() {
  init {
    given("a stack") {
      val stack = Stack<String>()
      `when`("an item is pushed") {
        stack.push("kotlin")
        then("the stack should not be empty") {
          stack.isEmpty() shouldBe true
        }
      }
      `when`("the stack is popped") {
        stack.pop()
        then("it should be empty") {
          stack.isEmpty() shouldBe false
        }
      }
    }
  }
}
```

The next spec we will cover is called `FeatureSpec`, which is similar to `BehaviorSpec`. The difference is that it uses the keywords `feature` and `scenario`:

```
class MyFeatureSpec : FeatureSpec() {
  init {
    feature("a stack") {
      val stack = Stack<String>()
      scenario("should be non-empty when an item is pushed") {
        stack.push("kotlin")
        stack.isEmpty() shouldBe true
      }
      scenario("should be empty when the item is popped") {
        stack.pop()
        stack.isEmpty() shouldBe false
      }
    }
  }
}
```

The final spec style is `String`. As the name implies, it simply uses Strings to group tests. This style is the simplest of all:

```
class MyStringSpec : StringSpec() {
  init {
    "strings.length should return size of string" {
      "hello".length shouldBe 5
    }
  }
}
```

When you're not sure which spec to pick, go with `StringSpec`. This is recommended by the KotlinTest authors.

Matchers

Matchers test for some property, indicated by the name of the matcher, beyond simple equality. For example, a matcher may check whether a string is empty or whether an integer is positive. In the getting started guide, we used the assertion `shouldBe` to check for equality. In fact, the assertion `shouldBe` also accepts a matcher that provides for more complicated assertions.

The idea behind the `shouldBe` naming convention is to lead to readable assertions, such as `thisString shouldBe empty()`. To further this goal, there is an equivalent of `shouldBe`, named `should`; with this, matchers such as `thisString` should `startWith("foo")` could be read as natural language.

Many matchers are provided by KotlinTest out of the box, and each one checks for some specific property or condition. In the rest of this section, we will cover some of the most fundamental matchers.

String matchers

One of the most common set of matchers is undoubtedly the String matchers. This is not surprising, given how fundamental String usage is throughout software development. This following table lists the common string matchers:

Matcher example	**Description**
`"hello world" should startWith("he")`	Tests string prefixes
`"hello" should include("ell")`	Tests substrings
`"hello" should endWith("ello")`	Test string suffixes
`"hello" should haveLength(5)`	Tests the length of a string
`"hello" should match("he...")`	Tests the equality, using a regular expression

Collection matchers

The next most useful set of matchers operate on collections, including lists, sets, maps, and so on:

Matcher example	**Description**
`col should contain(element)`	Tests that a collection should contain the given element.
`col1 should haveSize(3)`	Tests the sizes of the collections.
`list shouldBe sorted<Int>()`	Tests that the collections should be sorted. This only works for lists that contain the subclasses of `Comparable`.

`col shouldBe singleElement(element)`	Tests that the collection has a single element that is equal to the given element.
`col should containsAll(1, 2, 3)`	Tests that the collection contains all the given elements. The order of these elements does not matter.
`col should beEmpty()`	Tests whether the collection is empty or not.
`map should haveKey(key)`	Tests whether the map contains mapping from a key to any value.
`map should haveValue(key)`	Tests whether the map contains the value for at least one key.
`map should contain(key, value)`	Tests that the map contains the exact mapping of the key to the value.

Floating point matchers

A very useful matcher is the tolerance matcher, which is defined on doubles. When testing the equality of doubles, one should not use simple equals. This is because of the imprecise nature of storing some values, mainly repeating decimals in base 2 (just like one-third cannot be exactly represented in base 10).

The safest and most correct way to do floating point comparison is to assert that the difference between two numbers is below some value. The value chosen is the *tolerance,* and it should be low enough to satisfy your criteria that the numbers are equal. KotlinTest has built-in support for this:

```
a shouldBe 1.0
a shouldBe (1.0 plusOrMinus 0.001)
```

The first example can lead to errors if the result stored was not exactly `0.1`. The second example uses the tolerance factor of `0.001` and performs an absolute difference comparison.

Expecting exceptions

Sometimes, we want to assert that a function will throw an exception, perhaps to test a precondition we may have added. A naive approach to this would be to wrap the function invocation in a try...catch block and throw an exception in the try part. Here is a function that will throw an exception when invoked with a non-positive number:

```
fun squareRoot(k: Int): Int {
  require(k >= 0)
  return Math.sqrt(k.toDouble()).toInt()
}
```

Here is our initial approach to testing it:

```
try {
  squareRoot(-1)
  throw RuntimeException("This test should not pass")
} catch (e: Exception) {
  // noop
}
```

However, as you may have probably guessed, KotlinTest can take care of this for us. It provides the `shouldThrow` block, which will check that an exception was thrown, and if not, will fail the test for us:

```
shouldThrow<IllegalArgumentException> {
  squareRoot(-1)
}
```

Note that `shouldThrow` will also fail the test if the wrong type of exception is thrown. Here, we expect only `IllegalArgumentException`. So, for example, a generic `RuntimeException` would cause the test to fail.

Combining matchers

Matchers can be combined together using the usual Boolean logical operators of conjunction (`and`) and disjunction (`or`). We can do this using the infix functions that are named for those operators:

```
val thisString = "hello world"
thisString should (haveLength(11) and include("llo wor"))
```

In the preceding example, both the matchers must pass or the test will fail. Notice the parentheses around the matchers; also, we must use the `should` or `shouldBe` keywords only once:

```
val thisString = "hello world"
thisString should (haveLength(11) or include("goodbye"))
```

In the second example, only one test must pass, just like we're used to seeing. Also, the matchers are lazily evaluated; therefore, if the first matcher passes, the second will not be invoked.

Custom matchers

You may have seen the usage of some of the many built-in matchers that KotlinTest provides, but you don't need to stop there. KotlinTest also supports writing your own matchers, and this is extremely straightforward.

Every matcher is just an instance of the `Matcher` interface:

```
interface Matcher<T> {
  fun test(value: T): Result
}
```

Each matcher must implement a single function test that would receive the value as a parameter on the left-hand side of the `shouldBe` function. The values on the right-hand side of the `shouldBe` function are just constructor parameters for the matcher passed in via a function that is responsible for creating the matcher. The test function should return an instance of `Result`, which just contains a Boolean flag for whether the test has passed or not and a message to be outputted if it has not.

For demonstration purposes, we'll try to improve the experience of testing files. Let's say we are writing a unit test and we want to test that a file exists and that the file is an image file. For our example custom matcher, it is sufficient for us to assume that a file is an image if it has a well-known image file extension. In the real world, you might wish to go further by trying to load the file contents to confirm whether it is really an image.

The first step is to create a function that will return the matcher. The function will be what the users would see on the right-hand side of `shouldBe`, so it is best if it has a name that reads well:

```
fun anImageFile() = object : Matcher<File> {
  override fun test(value: File): Result {
  }
```

Notice that the matcher has a type parameter, which is the type of value the matcher can be used to verify. The `shouldBe` function is an extension function defined on this type parameter, so the compiler will helpfully restrict the usage of matchers to only those types that are valid. In other words, our file matcher here would only work on a file variable, and so you would not be able to be use it on a String accidentally, for example.

The implementation of the custom matcher is simple. We just need to use the `exists` function on the `File` object and also check the name:

```
val anImageFile = object : Matcher<File> {
  private val suffixes = setOf("jpeg", "jpg", "png", "gif")
  override fun test(value: File): Result {
    val fileExists = value.exists()
    val hasImageSuffix = suffixes.any {
    value.name.toLowerCase().endsWith(it) }
    if (fileExists.not()) {
      return Result(false, "File $value should exist")
    }
    if (!hasImageSuffix) {
      return Result(false, "File $value should have a well known
      image suffix")
    }
    return Result(true, "Test passed")
  }
}
```

Once the matcher is implemented, all that remains is that you use it. The function must be imported into a scope, so it needs to be either a top-level function with an import or should be placed in a `supertype` and inherited:

```
class MatcherTest : FunSpec() {
  init {
    test("testing our file matcher") {
      val file = File("/home/packt/kotlin.jpg")
      file shouldBe anImageFile
    }
  }
}
```

Notice how the assertion now reads as a grammatically correct statement. Although there is no requirement to name your functions in such a way, it does mean it would make the test easier to read for someone not familiar with the code.

By writing your matchers to the `Matcher` interface, they can automatically be used in logical operators. Let's imagine we want to bring the `exists` functionality out in a separate matcher and then introduce a matcher to test a specific file type:

```
fun exist() = object : Matcher<File> {
  override fun test(value: File): Result {
    val fileExists = value.exists()
    return if (!fileExists) {
      return Result(false, "File $value should exist")
    } else {
      Result(true, "Test passed")
    }
  }
}
```

Now add a matcher to test that the file has the given file extension:

```
fun ofFileType(ext: String) = object : Matcher<File> {
  override fun test(value: File): Result {
    val isOfType = value.name.toLowerCase().endsWith(ext)
    return if (!isOfType) {
      Result(false, "File $value is not of type $ext")
    } else {
      Result(true, "Test passed")
    }
  }
}
```

Then use these two matchers together using the normal and and/or operators:

```
class MultipleMatcherTest : FunSpec() {
  init {
    test("testing our file matcher") {
      val dir = File("/home/packt/images")
      for (file in dir.listFiles()) {
        (file should exist()) and (file shouldBe
        ofFileType("jpeg"))
      }
    }
  }
}
```

This shows how quickly you can add custom matchers to encapsulate your testing logic, making it reusable across multiple test files.

Inspectors

KotlinTest inspectors are an easy way to test the contents of collections. Sometimes, you may wish to assert that only some elements of a collection should pass an assertion. Other times, you may want no elements to pass an assertion, just one, or two, and so on. Of course, we can do this ourselves by just iterating over the collection and keeping track of how many items have passed the assertions; however, inspectors do this for us.

Let's start with the usual case that we want all the elements of a collection to pass the assertions. For this, first of all, we'll define a list that we'll work with throughout the rest of the section:

```
val kings = listOf("Stephen I", "Henry I", "Henry II", "Henry III",
"William I", "William II")
```

Then, we'll assert that every king has a regal number that ends with the letter `"I"`. Refer to the following:

```
class InspectorTests : StringSpec() {
  init {
    "all kings should have a regal number" {
      forAll(kings) {
        it should endWith("I")
      }
    }
  }
}
```

This particular test could have also been achieved with the function `All` on the collections. Other cases are not so easy without inspectors, and the next example will show this:

```
class InspectorTests : StringSpec() {
  init {
    "only one king has the name Stephen" {
      forOne(kings) {
        it should startWith("Stephen")
      }
    }
  }
}
```

Without an inspector, we will have to catch the exceptions and keep a count of how many `kings` have passed the test. The inspector hides this piece of boilerplate for us. The next inspector is quite interesting:

```
class InspectorTests : StringSpec() {
```

```
    init {
      "some kings have regal number II" {
        forSome(kings) {
          it should endWith("II")
        }
      }
    }
  }
```

This is an example of the `forSome` inspector that asserts that at least one element, not all the elements, has passed the test. So for *n* elements in a collection, the test will pass if between *1* and *n-1* elements matched the assertion.

There are many different inspectors, but we'll show just one more:

```
  class InspectorTests : StringSpec() {
    init {
      "at least one King has the name Henry" {
        forAtLeastOne(kings) {
          it should startWith("Henry")
        }
      }
    }
  }
```

The `forAtLeastOne` inspector, as the name implies, simply checks that one element has passed the test. It differs from the `forSome` inspector in that it allows all the elements to pass.

Interceptors

When moving beyond the scope of standalone unit tests and into tests that require resources, it is often the case that we would need to set up these resources before a test and tear them down again later. For example, a database connection may need to be initialized for use by a test and then closed properly once the test is finished. We can do this manually in a test, but if we have a suite of tests, then this soon becomes laborious.

Wouldn't it be nicer if we could just define a function once and and then have it run before and after each test or each suite of tests. This functionality exists in KotlinTest under the name of *interceptors*. Each type of interceptor is defined to run before and after the code is tested. Let's discuss the different types of interceptors.

The test case interceptor

The first type of interceptor is the test case interceptor. These are interceptors added directly to test cases themselves, and they only apply to the test cases they were added to. A test case interceptor receives two parameters. The first is the *test case context*. This contains details of the test, such as the name of the test, which spec file it is located in, how many invocations it should have, and so on. The second parameter is the test itself in the form of a zero arity function. This function must be invoked by the interceptor or the test will be skipped. This gives test interceptors the power to choose whether to run the test or not.

In the following example, we will define an interceptor that will output the time taken to run a test:

```
val myinterceptor: (TestCaseContext, () -> Unit) -> Unit = {
  context, test ->
  val start = System.currentTimeMillis()
  test()
  val end = System.currentTimeMillis()
  val duration = end - start
  println("This test took $duration millis")
}
```

Notice how the test is invoked inside the interceptor. The next step is to add the interceptor to any tests we want to be timed:

```
"this test has an interceptor" {
  // test logic here
}.config(interceptors = listOf(myinterceptor))
"so does this test" {
  // test logic here
}.config(interceptors = listOf(myinterceptor))
```

Notice that each test case accepts a list of interceptors. Although in this case we've only used one, we can add an arbitrary number.

The spec interceptor

The next type of interceptor is the spec interceptor. It is used to intercept all the tests in a single test class. The spec interceptor is very similar to the test case interceptor; the only difference is that the test case context is replaced by spec context. Just like the earlier interceptor, you must invoke the provided function; otherwise, the entire spec will be skipped. So this gives you the ability to use custom logic to determine whether a spec will run or not:

```
val mySpecInterceptor: (Spec, () -> Unit) -> Unit = {
  spec, tests ->
  val start = System.currentTimeMillis()
  tests()
  val end = System.currentTimeMillis()
  val duration = end - start
  println("The spec took $duration millis")
}
```

Here we have implemented our timing interceptor again, this time to time the entire spec. To use this, override a property called `specInterceptors` providing a list of the interceptors:

```
override val specInterceptors: List<(Spec, () -> Unit) -> Unit> =
listOf(mySpecInterceptor)
```

This is all very similar to the test case example.

Project config

Sometimes you may wish to execute some code before any tests are run at all or after all the tests are completed (whether successful or not). This can be achieved through the use of the `ProjectConfig` abstract class. To use this, simply create an object that will extend from this abstract class and ensure it is on the class path. Then, KotlinTest will automatically find it and invoke it:

```
object MyProjectConfig : ProjectConfig() {
  var server: HttpServer? = null
  override fun beforeAll() {
    val addr = InetSocketAddress(8080)
    val server = HttpServer.create(addr, 0)
    server.executor = Executors.newCachedThreadPool()
    server.start()
    println("Server is listening on port 8080")
  }
  override fun afterAll() {
    server!!.stop(0)
  }
}
```

In this case, we've made a `ProjectConfig` instance that creates an embedded HTTP server so that all the tests can use this server without the need to create their own. After all the tests are completed, the server will be shut down again.

We couldn't put this code into any particular spec (suite of tests) because we don't know the order in which the specs will be executed. So how do we know which file will contain it? Even if there was a deterministic order, there's nothing you could do to stop another spec from being added, whichever one comes first in the ordering.

Property testing

An alternative method of testing that is popular in frameworks, such as `QuickCheck` in Haskell and `ScalaCheck` in Scala, is the idea of property testing. Property testing is aimed at testing a single property of a function at a time. For example, when concatenating two strings together, the length property should always remain consistent as the sum of the original two lengths. This is in contrast to the normal style of testing, which is example-driven.

Note that a property in this case doesn't refer to the properties of objects, as in fields or members. Instead, it refers to some invariant or predicate that should be true.

Given that we are going to test that a property holds for multiple input values, it follows that we would want to use as many different values as possible. For this reason, property-based testing is often associated with the automatic generation of input values. In KotlinTest, these values are provided through the aptly named generators.

To use a generator for property testing, we need to use an inspector-style call to which we will pass another test function. This test function must have the parameter types specified because the compiler will not be able to infer them. The same function must return a Boolean, and the Boolean will indicate whether the property is held for the input values. That is, we don't need to use matchers in property testing; the return value of the function will itself indicate the correctness of the property.

In the following example, we will test the length of a concatenated string, as mentioned earlier, as an example:

```
"String.size" {
  forAll({ a: String, b: String ->
    (a + b).length == a.length + b.length
  })
}
```

Notice that the parameters have type ascriptions. KotlinTest uses the parameter types to work out which kind of generators to use for each input. Each input receives its own instance of a generator even if the types are the same. We used `forAll` in this example, but we could have used `forNone` instead, which is just the inverse.

When the test case is executed, the framework will rerun this test hundreds of times, each time requesting new values from the generators. The input will not only be between a-z or alphanumeric, but it could be any unicode value or values. This kind of generator is useful for generating input that we might overlook when writing an example-based unit test.

The obvious benefit to this approach is that we can test many more combinations manually, giving us greater confidence in the robustness of our code. The downside is that we don't have control over specific values, so an edge case may slip through many times before it is finally chosen as a random value.

Specifying a generator

As we've seen, property testing is often used to quickly test multiple input values. However, sometimes the automatically provided generators may not be exactly what we want. For example, if we're testing a square root function, we would not want to generate negative numbers. So instead of allowing KotlinTest to pick a default generator, we just provide one manually when writing the test:

```
"squareRoot" {
  forAll(Gen.int(), { k ->
    val square = squareRoot(k)
    square * square == k
  })
}
```

KotlinTest comes with many built-in generators, such as natural numbers, negative integers, random files, and so on.

A custom generator

Sometimes, we want to specify our own input ranges or values completely and the built-in generators are not sufficient enough; this is where custom generators come in handy. KotlinTest has several ways to conveniently create a generator. For example, we can create a generator that returns a random element from a collection each time it is invoked:

```
val values = listOf("pick", "one", "of", "these")
forAll(Gen.oneOf(values), { element ->
```

```
    // test logic
})
```

Or, we can create a generator over a range of numbers and have the generator pick a random number from that range:

```
forAll(Gen.choose(1, 10000), { k ->
  // test logic
})
```

Alternatively, if the built-in helpers are not sufficient, we can always create one ourselves from scratch. All we need to do is extend the `Generator<T>` interface, with `T` being the type returned, and implement the `generate` function. The `generate` function is invoked each time the framework requires another number, so the results should not be cached. In the next example, our custom generator returns a random even integer each time:

```
fun evenInts() = object : Gen<Int> {
  override fun generate(): Int {
    while (true) {
      val next = Random.default.nextInt()
      if (next % 2 == 0)
      return next
    }
  }
}
```

Once you get the integer, you can drop it at the right place:

```
forAll(evenInts(), { k ->
  val square = squareRoot(k)
  square * square == k
})
```

Table-driven testing

The idea behind table-driven tests is similar to property-based testing. The difference here is that instead of generators providing random values, the set of input values is manually specified. The way we do this is by declaring a table structure that can be hardcoded into the test or loaded from a file.

The easiest approach is to simply hardcode the table, and this works fine if we have a small range of input values or edge cases we want to test. For example, we may have a function with three Boolean input values and want to test the combinations. The first step is to define the table that contains the combinations we want to test:

```
val table = table(
  headers("a", "b", "c"),
  row(true, true, true),
  row(true, false, true),
  row(true, false, false)
)
```

Notice that we use the headers and row helper functions. The header is important. It is not used for the input but is used to label the values that will fail when a test does not pass. To this table, we pass it as blocks, which will resemble the inspector functions once again:

```
forAll(table) { a, b, c ->
  a shouldBe true
  if (b)
  c shouldBe true
}
```

Note that in table-driven testing, a function does not need to return a Boolean value. So unlike property-based testing, we should use regular matchers.

As mentioned earlier, headers are used for error reporting. If a particular row fails, then the output will be something like the following:

```
Test failed for (x, 9), (y, 12), (z, 18) with error 225 did not equal 324
```

There are row and header implementations that cover tuples up to 22 elements. If this isn't enough, then the function under the test is probably too large and would benefit from being split out.

Testing non-deterministic code

When testing non-deterministic code — such as futures, actors, or consistent data stores — it is useful to be able to assert that at some point, a test is expected to pass, even if that test had failed at first. A common way to achieve this is to use a countdown latch and adapt the code under the test to release the latch once the code is completed:

```
val latch = CountDownLatch(1)
```

```
createFile("/home/davidcopperfield.txt", { latch.countDown() })
latch.await(1, TimeUnit.MINUTES)
// continue with test
```

In the preceding example, we are able to use a latch in the `createFile` function because it accepts a listener that is invoked when the file is created.

Note that a countdown latch is a concurrency primitive that will block any thread calling `await` on it, until it has been counted down the appropriate number of times.

This trick doesn't work if we're not able to change the code under the test to be able to accept some function, callback, or listener. Sometimes, we are forced to fall back to the most naive approach, which is to make the thread sleep for a period of time:

```
createFile("/home/davidcopperfield.txt")
Thread.sleep(5000)
// continue with test
```

This approach is problematic because the sleep timeout must be large enough so that we don't wake up too early and fail the build. On the other hand, if an extremely large value is picked, our test throughput drops right off as we wait for the sleep to expire, even though we might be able to continue earlier.

What we really want is some way to have a test wait while a condition is `false` and then finish the test as soon as it flips to true. KotlinTest performs this trick by introducing a neat feature called `Eventually`, which was inspired by a similar functionality in ScalaTest.

To use `eventually` feature, we must first extend the `Eventually` interface which provide the functionality:

```
class EventuallyExample : WordSpec(), Eventually
```

Then, invoke the `eventually` function passing in a duration first and a function literal to be executed second. The function will be executed repeatedly until either the duration is expired or the function literal is completed successfully. Let's revisit the file create example; it could be rewritten using `eventually` method like this:

```
class FileCreateWithEventually : ShouldSpec(), Eventually {
  init {
    should("create file") {
      eventually(60.seconds) {
        createFile("/home/davidcopperfield.txt")
      }
    }
```

```
    }
}
```

Note that since the function is evaluated multiple times, it shouldn't rely on any state that has been changed by a prior run.

Tags, conditions, and config

In this section, we'll briefly cover the various configuration options that can be used to control *how* tests are executed and *which* tests are executed.

Config

Each test case makes a config function available, which can be used to set specific configurations for that test, such as threading, tags, and whether the test is enabled or not. For example, we can change the number of times a test is executed:

```
class ConfigExample : ShouldSpec(), Eventually {
  init {
    should("run multiple times") {
      // test logic
    }.config(invocations = 5)
  }
}
```

We set the number of invocations to five. This is the number of times the same test will be executed each time the unit tests phase is invoked. A complement to the number of invocations is the number of threads those invocations will use. By default, this is one:

```
should("run multiple times in multiple threads") {
  // test logic
}.config(invocations = 20, threads = 4)
```

In this example, the test will run 20 times, but a thread pool of four threads will be used to execute the tests. When using this option, we must of course make sure that the tests are thread-safe.

The other useful option is to set a timeout so that a thread can be killed if it is taking too long to complete. Each individual test can have their own configuration settings independent of the others.

Conditions

Conditions are a simple way of enabling or disabling a test based on runtime evaluation. The config block contains an *enabled* property, which is invoked before a test is executed in order to access whether that test should be executed or skipped (not withstanding any additional logic in an interceptor).

The simplest case is to just set the value to `false`:

```
should("be disabled") {
  // test logic
}.config(enabled = false)
```

The default, if omitted, is true. Generally speaking, the option to turn off a test completely by hardcoding the value to `false` should be used sparingly. Perhaps you can restore a green build while investigating why a test had failed.

We can extend this to use runtime lookup by defining a function instead of a hardcoded value. In fact, anything that is an expression can be used. For instance, we may decide that we only want to execute a test on a multicore system:

```
fun isMultiCore(): Boolean =
Runtime.getRuntime().availableProcessors() > 1
should("only run on multicore machines") {
  // test logic
}.config(enabled = isMultiCore())
```

Conditions can be written to support many use cases, such as limiting tests to certain operating systems or machines with certain hardware requirements or running tests only at a certain time of the day.

Tags

Similar to conditions, tags allow a way of grouping tests so they can be enabled or disabled at runtime. Each test case can have its own tag or tags set (can be one or several); it can also be left without a tag. At runtime, a system property can be set–which would determine which tags are included or excluded–indicating that only tests that match the requirements will be executed.

A tag is just an object that extends from the abstract class `Tag`. The name of the tag is then taken as the class name without any package namespace. For example, we can tag a test with a database and operating system requirement:

```
object ElasticSearch : Tag()
```

```
object Windows : Tag()
should("this test is tagged") {
  // test logic
}.config(tags = setOf(ElasticSearch, Windows))
```

If we were using Gradle, we could execute only these tests using the following command:

```
gradle test -DincludeTags=Windows,ElasticSearch
```

If we want to exclude any test that requires Windows, because we want to run a Linux build job, then we could use the following command:

```
gradle test -DexcludeTags=Windows
```

If you set both the include and exclude properties, then only tags that match both the sets of requirements will be run. If the runtime properties are omitted entirely, then all the tests will be executed, which is the normal mode.

Because the simple name of the tag is used, if you define multiple tags with the same name in different packages, they will appear as the same tag to KotlinTest.

One instance

Sometimes, you may wish to have a fresh instance of a test class for each test that is executed. Perhaps you have some initialization code outside of the `init {}` block and want this to be reset for each test. An easy way to do this is to just have KotlinTest instantiate a new instance of the class.

To do this, simply override the `oneInstancePerTest` property and set it to `true`:

```
class OneInstanceOfTheseTests : ShouldSpec() {
  override val oneInstancePerTest = true
  init {
    // tests here
  }
}
```

Resources

One final neat feature of KotlinTest is the ability to automatically close resources once all the tests are completed. This is essentially a shortcut to writing an interceptor and closing them yourself, and is useful if all you need to do is ensure that some handle is closed:

```
class ResourceExample : StringSpec() {
  val input = autoClose(javaClass.getResourceAsStream("data.csv"))
  init {
    "your test case" {
      // use input stream here
    }
  }
}
```

The usage is straightforward. Simply wrap the resource, such as the input stream in this example, with the `autoClose` function. Regardless of the outcome of the tests, the resources will be properly shut down.

Summary

This chapter focused on how Kotlin can be leveraged to write cleaner and more readable tests. We saw the popular KotlinTest framework in action and how it can be extended to fit your use cases. KotlinTest is continually being improved, so it is worth checking out the readme files on the GitHub website for new features that have been added since the date of its publication.

12
Microservices with Kotlin

Kotlin is not meant to be used only for Android development. There is a lot of back-end code out there, all written in Java, and nothing should stop you adding Kotlin into the mix whenever you have to add new functionality. Don't get locked into Java as your only option when it comes to deciding on the JVM language to be used in your new project. When your new microservices-oriented system gets the green light for you to start coding, why not actually rely on Kotlin?

This chapter is not meant to be a deep dive into the realm of designing microservices, but rather a brush up on the terminology. There is a lot of documentation written on the topic of microservices and you might have already been exposed to the principles; however, I encourage you to read *Reactive Microservices Architecture: Design Principles for Distributed Systems* by Jonas Bonér. The book can be obtained for free in pdf format from O'Reilly, so thank you to Jonas (`https://info.lightbend.com/COLL-20XX-Reactive-Microservices-Architecture-RES-LP.html`).

In this chapter you will learn:

- What microservices architecture is
- Why you would use such an approach and what are the drawbacks
- Setting up a Lagom maven project to allow coding with Kotlin
- Defining Lagom services
- Running a Lagom dev cluster

Definition

The way we design and build software has changed in the past few years. We are developing software designed to run in the cloud and it is driven by fast-changing business needs. If you are already familiar with this world, you will recognize some of the drivers behind the approach we take these days:

- There is a demand for reducing the costs while still improving performance
- You have to continuously deliver new functionality to meet business growth, and the turnaround needs to be fast
- The software has to reach customers around the globe and cope with the high demand it might produce while running at such a scale

To see a definition of what microservices are and how we arrived at such principles, let's do an exercise. Imagine you had the amazing idea of Airbnb, and there wasn't anything like it on the market. Now you are in the position to define a high-level view of your system architecture. Taking a very simplistic approach, you might produce something similar to this:

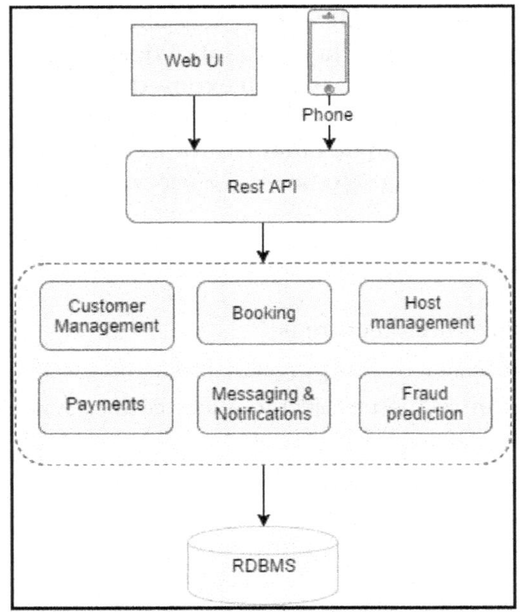

Monolithic system design

I am sure you have identified the typical three-tier-level design:

- UI layer
- Domain/business layer
- Storage layer

Initially this could easily prove to be the right solution, since you can package and deploy the application as one. You can even run multiple instances of it once you have configured a load balancer. It all sounds easy and right… at the beginning. But your idea is revolutionary and your business grows exponentially. If you are curious, I suggest you do a quick search on Airbnb customer-base growth. Seeing the impressive figures, you will understand that if you achieve such success, you have to push out more and new functionality to cope with the demand. As you do that, your lines of code count will grow considerably and with that the complexity of your software. Before you know it, you will start to pay the cost. Fixing bugs and adding functionality will prove to be more and more challenging. Your development speed will suffer and, since you own the business, you won't be impressed; and of course your revenue won't reach its maximum potential. Your deployment will also take longer because your application will most likely take longer to start, and therefore your continuous delivery will be affected considerably. Then think about reliability. You have all your modules running under the same process. While it is certainly advantageous to some degree, all it takes is a memory leak in one of the modules to bring your entire system down. I do not need to tell you how annoying it is to see *service unavailable* if you are sitting in the customer's position. One of the other big downsides of this monolithic approach is refactoring. Having to upgrade or even replace a framework may prove to be quite a task; most likely it will impact the whole application and it will require full testing as well.

This is where the new approach of microservices is helping. The idea is quite simple and some people will argue microservices is just a buzzword for what is already known as **Service Oriented Architecture** (**SOA**). The design principle for SOA is driven by these four tenants:

- Boundaries are explicit
- Services are autonomous
- Services share schema and contract, not class
- Service compatibility is based on policy

In the next two paragraphs we will define the principles for microservices and you will notice the real difference to SOA lies in the size and scope of your services.

To avoid pain down the road, you are supposed to split your application into many small services, each one focusing on a specific functionality; the services will interact with each other in order to provide all of the business requirements.

There isn't a bog-standard definition for microservices; searching the Internet will give various definitions of what they are and what they do. But all of them share some common ground:

- Can be developed in the language of choice and use the framework of choice
- Communicate between themselves using a well-defined protocol and over an established set of interfaces
- Provide for one business scenario only
- Can be independently versioned
- Can be independently deployed and upgraded
- Can be scaled out
- Can hold a state, if required
- Are resilient to failures
- Report the current state, metrics, and diagnostics

Putting all the above together will give you an idea of what microservices are.

Now we have covered the definition of microservices, let's revisit our earlier high-level diagram for an Airbnb-like system. The following is one approach for breaking down the monolithic app into smaller pieces:

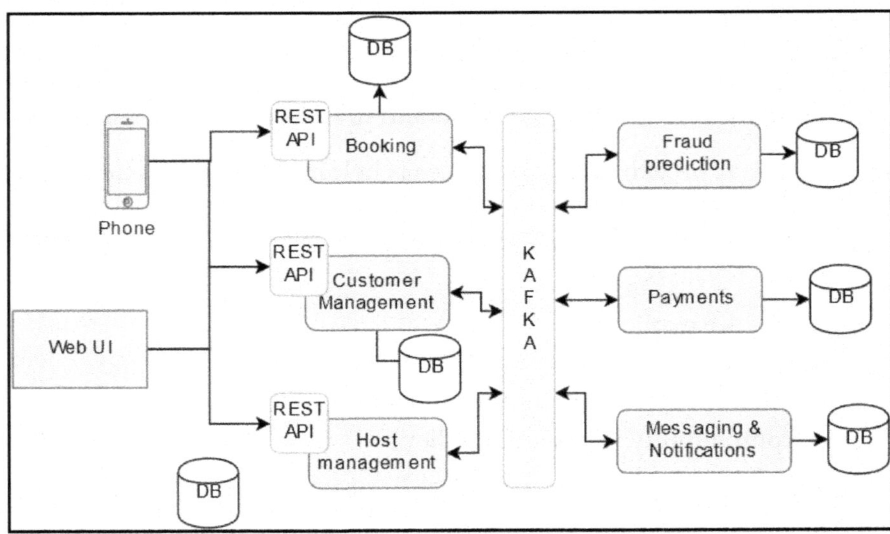

Microservices architecture

You might have noticed the earlier database storage has been left out. There is a reason for it. To ensure a loose coupling between your microservices, having a database schema per service is the way to go. This way you can't have an application-wide data model and you will end up duplicating data for sure. But there are a few reasons as to why you would want to do something like this. They are a consequence of not having tightly coupled components. This way, each service can work with their own database instance (to the extreme) and it doesn't have to be of the same database type. You can have the customer and host services working with a database such as MongoDB or RethinkDB, while the payments service can rely on a MySQL database. Evolving a database schema will have no impact on another service. This will add more complexity to the DevOps side by having to maintain more than one database instance.

Many references about a microservices architecture will talk about having an **RPC** (**remote procedure call**) as the means of communicating between services. RPCs are meant for inter process communications. RPC enables applications to call functions remotely and they can operates between processes on a single computer or on different computers on a network. A typical approach is where each component has an exposed REST endpoint, which can be called in order to trigger a set of actions. As your system grows in complexity, you will easily end up with spaghetti-like data pipelines. If you are familiar with the Kafka framework you will know the challenges LinkedIn faced and the reasons why it was built. If this is not something you are familiar with, please have a quick read or listen to some of the talks from Jay Kreps.

Drawbacks

No technology is perfect and using microservices has its drawbacks. As one would say, there are no silver bullets.

We mentioned that microservices have their own database schema. Therefore, you can't have transactional updates for your domain models like you usually do when dealing with a monolithic application using one database. Your system will eventually end up being consistent and that comes with its own bag of challenges.

Implementing a change that will end up touching more than one service has its own complexity. In a monolithic application, these things are quite straightforward. All you have to do is change the modules required and then deploy all of them in one go. But for a distributed microservices system, where there are dependencies between services, you need to plan the upgrade. You will end up deploying the service that all the other ones depend upon first and then repeat this step until the last required service is upgraded. Luckily, such changes are not very common. Usually the changes are self-contained to one service only.

Since we are on the subject of deploying, let's expand a bit more on the drawbacks of a system with a microservices architecture. Deploying a monolithic application is quite simple since it involves distributing the build artefacts and, if high availability is a requirement, then you would do that on a set of servers that have a load balancer in front of them. Things are a lot different for a system consisting of many separate services. Some of the well-known applications have different services in the hundreds, and each of the services has multiple instances to ensure high availability. To configure, deploy, scale, or monitor requires more deployment control and a higher level of automation. To achieve this automation, you might go with a PaaS solution, or implement your own through the combination of Docker and Kubernetes.

One other challenge for a microservices architecture comes when trying to test your application. A monolithic app is easy to spin up, but for microservices things are slightly different. In this case the tests need to launch the service and stub all its dependent services, and, of course, that takes more effort from you, the developer.

These points should not disarm you and make you avoid a microservices architecture. The benefits outweigh the challenges presented here. If the big names are doing it, they must know a thing or two. Uber didn't used to have a microservices architecture, but has slowly moved in that direction to cope with its business demands. So, plan well at the beginning to ensure the architecture empowers your business to thrive as opposed to being a bottleneck for its growth.

Why microservices?

While you might have been put off by the list of drawbacks presented earlier, you should keep in mind that there are real benefits for taking this approach; and if it wasn't paying off, people wouldn't do it.

One of the main benefits of a design like this is breaking down the complexity of a monolithic application. It will end up providing a finite set of services allowing one to achieve the same functionality while having code that is easier to understand, maintain, and evolve.

You will find that with the microservices approach you are not restricted to a specific technology and language. Because a service can be developed independently by one team, its members get to decide on the tech stack that makes the most sense for the problem at hand. How many times did you want to use a newer framework and/or language because it adds value, but you have been stuck with a framework or language that is old because the cost of change is so high that it is not justified?

A microservices design supports continuous deployment. A microservice can be deployed independently. As soon as changes have been tested, they can be shipped to production. Because deployment is isolated, you can have many upgrades during the day without even stopping your application.

To achieve throughput, each microservice can be scaled independently. Furthermore, the server hosting your service can be configured based on the resources required. If your service is memory hungry, you can have a machine with a lot more RAM than CPUs and vice versa, thus optimizing your costs.

There are other reasons why you would design your system using microservices principles, but it is for you to go and read more in-depth papers about the subject. At least, by now, you should see the value added by the approach.

Lagom

Lagom is a new JVM framework from Lightbend for writing microservices. This is a new open-source framework released at the beginning of 2016. At the time of writing this book, version 1.2 is out. You can find the source code on GitHub `https://github.com/lagom/lagom`. From there you can navigate to the framework website, which contains more details and its documentation.

Lagom comes with support for four main features: **Service API**, **Persistence API**, **Development Environment**, and **Production Environment**.

Through Service API you declare and implement the services to be consumed by the clients. A service-locator component allows the services to be discovered. Furthermore, the API allows for a synchronous request-response protocol as well as asynchronous streaming.

The Persistence API provides support for persisting your domain entities in your services. Lagom takes care of the distribution of those persisted entities across a cluster of nodes, enabling sharding and horizontal scaling with Cassandra database out-of-the-box. Nothing is stopping you from plugging in your own required storage type. The term sharding, for those who have never came across it before, is a way of partitioning the data for a database over multiple machines. The reason for this is to spread the load and achieve linear scaling in order to meet the performance requirements.

The Development Environment allows the running of all your services and the supporting Lagom infrastructure through the use of one command. With Lagom, a developer can bring up a new service or join an existing Lagom development team in just a few minutes.

Lagom provides out-of-the-box support for Production Environment through **Lightbend ConductR**, which allows the simple deployment, monitoring, and scaling of Lagom services in a container environment.

Lagom has full support for two of the build tools available on the market: SBT and Maven. Since SBT is not everyone's cup of tea, we will be focusing on Maven. The easiest way to get started and learn about Lagom is to make use of the Maven archetype plugin to generate a basic project. Once you grow accustomed to the layout and dependencies, you can create the `pom` file yourself. Since there is no support for a Kotlin-based project yet, we will have to start with a Java-based project and then amend the `pom` to enable Kotlin. It is expected that you already have Apache Maven installed on your machine. If not, please follow the instructions on the Apache Maven website to get it installed.

From your terminal window, type the following command:

```
mvn archetype:generate -DarchetypeGroupId=com.lightbend.lagom \ -
DarchetypeArtifactId=maven-archetype-lagom-java -DarchetypeVersion=1.2.0
```

This will prompt you to provide **GroupId** (`com.programming.kotlin`), **ArtifactId** (`chapter12`), and **version** (left blank). Once you have run this, you should see the following folder layout structure:

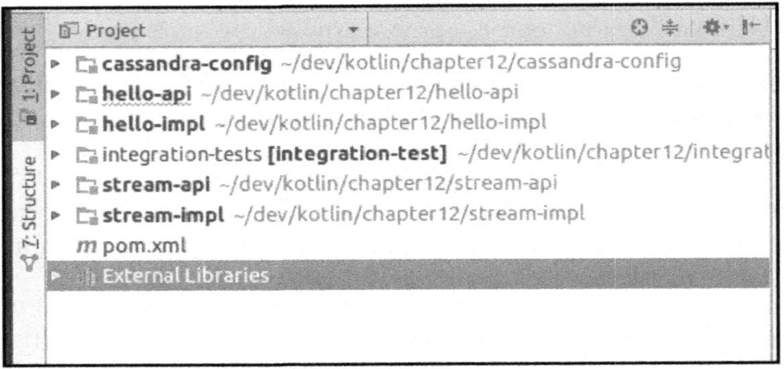

Modules layout

Next we need to add the Maven plugin for the Kotlin compiler. `Chapter 1`, *Getting started with Kotlin*, has already covered this, so let's go and modify the pom file accordingly.

For this project, `Kotlin 1.1-M04` will be used. This is the latest release for version 1.1 at the time this is written. If you attempt to use it with any of the 1.0.x versions, it won't work since Java 8 support comes only with the 1.1 version. You might know by now that this version comes with a bag of improvements and, most importantly, support for co-routines. The C# developer in me misses this kind of functionality whenever I code for JVM. So, the first thing you should do is add a new property in your `pom` file for the Kotlin version:

```
<properties>
  ...
  <kotlin.version>1.1-M04</kotlin.version>
  <lagom.version>1.2.0</lagom.version>
  ...
</properties>
```

The milestone builds are not stored in the default Maven repo, and we would need to add them in order to get the dependencies resolved. The following needs to be added to the `pom` file:

```
<project>
  <modelVersion>4.0.0</modelVersion>
  <groupId>com.programming.kotlin</groupId>
  <artifactId>chapter12</artifactId>
  <version>1.0-SNAPSHOT</version>

  <packaging>pom</packaging>

  <pluginRepositories>
    <pluginRepository>
      <snapshots>
        <enabled>true</enabled>
      </snapshots>
      <id>bintray-kotlin-kotlin-dev</id>
      <name>bintray</name>
      <url>http://dl.bintray.com/kotlin/kotlin-dev</url>
    </pluginRepository>
  </pluginRepositories>

  <repositories>
    <repository>
      <snapshots>
        <enabled>true</enabled>
      </snapshots>
      <id>bintray-kotlin-kotlin-dev</id>
      <name>bintray</name>
```

```
        <url>http://dl.bintray.com/kotlin/kotlin-dev</url>
      </repository>
    </repositories>
  ...
```

Next, we need to enable the Kotlin compiler and allow the Java compiler to run after during the Maven build. Hence, the following changes have been made to the `pom` file. Please revisit `Chapter 1`, *Getting started with Kotlin*, for more details on why this is required.

```
<build>
<plugins>
...
<plugin>
  <groupId>com.lightbend.lagom</groupId>
  <artifactId>lagom-maven-plugin</artifactId>
  <version>${lagom.version}</version>
 </plugin>
 <plugin>
  <groupId>org.apache.maven.plugins</groupId>
  <artifactId>maven-compiler-plugin</artifactId>
  <version>3.5.1</version>
  <configuration>
    <source>1.8</source>
    <target>1.8</target>
    <compilerArgs>
      <arg>-parameters</arg>
    </compilerArgs>
  </configuration>
  <executions>
      ...
  </executions>
</plugin>
</plugins>
...
```

Don't worry about typing this in yourself. You will find it all in the source code accompanying the book. Hopefully, soon we will see a Maven archetype template allowing a Lagom project to support Kotlin.

So far, we can build the code and run the services. From the terminal, execute the following to start all the services:

```
mvn lagom:runAll
```

This will compile the code, run the tests, and start all the services. We will cover each one in a moment. To validate all of them is fine, and to run this you should type `localhost:9000/api/hello/World` into your browser and you will see **Hello, World** printed on the screen. There are two endpoints for `/api/hello`, as you will find out later. To verify the HTTP `POST` works, fire off this curl command:

```
curl -H "Content-Type: application/json" -X POST -d '{"message":"Hi"}'
http://localhost:9000/api/hello/Gabriela
```

Since we enabled Kotlin, we might as well translate the code from Java to Kotlin. Let's start with the `hello-api` project and the `GreetingMessage` class. First you need to create a `kotlin` folder, a sibling of the Java one, which will contain the Kotlin source files. Next, add the following package to the newly created folder: `com.programming.kotlin.chapter12.hello.api`. Create a new Kotlin file and paste in the following code, while commenting out the corresponding Java file:

```
@JsonDeserialize data class GreetingMessage(val message: String)
```

Immutable classes are important for Lagom and there are a few places where they need to be used:

- Service request and response types
- Persistent entity commands, events, and states
- Publish and subscribe messages

If you are using Java and you want the boilerplate code handled, you would need to use and set up the **Immutables** tool (`http://immutables.github.io/`). But, luckily, Kotlin does allow us to quickly create an immutable class with all the `equals`, `hashCode` and `toString` generated for us out of the box. Remember, if an immutable class contains a member which is a collection, this collection needs to be immutable if the class provides a getter for it and otherwise the immutability guarantee is broken. As you know already, Kotlin offers support for immutable collection in the standard library, so it's very easy to provided a proper immutable class even if contains a collection.

Next, let's translate the `HelloService.java` to Kotlin:

```
interface HelloService : Service {
  fun hello(id: String): ServiceCall<NotUsed, String>

  fun useGreeting(id: String): ServiceCall<GreetingMessage, Done>

  override fun descriptor(): Descriptor {
    val helloCall: (String) -> ServiceCall<NotUsed, String> = {
this.hello(it) }
```

```
        val helloGreetings: (String) -> ServiceCall<GreetingMessage, Done>
= { this.useGreeting(it) }

         return named("hello")
         .withCalls(
           pathCall("/api/hello/:id", helloCall),
           pathCall("/api/hello/:id", helloGreetings))
          .withAutoAcl(true)
      }
    }
```

Now let's move our focus to the `hello-impl` project and provide the Kotlin implementation for `HelloServiceImpl` class (you need to comment out the Java implementation generated for you):

```
    class HelloServiceImpl
    @Inject
    constructor(private val persistentEntityRegistry:
PersistentEntityRegistry) : HelloService {
      init {
        persistentEntityRegistry.register(HelloEntity::class.java)
      }

      override fun hello(id: String): ServiceCall<NotUsed, String> {
        return ServiceCall<NotUsed, String>{
          val ref =
persistentEntityRegistry.refFor(HelloEntity::class.java, id)
          ref.ask<String, Hello>(Hello(id, Optional.empty<String>()))
        }
      }

      override fun useGreeting(id: String): ServiceCall<GreetingMessage,
Done> {
        return ServiceCall<GreetingMessage, Done>{
          val ref =
persistentEntityRegistry.refFor(HelloEntity::class.java, id)
          ref.ask<Done, UseGreetingMessage>(UseGreetingMessage(it.message))
        }
      }
    }
```

If you are running `mvn lagom:runAll` in your terminal, you will see every code change is picked automatically. The Maven Lagom plugin is responsible for watching file changes and recompile your code automatically. With the preceding code changes, you will see that there is now an error as it tries to launch the services again:

```
Error in custom provider, java.lang.IllegalArgumentException:
```

```
Service.descriptor must be implemented as a default method
  at
com.lightbend.lagom.javadsl.server.ServiceGuiceSupport.bindServices(Service
GuiceSupport.java:33) ...
Caused by: java.lang.IllegalArgumentException: Service.descriptor must be
implemented as a default method at
com.lightbend.lagom.internal.api.ServiceReader$ServiceInvocationHandler.inv
oke(ServiceReader.scala:280)
```

The code where the exception is thrown first checks to see if the `descriptor` method has a Java 8 interface default method, and if not, checks if it has been created with Scala (Lagom is written in Scala and on top of the Akka framework). Unfortunately, the Java 8 interop coming next to Kotlin is not yet perfect and it doesn't handle default interface methods. There is no way to tell the compiler the `descriptor` method in the earlier code should be compiled as a Java 8 default method. So, for the time being, we have to rely on Java to define the service interface. Hence, if you uncomment the Java code for `HelloService` and remove the Kotlin implementation, you will be able to get the environment up and running again.

The `api-impl` project is next in line to have its code translated to Kotlin. Most of the code is quite straight forward to change. It ends up reducing the number of lines of code quite a bit. Below, you will see the listings of the new files for `HelloCommand`, `HelloEvent`, `HelloState`:

```
    //HelloCommand.kt
    interface HelloCommand : Jsonable

    @JsonDeserialize data class UseGreetingMessage @JsonCreator
constructor(val message: String) : HelloCommand, CompressedJsonable,
PersistentEntity.ReplyType<Done>

    @JsonDeserialize data class Hello @JsonCreator constructor(val name:
String, val organization: Optional<String>) : HelloCommand,
PersistentEntity.ReplyType<String>

    //HelloEvent.kt
    interface HelloEvent : Jsonable

    @JsonDeserialize data class GreetingMessageChanged @JsonCreator
constructor(val message: String) : HelloEvent

    //HelloState.kt
    @JsonDeserialize data class GreetingMessage @JsonCreator
constructor(val message: String)
```

The `HelloEntity` class is slightly more challenging to convert. The editor doesn't do a great job when converting the Java code to Kotlin. It ends up producing code that doesn't compile. Because it is trickier to convert from Java (the editor is misleading as it falsely highlights errors), we are listing it next. At the time of writing these lines, Kotlin 1.1 hasn't been released and the IDE is not fully compatible with the upcoming version. I am sure by the time you read these lines it will all be sorted out.

```
    class HelloEntity : PersistentEntity<HelloCommand, HelloEvent,
HelloState>() {

      override fun initialBehavior(snapshotState: Optional<HelloState>):
PersistentEntity<HelloCommand, HelloEvent, HelloState>.Behavior {

        val b = newBehaviorBuilder(snapshotState.orElse(HelloState("Hello",
LocalDateTime.now().toString())))

        b.setCommandHandler(
          UseGreetingMessage::class.java,
          { cmd, ctx ->
          ctx.thenPersist(
            GreetingMessageChanged(cmd.message),
            { evt -> ctx.reply(Done.getInstance()) })
          }
        )

        b.setEventHandler(GreetingMessageChanged::class.java,
          { evt -> HelloState(evt.message, LocalDateTime.now().toString())
}
        )

        b.setReadOnlyCommandHandler(Hello::class.java,
          { cmd, ctx -> ctx.reply(state().message + ", " + cmd.name + "!")
}
        )

        return b.build()
      }
    }
```

You should be able to handle the rest of the conversions yourself; you can always cross check with the source code provided for this chapter.

Before moving on, fire the curl command mentioned earlier in the chapter to do a post on the `/api/hello`. You will notice it will now throw an exception because it can't map the JSON payload to the `GreetingMessage` class. This happens even despite of adding the json annotations to the class. We need to handle the serialization and deserialization ourselves.

First, we need to add the Jackson Kotlin (offers one of the best support for JSON for the JVM) library module dependency to the `hello-api` project. We are using version 2.7.8 because this is the version Lagom uses for core Jackson library:

```
<dependency>
  <groupId>com.fasterxml.jackson.module</groupId>
  <artifactId>jackson-module-kotlin</artifactId>
  <version>2.7.8</version>
  <exclusions>
    <exclusion>
      <groupId>org.jetbrains.kotlin</groupId>
      <artifactId>kotlin-stdlib</artifactId>
    </exclusion>
    <exclusion>
      <groupId>org.jetbrains.kotlin</groupId>
      <artifactId>kotlin-reflect</artifactId>
    </exclusion>
  </exclusions>
</dependency>
```

The next step is to create an instance of the `ObjectMapper` via the singleton pattern:

```
object Jackson{
  val mapper: ObjectMapper = {
    ObjectMapper().registerKotlinModule()
  }()
}
```

To support the `GreetingMessage` class serialization, a class-inheriting `StrictMessageSerializer` must be provided. The code is straight forward, as you can see here:

```
    class GreetingMessageSerializer :
StrictMessageSerializer<GreetingMessage> {

      internal var serializer:
MessageSerializer.NegotiatedSerializer<GreetingMessage, ByteString> =
object : MessageSerializer.NegotiatedSerializer<GreetingMessage,
ByteString> {
        override fun protocol(): MessageProtocol {
          return MessageProtocol().withContentType("application/json")
        }

        @Throws(SerializationException::class)
        override fun serialize(messageEntity: GreetingMessage): ByteString
{
          return
```

```
ByteString.fromArray(Jackson.mapper.writeValueAsBytes(messageEntity))
        }
      }

      internal var deserializer =
MessageSerializer.NegotiatedDeserializer<GreetingMessage, ByteString> {
          bytes ->
Jackson.mapper.readValue(bytes.iterator().asInputStream(),
GreetingMessage::class.java)
      }

      override fun serializerForRequest():
MessageSerializer.NegotiatedSerializer<GreetingMessage, ByteString> =
serializer

      @Throws(UnsupportedMediaType::class)
      override fun deserializer(protocol: MessageProtocol):
MessageSerializer.NegotiatedDeserializer<GreetingMessage, ByteString> =
deserializer
      @Throws(NotAcceptable::class)
      override fun serializerForResponse(acceptedMessageProtocols:
List<MessageProtocol>):
MessageSerializer.NegotiatedSerializer<GreetingMessage, ByteString> =
serializer
    }
```

To let the framework use this class, the `HelloService` descriptor code needs to be amended to map the class to the serializer-deserializer. The documentation for Lagom provides a detailed view on how you can provide your own custom serialization; if you want to know more please read the documentation.

```
    @Override
    default Descriptor descriptor() {
      return named("hello").withCalls(
        namedCall("hi", this::sayHi),
        pathCall("/api/hello/:id", this::hello),
        pathCall("/api/hello/:id", this::useGreeting)
      ).withAutoAcl(true)
      .withMessageSerializer(GreetingMessage.class, new
GreetingMessageSerializer());
  }
```

Now we are in a position where we can say we have full support for a Lagom-based project using Kotlin. You can re-launch the services via the `maven` command and check they are running.

Defining services

When writing your project, you should adhere to best practices and standards. A service interface should always be placed in a `*-api` project. You can see the `HelloService` interface follows the same rule. The requirement is for your service interface to extend the Lagom service interface and provide a default implementation for the descriptor method. The descriptor is responsible for mapping the service to the underlying transport protocol.

```
public interface HelloService extends Service {
  ServiceCall<NotUsed, String> hello(String id);
  ServiceCall<GreetingMessage, Done> useGreeting(String id);

  @Override
  default Descriptor descriptor() {
    return named("hello").withCalls(
      pathCall("/api/hello/:id",  this::hello),
      pathCall("/api/hello/:id", this::useGreeting)
    ).withAutoAcl(true);
  }
}
```

This is quite a simple description of a service exposing two service calls: `hello` and `useGreeting`. Both methods return an instance of a `ServiceCall` representing the handle to the method call that can be invoked when consuming the service. The definition of the `ServiceCall` is as follows:

```
interface ServiceCall<Request, Response> {
  CompletionStage<Response> invoke(Request request);
}
```

This interface definition is simple and, as you can see, it encapsulates the concept of the request-response paradigm.

A service implementation should be agnostic to what transport protocol is used. In the code generated, the protocol is HTTP; however, nothing is stopping you from changing that to WebSockets or any other one that better suits your needs.

Each call to a service needs to carry an identifier. This identifier will map the call to the appropriate method on the interface. These identifiers can take the form of static names or paths (as we have seen in the code generated), but they can carry dynamic parameters that are handed over to the service call methods.

The simplest identifier is the one defined via `namedCall` method – as the naming suggests, you label your service call. Let's extend `HelloService` to include such a call. The `sayHi` method has been added to the interface, and this time the code is using `namedCall` instead of `pathCall`:

```
public interface HelloService extends Service {
  ServiceCall<NotUsed, String> sayHi();
  ...
  @Override
  default Descriptor descriptor() {
    return named("hello").withCalls(
      namedCall("hi", this::sayHi),
      ...
    ).withAutoAcl(true);
  }
}
```

Now the `HelloServiceImpl` class needs to be updated to provide the implementation for `sayHi`:

```
    override fun sayHi(): ServiceCall<NotUsed, String> =
ServiceCall<NotUsed, String>{
      completedFuture("Hi!")
    }
```

Once the has been recompiled, you should be able to paste the following URL: `http://localhost:9000/hi` into your browser and see the text **Hi!** on the screen.

The template project has used path-based identifiers – you can see that in the `HelloService` code snippet preceding. This type of identifier uses a URI path and query string to route calls, and can optionally provide parameters that can be extracted out. If you have worked with a REST service, you will be familiar with the concept. Say you are working on a health insurance system and you want to be able to return the customers for an insurance policy. Your service definition will probably look like this:

```
    ServiceCall<NotUsed, PSequence<Customer>> getDependents(long
policyHolderId, int pageNo, int pageSize);

    default Descriptor descriptor() {
      return named("customers").withCalls(
        pathCall("/customer/:policyHolderId/dependencies?pageNo&pageSize",
this::getDependents)
      );
    }
```

Lagom framework will make sure your service method map to the appropriate REST method types. Type `http://localhost:9000` into your browser and you will get a list of all the endpoints available:

1. GET \Q/hi\E Service: hello (`http://0.0.0.0:57797`)
2. GET \Q/api/hello/\E([^/]+) Service: hello (`http://0.0.0.0:57797`)
3. POST \Q/api/hello/\E([^/]+) Service: hello (`http://0.0.0.0:57797`)
4. GET \Q/stream\E Service: stream (`http://0.0.0.0:58445`)

You can see both `POST` and `GET` are supported for the `/api/hello` path. You might wonder where is that defined. This is provided by Lagom framework itself. It will look at the `ServiceCall` definition and if the incoming parameter is not set to `NotUsed`, then it will map the service call to the `POST` request type.

There is one last type of call identifier supported by the framework. These are REST call identifiers and they offer you finer-grained definition of your service call mappings to REST calls. Imagine you have a service to provide **Create**, **Read**, **Update**, and **Delete** (**CRUD**) for a customer base. Then your service interface will take the following shape:

```
ServiceCall<Customer, NotUsed> addCustomer(long customerId);
ServiceCall<NotUsed, Customer> getCustomer(long customerId);
ServiceCall<NotUsed, NotUsed> deleteCustomer(long customerId);

default Descriptor descriptor() {
  return named("orders")
  .withCalls(
    restCall(Method.POST,    "/api/customer", this::addCustomer),
    restCall(Method.GET,     "/api/customer/:customerId/",
this::getCustomer),
    restCall(Method.PUT,     "/api/customer/:customerId",
this::updateCustomer)
    restCall(Method.DELETE, "/api/customer/:customerId",
this::deleteCustomer)
  );
}
```

You might have noticed in the `descriptor` definition the presence of `NotUsed` class. This type instructs the framework that the incoming request parameter or outgoing response object is not used. If you look at the definition for deleting a customer, you will notice both the request and the response are not used. All the examples of code presented so far use what is known as *strict messages*. A message is considered to be strict if it can be mapped to a JVM class. There is also another type of message, which is **stream**. Streaming functionality is built on top of Akka Streams API. You will recognize a stream message when you see the usage of the type `Source` type. The API is offering an intuitive way of describing data-stream processing setups, and can execute them efficiently and with bounded resource usage.

```
ServiceCall<String, Source<String, ?>> gbpToUsd()
ServiceCall<Source<String, ?>, Source<String, ?>> chatRoom()
```

The first entry describes a unidirectional stream, whereas the second one is a bidirectional one. By default, Lagom uses WebSockets to provide the transport layer for the data streams but you are free to hook in your own transport mechanism. We are not going into the details of Lagom streaming support, but you are more than welcome to go and learn more using the documentation provided with the framework.

Implementing a Lagom service

We have seen already how to define a service. The next natural step is to implement the service interface, and this is materialized in the `hello-impl` project. The `HelloServiceImpl` class is responsible for implementing your API interface. We have seen this throughout the code snippets listed earlier. One important thing to notice is that all the methods don't actually execute the call, but rather return a method handle via the instance of `ServiceCall`. The reason behind this approach is to allows function composition in order to achieve a processing pipeline where authentication, authorization, logging, and exception handling can easily be added.

Let's move the focus back to `ServiceCall` class. From the definition presented already, you can see it takes a request object and returns a `CompletionStage<Response>`. This container is nothing but a promise the API makes. At some point in the future, the `Response` will be computed and therefore will be available to be consumed. Through the API methods, `thenApply` and `thenComponse`, you can morph the response type. This will, of course, yield another promise. The `CompletionStage` type and its methods allow you to build reactive applications that are fully asynchronous. The simple implementation for the `sayHi` method introduced earlier, should make more sense now.

Once your service is implemented, you need to register it with the framework in order to make use of it. Lagom is built on top of the Play framework, which allows you to build scalable web applications using Java or Scala. By default, the framework uses Guice as the dependency injection framework and therefore Lagom relies on it as well. This is why the `HelloModule` class exists and it inherits both `AbstractModule` (a Guice-specific class) and `ServiceGuiceSupport` (Lagom-specific).

```
class HelloModule : AbstractModule(), ServiceGuiceSupport {
  override fun configure() {
    bindServices(serviceBinding(HelloService::class.java,
HelloServiceImpl::class.java))
  }
}
```

The `bindServices` method can take multiple `ServiceBinding` instances. However, in the example we have provided only one. But this should not stop you providing as many service bindings as you require. But, make sure you only call `bindServices` once, otherwise you will end up with a Guice runtime-configuration error.

When you start working with Lagom, you will come across the terms **Event Sourcing** (**ES**) and **Command Query Responsibility Segregation** (**CQRS**). Before defining what ES is, let's see the basic traits of an event:

- It represents a business action. Think about booking a flight; you would say, "the seat on flight BA0193 was booked by Alex Smith."
- It carries some description information with it. Carrying on with the example earlier, the you attach data to your event in the form of your personal information, baggage allowance, flight dates, and so on.
- It is an immutable, one-way messages. A publisher, in this case the booking website, will broadcast the message and *N* number of subscribers will receive it.
- It happened in the past. When you describe an event, you will always use the past tense.

ES is an approach for persisting your application state by storing the history that determines its current state. Caring on with the example of buying a flight ticket, the booking system will track the number of completed bookings for the flights involved and the remaining available seats. There are two options for tracking available seats: either start with the total available and decrease this number until it reaches zero, or always sum the existing bookings to see if it has reached the maximum number of seats available on the aircraft.

You might ask yourself what is the benefit of ES, other than building the audit trail for all your data. If you are developing software for a financial institution, this is already an important gain. However, there are other benefits as well:

- **Performance**: Since the events are immutable, the write can make use of append-only mode, thus making them faster to store. But you must pay attention using this approach because you need to recreate the application state by walking through all the records. That could be costly and is sometimes unacceptable, however there are ways to overcome the drawbacks.
- **Simplicity**: Storing events could save you the complexity of having to deal with complex domain models.
- **Data replay-ability**: You have your sequence of events and any bug, let's say some aggregated value is wrong, can be fixed by walking through the data stored and applying the new codebase.

Of course, ES comes with its own challenges. You need to make sure your system can cope with multiple versions of a given message/event type. Then how would you handle complex queries. Imagine a system like Airbnb, one question you might want to answer is: What are all the bookings made for Rome for July 2015 with a price per night higher than 100 euros? This is where CQRS will come into play.

CQRS is a pattern that originated in the **Domain Driven Design** (**DDD**) pattern. DDD is an approach for designing complex systems with ever-changing business rules; you analyse the domain problem to produce a conceptual model, which becomes the basis of your solution.

We will not go into the depths of DDD (it goes far beyond the scope of this chapter), but we will define a few specific terms that you will come across while working with Lagom. While defining your domain model, you will use the following terms:

- **Entities**: Objects that can be described by an identity that will never change. Your flight booking reference is one of these.
- **Value-objects**: Not all your objects can be entities. For these objects, the value of their attributes is important. For example, the flight booking system doesn't have to provide a unique identifier for the customer's address.
- **Services**: You can't model everything as an object. The payment system will most likely rely on third-party payment processing. Most likely you will build a stateless service, which is responsible for passing all the information required by the third party to process the payment.

In the DDD world, the term aggregate defines a cluster of entities and value objects which form a consistency boundary within the system. The entities and value objects are related to each other.

The access to the objects within an aggregate must go through an aggregate root. This basically becomes the gatekeeper. Through the aggregates, DDD describes and manages the set of type relationships part of a typical domain model.

Going back to the CQRS pattern, its goal is to allocate the responsibility for modifying and querying your different object types. It ends up creating a `write` and a `read` model. Since the objects have a single responsibility, either to modify or read data, it will make your code a lot simpler and easier to maintain.

Now that we have the context covered, we can talk in more detail about persisting entities. In the source code generated you get the `HelloEntity` class derived from `PersistentEntity`, a base class providing never-changing identifier. Through this identifier, any object can be accessed. Behind the scenes, the framework uses ES to persist the entity. Of course, all state changes are recorded in the sequence they appeared by appending them to an event log. A persistent entity is the equivalent of the aggregate root we discussed earlier.

Interacting with a `PersistentEntity` comes in the form of a command message. These are messages you send and they get processed one by one. A command message could result in a state change, which is then recorded:

```
b.setCommandHandler(UseGreetingMessage::class.java, {
  cmd, ctx -> ctx.thenPersist(GreetingMessageChanged(cmd.message), {
    evt -> ctx.reply(Done.getInstance()) })
})
```

You should provide a command handler for each message type. In this case, we have only one. Each command handler is responsible for returning a `Persist` instance, which describes what event(s) to persist if there is such requirement. The code sample is instructing the persistence for only one event; however, there is support for persisting more than one event through `thenPersistAll`.

If the incoming message is not correct, you can reject it by using `ctx.invalidCommand` or `ctx.failedCommand`. For example, if the `GreetingMessage` has an empty message field you would want to reject the command.

Not all the messages end up modifying the state. This is specific to query messages. In this case, you will use `setReadonlyCommandHandler` to register your command handler:

```
b.setReadOnlyCommandHandler(Hello::class.java,{
  cmd, ctx -> ctx.reply(state().message + ", " + cmd.name + "!") })
```

Once the event has been stored, the current entity store is updated by combining the current state with the incoming event. You will use `setEventHandler` to register your handler, which should return a new immutable state. `PersistentEntity` provides a state method to get your latest entity's state. You should provide a state event handler for each command message type. In the code example, there is only one message type and all it does is retain the latest message and the time it was received:

```
b.setEventHandler(GreetingMessageChanged::class.java, {
  evt -> HelloState(evt.message, LocalDateTime.now().toString())
})
```

Normally, you would run a few instances of your service and each entity would be located automatically to one of the nodes. If a node is going down, then those entities allocated to it will be rerouted to another working node. One good thing is that a command producer doesn't have to know about the actual location. The framework will take care of routing it to the appropriate node. For optimization purposes, the framework will cache the entity and its state if is used, and will release the resources after it hasn't been accessed for a given time window. When an entity is loaded, it might replay all the events ever stored or use a snapshot approach to get its latest state.

Summary

In this chapter, you have learned how a microservice architecture recommends building a system as a collection of small and isolated services, where each service owns its own data and can be independently scaled to provide resilience to failure. These services interact with each other to form a cohesive system. This chapter was a quick introduction to Lagom, which is the new framework for developing reactive microservices on the JVM. There is far more to talk about when it comes to Lagom. It is a book on its own. Hopefully, this quick introduction has given you the appetite to go and learn more about it. You have seen how to enable Kotlin for the Lagom project, and now you can go on and utilize all the benefits of Kotlin to more quickly develop your next distributed system.

The last chapter of this book will be an introduction to concurrency. It will go over the terminology and how concurrency common problems can be solved in Kotlin. You will get to read about Akka and discover what it is and how it helps with concurrency and of course how they integrate with Kotlin.

13
Concurrency

You've most likely heard of Moore's Law. In 1965, Gordon Moore noticed that the number of transistors that could be fit on a circuit board per square inch had doubled every year since their invention. Moore's Law was the name given to the belief that this would continue, albeit every 18 months. So far, this has been remarkably correct. The upshot is that computers are getting faster and smaller, and they use less power; one example is the ubiquity of mobile phones.

However, nothing lasts forever. The exponential growth in the context of processing power is already tailing off. If we are unable to continually make systems work faster by increasing raw speed, we must look for an alternative.

One such alternative is to split programs into parts that could run concurrently and then use multiple processors. Together, a collection of slower chips can perform as fast as one faster chip as long as the programs are able to parallelize their code to take advantage. A collection of chips on a single CPU is referred to as a multicore processor.

Structuring programs that allow them to be run concurrently requires new approaches and techniques. Many of the ideas that underpin concurrency are not new and have been around since the 1970s. What's new is that modern languages allow us to use these ideas more easily than we can in lower level languages.

Concurrency is such a large subject that an entire book can be dedicated to it, so this chapter focuses on a few key fundamentals. This chapter will cover the following topics:

- Threading
- Synchronization and monitors
- Concurrency primitives
- Asynchronous and non-blocking techniques

Threads

A thread is one of the most basic building blocks of concurrent code. It is a part of a program that can execute threads *concurrently* to the rest of the code. Each thread can share resources, such as memory and file handles. In a system that allows threading, each process is divided into one or more threads. If the program was not written to use multiple threads and run concurrently, then it is called a **single thread process**.

In a single CPU system, multiple threads are interleaved, with each thread receiving a small amount of time called a **quantum**. This is called **time slicing** and happens so quickly that to the user, it appears as if the threads are running in parallel. For example, one thread might be updating a file while another is redrawing a window on the screen. To the user, they appear in parallel but may only be running sequentially. It is the same principle that is applied to running processes using the operating system scheduler.

When a thread expires, it's referred to as a time slice; when complete, the thread scheduler switches the thread with another one. This is called a **thread-context-switch** and is analogous to the context switch that the processes undergo. A thread context switch is more lightweight than a full process switch. This is because threads share many resources, and thus they have the data that needs to be saved and swapped out.

Concurrency is a general term that means two tasks are active and making progress at the same time, whereas parallelism is a stricter term that means two tasks are both executing at a particular instant. The two are often used interchangeably, but true parallelism is the goal of concurrent programming.

On a JVM, each `Thread` object has an associated state. A thread only has one state at a particular time. These states are listed in the following table:

State	**Description**
NEW	The thread has been created but not yet started.
RUNNABLE	A thread in this state is running from the point of view of the JVM. This does not necessarily mean it is executing the programming, as it may be waiting for a resource from the operating system, such as a time slice from the processor.
BLOCKED	A thread that is waiting to take ownership of a resource called monitor.
WAITING	A thread that has entered a waiting state. In this state, the thread will not be awakened until it has been notified by some other thread.

TIMED_WAITING	This is the same as WAITING, except that the thread here will exit the waiting state after a period of time has passed, if it has not already been notified.
TERMINATED	A thread that has exited.

Blocking

A thread that is running is consuming CPU resources. If a running thread is unable to make progress, it means it is consuming resources that could ideally be allocated to another thread that is ready to make meaningful use of the resource. An example would be a thread that is reading data from a network. A wireless network could be as much as 1,000 to 10,000 times slower than reading from the RAM; therefore, the majority of the time, the thread will simply be waiting for the network to deliver data.

In a naive threading implementation, the thread would keep looping, checking for the presence of more bytes until the operation is completed or checking whether the thread has expired its time slice. This is an example of busy-waiting, where although a thread is technically busy (using CPU time), it is not doing anything useful.

In a JVM, we are able to indicate that a thread is currently unable to progress and thus take it out of the set of threads that are eligible for scheduling. This is called blocking a thread. The advantage now is that when a thread is blocked, the thread scheduler knows to skip it, and so the thread won't waste CPU time busy-waiting.

Many I/O operations in the standard library perform the blocking operation, for example, `InputStream.read()`, `Thread.sleep(time)`, or `ServerSocket.accept()`.

Creating a thread

Kotlin has an extension function to make the process of creating a thread very easy. This top-level function, as part of the Kotlin standard library, is simply called **thread**. It accepts a function literal to execute as well as several named parameters to control the setup of the thread:

```
thread(start = true, name = "mythread") {
  while (true) {
    println("Hello, I am running on a thread")
  }
}
```

In the preceding example, we created a named thread that will begin executing immediately. If we want to delay the execution of a thread until some time in the future, we can store a handle in the thread instance and then call `start`:

```
val t = thread(start = false, name = "mythread") {
  while (true) {
    println("Hello, I am running on a thread sometime later")
  }
}
t.start()
```

If you do not name a thread, it will have the default name supplied by the JVM.

Stopping a thread

A thread will naturally stop once the function literal is returned. To preemptively stop a thread, we should not use the `stop` function available on the `Thread` class. This has been a deprecated method for many years. Instead, we should use a condition that we could loop on; alternatively, if your thread invokes blocking functions, use an interrupt and then allow the function to return.

For the former, we declare a property, say a `var` named `running`, which we set to true. Then, allow this variable to be mutated by whichever code needs to stop the thread. We must ensure that the thread regularly checks the state of this variable; otherwise, the thread might get into a state where it would never stop:

```
class StoppableTask : Runnable {

  @Volatile var running = true

  override fun run() {
    thread {
      while (running) {
        println("Hello, I am running on a thread until I am stopped")
      }
    }
  }
}
```

An important point to mention here is the use of the `@Volatile` annotation on the state variable. This is crucial to ensuring that the state of the variable is propagated between threads. Without the volatile annotation, outside threads may set the variable to false; however, a running thread may not see the change. This is part of the **Java Memory**

Model (JMM), which is out of the scope of this book. But if you are interested, an Internet search for JMM will get you enough material to have a good understanding.

If we have a thread that invokes blocking calls, then using a `running` variable alone will not work as the thread may be blocked when we set `running` to `false`. Consider the following example of a producer and consumer:

```
class ProducerTask(val queue: BlockingQueue<Int>) {

  @Volatile var running = true
  private val random = Random()

  fun run() {
    while (running) {
      Thread.sleep(1000)
      queue.put(random.nextInt())
    }
  }
}

class ConsumerTask(val queue: BlockingQueue<Int>) {

  @Volatile var running = true

  fun run() {
    while (running) {
      val element = queue.take()
      println("I am processing element $element")
    }
  }
}
```

The producer and consumer both share a queue. This queue is an instance of `BlockingQueue`, which offers blocking functions for getting and putting values into the queue — `take()` and `put()`, respectively. If there are no elements to take from the queue, the thread will be blocked until one is available. Notice the thread sleep on the producer, which is designed to slow the producer down. This is an example of *slow-producer fast-consumer*.

To start the example, we create instances of the tasks and begin the execution of multiple consumers and a single producer, each on their own thread:

```
val queue = LinkedBlockingQueue<Int>()

val consumerTasks = (1..6).map { ConsumerTask(queue) }
```

```
val producerTask = ProducerTask(queue)

val consumerThreads = consumerTasks.map { thread { it.run() } }
val producerThread = thread { producerTask.run() }

consumerTasks.forEach { it.running = false }
producerTask.running = false
```

At some point in the future, we may decide to shut down the producer and the consumer. We will do this using a control variable:

```
consumerTasks.forEach { it.running = false }
producerTask.running = false
```

Now let's imagine that one of our consumers was in the following state: it had called `take`, but the queue was empty and now it is in the blocking state. Since the producer is now shut down, it will never receive an item and so it will stay blocked. Because it stays blocked, it will never check for the control variable and so our program will never exit normally.

Note that in this example, this problem only affects the consumer and not the producer because the producer only ever blocks for a limited period of time and so will always wake up to check the control variable.

Thread interrupts

To avoid these issues, we must perform an *interrupt* on the thread. An interrupt is a way of forcing a thread that is currently blocked to wake up and continue. It literally interrupts the thread. When this happens, the blocking function will throw an exception `InterruptedException`, which must be handled. `InterruptedException` is your way of knowing that the thread was interrupted.

Let's change our consumer to use interrupts:

```
    class InterruptableConsumerTask(val queue: BlockingQueue<Int>) :
Runnable {

      override fun run() {
        try {
          while (!Thread.interrupted()) {
            val element = queue.take()
            println("I am processing element $element")
          }
        } catch (e: InterruptedException) {
          // shutting down
        }
```

```
    }
}
```

As you can see, the loop is now enclosed in a `try...catch` block; if caught, this allows the run function to return normally, ending the thread. Notice that the infinite `while` loop has become a `while` statement with a condition as well. The `Thread.interrupted()` condition checks to see whether the thread has been interrupted since the last time the function was invoked. This is required because if the thread was not currently blocked in `take()`, when the interrupt had occurred, then no exception would be thrown and we would not be able to exit. This is very important when using interrupts to handle both cases.

To perform an interrupt, we call `interrupt` on an instance of `Thread`. Therefore, our shutdown code needs to operate on the thread instances themselves and not the tasks:

```
val queue = LinkedBlockingDeque<Int>()

val consumerTasks = (1..6).map {
  InterruptableConsumerTask(queue)
}
val producerTask = ProducerTask(queue)

val consumerThreads = consumerTasks.map {
  thread { it.run() }
}
val producerThread = thread { producerTask.run() }

consumerThreads.forEach { it.interrupt() }
producerTask.running = false
```

Notice that for the producer, we don't perform `interrupt` as the control variables work fine.

CPU-bound versus I/O-bound

One common piece of terminology in the threading world is the concept of CPU-bound and I/O-bound computations. This simply means that a particular task is dominated by either the use of CPU or I/O, irrespective of whether it is a network, file, or whatever else. For example, a CPU-bound computation is the one where you could calculate the digits of Pi. An example of an I/O-bound computation is the one where you could download files from the Internet and save them locally.

In the first example, we can make progress as fast as the CPU can process the math operations. In the second example, we can only make progress as fast as the network can supply us with bytes. The latter case would be much slower.

The concept is important when deciding how to split up executions into threads. Let's say we had a thread pool of eight threads and we allocated this pool to both our CPU- and I/O-bounded computations.

If this is the case, then it is possible we could have a situation where we could have all the eight threads blocked on a slow network to deliver bytes while the the Pi calculation would make no progress despite the CPU being idle.

A common solution to this is to have two thread pools. Have one for CPU-bound operations, which might have its size limited to the number of CPU cores. And have another pool for IO-bound operations, which would typically be larger since these threads would often be in the blocked state, waiting on data.

Deadlocks and livelocks

When a thread cannot continue because it requires some resource that another thread has ownership of, it blocks waiting for that resource. The thread that owns that resource in turn requires something the first thread owns and so it blocks the initial one. Neither can make progress, and this is called a **deadlock**.

If the resource is preemptable, then the operating system or virtual machine can take the lock away from one of the threads and then another thread will be able to grab it; with this, progress would be made eventually. This is not a deadlock. Also, the resources in question must not be shareable, otherwise both threads could simply acquire the lock at the same time, which would also not be a deadlock.

One way to avoid a deadlock is to ensure that threads request the ownership of a resource in the same order. If we have threads *t1* and *t2* and they both require *r1* and *r2*, then if they always request *lock(r1)* followed by *lock(r2)*, it is impossible to get into a situation where one thread has *r1* and another thread has *r2*. This is because the thread that gets the ownership of *r1* will block the other thread from requesting *r2* until it itself has *r1*.

A livelock is a situation where threads are able to change their state but ultimately make no progress. For example, if we had code to detect when a deadlock had occurred, one that forced both the threads to release the locks, we could get into a situation where the threads would continually re-request the locks in the same order as before, going back to the deadlock state. Although the threads are moving between blocked and running and seem to be doing something, they would ultimately not make any progress to complete their computations.

correctness and performance. This is especially true since these kinds of bugs can sometimes only appear when running on certain systems and under certain conditions, so it might appear that the code is correct when what it really doing is harboring a subtle bug.

It is important to consider deadlocks and livelocks when writing concurrent code to ensure program correctness and performance. This is especially true since these kinds of bugs can sometimes only appear when running on certain systems and under certain conditions, so it might appear that the code is correct when what it really doing is harboring a subtle bug.
Dining philosophers problem

The dining philosophers problem is a classic in computer science. The problem was initially stated by Edsger Dijkstra, famous for many contributions to software development. It is often used to show how synchronization issues can result in a deadlock and that coming up with a solution is not always simple.

The problem in its current form is stated like this. Imagine a table of five philosophers, each sitting in front of a bowl of spaghetti. Placed between each philosopher is a fork, so each one of them has access to two forks, one on either side of him or her. A philosopher can think, eat, and move between these states at random. In order to eat, he or she must hold both of their forks at the same time, but each fork can only be used by one philosopher at any time. If a fork is not available — it is being held by another philosopher — then that philosopher will wait until it is free, holding the other fork as soon as it becomes available. It is assumed that the bowl would never empty and that the philosophers will always be hungry.

To show that the obvious solution results in a deadlock, consider the following erroneous solution:

Each philosopher should:

- Think for a random period of time
- Try to acquire the left fork, blocking until it is available
- Try to acquire the right fork, blocking until it is available
- Eat for a random period of time

- Release both the forks
- Repeat

This is erroneous because it is easy to get into a state where every philosopher has acquired their left forks, which means no philosopher can then acquire their right fork (because every right fork is another philosopher's left fork).

The problem can further be used as an example of a livelock. Imagine we enhance our first solution with an extra rule: if the process of acquiring a fork is blocked for more than a minute, all the forks should be dropped and the procedure should be restarted. Then no deadlock is possible, as the system can always make progress (from being blocked back to running). However, it is also possible that all the philosophers would acquire and drop the forks at the same time, meaning they would continually move back to the blocking state.

Executors

Creating a thread manually is fine when we want a single thread to do some work, perhaps a long-lived thread or a very simple one-off task that would run concurrently. However, when we want to run many different tasks concurrently while sharing limited CPU time, track the process of tasks in an easy way, or simply want to abstract how each task will run, we can turn to `ExecutorService`; this is commonly called an **executor** as well. An executor is part of the standard Java library.

An executor is a more generic interface with a single function `run()`. An `ExecutorService` is a more fully featured interface and is usually the abstraction used. It is common for people to use the term executor when referring to either.

An `ExecutorService` is simply an object that executes submitted tasks while allowing us to control the life cycle of the executor, that is, rejecting new tasks or interrupting already running tasks. Executors also allow us to abstract the mechanism of allocating threads to tasks. For example, we may have an executor with a fixed number of threads or an executor that creates a new thread for each submitted task. Any task that is not currently executing will be queued up internally in the executor.

Executors work with two main interfaces. The first, `Runnable`, is the most generic and used interface when we just want to wrap some code to be able to run in an executor. The second, `Callable`, adds a return value for when the task is completed. Since both of these are single-abstract-method interfaces, we can just pass in a function literal in Kotlin.

The Java standard library comes with several built-in executors, created from helper methods in `Executors`, that allow you to create custom executors very easily. The most common executors used are `Executors.newSingleThreadExecutor()`, which creates an executor that will process a single task at a time, and `Executors.newFixedThreadPool(n)`, which creates an executor with an internal pool of threads running up to *n* tasks concurrently.

Let's see how to handle the life cycle of an executor:

```
val executor = Executors.newFixedThreadPool(4)
for (k in 1..10) {
  executor.submit {
    println("Processing element $k on thread
${Thread.currentThread()}")
  }
}
```

In this example, we created a thread pool of four threads and then submitted ten tasks. Each task should print out the ID of the thread it ran on. The static method `Thread.currentThread()` just returns the thread that the code is currently executing on. The output should look something like the following:

```
Processing element 2 on thread Thread[pool-1-thread-2,5,main]
Processing element 5 on thread Thread[pool-1-thread-2,5,main]
Processing element 1 on thread Thread[pool-1-thread-1,5,main]
Processing element 7 on thread Thread[pool-1-thread-1,5,main]
Processing element 8 on thread Thread[pool-1-thread-1,5,main]
Processing element 9 on thread Thread[pool-1-thread-1,5,main]
Processing element 10 on thread Thread[pool-1-thread-1,5,main]
Processing element 3 on thread Thread[pool-1-thread-3,5,main]
Processing element 4 on thread Thread[pool-1-thread-4,5,main]
Processing element 6 on thread Thread[pool-1-thread-2,5,main]
```

It wouldn't be in exactly the same order, as the output is non-deterministic; this shows how the different tasks are being interleaved:

```
executor.shutdown()
executor.awaitTermination(1, TimeUnit.MINUTES)
```

Once we are finished with the example, we call `shutdown()` so that further tasks could be rejected and then use `await()`, which would block the program until the executor has finished executing all the tasks. If we want to cancel running tasks, then we could use the `shutdownNow()` function on the executor, which will reject further tasks and interrupt running tasks before they are returned.

Race conditions

A race condition is another type of concurrency bug that occurs when two or more threads access shared data and try to change it at the same time. This means a situation where the output of a piece of logic requires that interleaved code is run in a particular order — an order that cannot be guaranteed.

A classic example is of a bank account, where one thread is crediting the account and another is debiting the account. An account operation requires us to retrieve the value, update it, and set it back, which means the ordering of these instructions can interleave with each other.

For example, assume an account starts with $100. Then, we want to credit $50 and debit $100. One possible ordering of the instructions can be something like this:

`<credit thread>`	`<account balance>`	`<debit thread>`
	start value = 100	
get current balance = 100		
		get current balance = 100
set new balance = 100 + 50		
	Updated = 150	
		set new balance = 100 – 100
	Updated = 0	

As you can see, our customer has lost their deposit! (They might not be as concerned if they had lost the withdrawal.)

The actual ordering can differ each time we run it. This is because if each thread were running on a separate processor, then the timings would never be exactly in sync. And if the threads were running on the same core, then we could never be quite sure how far each thread would get before a context switch is occurred.

One of the particular issues with race conditions is that by their very nature, they may not be apparent immediately. That is to say they are *non-deterministic*. A machine used for development will have different processing speeds than a server, and this, or the number of concurrent users, may be enough to trigger a race condition that you don't see in development.

Monitors

In a JVM, all instances have what is known as a **monitor**. A monitor can be thought of as a special token, which only one thread is allowed to own at any particular moment. Any thread can request the monitor for any instance, in which case they will either receive it or block it until they make the request. Once a thread has ownership of a particular monitor, it is said to hold the monitor.

To request the monitor, we use the `synchronized` function, which in Kotlin is a standard library function rather than a built-in feature as in Java. This function accepts two parameters: the first being the object whose monitor we wish to own and the second a function literal, which will be executed once we are assigned the monitor. Refer to the following code:

```
val obj = Any()
synchronized(obj) {
  println("I hold the monitor for $obj")
}
```

If we examine the bytecode for this, we would see that the monitor is being acquired (`monitorenter`) and released (`monitorexit`):

```
0: new
3: dup
4: invokespecial
7: astore_0
9: aload_0
10: monitorenter
13: getstatic
16: astore_2
17: aload_0
18: monitorexit
19: aload_2
20: goto
23: astore_2
24: aload_0
25: monitorexit
26: aload_2
27: athrow
28: pop
29: return
```

Any code that is executed when inside the monitor is guaranteed to complete (either normally or by throwing an exception) before the monitor is released and before any other thread takes ownership of that monitor. The code that we run when we hold a monitor is referred to as a critical section.

When a thread reaches a synchronized call for a monitor that is already held by another thread, it is placed in a set of waiting threads. Once the holding thread gives up the monitor, one of the waiting threads is chosen. There is no guaranteed ordering as to which the waiting thread will acquire the monitor, that is, the thread that arrives first does not have any priority over the one that arrives at the end.

The main use of a synchronized block is to ensure only one thread can mutate shared variables at the same time. If we were to revisit our bank account example and this time update it to use synchronization on some common instance, we would see a difference in the interleaving of the code:

`<credit thread>`	`<account balance>`	`<debit thread>`
	start value = 100	
request monitor for account		
		request monitor for account
monitor acquired		
get current balance = 100		
set new balance = 100 + 50		
	updated = 150	
monitor released		
		monitor acquired
		get current balance = 150
		set new balance = 150 + 50
	updated = 200	
		monitor released

To be clear, synchronization as a technique only works if the threads are requesting the monitor for the same exact instance. Every instance of a class has its own monitor, so there is no benefit of having two threads request the monitor of different instances of the same class. This is a common cause of errors made by beginners.

Synchronization is somewhat of a blunt concurrency technique. This is because it is typically used to synchronize over a relatively large set of instructions that are blocking other threads for a long time. As we seek to achieve greater throughput in concurrent code, we should try to minimize the amount of time we are in a critical section of code.

Locks

An alternative to synchronization is to use one of the lock implementations provided in the `java.util.concurrent.locks` package. Typically, the implementation is `ReentrantLock`. A reentrant lock is one that allows the current owner of the lock to request the lock again without causing a deadlock. This simplifies code which uses recursion or passes the lock to other functions.

Although locks and synchronization have very similar uses, in that they both restrict access to a block of code, the lock interface is more powerful. For example, a lock allows us to attempt to acquire ownership and then back off if it is not successful; however, a synchronized call will only block.

In the following example, if we do not get the `lock` immediately, we continue. The return value of the `tryLock()` function indicates whether the lock was acquired or not:

```
val lock = ReentrantLock()
  if (lock.tryLock()) {
    println("I have the lock")
    lock.unlock()
  } else {
    println("I do not have the lock")
  }
```

Remember to always release a `lock` after using it. A `lock` can also block, but it allows you to interrupt:

```
val lock = ReentrantLock()
try {
  lock.lockInterruptibly()
  println("I have the lock")
  lock.unlock()
} catch (e: InterruptedException) {
  println("I was interrupted")
}
```

Kotlin provides an extension function that allows us to use the `lock` and have it automatically released:

```
val lock = ReentrantLock()
lock.withLock {
  println("I have the lock")
}
```

Another advantage is that a lock allows us to enforce fair ordering, which ensures that no particular thread will starve while waiting for the lock. This is done by allocating the lock to the thread that has been waiting for the longest period of time, but this can have a performance penalty, especially on highly contended locks.

Contention is the term given to how much demand there is for a lock or monitor. A high amount of contention means many threads are competing for the same lock at the same time.

Read-write locks

A more sophisticated type of lock provided by the standard library is `ReadWriteLock`. This is a specialized lock aimed at problems involving groups of readers and writers. Imagine a program that reads data from a file and sometimes updates that file. It is perfectly safe for multiple threads to be reading from the file at once but only as long as no one is modifying the file. In addition, only one writer should be writing at any time.

To accomplish this, the read-write lock has two locks: a read lock and a write lock. The read lock can be requested by multiple threads. The write lock can only be held by a single thread. If the read lock is being held, then the write lock cannot be acquired. Once the write lock has been acquired, no other threads can acquire it or a read lock until the write lock has been released.

The basic design of a read-write lock should also take into account whether a second reader requesting a read lock should take preference over a waiting writer. To explain, imagine that the first thread holds the read lock and the second thread then requests the write lock. While the second thread is waiting for the first reader to finish, another reader could come in and request the read lock. Should it be allocated then? It could be since having multiple readers is fine, but what if this happens indefinitely? The writer will definitely starve then.

To avoid this, we can create the read-write lock in fair mode. Similar to the standard lock implementation, when in fair mode, the writer who has been waiting for the longest period of time will be allocated the writer lock. And if a reader has been waiting for the longest period of time, then all the waiting readers are given the read lock at the same time.

Semaphores

The semaphore was again invented by our old friend Edsger Dijkstra. Although these days, with higher level programming languages, the humble semaphore may not be used as much as it was, it is still useful to understand how it works and why it is useful. This is because semaphores are often used as the basis for higher level abstractions.

A semaphore is a mechanism to keep a count of the number of resources and allow the counter to be changed in a thread-safe manner: either request resources or return them, with the additional ability to optionally wait until the requested number of resources are available. In the original design, the operation to request a resource was called **p** and the operation to return a resource was called **v**. The letters come from the original Dutch terms, Dijkstra being Dutch. In other languages, the terms are often called up and down or signal and wait.

The Java standard library exposes a semaphore implementation in the `java.util.concurrent.Semaphore` class. In Java terms, the count is called the number of **permits**; p or up is called **acquire** and v or down is called **release**.

The advantage of a semaphore is not only that they can be safely used from multiple threads at once without running into a race condition, but that any thread waiting on an acquire operation will be blocked, avoiding the need to spin lock and waste CPU time.

A spin lock is a type of lock where a thread repeatedly tests a condition until it is true. Since the thread is active, it is consuming CPU time without making process. This is an example of the so-called **busy-waiting** process and is an inferior solution to correctly block a thread.

A special case of the semaphore is the so-called binary semaphore, which only contains a single resource and so has the states `0` and `1` or unlocked and locked. These can be used to implement a lock or restrict access to a resource to a single consumer at any moment.

The bounded buffer problem

The **bounded buffer** (or producer-consumer) problem is a classic in concurrency. The problem to be solved is this: having a producer who would generate items to be put into a fixed size buffer and a consumer who would read these items. The producer should not try to generate items if the buffer is full, and the consumer should not try to read items if the buffer is empty.

An initial naive attempt, without the use of concurrency primitives, may be something like the following:

```
val buffer = mutableListOf<Int>()
val maxSize = 8

(1..2).forEach {
  thread {
    val random = Random()
    while (true) {
      if (buffer.size < maxSize)
        buffer.plus(random.nextInt())
    }
  }
}

(1..2).forEach {
  thread {
    while (true) {
      if (buffer.size > 0) {
        val item = buffer.remove(0)
        println("Consumed item $item")
      }
    }
  }
}
```

There is a shared buffer with two producers and two consumers each accessing it. The producers and consumers respectively check whether there is space to produce an item or an item to consume. They do this by just checking the size of the list. The problem with this solution is that we are spin locking, waiting for an item each time. If the buffer is empty, the consumer threads will continue to just check the condition, wasting CPU time.

So we need another implementation. Since we have a number of *slots* in the buffer, it seems that semaphores are a good fit. This is due to their ability to hold a count. The idea behind the next iteration is that we have two semaphores: one containing the number of empty slots and another containing the number of filled slots. A producer will wait for an empty slot before producing an item, after which it will increase the number of filled slots. The consumer will wait for a filled slot before consuming an item; after this, it will increase the number of empty slots:

```
val emptyCount = Semaphore(8)
val fillCount = Semaphore(0)
val buffer = mutableSetOf<Int>()

thread {
```

```
        val random = Random()
        while (true) {
          emptyCount.acquire()
          buffer.plus(random.nextInt())
          fillCount.release()
        }
      }

      thread {
        while (true) {
          fillCount.acquire()
          val item = buffer.remove(0)
          println("Consumed item $item")
          emptyCount.release()
        }
      }
```

This is certainly an improvement and avoids spin locking. However, since multiple threads can still access the list concurrently, the list could be modified by different threads at the same time. We can see this through a table of instructions showing one possible interleaving of instructions:

`<producer 1>`	`<list>`	`<producer 2>`
	size = 6	
request empty slot		
		request empty slot
empty slot acquired		
		empty slot acquired
set slot 7 to "x"		
	size = 7	
		set slot 7 to "y"
	size = 7	

This is an issue because of the fact that multiple threads will be mutating the list internally at the same time. Updating a list is not atomic and requires several instructions, which themselves are subject to race conditions.

An operation is said to be atomic if it appears to the rest of the system as if it is one single operation and any intermediate state is never visible outside of the thread.

Therefore, the safe solution is to further limit access to the list to a single thread at a time, and we can do this by introducing `mutex`:

```
val emptyCount = Semaphore(8)
val fillCount = Semaphore(0)
val mutex = Semaphore(1)
val buffer = mutableSetOf<Int>()

thread {
  val random = Random()
  while (true) {
    emptyCount.acquire()
    mutex.acquire()
    buffer.plus(random.nextInt())
    mutex.release()
    fillCount.release()
  }
}
thread {
  while (true) {
    fillCount.acquire()
    mutex.acquire()
    val item = buffer.remove(0)
    mutex.release()
    println("Consumed item $item")
    emptyCount.release()
  }
}
```

In the final iteration, we've added a `mutex` acquire and release around each mutation of the buffer. This solution is now thread-safe.

Concurrent collections

As discovered in the section on race conditions, multiple threads accessing shared data can result in an inconsistent state. As we further saw in the section on monitors and locking, writing thread-safe code for updating collections can be tricky. Luckily, the Java standard library has solved many of these problems for us. In Java 1.5 (or version 5) onward, the standard library comes with a large number of concurrency primitives and concurrent collections.

The following several sections will cover some of these primitives, with this chapter on collections specifically and the next three on other non-collection primitives.

A *concurrent* collection is the term given to collections that are thread-safe and specifically designed for use in multithreaded code. They are less performant than a *normal* collection would be in a single thread environment, but more performant than wrapping normal collections in synchronized blocks (which was the pre-Java 1.5 solution).

ConcurrentHashMap

The first such collection is `java.util.concurrent.ConcurrentHashMap` and is possibly the most used of all the concurrent collections. As the name implies, this is an implementation of the `Map` interface that is thread-safe. The issue with a normal map is that two threads may both try to put an element into the map, one overwriting the other if their keys both hash to the same value. The other, less obvious, issue is that if the map reaches the capacity of putting the first thread, then it will perform a resize operation, which will involve rehashing each element into a new bucket. While this is going on, the put operation from the second thread can be lost.

A concurrent hash map avoids these issues. It maintains a set of locks, and each lock is used to restrict access to a stripe of the map. This way, multiple updates can occur at the same time safely, reducing the amount of code that has to be performed serially. Additionally, a `get()` operation does not require a lock at all, and it will return the result of the latest completed update.

A blocking queue

A blocking queue is another well-trodden collection. It is an extension of the `java.util.Queue` interface to support thread-safe blocking operations. It defines an operation called `take()`, which will block until the queue is non-empty, and `put()`, which will block until there is capacity in the queue to accept the item. If multiple threads perform the block action on the same operation, say three threads trying to take an item and one becomes available, only one thread will succeed and the others will safely continue to block.

There are two implementations in the Java standard library. The first implementation `java.util.concurrent.ArrayListBlockingQueue` is backed by an `Array` implementation. The second `java.util.concurrent.LinkedBlockingQueue` is backed by `LinkedList`. Each offers trade-offs of course, the latter being particularly useful as it uses two locks internally, one for the head of the list and one for the tail.

Using a blocking queue would dramatically simplify our earlier, bounded buffer problem. Let's rework that problem using `LinkedBlockingQueue` so we can see the difference:

```
val buffer = LinkedBlockingQueue<Int>()

thread {
  val random = Random()
  while (true) {
    buffer.put(random.nextInt())
  }
}

thread {
  while (true) {
    val item = buffer.take(0)
    println("Consumed item $item")
  }
}
```

As you can see, all the concurrency-related complication has been taken away for us. We can use the queue as if we were in a single threaded environment:

```
13.7.x
```

Atomic variables

Quite often, we will find ourselves wanting a single value that we can atomically update between threads. A collection seems overkill for that purpose and probably slower than a special purpose primitive. he standard library provides such primitives in the `java.util.concurrent.atomic` package.

There are different implementations for each basic type, plus one for object references. For example, `AtomicLong` contains a `Long` counter and provides operations to retrieve the current value or update the value in a thread safe manner. A typical use case is a counter shared between threads, perhaps as an increasing ID generator:

```
val counter = AtomicLong(0)
(1..8).forEach {
  thread {
    while (true) {
      val id = counter.incrementAndGet()
      println("Creating item with id $id")
    }
  }
}
```

If you are using JDK 1.8 or higher, they ship with a primitive called **LongAdder** and **DoubleAdder**, which are even more efficient for summing values, with the drawback of being eventually consistent.

The `AtomicReference` class is similar, but rather than a number, it allows any reference type. It is useful for allowing multiple threads to share a single object and allow them all to update the object safely. One such use case is lazy initialization between threads. The initial value is null and then each thread can check for null, and if found, update to a proper value:

```
val ref = AtomicReference<Connection>()
(1..8).forEach {
  thread {
    ref.compareAndSet(null, openConnection())
    val conn = ref.get()
   }
}
```

Now only one thread would call the `openConnection()` function. And it would occur lazily the first time a thread is executed.

CountDownLatch

The `CountDownLatch` object is a very useful concurrency primitive that has existed in Java since version 1.5 (or version 5, depending on which Java numbering scheme you prefer). The basic idea of the latch is that it allows one or more threads to block until the latch is released. You can imagine that the naming comes from the latch we see on a gate — once the latch is opened, the sheep behind the gate can escape. So similarly, the threads are queued up behind the gate, and once the latch is released, the threads are allowed to move through.

A latch is initialized with a count, and the `countDown()` method can be used to decrement the count. Once the count hits zero, any threads waiting on the latch are unblocked. A thread can block the latch using the `await` method; in fact, any number of threads can block the latch and they will all be released at the same time.

Any thread calling `countDown` is free to continue. Only threads calling `await` are blocked. Also note that any thread can call `countDown` multiple times, which is often the case when we have many tasks that are processed by several threads in turn.

Latches have many uses. We briefly mentioned one in `Chapter 11`, *Testing in Kotlin,* when we showed that latches are a useful tool for testing asynchronous functions. Recall that we wanted to prevent assertions from being executed until the asynchronous code that they depended on had finished executing.

Another canonical use of latches is to prevent some main thread from proceeding until worker threads are utilized. Let's say we have an application that needs to download and process multiple feeds before sending a notification via a queue. We want to multithread the processing of the feeds, especially since they are CPU-bound and we happen to be running on a multicore processor. The final notification should only be sent once all the feeds are processed. We don't know in advance which feeds will complete first or in what order. Since the order is unspecified we can't rely on the logic that the last feed started will be the last feed to complete.

This is an example of the workpile pattern. The feeds to be processed can be imagined as a pile of tasks and a thread can take a task from this pile. Just like if you had a to-do list and each one was represented by a post-it note. You would pick up the top post and do whatever needs to be done before moving on to the next one. This is how the workpile pattern works.

We will model our tasks as a function called `processFeed`, which accepts a `Feed` object that describes the feed to be processed. The implementation of this function is not important for this example:

```
fun processFeed(feed: Feed): Unit {
  println("Processing feed ${feed.name}")
}
```

We will assume we are somehow given a list of feeds, perhaps we could read them from a database. Each feed in turn will be submitted to an `Executor`. Our `Executor` will happen to be a cached thread pool:

```
val executor = Executors.newCachedThreadPool()
```

Finally, we'll need a function to send across the notification once all the feeds are completed:

```
fun sendNotificaticn(): Unit {
  println("Sending notification")
}
```

So far, we've multithreaded the processing of each feed. But how do we now make sure the `sendNotification` function is only invoked once all the feeds are complete. The first thought might be to use a counter and have each feed task update the counter as it finishes. However, how do we wait for the counter? Again, naively, we could simply spin lock on the counter until it hits the required number.

A better solution would be to block the thread until it is ready. This is where the countdown latch comes into play. If we create a latch with the count set to the number of feeds and have each task count it down before it finishes, we can then have the main thread wait on the latch. Here is the full example:

```
fun processFeed(feed: Feed): Unit {
  println("Processing feed ${feed.name}")
}

fun sendNotification(): Unit {
  println("Sending notification")
}

val feeds = listOf(
  Feed("Great Vegetable Store",
"http://www.greatvegstore.co.uk/items.xml"),
  Feed("Super Food Shop", "http://www.superfoodshop.com/products.csv")
)

val latch = CountDownLatch(feeds.size)

val executor = Executors.newCachedThreadPool()
for (feed in feeds) {
  executor.submit {
    processFeed(feed)
    latch.countDown()
  }
}

latch.await()
println("All feeds completed")
sendNotification()
```

Now the main thread will block at the `latch.await` line and consume no more CPU time until it is ready to proceed past the `latch`.

Cyclic Barrier

Another concurrency primitive along the lines of the countdown latch is `CyclicBarrier`, which allows multiple threads to wait until they all reach the required point. The common use for a barrier is when you have a set of threads that must perform some logic and then wait until everyone is ready before moving on.

Let's imagine we are writing a system that copies a file at multiple places. We don't want to start the next file until the first one has been successfully written out at all places. Each task is running on a separate thread that writes out to a single location. An implementation for this use case may decide to run multiple tasks on multiple threads, each task taking care of one particular output location. Each task can then wait on the barrier so that the next file is started only once they are all complete.

First, let's define a task that will repeatedly copy a file and then wait on a barrier:

```
    class CopyTask(val dir: Path, val paths: List<Path>, val barrier:
CyclicBarrier) : Runnable {

      override fun run() {
        for (path in paths) {
          val dest = dir.resolve(path)
          Files.copy(path, dest, StandardCopyOption.REPLACE_EXISTING)
          barrier.await()
        }
      }
    }
```

Next, set up an executor and submit the tasks for each of the output locations:

```
    fun copyUsingBarrier(inputFiles: List<Path>, outputDirectories:
List<Path>) {

      val executor = Executors.newFixedThreadPool(outputDirectories.size)
      val barrier = CyclicBarrier(outputDirectories.size)

      for (dir in outputDirectories) {
        executor.submit {
          CopyTask(dir, inputFiles, barrier)
        }
      }
    }
```

As you can see, one of the advantages of a barrier is that it can be reused. Each time it is released, it is ready to be used again. We could also use a countdown latch here, but we'd have to create a new one each time and then we have the issue of sharing the new instance.

Non-blocking I/O and asynchronous programming

Throughout this chapter, we focused on threads as the main instrument of concurrency. As crucial as they are, as the number of threads increases, the marginal benefit decreases. The more threads exist, the more time is spent on context switching between them. Ideally, we would want to be in a situation where we have one thread per CPU core, avoiding context switching entirely. This is somewhat of an impossible goal, but we can reduce the number of threads in use significantly.

Imagine a problem where we want to download ten feeds from a supplier's website. Once these are downloaded, we want to write them out to our database. One solution would be to create ten threads and have each thread read a single feed.

As each thread waits for more data to become available, it blocks. As the threads block or as their time slice expires, the system will context switch between the threads. If we were to scale out this system to a thousand feeds, that's a lot of switching, when the bulk of the time will still be spent waiting on the network.

A better solution might be to have the I/O system inform us when the data is made available, then we could allocate a thread to process that data. For us to be notified, we must provide a function that the I/O system knows to run when ready, and that function or block is commonly referred to as a *callback*. This is the idea behind non-blocking I/O. Java introduced non-blocking I/O in the 1.4 edition of the JDK.

If you were to use non-blocking I/O to download all the feeds from our supplier, we would have provided multiple callbacks. Since we have no idea about the order they will execute — this would be determined by the order in which they finish downloading, and some may be much larger than others — this kind of programming is referred to as **asynchronous programming**.

Asynchronous programming doesn't only work on I/O. It may be the case that we have a callback on a thread that runs once we finish a CPU-bound operation. For example, calculate the Pi to one hundred thousand places and then run a completion callback.

While this technique is very powerful, it can also result in what is known as **callback hell**. This is where we have multiple levels of nested callbacks, as each callback triggers a further operation:

```
fun persistOrder(order: Order, callback: (String) -> Unit): Unit = ...
fun chargeCard(card: Card, callback: (Boolean) -> Unit): Unit = ...
fun printInvoice(order: Order, callback: (Unit) -> Unit): Unit = ...
```

```
persistOrder(order, {
  println("Order has been saved; charging card")
  chargeCard(order.card, { result ->
  if (result) {
    println("Order has been charged; printing invoice")
    printInvoice(order, {
      println("Invoice has been printed")
    })
  }
})
})
```

As you can see, this code has three levels of callbacks. In the extreme case, this could be in dozens. While this is very efficient, as each further operation will only run once the previous one is completed and won't block any resources while waiting, it does result in somewhat unreadable code.

Futures

Imagine we want to submit tasks to an executor, but we want to know when they would be complete. One way would be to pass some kind of variable into each task, which we could interrogate to check on the status. However, this would require us to manage the volatility of that variable, and potentially spin locking to check on it.

A better solution would be some kind of structure that would represent a computation that hasn't yet completed. This structure would allow us to get the return value once it is completed, queue up an operation to run on it once it was ready, or block until it is finished. This kind of structure is called a **future**. The naming comes from the fact that it represents a value that will be available sometime in the future. (Futures are sometimes called promises in other languages, although in languages such as Scala, a promise and a future are different but related structures.)

We'd need the support of `ExecutorService` to return a future when we submit a task. To do this, we need to use the `Callable` interface rather than `Runnable`:

```
val executor = Executors.newFixedThreadPool(4)

val future: Future<Double> = executor.submit(Callable<Double> {
  Math.sqrt(15.64)
})
```

The basic `Future` returned here offers functions to test whether it has been completed and to get the value, blocking the calling thread until it is ready.

The real power, however, lies in the `CompletableFuture` abstraction. This enhanced future supports asynchronous operations and so operates via callbacks rather than explicitly blocking the thread. To create such a future, use the static methods defined on the class, which optionally accept an executor:

```
    val executor = Executors.newFixedThreadPool(4)
    val future = CompletableFuture.supplyAsync(Supplier {  Math.sqrt(15.64)
}, executor)
```

With this future, we can now attach a callback:

```
future.thenApply {
  println("The square root has been calculated")
}
```

Callbacks can be chained so that the results of one future could be fed into another future. If we revisit the order-processing example from earlier, it can be rewritten as such:

```
fun persistOrder(order: Order): String = TODO()
fun chargeCard(card: Card): Boolean = TODO()
fun printInvoice(order: Order): Unit = TODO()

CompletableFuture.supplyAsync {
  persistOrder(order)
}.thenApply { id ->
  println("Order has been saved; id is $id")
  chargeCard(order.card)
}.thenApply { result ->
if (result) {
  println("Order has been charged; printing invoice")
  printInvoice(order)
}
}
```

This is more readable and avoids the many nested levels of callbacks in the case of an ordered series of callbacks. Futures can also be executed together with the results merged back into a single future. Imagine we decided that we wanted to persist the order, charge the card, and print the invoice simultaneously:

```
fun persistOrder(order: Order): CompletableFuture<String> = TODO()
fun chargeCard(card: Card): CompletableFuture<Boolean> = TODO()
fun printInvoice(order: Order): CompletableFuture<Unit> = TODO()

CompletableFuture.allOf(
  persistOrder(order),
  chargeCard(order.card),
  printInvoice(order)
```

```
    ).thenApply {
      println("Order is saved, charged and printed")
    }
```

The `CompletableFuture` has many more functions, such as accepting the first completed value of multiple futures, mapping of results, and handling errors.

Summary

This chapter has focused on the core underpinnings of concurrency in the JVM and how to use them effectively in Kotlin. Concurrency is a large subject, and this chapter should have given a solid footing to anyone who is new to using concurrency. Those who already are very familiar with concurrent code can see how Kotlin offers small but useful helper functions in the concurrent package.

Index

D

E

F

G

H

I

J

K

L

M

N

T

U

V

W

Lightning Source UK Ltd.
Milton Keynes UK
UKOW04f2140200117
292544UK00002B/50/P